ABORTION

A Documentary and Reference Guide

Melody Rose

Greenwood Press

Wesport Connecticut • London

Library of Congress Cataloging-in-Publication Data

Rose, Melody.
    Abortion : a documentary and reference guide / Melody Rose.
       p. cm.
    Includes bibliographical references and index.
    ISBN: 978–0–313–34032–1 (alk. paper)
    1. Abortion—United States—History.   I. Title.
    HQ767.5.U5R66   2008
    363.460973—dc22   2007037489

British Library Cataloguing in Publication Data is available.

Library of Congress Catalog Card Number: 2007037489
ISBN: 978–0–313–34032–1

First published in 2008

Greenwood Press, 88 Post Road West, Westport, CT 06881
An imprint of Greenwood Publishing Group, Inc.
www.greenwood.com

Printed in the United States of America

∞™

The paper used in this book complies with the
Permanent Paper Standard issued by the National
Information Standards Organization (Z39.48–1984).

10 9 8 7 6 5 4 3 2 1

CONTENTS

PREFACE

As the United States entered the twenty-first century, the sands of abortion politics were shifting in a discernible way. Both states and the federal government were crafting novel restrictions on abortion access, testing the Supreme Court's resolve to protect a woman's right to end her pregnancy. Then, in 2006, President George W. Bush received word of not one, but two, departures from the Supreme Court. After some controversy, the President's nominees were confirmed by the Senate, and in early 2007 Justice Samuel A. Alito and Chief Justice John G. Roberts took their places on the nation's highest court.

Later that year, the new court heard *Gonzales v. Carhart*, the product of a 10-year battle over a single abortion procedure used in the latter half of pregnancy. By a five to four decision, the majority (which includes the court's two newest members) ruled to uphold the federal ban despite the fact that the ban did not include an exception to preserve a woman's health. This decision marked not just another chapter in the epic of abortion politics, but a sea-change in the court's more than 30-year history of preserving a woman's health before the state's interest in fetal life.

Following that ruling, state legislatures ushered in a myriad of abortion restrictions. From mandates requiring that abortion facilities purchase ultrasound equipment to state-level abortion procedure bans, the states where abortion practice is not widely supported have pursued a roll-back of abortion access not seen since the early twentieth century.

This text seeks to put these recent abortion policy changes into a larger historical context. By placing recent primary source documents alongside older documents, the reader is invited to take a step back from contemporary events, which appear to those who are invested in them to be unique, and entertain the broader spectrum of abortion history in America. Looking broadly across time allows the reader to discern certain patterns and nuances that may not be readily observable to the contemporary activist or attentive layperson.

One lesson to be drawn from the documents I have selected for this text is that abortion has been a common medical practice in Western civilization. And despite the rancorous contemporary debate over abortion policy in contemporary America, this country's policies appear neither stable nor predictable. With 200 years of history in this policy terrain, our nation has not settled on an abortion resolution that has much longevity.

Another lesson here is that, as with other issues that stir the conscience of our citizens, the topic of abortion inspires vitriolic and ideological debate. And although our institutions of science and religion have not uncovered a consensus policy, our policymakers often argue in terms that sound both unyielding and extreme. The trouble with that is, most average Americans' views on abortion are neither unyielding nor extreme.

This text offers a wide array of voices on the subject of abortion policy. I have chosen each selection deliberately for its impact on public policy and the public abortion debate. Containing primary source documents on the abortion question from before the American founding up through the present day, this text strives to incorporate a far-reaching set of materials that offer the full texture of the American abortion debate. From modern-day extreme antiabortion forces who justify violence for the sake of preventing abortion, to the earliest advertisements for abortion providers in the nineteenth century, this text seeks to represent the full course of American abortion policy, and its many iterations, through the voices of those who have participated in the debate. Inclusion of these voices gives life to the full debate in a larger context than is often unavailable in the current din of abortion politics.

The motivation to create such a text stems from the practical discovery that no such similar text is in print today. Scholars and interested citizens who seek to understand the abortion contest, or abortion policy, may use this guide as a reference for the most commonly visited and influential artifacts in this 200-year debate. For the first time in a single location, papal encyclicals sit next to activist pleas and court proceedings. While previous such tomes have accumulated only legal resources, this text seeks explicitly to review a wider set of documents from legal, to religious, to scientific, to activist accounts. The reason for such a broad array of source materials is simply to expose a wide variety of perspectives.

The materials are grouped chronologically into chapters, and are designed to reflect distinct epochs in American abortion debate. Each chapter contains documents pertinent to its period, but the documents within are juxtaposed to reflect distinct trends or views within the period, shedding light on the tensions emblematic of each era. Chapter 1 reveals the minimal role of the state in abortion practices of the nineteenth century and the role of the nascent women's movement positioned against a medical movement to restrict abortion provision. In chapter 2 the documents reveal America's strictest era of abortion policy, where the ideology of motherhood pushed against postsuffrage women's desire to control and regulate their fertility. Chapter 3 focuses on an emergent demand for less restrictive policies, illustrating the voices for reform and the sometimes tragic consequences of restriction. The product of that movement to liberalize abortion policy is reflected in chapter 4, as are some of the immediate academic responses to liberalization. In chapter 5, the documents expose the growing role of party politics in abortion politics, while chapter 6 focuses on the movement to protect the fetus. Finally, chapter 7 conveys the impact of the fetal rights movement and the recent successes of that movement to restrict abortion access. And for those who wish to delve more deeply into this policy arena, a chronology and bibliography yield additional sources that will illuminate further avenues of research.

There are two primary ways to use this book. The text may be used selectively: by utilizing the index, the reader may find particular documents within. Alternatively, the reader might choose to read the whole book or entire sections that reflect specific periods of time. When used this way, the reader will likely observe large trends in policy and perspective that can only be seen by viewing from a distance.

Several trends and themes emerge for the reader who avails herself of the whole book. Nineteenth-century statutory permissiveness on abortion gives way to early-twentieth-century controls. From the turn of the twentieth-century to the mid-1960s, restrictions on abortion are the rule, and the selections will indicate a range of beliefs regarding this strict era. Then, in the 1960s, the pendulum begins to swing again; doctors and women's groups organize to oppose restrictive laws and *Roe v. Wade* ushers in a new era of relatively easier access to abortion. Then, once again, in 1989, a new trend is evident: a remade Supreme Court permits more abortion restrictions until, in 2007, a landmark decision steps away from 34 years of abortion jurisprudence.

Other trends around the nature of government's various roles in abortion policy and practice, the influence of political parties and interest groups, and the roles of science and religion in the debate are familiar themes in these pages. And the most constant theme of all, the interminable search for policy resolution, remains throughout the text.

Creating a reference guide such as this is a rewarding experience, both for the materials found and analyzed, and for the team required to produce it. At Portland State University, graduate students Suzanne Laberge and Bonnie Lander provided able support with copyright clearance and document location. Graduate student and instructor Jim Hite went beyond what was required of him, and assisted at every stage of the book's development. From proposing and searching for critical documents, to pursuing tricky copyright clearance, to proofreading the final copy, his help was essential to the content and quality of the book. I am deeply indebted to these helpers, although any flaws remaining here are mine alone.

I have learned that no book is produced without full family support. For their unfailing patience, inspiration, good natures, and forbearance, I thank my beautiful family: Bella, Cloe, Eric, Madison, and Simone.

CHRONOLOGY

1588–1591	Pope Sixtus V issued a papal bull forbidding abortion as punishment for the sexual sin of intercourse.
1591	Pope Gregory XIV succeeded Sixtus V, rescinding the penalties (including excommunication) imposed for abortion.
1869	Pope Pius IX returned to Sixtus V's old bull and reinstated abortion as murder, establishing the rule of ensoulment.
1873	March 3: President Ulysses S. Grant signs "An Act for Suppression of Trade in and Circulation of Obscene Literatures and Articles of Immoral Use," also known as the Comstock Act.
1914	Margaret Sanger launches "The Woman Rebel," and coins the term *birth control*.
1918–1968	Ruth Barnett performs tens of thousands of illicit, but safe, abortions in Portland, Oregon.
1940s–1950s	An estimated 200,000 to 1.3 million illegal abortions are performed annually in the United States.
1953	Alfred Kinsey's revolutionary book, *Sexual Behavior in the Human Female*, reports that 9 out of 10 premarital pregnancies end in abortion, and 22 percent of all married women have abortions.
1960	The American Medical Association (AMA) argues that abortion bans are not enforceable.
	The American Law Institute (ALI) creates a model penal code that would soften abortion laws to allow more flexibility for physicians.
1962	Sherri Finkbine goes to Sweden to have a legal abortion after discovering her fetus was badly damaged by the drug thalidomide.
	Pat Maginnis forms the women's rights group Citizens for Humane Abortion Laws in California.
1965	February 13: Society for Human Abortions (SHA) is founded. The *New York Times* embraces abortion reform on its editorial page.
	Rubella outbreaks lead to abortions and galvanize physician support for reform.

	Griswold v. Connecticut rules that Connecticut's ban on contraception infringes on a fundamental right of privacy.
1966	The National Organization for Women (NOW) is founded.
	The Association to Repeal Abortion Laws in California is founded.
1967	The *Journal of the American Medical Association* advocates for abortion policy reform.
	21 New York ministers and rabbis found Clergy Consultation Service on Abortion, providing abortion referrals while abortion was illegal.
	National Organization for Women adds abortion rights to its demands.
	Colorado, North Carolina, and California enact the ALI abortion reform law.
1969	The underground abortion provider network, Jane, is formed in Chicago.
	The National Conference on Abortion Laws forms the National Association for Repeal of Abortion Laws (NARAL).
	Redstockings, a radical feminist group in New York, holds an abortion speak-out.
1970	New York, Hawaii, and Washington legalize abortion.
	Our Bodies, Ourselves first published.
1971	American Bar Association endorses abortion until the twentieth week of pregnancy.
	Dr. Jane Hodgson convicted for performing abortions in a hospital—the only doctor ever so convicted.
	The Comstock Act is repealed.
	The Feminist Women's Health Center is formed in Los Angeles; the group teaches women how to perform "menstrual extraction."
1972	Television character "Maude" has an abortion.
1973	*Roe v. Wade*, and its lesser-known companion case *Doe v. Bolton*, legalize abortion.
	In response to the *Roe* ruling, antiabortion activists create the National Right to Life Committee, the nation's largest and longest-running antiabortion organization in the United States.
	NARAL changes its name to National Abortion Rights Action League.
	Religious Coalition for Abortion Rights founded.
1975	National Women's Health Network founded.
1976	The Hyde Amendment enacted, eliminating most federal funding for abortions, except "where the life of the mother would be endangered."
	First abortion clinic arson reported.

1980	The Republican Party platform drops its 40-year commitment to the Equal Rights Amendment and calls for the appointment of antiabortion judges.
	Direct-action group Pro-Life Action League formed.
1983	National Black Women's Health Project is formed.
1984	At the United National Population Conference in Mexico City, the Reagan administration announces its "Mexico City policy," which bans U.S. family planning funds to overseas nongovernmental organizations that use their own funds for abortion.
1985	The Religious Coalition for Abortion Rights creates the Women of Color Partnership Program.
1987	Reproductive Health Technologies Project formed.
	Randall Terry performs his first "rescue" at a women's health facility where abortions are performed.
1988	Randall Terry founds Operation Rescue, one of the nation's leading abortion-protest organizations.
1989	*Webster v. Reproductive Health Services* upholds Missouri's abortion restrictions and inspires the states to experiment with further limitations.
	Teen Becky Bell dies after procuring an illegal abortion to avoid her state's parental involvement law.
1989–1992	Over 700 abortion restrictions are considered in state legislatures.
1990s	Abortion clinic violence increases.
1991	Operation Rescue blockades clinics in Wichita, Kansas.
1992	National Network of Abortion Funds established to provide private funds for indigent women seeking abortion care.
	The March for Women's Lives brings 750,000 demonstrators to Washington, D.C. for women's reproductive rights.
	Planned Parenthood v. Casey upholds Pennsylvania restrictions on abortion and lowers the legal barriers to similar restrictions.
1993	NARAL changes its name to National Abortion and Reproductive Rights Action League.
	Dr. David Gunn, of Florida, becomes the first abortion provider to be murdered.
	The Hyde Amendment expands to offer abortion assistance in cases of rape and incest.
	On the twentieth anniversary of *Roe v. Wade*, President Clinton reverses five Reagan and Bush administration restrictions on abortion.

1994	Freedom of Access to Clinic Entrances (FACE) signed by President Clinton, limiting protest actions at abortion clinic entrances.
	Medical Students for Choice formed to address the declining practice of abortion medicine.
1995	Two abortion clinic employees, Shannon Lowney and Leanne Nichols, are murdered in Massachusetts.
1996 and 1997	President Clinton twice vetoes the Partial Birth Abortion Ban Act.
2001	President George W. Bush reinstates two abortion restrictions on his first day in office.
2003	The Supreme Court lets stand a lower court ruling against the Nuremberg Files Web site, which encouraged violence against abortion providers.
	President Bush signs the Partial Birth Abortion Ban.
	Paul Hill becomes the first antiabortion extremist executed for his crime of murdering two clinic workers in Pensacola, Florida.
2006	In March, South Dakota bans abortion in all cases except to save the life of the pregnant woman; voters overturn the ban in November.
2007	*Gonzales v. Planned Parenthood* upholds the federal Partial Birth Abortion Ban, despite not containing a health exception.
	New Hampshire becomes the first state in the nation to repeal its parental involvement law.

1

ABORTION IN EARLY AMERICA

Students of contemporary American history are well acquainted with the abortion debate. Not a week goes by, it seems, without a government entity making policy on abortion. This observation stands in stark contrast to nineteenth-century America, where policy on abortion was rare and talk of the practice rarer still. Thus, this book's first chapter focuses on a handful of unusual but prominent primary sources, the first to characterize abortion practices in America.

The absence of public policy on abortion is the direct result of three conspiring variables. First, early American political theory located such issues of morality squarely in the states, so very little discussion of abortion would occur in the national branches until much later in our history. Second, American law was founded on British Common Law, which also had little to say about abortion. What it did say was moderate and by default delegated a fair amount of discretion to women and their caregivers: midwives. Third, polite society simply did not discuss issues related to sexuality with any regularity, which made public policy consideration of abortion unlikely.

Still, this chapter will document a growing public interest in abortion toward the mid- to late-nineteenth century. As a function of changing immigration patterns, increased scrutiny of women's sexuality and childbearing decisions, and the development of a "regular" medical industry, public policy makers began to take notice of abortion. The consequence is that while in 1800 not a single American state outlawed abortion, by 1900, such bans were the rule.

Document: Excerpt from S. K. Jennings' *The Married Lady's Companion, Or Poor Man's Friend,* a text on issues confronting the nineteenth-century American wife.

Date: 1808.

Where: First published in New York; selections were reprinted elsewhere.

Significance: This early-nineteenth-century tract on married women's etiquette reveals the prevailing sentiment at that time that pregnancy reflected an unnatural condition, the relief of which allowed the return of menses by removal of the "blockage."

CHAPTER XVIII

Obstructed menses.

If by alternate exposure to heat and cold, or by any other accidental means, the menses cease to flow, they are said to be obstructed.

There are different appearances in this disease, according to the state of the general system. I shall mark three variations for the sake of distinction.

The first is generally brought on by some kind of exposure or accident. In this case, there will be a sensible fullness or increased motion of the blood, producing a swimming and dull heavy pain of the head, which are increased on stooping down, a redness, a fullness, with a sense of weight across the eyes, an aversion to motion, an unusual sense of weakness and heaviness of all the limbs, and sometimes a bleeding at the nose, &c.

Where these, or most of these symptoms occur,

1st. Let blood from the foot ten or twelve ounces, to be repeated as occasion may require.
2d. Bathe her feet half an hour on going to bed.
3d. Then give a portion of calomel and aloes three grains of each. Syrrup of some kind may be added so as to form it into a pill or two, or so much as to make it of the consistence of honey. Continue the bath and calomel and aloes, for three successive nights.

If the disorder came on suddenly, and especially if she was a healthy girl, before the attack, you may use the lancet the more freely.

There is no danger from the use of calomel. The only necessary precautions are, to avoid improper exposure to cold and wet, and abstain from large draughts of cold water. And these would be equally necessary if no calomel were used. At the next period proceed a second time through the same course, viz. bleed, bathe, and give calomel and aloes for three successive nights, and if there be not something more amiss than what you call a *common cold*, she will probably be relieved. It might not be amiss however to repeat it a third time if necessary (43–45).

CHAPTER XXI

I. Floodings in abortion

If the foetus be expelled at any time before the end of the sixth month, it may be called an abortion. But an expulsion in any of the last three months, may be considered a labour premature or irregular.

Cases of abortion neither require nor admit of any manual assistance; for the proper treatment in this case see chap. XXIV. Part II.

But when a woman is miscarrying with a considerable and apparently dangerous flooding, is so far advanced in pregnancy that it may be difficult to determine, whether the case be an abortion or a premature labour; the circumstances being such at the same time as to render it unsafe to depend on the common remedies, it may become necessary to hasten her delivery. For this purpose the membranes may be broken and waters discharged. By this evacuation, the uterus will be made to contract, and the flooding will be stayed until the *foetus* can be expelled by the natural efforts of the constitution (147).

SOURCE: S. K. Jennings, *The Married Lady's Companion, Or Poor Man's Friend.* 2nd ed. (New York: Lorenzo Dow, 1808). Republished by Arno Press and The New York Times, 1972. 4345, 147. All page numbers refer to the 1808 edition.

DOCUMENT ANALYSIS

This guide to proper women's etiquette reveals much about nineteenth-century medical and popular responses to the practice of abortion. The language, and even some of the spellings, may appear foreign to the twenty-first-century sensibility, but to the nineteenth-century woman would affirm common practices and standards of behavior.

First, this passage reveals a much broader concern with proper women's conduct. The guide was intended to shepherd married women through the social practices and expectations of the day, offering them guidance on a large number of subjects ranging from cooking practices to abortion care. Societal expectations of the nineteenth-century woman were well guarded, and generally protected men's superior civic and economic status. Still, within the home, women emerged through the nineteenth century's industrialization period with some authority, given that their social and personal behaviors met with society's expectations for piety and a focus on motherhood as well as hearth and home.

Still, within this rigid paradigm, women in the early part of the century experienced surprisingly wide acceptance of abortion. In part, this acceptance stems from the structure of medicine at that time. Largely controlled in the early nineteenth century by female midwives, abortion was considered part of a woman's overall healthcare needs. Abortion care was delivered exclusively by midwives, who were trained in herbal remedies, as the passage indicates.

What is more, abortion care reflected prevailing notions of human development: at this time both legal and religious traditions assumed a belief that human value evolved throughout the pregnancy. While today's fundamentalist Christians maintain that human life, or *hominization,* begins at conception, at that time both medicine and major religious traditions supported a view that life evolved within the womb, reaching full human scale at the point of "quickening," or about midway through a pregnancy when the woman could sense independent movement of her fetus. Jennings' focus on the six-month demarcation of pregnancy loosely reflects this belief.

The passage also reveals the perils of abortion at this time. The practices of "restoring menses," were sometimes hazardous and often unpredictable both in terms of efficacy and danger. Hence the focus on safety: the guidebook is intended to improve women's health, recognizing that abortion (and childbearing itself) could be a treacherous undertaking at this time.

IN HISTORY

HIPPOCRATIC OATH (CLASSICAL VERSION)

I swear by Apollo Physician and Asclepius and Hygieia and Panaceia and all the gods and goddesses, making them my witnesses, that I will fulfil according to my ability and judgment this oath and this covenant:

To hold him who has taught me this art as equal to my parents and to live my life in partnership with him, and if he is in need of money to give him a share of mine, and to regard his offspring as equal to my brothers in male lineage and to teach them this art—if they desire to learn it—without fee and covenant; to give a share of precepts and oral instruction and all the other learning to my sons and to the sons of him who has instructed me and to pupils who have signed the covenant and have taken an oath according to the medical law, but no one else.

I will apply dietetic measures for the benefit of the sick according to my ability and judgment; I will keep them from harm and injustice.

I will neither give a deadly drug to anybody who asked for it, nor will I make a suggestion to this effect. Similarly I will not give to a woman an abortive remedy. In purity and holiness I will guard my life and my art.

I will not use the knife, not even on sufferers from stone, but will withdraw in favor of such men as are engaged in this work.

Whatever houses I may visit, I will come for the benefit of the sick, remaining free of all intentional injustice, of all mischief and in particular of sexual relations with both female and male persons, be they free or slaves.

What I may see or hear in the course of the treatment or even outside of the treatment in regard to the life of men, which on no account one must spread abroad, I will keep to myself, holding such things shameful to be spoken about.

If I fulfil this oath and do not violate it, may it be granted to me to enjoy life and art, being honored with fame among all men for all time to come; if I transgress it and swear falsely, may the opposite of all this be my lot.

Source: Ludwig Edelstein. *The Hippocratic Oath: Text, Translation, and Interpretation,* trans. from the Greek by Ludwig Edelstein (Baltimore: Johns Hopkins Press, 1943). ©1996 Prof. Harold Cherniss. Reprinted with permission of The Johns Hopkins University Press.

Document: Commonwealth v. Isaiah Bangs, the first known American judicial ruling on abortion (footnotes omitted).
Date: 1812.
Where: Supreme Judicial Court of Massachusetts.
Significance: Indicates the contemporary emphasis on quickening.

Supreme Judicial Court of Massachusetts.

Commonwealth v. Isaiah Bangs.

October Term, 1812.

**1 *387 An indictment for administering a potion with intent to procure an abortion, must contain an allegation that an abortion ensued, and that the woman was quick with child.

THE defendant was indicted, October term, 1810, for assaulting and beating one *Lucy Holman,* and administering to her a certain dangerous and deleterious draught or potion, against her will, with intent to procure the abortion and premature birth of a bastard child, of which she was then pregnant, and which the defendant had before that time begotten of her body, *et alia enormia,* &c., to the great damage of the said *Lucy,* against good morals and good manners, in evil example to others in like case to offend, *contra pacem,* &c.

The *Solicitor-General,* at the trial, entered a *noli prosequi* as to the assault and battery charged in the indictment.

A verdict was found, at the same term, that the defendant was guilty of all the several matters charged in the indictment, excepting that the said potion was taken by the said *Lucy* voluntarily.

After the verdict was returned, the defendant moved the Court to arrest the judgment, on the ground that no indictable offence was described in the indictment, except the part *non pros'd* by the *Solicitor-General,* and the cause stood over to this term for the consideration of that motion.

Fay, in support of the motion, contended that the principal charge in the indictment, amounting to no more than an aggravated assault and battery, as to which the *Solicitor-General* had entered a *noli prosequi*, and of which there was no evidence at the trial, there remained nothing against the defendant but the administering, with the patient's consent, some potion, with intent that the same should produce an abortion. No abortion was produced; and if there had been, there is no averment that the woman was quick with child; both which circumstances are *388 necessary ingredients in the offence intended to be charged in the indictment.

The Solicitor-General argued that any overt act, perpetrated with the intent to procure a misdemeanor to be committed, was itself a misdemeanor, and the patient's consent to take the deleterious draught did not make the administering of it lawful.

There can be no sentence upon this verdict. The assault and battery are out of the case, and no abortion is alleged to have followed the taking of the potion; and if an abortion had been alleged and proved to have ensued, the averment that the woman was quick with child at the time is a necessary part of the indictment.

Mass. 1812.

COMMONWEALTH v. ISAIAH BANGS.

9 Mass. 387, 1812 WL 1295 (Mass.)

SOURCE: *Commonwealth v. Isaiah Bangs* 9 Mass. 387, 1812 WL 1295 (Mass.).

DOCUMENT ANALYSIS

This case from Massachusetts exemplifies the concern with quickening, the point at which the pregnant woman can feel her fetus move in the womb. The facts of the case are quite simple, although the old English language can make them hard to interpret: the father of Lucy's fetus was alleged to have assaulted her and forced her to drink a poison that would cause her to miscarry. The court found, after investigating these allegations, that Lucy had willingly taken the poison, absolving her partner of liability in that charge. More importantly for the purposes of this text, however, is the consistent comment that whether abortion is a crime depends on the establishment of quickening.

IN HISTORY

CONNECTICUT ABORTION LAW

With the following statute, Connecticut became the first state in the nation to criminalize postquickening abortions in America in 1821.

Title 22

SECT. 14 Every person who shall, wilfully and maliciously, administer to, or cause to be administered to, or taken by, any person or persons, any deadly poison, or other noxious and destructive substance, with an intention him, her, or them, thereby to murder, or thereby to cause or procure the miscarriage of any woman, then being quick with child, and shall be thereof be duly convicted, shall suffer imprisonment, in newgate prison, during this natural life, or for such other term as the court having cognizance of the offence shall determine.

Source: The Public Statute Laws of the State of Connecticut, 1821 (Hartford, 1821), 152–153.

Ironically, quickening can only be confirmed by the pregnant woman, who may herself not wish to establish the unlawfulness of her abortion. Quickening was an unreliable demarcation of pregnancy for another reason: not all women experience quickening at the same moment of fetal development. Factors affecting quickening include a woman's physiological condition—including her stature and weight and whether she has had previous pregnancies—and the overall activity level of the individual fetus. So while the quickening doctrine afforded women a fair amount of latitude in managing their own pregnancy decisions, it was a rather imprecise scientific measure of fetal development.

The court's judgment here reflects one additional development: that the issue of abortion was beginning to take on a public dimension. Once moved from the home-care of the midwife and into the courtroom, abortion would begin to incite a public dialogue—and debate—about its proper use and place within American society, as seen in the following documents.

Document: The Declaration of Sentiments.
Date: 1848.
Where: Seneca Falls, New York.
Significance: This statement was drafted at the Seneca Falls Convention, which marked the beginning of the American movement for women's rights. The document follows the tone and structure of the Declaration of Independence and lists many grievances against women, including forcing women to adhere to laws to which they did not consent.

When, in the course of human events, it becomes necessary for one portion of the family of man to assume among the people of the earth a position different from that which they have hitherto occupied, but one to which the laws of nature and of nature's God entitle them, a decent respect to the opinions of mankind requires that they should declare the causes that impel them to such a course.

We hold these truths to be self-evident: that all men and women are created equal; that they are endowed by their Creator with certain inalienable rights; that among these are life, liberty, and the pursuit of happiness; that to secure these rights governments are instituted, deriving their just powers from the consent of the governed. Whenever any form of government becomes destructive of these ends, it is the right of those who suffer from it to refuse allegiance to it, and to insist upon the institution of a new government, laying its foundation on such principles, and organizing its powers in such form, as to them shall seem most likely to effect their safety and happiness. Prudence, indeed, will dictate that governments long established should not be changed for light and transient causes; and accordingly all experience hath shown that mankind are more disposed to suffer. while evils are sufferable, than to right themselves by abolishing the forms to which they are accustomed. But when a long train of abuses and usurpations, pursuing invariably the same object, evinces a design to reduce them under absolute despotism, it is their duty to throw off such government, and to provide new guards for their future security. Such has been the patient sufferance of the women under this government, and such is now the necessity which constrains them to demand the equal station to which they are entitled. The history of mankind is a history of repeated injuries and usurpations on the part of man toward woman, having in direct object the establishment of an absolute tyranny over her. To prove this, let facts be submitted to a candid world.

The history of mankind is a history of repeated injuries and usurpations on the part of man toward woman, having in direct object the establishment of an absolute tyranny over her. To prove this, let facts be submitted to a candid world.

He has never permitted her to exercise her inalienable right to the elective franchise.

He has compelled her to submit to laws, in the formation of which she had no voice.

He has withheld from her rights which are given to the most ignorant and degraded men—both natives and foreigners.

Having deprived her of this first right of a citizen, the elective franchise, thereby leaving her without representation in the halls of legislation, he has oppressed her on all sides.

He has made her, if married, in the eye of the law, civilly dead.

He has taken from her all right in property, even to the wages she earns.

He has made her, morally, an irresponsible being, as she can commit many crimes with impunity, provided they be done in the presence of her husband. In the covenant of marriage, she is compelled to promise obedience to her husband, he becoming, to all intents and purposes, her master—the law giving him power to deprive her of her liberty, and to administer chastisement.

He has so framed the laws of divorce, as to what shall be the proper causes, and in case of separation, to whom the guardianship of the children shall be given, as to be wholly regardles of the happiness of women—the law, in all cases, going upon a flase supposition of the supremacy of man, and giving all power into his hands.

After depriving her of all rights as a married woman, if single, and the owner of property, he has taxed her to support a government which recognizes her only when her property can be made profitable to it.

He has monopolized nearly all the profitable employments, and from those she is permitted to follow, she receives but a scanty remuneration. He closes against her all the avenues to wealth and distinction which he considers most honorable to himself. As a teacher of theology, medicine, or law, she is not known.

He has denied her the facilities for obtaining a thorough education, all colleges being closed against her.

He allows her in church, as well as state, but a subordinate position, claiming apostolic authority for her exclusion from the ministry, and, with some exceptions, from any public participation in the affairs of the church.

He has created a false public sentiment by giving to the world a different code of morals for men and women, by which moral delinquencies which exclude women from society, are not only tolerated, but deemed of little account in man.

He has usurped the prerogative of Jehovah himself, claiming it as his right to assign for her a sphere of action, when that belongs to her conscience and to her God.

He has endeavored, in every way that he could, to destroy her confidence in her own powers, to lessen her self-respect, and to make her willing to lead a dependent and abject life.

Now, in view of this entire disfranchisement of one-half the people of this country, their social and religious degradation—in view of the unjust laws above mentioned, and because women do feel themselves aggrieved, oppressed, and fraudulently deprived of their most sacred rights, we insist that they have immediate admission to all the rights and privileges which belong to them as citizens of the United States.

SOURCE: Elizabeth Cady Stanton, *A History of Woman Suffrage*, vol. 1 (Rochester, N.Y.: Fowler and Wells, 1889), 70–71.

DOCUMENT ANALYSIS

The Declaration of Sentiments is widely heralded as the beginning of organized feminism in the United States. The document was the product of a convention at Seneca Falls, New York, organized by activists Lucretia Mott and Elizabeth Cady Stanton, who were inspired to begin the women's movement because of their poor treatment in the abolition movement. The document was signed by 32 men and 68 women.

The impact of the Declaration is enormous. Because of its reach and the strategically savvy use of the Declaration of Independence as its model, a feminist movement began in earnest to demand voting rights, among other things. Foremost among the claims of the Declaration is its emphasis on voting rights as a means to secure other meaningful legal protections.

The fact that the Declaration does not explicitly mention abortion reflects several dynamics. First, abortion was still considered a very private experience, and many Americans, women and men alike, would have been reluctant to discuss it in public. What is more, to have included abortion in this statement would surely have made the movement more divisive; by focusing on rights of property, education, and representation, the authors called on the great demands of the revolution itself, and therefore afforded themselves wider public acceptance.

Although it does not include reference to abortion, this document is central in this chapter in illustrating the countervailing social pressures of the nineteenth century: while on the one hand, women were clamoring for a wide variety of rights, simultaneously a movement to restrict their ability to control fertility was in full swing.

Document: American Medical Association (AMA) Report on Criminal Abortion.

Date: 1859.

Where: Read to the AMA membership at its Louisville meeting.

Significance: The report reveals the role of the AMA, founded in 1847, in criminalizing abortion during the latter half of the nineteenth century, as well as the erosion of society's focus on quickening as the point of human ensoulment or hominization.

The heinous guilt of criminal abortion, however viewed by the community, is everywhere acknowledged by medical men.

Its frequency—among all classes of society, rich and poor, single and married—most physicians have been led to suspect; very many, from their own experience of its deplorable results, have known. Were any doubt, however, entertained upon this point, it is at once removed by comparisons of the present with our past rates of increase in population, the size of our families, the statistics of our foetal deaths, by themselves considered, and relatively to the births and to the general mortality. The evidence from these sources is too constant and too overwhelming to be explained on the ground that pregnancies are merely prevented; or on any other supposition than that of fearfully extended crime.

The causes of this general demoralization are manifold. There are three of them, however, and they are the most important, with which the medical profession have especially to do.

The first of these causes is a wide-spread popular ignorance of the true character of the crime—a belief, even among mothers themselves, that the foetus is not alive till after the period of quickening.

The second of the agents alluded to is the fact that the profession themselves are frequently supposed careless of foetal life; not that its respectable members are ever knowingly and intentionally accessory to the unjustifiable commission of abortion, but that they are thought at times to omit precautions or measures that might prevent the occurrence of so unfortunate an event.

The third reason of the frightful extent of this crime is found in the grave defects of our laws, both common and statute, as regards the independent and actual existence of the child before birth, as a living being. These errors, which are sufficient in most instances to prevent conviction, are based, and only based, upon mistaken and exploded medical dogmas. With strange inconsistency, the law fully acknowledges the foetus in utero and its inherent rights, for civil purposes; while personally and as criminally affected, it fails to recognize it, and to its life as yet denies all protection.

Abundant proof upon each of these points has been prepared by the Committee, and is elsewhere* [Report Footnote: *North American Medico-Chirurgical Review, Jan. 1859, et seq.] being published to the profession; but as the statements now made are almost axiomatic, recapitulation would be here wearisome and is unnecessary.

Our duty is plain. If, by any act, we can effect aught towards the suppression of this crime, it must be done. In questions of abstract right, the medical profession do not acknowledge such words as expediency, time service, cowardice. We are the physical guardians of women; we, alone, thus far, of their offspring in utero. The case is here of life or death—the life or death of thousands—and it depends, almost wholly, upon ourselves.

As a profession we are unanimous in our condemnation of the crime. Mere resolutions to this effect, and nothing more, are therefore useless, evasive, and cruel.

If to want of knowledge on a medical point, the slaughter of countless children now steadily perpetrated in our midst, is to be attributed, it is our duty, as physicians, and as good and true men, both publicly and privately, and by every means in our power, to enlighten this ignorance.

If we have ever been thought negligent of the sanctity of foetal life, the means of correcting the error are before us. If we have ever been so in deed, there are materials, and there is good occasion for the establishment of an obstetric code; which, rigorously kept to the standard of our attainments in knowledge, and generally accepted by the profession, would tend to prevent such unnecessary and unjustifiable destruction of human life.

If the tenets of the law, here unscientific, unjust, inhuman, can be bettered—as citizens, and to the best of our ability we should seek this end. If the evidence upon this point is especially of a medical character, it is our duty to proffer our aid, and in so important a matter to urge it. But if, as is also true, these great fundamental, and fatal faults of the law are owing to doctrinal errors of the profession in a former age, it devolves upon us, by every bond we hold sacred, by our reverence for the fathers in medicine, by our love for our race, and by our responsibility as accountable beings, to see these errors removed and their grievous results abated.

In accordance, therefore, with the facts in the case, the Committee would advise that this body, representing, as it does, the physicians of the land, publicly express its abhorrence of the unnatural and now rapidly increasing crime of abortion; that it avow its true nature, as no simple offence against public morality and decency, no mere misdemeanor, no attempt upon the life of the mother, but the wanton and murderous destruction of her child; and that while it would in no wise transcend its legitimate province or invade the precincts of the law, the Association recommend, by memorial, to the governors and legislatures of the several States, and, as representing the federal district, to the President and Congress, a careful examination and revision of the statutory and of so much of the common law, as relates to this crime. For we hold it to be a thing deserving all hate and detestation, that a man in his very originall, whiles he is framed, whiles he is enlived, should be put to death under the very hands, and in the shop, of Nature.

In the belief that we have expressed the unanimous opinion of the Association, our report is respectfully submitted.

> Horatio R Storer of, Massachusetts.
> Thomas W. Blatchford, of New York.
> Hugh L. Hodge, of Pennsylvania.
> Charles A. Pope, of Missouri.
> Edward H. Barton, of South Carolina.
> A. Lopez, of Alabama.
> Wm. Henry Brisbane, of Wisconsin.
> A. J. Semmes, of District of Columbia.

If the recommendation of the report are adopted, the Committee would offer the following resolutions:

Resolved, That while physicians have long been united in condemning the act of producing abortion, at every period of gestation, except as necessary for preserving the life of either mother or child, it has become the duty of this Association, in view of the prevalence and increasing frequency of the crime, publicly to enter an earnest and solemn protest against such unwarrantable destruction of human life.

Resolved, That in pursuance of the grand and noble calling we profess, the saving of human lives, and of the sacred responsibilities thereby devolving upon us, the Association present this subject to the attention of the several legislative assemblies of the Union, with the prayer that the laws by which the crime of procuring abortion is attempted to be controlled may be revised, and that such other action may be taken in the premises as they in their wisdom may deem necessary.

Resolved, That the Association request the zealous co-operation of the various State Medical Societies in pressing this subject upon the legislatures of either respective States, and that the President and Secretaries of the Association are hereby authorized to carry out, by memorial, these resolutions. (pp. 75–8).

SOURCE: AMA Report on Criminal Abortion (1859), available at: http://www.abortionessay.com/files/1859ama.html.

DOCUMENT ANALYSIS

The American Medical Association (AMA) was founded in 1847; from its inception, this professional association had opposed the practice of abortion for a number of reasons. First, this new association of "regular doctors" used its opposition to abortion to distinguish itself, both morally and medically, from the midwives who had dominated female health care since colonial times. Arguing that abortion was dangerous and morally repugnant, the doctors could assert that anyone providing abortion (midwives) was both morally questionable and professionally inferior. The result is that physicians competed for the business of women, and by the end of the nineteenth century, they were successful in generating business, particularly from the middle and upper class families who identified with the specialized training required of physicians.

This particular document also reflects the influence of one of its signatories: Horatio Storer. Dr. Storer, whose award-winning essay, *Why Not? A Book for Every Woman*, is reviewed in this chapter, had urged the AMA to more directly address the question of abortion in the medical profession, calling on the AMA to establish a committee to investigate the procedure and its practice. By 1857, the AMA had established such a committee; the product of their work is this report.

The report primarily condemns the wrongful thinking of the quickening doctrine. For much of Western civilization, at least dating back to the Greeks, the quickening doctrine had guided both religious and medical institutions. The AMA report marks the first major professional organization to attack the quickening doctrine head-on, calls instead for an appreciation of human life beginning at conception, and indicates the serious role played by midcentury doctors in effecting abortion restrictions.

The consequence of the report is hard to overstate. Offered up at midcentury, the report turned the tide of legal opinion, and created a catalyst for change in the state legislatures. It is important to remember, however, that this document emphasizes male understanding of pregnancy and abortion; women themselves, most deeply affected by abortion policy, would wait another 60 years before gaining the right to vote. Still, beginning in the 1860s, states began to criminalize abortion from the point of conception, fundamentally changing the legal context in which abortion would continue to occur. For although there is little evidence that criminalization stops abortion, there is significant evidence that criminalization makes provision much riskier for both provider and patient.

Document: Excerpt from Dr. Horatio Storer's *Why Not? A Book for Every Woman: A Proper Bostonian on Sex and Birth Control.*
Date: 1868.
Where: Originally appeared as a pamphlet in Boston in 1866 published by Lee and Shepard Publishers.
Significance: During the 1864 annual meeting of the AMA, attending physicians who were distressed about the continuance of abortion in America decided to produce "a short and comprehensive tract, for circulation among females, for the purpose of enlightening them upon the criminality and physical evils of forced abortions." The AMA chose to create a competition for best essay; the resulting document, which received the gold medal, is written by Dr. Horatio Storer, antiabortion activist, surgeon to the Franciscan Hospital for Women, and professor of obstetrics and the diseases of women in Berkshire Medical College.

V. — THE FREQUENCY OF FORCED ABORTIONS, EVEN AMONG THE MARRIED.

All are familiar with the fact, to be perceived everywhere upon the most casual scrutiny, that the standard size of families is not on the average what used to be seen; in other words, that instances of an excess over three or four children are not nearly as common as we know was the case a generation or two back. No one supposes that men or women have, as a whole, so deteriorated in procreative ability as this might otherwise seem to imply.

There can be but one solution to the problem, either that pregnancies are very generally prevented, or that, occurring, they are prematurely cut short. We have seen that countless confessions prove that this surmise is true.

In the treatise to which we have already alluded, its author has shown by a series of un-answerable deductions, based on material gathered from many sources both at home and abroad, that forced abortions in America are of very frequent occurrence, and that this frequency is rapidly increasing, not in the cities alone, but in the country districts, where there is less excuse on the ground of excessive expenditures, the claims of fashionable life, or an over-crowding of the population. It was proved, for instance, that in one State that was named, one of the wealthiest in the Union, the natural increase of the population, or the excess of the births over the deaths, has of late years been wholly by those of recent foreign origin. This was the state of things existing in 1850; three years later it was evident that the births in that commonwealth, with the usual increase, had resulted in favor of foreign parents in an increased ratio. In other words, it is found that, in so fir as depends upon the American and native element, and in the absence of the existing immigration from abroad, the population of our older States, even allowing for the loss by emigration, is stationary or decreasing.

Thus it is seen that abortion is a crime not merely against the life of the child and the health of its mother, and against good morals, but that it strikes a blow at the very foundation of society itself.

One of the strange and unexpected results at which the author we have so often referred to has arrived, but which he has both proved to a demonstration and satisfactorily explained, is that abortions are infinitely more frequent among Protestant women than among Catholic; a fact, however, that becomes less unaccountable in view of the known size, comparatively so great, of the families of the latter—in the Irish, for instance—the point being that the different frequency of the abortions depends not upon a difference in social position or in fecundity, but in the religion. We should suppose a priori that the Protestant, especially if of New England and Puritan stock, would be much the safer against all such assaults of the world, the flesh, and the devil. The following is the concise and convincing solution of the paradox that has been given:

> "It is not, of course, intended to imply that Protestantism, as such, in any way encourages, or, indeed, permits the practice of inducing abortion; its tenets are uncompromisingly hostile to all crime. So great, however, is the popular ignorance regarding this offence, that an abstract morality is here comparatively powerless; and there can be no doubt that the Romish ordinance, flanked on the one hand by the confessional, and by denouncement and excommunication on the other, has saved to the world thousands of infant lives."

There is another surprising result that must strike every candid observer whose position gives him extended and frequent observation of women, and of late years the study, and treatment of their special diseases has become so recognized that there are many physicians thus rendered competent to judge; it is this, but a second one of the many very frightful characteristics of induced abortion, that the act is proportionately much more common in the married than in the unmarried, basing the calculation upon an equal number of pregnancies in each case.

This fact also may be easily accounted for. Abortion is undoubtedly more common in the earlier than in the later months of pregnancy, because the sensible signs of foetal vitality are then less permanently present, and the conscience is then better able to persuade itself that the child may possibly be without life, or the alarm wholly a false one. It is less common with first than with subsequent children, though instances of its occurrence with the former are certainly not rare. A woman who has never been pregnant does not, -as a general rule, conceive as readily as one who has already been impregnated before, perhaps partly from the fact that intercourse, under certain circumstances, is more likely to be excessive in such cases, at times producing acute or subacute inflammation of the cervix uteri, and consequent sterility, as is so constantly observed in prostitutes, very many of whom, upon ceasing their trade, after accumulating a little property, as in France, or upon being sent to out-lying colonies, as in England, and becoming married, at once fall pregnant.

The unmarried woman, if enceinte, has not the opportunity of lying by for a few days' sickness, without exciting suspicion, that the married can easily seize for themselves. She is often not so conversant with the early symptoms of gestation, and is more prone to wait until its existence has been rendered certain by the sensation of quickening, in the hope, doubtless, not unfrequently, that this certainty may persuade her paramour to marriage, instead of deckling hire against it, as is so often the case. It may he allowed, I think, that infanticide, the murder of a child after its birth, or its exposure to the vicissitudes and perils of chance, is more common among the unmarried, but that destruction of the foetus in utero, the rather prevails where the rites of law and religion would seem to have extended to that foetus every possible safeguard.

In the latest of the papers upon the subject of abortion, to which we have already alluded, there is furnished additional evidence as to the frequency of induced miscarriage.

"The infrequency of abortions," it is said, "as compared with labors at the full period, is disproved by the experience of every physician in special or large general practice, who will faithfully investigate the subject. The truth of this statement has been fully verified, in the instance of abortion criminally induced, by many of my professional friends who were at first inclined to doubt the accuracy of my inferences on that point; with reference to abortions more naturally occurring, the evidence is of course more easily arrived at, and is in consequence proportionately more striking. In many cases of sterility it will be found that the number of abortions in a single patient have been almost innumerable; and, it way be added, in a large proportion of the cases of uterine disease occurring in the married, inquiry as to their past history will reveal abortions, unsuspected perhaps even by the family physician, as the cause. It is not so much the general practitioner, the hospital attendant, or the accoucheur, as such, who can testify as to the true frequency of abortion; for many cases, even of the most deplorably fatal results, do not seek for medical assistance at the time of the accident. The real balance sheet of these cases is to be made out by the hands which are more especially called to the treatment of chronic uterine disease."

But not only is abortion of excessively frequent occurrence; the nefarious practice is yearly extending, as does every vice that custom and habit have rendered familiar. It is foolish to trust that a change for the better may be spontaneously effected. "Longer silence and waiting by the profession would be criminal. If these wretched women, these married, lawful mothers, ay, and these Christian husbands, are thus murdering their children by thousands through ignorance, they must be taught the truth; but if, as there is reason to believe is too often the case, they have been influenced to do so by fashion, extravagance of living, or lust, no language of condemnation can be too strong."

VI. — The Excuses and Pretexts that are given for the Act.

I have already stated that in many instances it is alleged by the mother that she is ignorant of the true character of the act of willful abortion, and in some cases I am satisfied that the excuse is sincerely given, although, in these days of the general diffusion of a certain amount of physiological knowledge, such ignorance would seem incredible.

The above is, however, the only excuse that can be given with any show of plausibility, and even this holds for naught should the case by any chance come under the cognizance of the law, just as would a plea of ignorance of the low itself; it being always taken for granted that any intentional act implies a knowledge of its own nature and its consequences, be these trivial or grave.

I have stated that in no case should abortion be permitted, or allowed to be permitted, by the advice or approval of a single physician; that in all cases where such counsel is taken, it should be from a consultation of at least two competent men. Submitted to such a tribunal, seldom indeed would the sanction be given. Ill health would be no excuse, for there is hardly a conceivable case where the invalidism could either not be relieved in some other mode, or where by an abortion it would not be made worse.

The fear of childbed would be no excuse, for we have seen that its risks are in reality less than those of an abortion, and its pains and anguish can now be materially mitigated or entirely subdued by of aesthesia, which the skill of medical science can induce, and should induce, in every case of labor. My remarks apply not to first pregnancies alone, when one might expect that women would naturally be anxious and timid, but even to those cases of pregnancy that have been preceded by difficult and dangerous labors.

It has been urged, and not so absurdly as would at first sight appear, that the present possibilities of painless and so much safer delivery, by changing thus completely the primal curse, from anguish to a state frequently of positive pleasure, remove a drawback of actual advantage, and, by offering too many inducements for pregnancy, tend to keep women in that state the greater part of their menstrual lives.

Much of the low morale of the community, as regards the guilt of abortion, depends upon the very erroneous doctrines extensively inculcated by popular authors and lecturers for their own sinister purposes.

One of these is the doctrine that it is detrimental to a woman's health to bear children beyond a certain number, or oftener than at certain stated periods, and that any number of abortions are not merely excusable, as preventives, but advisable; it being entirely forgotten that the frequency of connection may be kept within bounds, and the times of its occurrence regulated, by those who are not willing to hazard its consequence's; that if women will, to escape trouble, or for fashion's sake, forego the duty and privilege of nursing,—a law entailed upon them by nature, and seldom neglected without disastrous results to their own constitutions,—they must expect more frequent impregnation; that the habit of aborting is generally attended with the habit of more readily conceiving; and that abortions, accidental, and still more if induced, are generally attended by the loss of subsequent health, if not of life.

This error is one which would justify abortion as necessary for the mother's own good; a selfish plea. The other is based on a more generous motive. It is, that the fewer one's children the more healthy they are likely to be, and the more worth to society. It is, however, equally fallacious with the first, and is without foundation in fact. The Spartans and Romans, so confidently appealed to, gave birth probably to a many weakly children as do our own women; that they destroyed many for this reason, in infancy, is notorious. The brawny Highlanders are not the only offspring of their parents; the others cannot endure the national processes of hardening by exposure and diet, and so die young from natural causes. Rut were this theory true even so far as it goes, the world, our own country, could ill spare its frailer—children, who oftenest, perhaps, represent its intellect and its genius.

VII.—Alternatives, Public and Private, and Measures of Relief.

It may be asked if there is no latitude to be allowed for extreme cases of the character already described. We are compelled to answer, None. If each woman were allowed to judge for herself in this matter, her decision upon the abstract question would be too sure to be warped by personal considerations, and those of the moment: Woman's mind is prone to depression, and, indeed, to temporary actual derangement, under the stimulus of uterine excitation, and this alike at the time of puberty and the final cessation of the menses, at the monthly period and at conception, during pregnancy, at labor, and during lactation; a matter that also seems to have been more thoroughly investigated by the authority I have so freely drawn from in reference to the question of abortion, than by any other writer in this country. During the state of gestation the woman is therefore liable to thoughts, convictions even, that at other times she would turn from in disgust or dismay; and in this fact, that must be as familiar to herself as it is to the physician, we find her most valid excuse for the crime.

Is there then no alternative but for women, when married and prone to conception, to occasionally bear children? This, as we have seen, is the end for which they are physiologically constituted and for which they are destined by nature. In it lies their most efficient safeguard for length of days and immunity from disease. Intentionally to prevent the occurrence of pregnancy, otherwise than by total abstinence from coition, intentionally to bring it, when begun, to a premature close, are alike disastrous to a woman's mental, moral, and physical well-being.

There are various alternatives to these so degrading habits of the community. To some of them equal objections apply. But, in reality, there is little difference between the immorality by which a man forsakes his home for an occasional visit to a house of prostitution, that he may preserve his wife from the chance of pregnancy, and the immorality by which that wife brings herself willfully to destroy the living fruit of her womb. Allowing for the weakness and frailty of human nature, the first were surely the preferable of the twain. But we need not compare these odious customs, each so common and each so wrong. With greater frugality of living, and greater self-denial, and self-control in more trivial matters, there need be no interference, at least no intentional interference, on the part of either husband or wife with the first great law of human weal and human happiness, in accordance with which, by the divine institution of home and its mutual joys, the due propagation and natural increase of the species was intended to be insured.

Were well-arranged foundling hospitals provided in all our large cities, they would prove a most efficient means of preventing the sacrifice of hundreds of the children of shame, and, so far from encouraging immorality, they would afford one of its surest preventives, for by keeping a woman from the crime of infanticide or the equally guilty intentional miscarriage, they would save her from one element of the self-condemnation and hatred which so often hurry the victim of seduction downward to the life of the brothel. A certain amount of illicit intercourse between the sexes will always take place, no matter how condemned by law, until the public standard of morals shall be so elevated as to render the practice unknown. This is a fact that is self-evident, and cannot be frowned out of existence. How much better to provide for its innocent victims, its irresponsible offspring, than, as now, to permit the so frequent destruction of both. It is foolish to assert that by such provision we but pander to sin. In many of these instances the woman is innocent of intentional wrong, being led astray by her perfect confidence in the constancy and good faith of a lover, and in others she is, doubtless, ignorant of the true character of the act she is committing. Should she be driven by what is comparatively a venial, and not so unnatural an offence, to one of the deadliest crimes?

But for the married, who have not this strong stimulus of necessity, and the excuse of having been led astray or deceived, there need be no public channel provided, through which to purchase safety for their children. Is it not, indeed, inconceivable that the very women, who, when their darlings of a month old, or a year, are snatched from them by disease, find the parting attended with so acute a pang, can so deliberately provide for, and congratulate themselves and each other, upon a willful abortion! Here, words fail us.

"Of the mother, by consent or by her own hand, imbrued with her infant's blood; of the equally guilty father, who counsels or allows the crime; of the wretches, who by their wholesale murders, far out-Herod Burke and Hare; of the public sentiment which palliates, pardons, and would even praise this, so common, violation of all law, human and divine, of all instinct, all reason, all pity, all mercy, all love, we leave those to speak who can."

SOURCE: Horatio Storer, *Why Not? A Book for Every Woman: A Proper Bostonian on Sex and Birth Control* (Reprint by Arno Press, New York, 1974).

DOCUMENT ANALYSIS

Dr. Storer's prize-winning essay, which is quite long in its entirety, touches on a number of important developments in mid-nineteenth-century abortion politics. Foremost among these points is the doctor's emphasis on the mistaken historic reliance on quickening as a justification for early abortion. He writes at length to describe the faulty logic and science of allowing abortion prior to that developmental milestone, in part reflecting the growing concern that a quickening doctrine ceded too much authority to women, the only individuals able to discern that the milestone had been achieved.

Beyond this contribution, Storer's comments reflect two additional observations that would become widely shared by the end of the century. One is rooted in ethnic bias: a growing number of commentators observed that as Irish and Italian immigration boomed toward the end of the century, the primarily Catholic immigrants would outnumber the "native born" Protestants if abortion rates continued to increase among them, as Storer claims they had. Likely a result of rising education and political opportunity, many historians have noted the likelihood that abortion rates climbed at the end of the century, allowing middle-class white women especially the opportunity to seek public lives through planned child-birth.

This trend is cause for another of Storer's concerns: the rising incidence of abortion among married women in particular. It is largely thought that abortion went unregulated in the first half of the century because it was mostly poor, immigrant, and single women who accessed abortion. Tighter restrictions on abortion coincide chronologically with a rising abortion incidence among married women, whose social, familial, and religious purpose was linked often with motherhood. With a cultural emphasis on "quality" child-rearing, many married women of means were trying to time, space, and limit their childbearing to conform with social expectations. This, in turn, caused Storer, and others, great concern over the proper role of married women, which by Storer's account, is to bear children.

Document: Abortionist Advertisement.
Date: 1866.
Where: The *New York Times*.
Significance: This advertisement is characteristic of abortion service advertising in the late-nineteenth century. The ads illustrate the commonness of abortion, indicate some of the common language used to describe unwanted pregnancy, and also provide authorities with locations of providers.

ABORTION ADVERTISEMENT IN THE NEW YORK TIMES, 1866.

Ann Trow was the most reknowned and successful abortion provider of the nineteenth century. Advertising under the name "Madame Restell," Trow was widely known to practice abortion at a time when abortion was under increasing political and legal scrutiny. The advertisement for "Madame Restell's" services in the *New York Times* some years after her arrest indicates how ubiquitous the practice of abortion was, even as lawmakers and those in the "regular" medical profession attempted to restrict access. Restell was one of the best-known abortion providers in her region, and although she openly advertised her services, Restell's euphemistic language is indicative of her time.

ADVICE TO MARRIED LADIES.—

MADAME RESTELL, Professor of Midwifery, having over thirty years' successful practice in this city, guarantees a safe and immediate removal of all special irregularities and obstructions in females, with or without medicine, at one interview, or by mail. Can be consulted with the utmost confidence at No. 64 West 34th-st., (under the Everett Rooms) a few doors from 6th-av. Her infallible French Female Pills, No. 1, price $1, or No. 2, which are four degrees stronger than No. 1, and can never fail, are safe and healthy, price $5. can be sent by mail. Madame RESTELL deams it her duty to caution ladies against imitators, who not only deprive them of their means, but their health.

Document: Madame Restell Charged.
Date: 1854.
Where: The *New York Daily Times*.
Significance: Madame Restell, like many other abortion providers during this time, was arrested and charged with a felony. Restell was particularly notorious in New York, mainly because she was financially successful in her illicit business. Tragically, Restell ultimately committed suicide in the midst of her troubles with the law.

MADAME RESTELL ARRESTED ON FELONY CHANGES OF CRIMINAL ABORTION.

Madame Restell, had a number of brushes with the law and was a target of the local press for many years. This story tells of one such incident and illustrates the dire situation in which many nineteenth-century women found themselves. Restell continued to perform abortions until she was arrested in 1878 for violation of the Comstock Act. Tragically, Restell took her own life on April 1, 1878 by slitting her throat to avoid standing trial.

NEW-YORK CITY.

New York Daily Times (1851-1857); Feb 14, 1854; ProQuest Historical Newspapers The New York Times (1851-2003) pg.1

NEW-YORK CITY.

The Seduction in High Life–Remarkable Disclosures of the Victim–Madame restell charged with a Felony—Surrender of the reputed husband.

Additional proceedings were had yesterday before Judge STUART, at the Jefferson Police Court, respecting the alleged seduction of a young girl named CORDELIA A. GRANT, by a person of wealth named GEORGE R. SHACKFORD, who resides at Fordham, Westchester County, N. Y. The complainant in this case is connected with a highly respectable family residing at Portland, Maine, and when first brought to this City was not quite 16 years of age. Thus six years or more have elapsed, and during that period her parents, relatives, friends, and all who knew her, were under the impression that she was the lawful wife of SHACKFORD. The girl states that she also believed the would eventually become the wife of said defendant, but latterly he manifested a desire to desert her, and she at once sought redress through the criminal authorities. As before stated, the notorious RESTELL was arrested by the police, and she now stands charged with the commission of a felony, which is punishable by imprisonment in the State Prison for a term not exceeding three years nor less than one in the penitentiary.

Yesterday morning SHACKFORD came before Justice STUART, in company with his counsel, ex-Recorder TALLMADOE, and surrendered himself to answer the charges preferred against him. Meanwhile the complainant made full disclosures of the affair in a sworn affidavit. We append such of the statements sworn to as are deemed fit for publication.

THE DISCLOSURES.

Cordelia A. Grant, of the City of New-York, being sworn, said: I am now 22 years of age; for the past seven years I have lived most of the time with George R. Shackford as his wife, and have been introduced by said George as his reputed wife; I have traveled with George R. Shackford, and boarded and lodged with him, as his wife; I have, during this time, been *enciente* five different times, and in each and every case an abortion has been procured, at the inhance of Shackford, so that my health and constitution are broken and greatly impaired; three of these abortions have been produced while in the City of New-York, (by the procurement of sail George,) at the house of Madame Restell, No. 162 chambers street, as follows: On the first occasion, myself and George were boarding at the house of Mr. Henry, in Wooter-street, as man and wife; I was approaching confinement, when George R. Shackford told me he had made arrangement: with Charles Lohman (the reputed husband of Madame Restell) to produce an abortion, and that he was waiting for me to come to his house; I then went to the residence of Restell, in Chambers street; Shackford and Lohman whispered together, and then he (Shackford) paid Lohman $50 in cash: the Madame's husband then spoke to me, and said I could have a lady attendent if I chose: at this moment, Madame Restell came into the room, and told me to walk upstairs with her; at this time Shackford told Restell I was his wife, or rather that we were married; after we got upstairs, Restell told me it was a pity for a married woman like me to love my children, as I was a pretty woman, and would have fine children; she then talked with me, on more lively matters, and remarked, "Keep up good spirits;" Restell soon after performed her operation, which threw me into an agony of pain; I was very sick for a long time after; when this abortion was produced as above stayed, it was on the night of 2nd of January, 1850; the second time Restell produced an abortion was on or about the 14th of January, 1851; at this time I was boarding with shackford, as No. 141 Greenwich-street; I passed as his noice, and he passed as my guardian; at this time I was attending school daily at Mrs. Hannah Parker's in Spring-street; said George told the school teacher and the parties where we boarded that I was his ward; I became advanced again towards confinement, and George insisted I should again submit to Restell's operation; I refused, but was finally compelled to go there with him; I went there with my trunk in a carriage, and permanent arrangements were made for me to stay there with Restell two weeks; in the meantime, George told our boarding-house keeper that we were going to Boston; it was at noon-day when we arrived at the house of Lohman, and in my presence Shackford paid Restell $100 in cash; about 6 o'clock that evening the painful operation was performed by Restell; I was in a room alone after this and fainted away; when I came to, I knocked on the wall for Restell, and she came and attended to me; Restell took the child away at this time, and afterwards informed me she had burnt it up; Restell told me "George has said I could be trusted, and all would be kept still;" when George returned form Boston I was a little recovered, and he took me back to the same house in Greenwich-street, where we remained until Spring, when we started on our Summer travelling tour; we visited Cape May, Saratoga and numerous other places, as man and wife; during the whole time I remained at Rostell's house; Lohman was there every day, and lived there as the husband of Festell; he saw me daily and knew (as well as I did) what object I was there for, except that the money in this case was paid to Restell; on the third occasion of being enciente. I was at Cape May, N. J. with Shackford, as his wife; for the purpose of having another abortion produced upon me, he brought me to the City and we stopped at the Girard House; we arrived here this time in the month of October, 1852; the next day George gave me $50 in cash and sent me to Restell's to have another abortion produced; he accompanied me part of the way to the house; I got to Restell's house at 9 o'clock in the morning, but she was not in and the servant said she had gone to Lohman's office in Liberty-street; I then went down there and found her with her brother-Lohman having gone to Europe; Restell and myself walked to her house together, and I told her "what I had come for again;" I then paid her the $50, and she performed the operation as before; I then left immediately, went back to the Girard House and met George, with the baggage, all ready to start, and we went for with to the Westchester House, corner of Broome-street and the Bowery, and I went immediately to bed; I was sick at the Westchester House about two weeks, and then paid a visit to my friends down East, where I remained three weeks, when George came out there and brought me back to the City; since this time of returning from the eastward, George has not had any intercourse with me; since we left the Westchester House, I continued to remain with him as his ward, and have been under his charge, boarding at the same houses; I further say that Shackford has recently built a new and costly house at Fordham, Westchester Co; N. Y, to which place he took me from the school in Twenty seventh street, in the month of October last, and I have remained as the mistress of the house since, until now; the other two abortions were not committed in this City or any part of the State; I was about 16 years of age when I first became acquainted with the said George R. Shockford, and most of the time since I have lived with him in the Character of a wife and as ward.

As will be observed, there are several criminal charges pending against the parties in this matter, and at 3 o'clock tomorrow (Wednesday) afternoon the investigation commences.

Document: The Comstock Act or "An Act for the Suppression of Trade in, and Circulation of, Obscene Literature and Articles of Immoral Use" (S. 1572, 42D Congress, 3D Session).

Date: 1873.

Where: U.S. Congress.

Significance: The Comstock Act, so named for its author and chief advocate, was the first action taken by the federal government to intervene in the regulation of abortion and marks a significant change in the scope of federal authority.

TITLE 18, UNITED STATES CODE

Section 1461. Mailing obscene or crime-inciting matter

Every obscene, lewd, lascivious, indecent, filthy or vile article, matter, thing, device, or substance; and—Every article or thing designed, adapted, or intended for producing abortion, or for any indecent or immoral use; and

Every article, instrument, substance, drug, medicine, or thing which is advertised or described in a manner calculated to lead another to use or apply it for producing abortion, or for any indecent or immoral purpose; and

Every written or printed card, letter, circular, book, pamphlet, advertisement, or notice of any kind giving information, directly or indirectly, where, or how, or from whom, or by what means any of such mentioned matters, articles, or things may be obtained or made, or where or by whom any act or operation of any kind for the procuring or producing of abortion will be done or performed, or how or by what means abortion may be produced, whether sealed or unsealed; and

Every paper, writing, advertisement, or representation that any article, instrument, substance, drug, medicine, or thing may, or can, be used or applied for producing abortion, or for any indecent or immoral purpose; and

Every description calculated to induce or incite a person to so use or apply any such article, instrument, substance, drug, medicine, or thing is declared to be nonmailable matter and shall not be conveyed in the mail or delivered from any post office or by any letter carrier.

Whoever knowingly uses the mail for the mailing, carriage in the mail, or delivery of anything declared by this section or section 3001(e) of title 39 to be nonmailable, or knowingly causes to be delivered by mail according to the direction thereon, or at the place at which it is directed to be delivered by the person to whom it is addressed, or knowingly takes any such thing from the mail for the purpose of circulating or disposing thereof, or of aiding in the circulation or disposition thereof, under this title or imprisoned not more than five years, or both, for the first such offense, and shall be fined under this title or imprisoned not more than 10 years, or both, for each such offense thereafter.

The term indecent, as used in this section includes matter of a character tending to incite arson, murder, or assassination.

Section 1463. Mailing indecent matter on wrappers or envelopes

All matter otherwise mailable by law, upon the envelope or outside cover or wrapper of which, and all postal cards upon which, any delineations, epithets, terms, or language of an indecent, lewd, lascivious, or obscene character are written or printed or otherwise impressed or apparent, are nonmailable matter, and shall not be conveyed in the mail nor delivered from any post office nor by any letter carrier, and shall be withdrawn from the mail under such regulations as the Postal Service shall prescribe.

Whoever knowingly deposits for mailing or delivery, anything declared by this section to be nonmailable matter, or knowingly takes the same from the mail for the purpose of circulating or disposing of or aiding in the circulation or disposition of the same, shall be fined under this title or imprisoned not more than five years, or both.

Section 1735. Sexually oriented advertisements

(a) Whoever—

 (1) willfully uses the mail for the mailing, carriage in the mail, or delivery of any sexually oriented advertisement in violation of section 3010 of title 39, or willfully violates any regulations of the Board of Governors issued under such section; or

 (2) sells, leases, rents, lends, exchanges, or licenses the use of, or, except for the purpose expressly authorized by section 3010 of title 39, uses a mailing list maintained by the Board of Governors under such section; shall be fined under this title or imprisoned not more than five years, or both, for the first offense, and shall be fined under this title or imprisoned not more than 10 years, or both, for any second or subsequent offense.

(b) For the purposes of this section, the term "sexually oriented advertisement" shall have the same meaning as given in section 3010(d) of title 39.

SOURCE: United States Code 17 stat. 598.

DOCUMENT ANALYSIS

Passage of the Comstock Act signified the changes that had occurred in abortion policy during the nineteenth century. At the beginning of that century, not a single state had an abortion statute on its books, and both religious and medical institutions assumed, along with the doctrine of quickening, that abortion was at least legitimate prior to that time. By century's end, every state had a restrictive policy reflective of Dr. Horatio Storer's argument (see previously in this chapter) and the Catholic Church's admonition that abortion was murder. With action by Congress to stem the flow of advertisements and information about abortion practices, the country entered the twentieth century in a very different abortion policy environment than it had in the nineteenth.

Anthony Comstock took to the floor of the U.S. Senate to present this bill himself. And while few would doubt his anti-vice credentials, it is believed he wrote and pursued passage of the bill in order to allow President Ulysses S. Grant, then mired in scandal, the opportunity to take the high moral ground by signing the legislation into law.

It is noteworthy that Congress banned transmission of "sexually oriented advertisement" through the mail system; giving the prevailing division of labor, the Congress could only control that which crossed state lines. Anything purely intrastate would remain within the authority of the states, limiting Congress' ability to ban abortion outright. Still, the Comstock Act inspired outrage in some, who saw it as an encroachment on the state's traditional authority to govern social policy, and it ultimately was allowed to expire, but was not officially overturned by the Supreme Court until *United States v. One Package of Japanese Pessaries* in 1936.

Further Reading

Gordon, Linda. *Woman's Body, Woman's Right*. New York: Penguin Books, 1974.

Mohr, James C. *Abortion in America: The Origins and Evolution of National Policy*. Oxford, England: Oxford University Press, 1978.

Petchesky, Rosalind. *Abortion and Woman's Choice: The State, Sexuality, and Reproductive Freedom*, 2nd ed. Boston: Northeastern University Press, 1990.

2

EARLY TWENTIETH-CENTURY TENSIONS AND TRENDS

Early in the twentieth century, America faced a philosophical crossroads: would the nation continue its policy of laissez-faire politics and economics, leaving most major policy decisions to the states, or would it set upon a path of centralized authority? As a consequence of the late nineteenth-century economic recessions and a growing chasm between rich and poor, some political figures began to advocate for greater national involvement in both our economy and society at large. Sometimes this impulse was motivated by a desire to assist the weak or the poor; at other times, the impulse was motivated by an interest in controlling behavior across the states.

In this chapter, we see instances of both impulses, sometimes within the same document. In President Theodore Roosevelt's speech, for instance, there is both concern for women's well-being and a clear position that motherhood is the fulfillment of women's destiny. This view reflects the dominant paradigm of the age, but also stands in contrast to the women's suffrage movement, which was arguing for women's wider inclusion in society.

In these early decades of the twentieth century, abortion politics itself was local and muted. In part because progressive women were focused so keenly on the achievement of national suffrage, no organized movement for women's abortion rights existed. Rather, the vocal advocates of the day would focus on prevention of unwanted children through birth control. Margaret Sanger, and later her organization Planned Parenthood, would stress the importance of discovering and disseminating effective methods of birth control as a way to prevent impoverishment of America's families and to protect women's health.

At the same time, certain groups of women found their reproductive choices not only discouraged, but prevented through forced sterilization practices. African American women, in particular, experienced such intrusions into their reproductive health in the early decades of the twentieth century, which may explain why even today, the African American community is less supportive of abortion rights than other communities.

Simultaneously, an industry of illegal abortion flourished. Pushed underground by the anti-vice movements of the late-nineteenth century, abortion provision became no less prevalent, but much less safe. Without regulation, abortion providers would take advantage of some women's desperation to end their pregnancies, sometimes leaving those women badly harmed or even dead. Because the practice was illegal, unsatisfied abortion clients would have a disincentive to report unethical business practices, and often times even delayed their own medical needs to avoid revealing that they had had abortions.

Of course, a few notable exceptions to the unethical provision of abortion did exist in some communities. One of the best known examples is that of Ruth Barnett of Portland, Oregon, who provided some 40,000 abortions during this illegal period and never lost a single patient.

Document: Excerpt from U.S. President Theodore Roosevelt's address "On American Motherhood," delivered to the National Congress of Mothers.
Date: March 13, 1905.
Where: Washington, D.C.
Significance: On the eve of women's suffrage, President Roosevelt's comments acknowledged the significant social role of women in their families, and their indirect influence on American culture, but simultaneously also reveal society's expectation that a proper woman's "first and greatest duty" is to bear children.

In our modern industrial civilization there are many and grave dangers to counterbalance the splendors and the triumphs. It is not a good thing to see cities grow at disproportionate speed relatively to the country; for the small land owners, the men who own their little homes, and therefore to a very large extent the men who till farms, the men of the soil, have hitherto made the foundation of lasting national life in every State; and, if the foundation becomes either too weak or too narrow, the superstructure, no matter how attractive, is in imminent danger of falling.

But far more important than the question of the occupation of our citizens is the question of how their family life is conducted. No matter what that occupation may be, as long as there is a real home and as long as those who make up that home do their duty to one another, to their neighbors and to the State, it is of minor consequence whether the man's trade is plied in the country or in the city, whether it calls for the work of the hands or for the work of the head.

No piled-up wealth, no splendor of material growth, no brilliance of artistic development, will permanently avail any people unless its home life is healthy, unless the average man possesses honesty, courage, common sense, and decency, unless he works hard and is willing at need to fight hard; and unless the average woman is a good wife, a good mother, able and willing to perform the first and greatest duty of womanhood, able and willing to bear, and to bring up as they should be brought up, healthy children, sound in body, mind, and character, and numerous enough so that the race shall increase and not decrease.

There are certain old truths which will be true as long as this world endures, and which no amount of progress can alter. One of these is the truth that the primary duty of the husband is to be the home-maker, the breadwinner for his wife and children, and that the primary duty of the woman is to be the helpmate, the housewife, and mother. The woman should have ample educational advantages; but save in exceptional cases the man must be, and she need not be, and generally ought not to be, trained for a lifelong career as the family breadwinner; and, therefore, after a certain point, the training of the two must normally be different because the duties of the two are normally different. This does not mean inequality of function, but it does mean that normally there must be dissimilarity of function. On the whole, I think the duty of the woman the more important, the more difficult, and the more honorable of the two; on the whole I respect the woman who does her duty even more than I respect the man who does his.

No ordinary work done by a man is either as hard or as responsible as the work of a woman who is bringing up a family of small children; for upon her time and strength demands are made not only every hour of the day but often every hour of the night. She may have to get up night after night to take care of a sick child, and yet must by day continue to do all her household duties as well; and if the family means are scant she must usually enjoy even her rare holidays taking her whole brood of children with her. The birth pangs make all men the debtors of all women. Above all our sympathy and regard are due to the struggling wives among those whom Abraham Lincoln called the plain people, and whom he so loved and trusted; for the lives of these women are often led on the lonely heights of quiet, self-sacrificing heroism.

Just as the happiest and most honorable and most useful task that can be set any man is to earn enough for the support of his wife and family, for the bringing up and starting in life of his children, so the most important, the most honorable and desirable task which can be set any woman is to be a good and wise mother in a home marked by self-respect and mutual forbearance, by willingness to perform duty, and by refusal to sink into self-indulgence or avoid that which entails effort and self-sacrifice. Of course there are exceptional men and exceptional women who can do and ought to do much more than this, who can lead and ought to lead great careers of outside usefulness in addition to—not as substitutes for—their home work; but I am not speaking of exceptions; I am speaking of the primary duties, I am speaking of the average citizens, the average men and women who make up the nation.

In as much as I am speaking to an assemblage of mothers, I shall have nothing whatever to say in praise of an easy life. Yours is the work which is never ended. No mother has an easy time, the most mothers have very hard times; and yet what true mother would barter her experience of joy and sorrow in exchange for a life of cold selfishness, which insists upon perpetual amusement and the avoidance of care, and which often finds its fit dwelling place in some flat designed to furnish with the least possible expenditure of effort the maximum of comfort and of luxury, but in which there is literally no place for children? The woman who is a good wife, a good mother, is entitled to our respect as is no one else; but he is entitled to it only because, and so long as, she is worthy of it. Effort and self-sacrifice are the law of worthy life for the man as for the woman; tho neither the effort nor the self-sacrifice may be the same for the one as for the other. I do not in the least believe in the patient Griselda type of woman, in the woman who submits to gross and long continued ill treatment, any more than I believe in a man who tamely submits to wrongful aggression. No wrong-doing is so abhorrent as wrong-doing by a man toward the wife and the children who should arouse every tender feeling in his nature. Selfishness toward them, lack of tenderness toward them, lack of consideration for them, above all, brutality in any form toward them, should arouse the heartiest scorn and indignation in every upright soul.

I believe in the woman keeping her self-respect just as I believe in the man doing so. I believe in her rights just as much as I believe in the man's, and indeed a little more; and I regard marriage as a partnership, in which each partner is in honor bound to think of the rights of the other as well as of his or her own. But I think that the duties are even more important than the rights; and in the long run I think that the reward is ampler and greater for duty well done, than for the insistence upon individual rights, necessary tho this, too, must often be. Your duty is hard, your responsibility great; but greatest of all is your reward. I do not pity you in the least. On the contrary, I feel respect and admiration for you.

Into the woman's keeping is committed the destiny of the generations to come after us. In bringing up your children you mothers must remember that while it is essential to be loving and tender it is no less essential to be wise and firm. Foolishness and affection must not be treated as interchangeable terms; and besides training your sons and daughters in the softer and milder virtues, you must seek to give them those stern and hardy qualities which in after life they will surely need. Some children will go wrong in spite of the best training; and some will go right even when their surroundings are most unfortunate; nevertheless an immense amount depends upon the family training. If you mothers through weakness bring up your sons to be selfish and to think only of themselves, you will be responsible for much sadness among the women who are to be their wives in the future. If you let your daughters grow up idle, perhaps under the mistaken impression that as you yourselves have had to work hard they shall know only enjoyment, you are preparing them to be useless to others and burdens to themselves. Teach boys and girls alike that they are not to look forward to live spent in avoiding difficulties, but to lives spent in overcoming difficulties. Teach them that work, for themselves and also for others, is not a curse but a blessing; seek to make them happy, to make them enjoy life, but seek also to make them face life with the steadfast resolution to wrest success from labor and adversity, and to do their whole duty before God and to man. Surely she who can thus train her sons and her daughters is thrice fortunate among women.

There are many good people who are denied the supreme blessing of children, and for these we have the respect and sympathy always due to those who, from no fault of their own, are denied any of the other great blessings of life. But the man or woman who deliberately forego these blessings, whether from viciousness, coldness, shallow-heartedness, self-indulgence, or mere failure to appreciate aright the difference between the all-important and the unimportant,—why, such a creature merits contempt as hearty as any visited upon the soldier who runs away in battle, or upon the man who refuses to work for the support of those dependent upon him, and who tho able-bodied is yet content to eat in idleness the bread which others provide.

The existence of women of this type forms one of the most unpleasant and unwholesome features of modern life. If any one is so dim of vision as to fail to see what a thoroughly unlovely creature such a woman is I wish they would read Judge Robert Grant's novel "Unleavened Bread," ponder seriously the character of Selma, and think of the fate that would surely overcome any nation which developed its average and typical woman along such lines. Unfortunately it would be untrue to say that this type exists only in American novels. That it also exists in American life is made unpleasantly evident by the statistics as to the dwindling families in some localities. It is made evident in equally sinister fashion by the census statistics as to divorce, which are fairly appalling; for easy divorce is now as it ever has been, a bane to any nation, a curse to society, a menace to the home, an incitement to married unhappiness and to immorality, an evil thing for men and a still more hideous evil for women.

These unpleasant tendencies in our American life are made evident by articles such as those which I actually read not long ago in a certain paper, where a clergyman was quoted, seemingly with approval, as expressing the general American attitude when he said that the ambition of any save a very rich man should be to rear two children only, so as to give his children an opportunity "to taste a few of the good things of life."

This man, whose profession and calling should have made him a moral teacher, actually set before others the ideal, not of training children to do their duty, not of sending them forth with stout hearts and ready minds to win triumphs for themselves and their country, not of allowing them the opportunity, and giving them the privilege of making their own place in the world, but, forsooth, of keeping the number of children so limited that they might "taste a few good things!" The way to give a child a fair chance in life is not to bring it up in luxury, but to see that it has the kind of training that will give it strength of character. Even apart from the vital question of national life, and regarding only the individual interest of the children themselves, happiness in the true sense is a hundredfold more apt to come to any given member of a healthy family of healthy-minded children, well brought up, well educated, but taught that they must shift up, well educated, but taught that they must shift for themselves, must win their own way, and by their own exertions make their own positions of usefulness, than it is apt to come to those whose parents themselves have acted on and have trained their children to act on, the selfish and sordid theory that the whole end of life is to "taste a few good things."

The intelligence of the remark is on a par with its morality; for the most rudimentary mental process would have shown the speaker that if the average family in which there are children contained but two children the nation as a whole would decrease in population so rapidly that in two or three generations it would very deservedly be on the point of extinction, so that the people who had acted on this base and selfish doctrine would be giving place to others with braver and more robust ideals. Nor would such a result be in any way regrettable; for a race that practised such doctrine—that is, a race that practised race suicide—would thereby conclusively show that it was unfit to exist, and that it had better give place to people who had not forgotten the primary laws of their being.

To sum up, then, the whole matter is simple enough. If either a race or an individual prefers the pleasure of more effortless ease, of self-indulgence, to the infinitely deeper, the infinitely higher pleasures that come to those who know the toil and the weariness, but also the joy, of hard duty well done, why, that race or that individual must inevitably in the end pay the penalty of leading a life both vapid and ignoble. No man and no woman really worthy of the name can care for the life spent solely or chiefly in the avoidance of risk and trouble and labor. Save in exceptional cases the prizes worth having in life must be paid for, and the life worth living must be a life of work for a worthy end, and ordinarily of work more for others than for one's self.

The woman's task is not easy—no task worth doing is easy—but in doing it, and when she has done it, there shall come to her the highest and holiest joy known to mankind; and having done it, she shall have the reward prophesied in Scripture; for her husband and her children, yes, and all people who realize that her work lies at the foundation of all national happiness and greatness, shall rise up and call her blessed.

SOURCE: Theodore Roosevelt, "On American Motherhood," March 13, 1905, available at National Center for Public Policy Research, http://www.nationalcenter.org/TRooseveltMotherhood.html.

DOCUMENT ANALYSIS

The National Congress of Mothers, established in 1897, is now known as the Parent Teacher Association. The organization was in its inception a maternalist organization, dedicated to the advancement of motherhood, and best known for its influence in the creation of mother's pensions and other benefits to "proper" mothers. The content of the president's speech echoes the organization's predisposition that "the primary duty of the woman is to be the helpmate, the housewife, and mother." At a time when other women's organizations were more directly demanding political inclusion through suffrage, the National Congress was accepting women's indirect influence over society as the only true fulfillment of women's better nature. Furthermore, the National Congress has been criticized by contemporary feminists both for focusing on women's maternal function as her sole contribution to society and for excluding women of color and of lesser means from their organization.

While in hindsight this speech has a conservative tone, and may have piqued the ire of some contemporary feminists who were trying to focus government on women's capacity as citizens and workers rather than motherhood, it is notable that this is the first major presidential address to focus on the status of women. That the president had concerns about the status of women was reflective of the major social upheaval of the time, and may have inspired the suffragists of that day onward in their last years before the vote for women was obtained in 1919.

Document: "Up to the Doctors."
Date: April 15, 1925.
Where: The Survey.
Significance: This piece documents Margaret Sanger's birth control conference in New York City, the first of its kind and a major accomplishment for women's health advocates.

Ten years ago the very idea of an international conference on birth control in New York city would have been unthinkable. Except to a few earnest propagandists and sociologists the term suggests only something rather daringly funny, even funnier than the activities of the "suffragettes" of those days. There was little public discussion of it except in the police courts, where Margaret Sanger bravely ignored the insults and innuendos of judges, audience and reporters alike. Every hand seemed raised against her except for a few loyal followers, among them many of the weary mothers of Brownsville who had parked their baby carriages in rows outside the doors of her first clinic, closed by the police.

The opposite picture of the conference just concluded gives faith in the vitality of an idea backed by one determined person. For a week a distinguished group of professional men and women of widely differing interests has met in the auditorium of a New York hotel, listening to papers on various aspects of birth control by persons whose names are known the wide world over. There has been only one free public meeting; all the other sessions have been for groups who came and paid a conference fee not hear propaganda or argument, but to learn of and contribute to an important sociological development. . . .

Through it all Mrs. Sanger smiled as quietly and as unconcerned as though she never had envisaged anything different from this focusing of all kinds of professional competence upon the subject which has been her life work. As Dr. Raymond Pearl of Johns Hopkins University declared: "This congress of leading scientific men and women from all over the world is also in large measure a tribute to the splendid work of Mrs. Margaret Sanger, the pioneer and leader of the birth control movement in America. Under difficulties and vicissitudes which would have completely disheartened a less courageous soul, she has kept up the fight and won a succession of victories which even a few years ago would have seemed impossible.". . .

A rapidly increasing professional interest and support was registered in the attendance at a meeting on contraceptive methods open only to licensed physicians, which jammed one hall, and necessitated an overflow meeting in another hotel, bringing together more than a thousand physicians, who acknowledged the interest and responsibility of the medical profession in birth control. . . .

Perhaps because birth control began as a lay movement the knowledge of its sociological implications has outrun progress in medical technique, so that there is great present need for a program of medical research and clinical trial . . . Mrs. Sanger herself has been among the first to recognize this need. *The Survey* already has noted her offer, in accord with generous and statesman like course of her ten year's campaign, to place the direction of the medical activities of the American Birth Control League in the hands of a representative medical group. Now it is up to the doctors. . . .

SOURCE: "Up to the Doctors." *The Survey*, April 15, 73.

DOCUMENT ANALYSIS

This report on Margaret Sanger's birth control conference reveals the significance of Sanger's career. As a nurse on the lower east side of New York, Sanger had witnessed staggering birth rates for some of America's poorest women. Convinced that women could better their own health and that of their children by controlling the number and timing of their children, Sanger left the practice of nursing to dedicate herself full-time to research and teaching in the area of birth control. The account in *The Survey* documents an historic training where Sanger presided over a conference dedicated to teaching physicians about emerging birth control methods and their use. Most notably, the argument calls on the doctors to assist women in limiting their childbearing.

Sanger's role in the history of reproductive rights is not without controversy, however. While heralded as the founder of the American Birth Control League, the predecessor of today's Planned Parenthood, her vocal opposition to abortion practices and her association with eugenics earned her much criticism.

Document: Excerpt from *United States v. One Package of Japanese Pessaries*.
Date: December 7, 1936.
Where: U.S. Circuit Court of Appeals, Second Circuit.
Significance: The court undermines the 1873 Comstock Act.

Appeal from the District Court of the United States for the Southern District of New York. Libel by the United States for the forfeiture of one package containing 120 rubber pessaries, more or less, being articles to prevent conception, which were imported into the United States by Dr. Hannah M. Stone, claimant, in alleged violation of the Tariff Act of 1930, Sec. 305(a), 19 U.S.C.A. 1305(a), 19 U.S.C.A. 1305(a). From a decree dismissing the libel (*13 F.Supp. 334*), the United States appeals.

Affirmed.

. . .

Before L. HAND, SWAN, and AUGUSTUS N. HAND, Circuit Judges.
AUGUSTUS N. HAND, Circuit Judge.

The United States filed this libel against a package containing 120 vaginal pessaries more or less, alleged to be imported contrary to section 305(a) of the Tariff Act of 1930

(*19 U.S.C.A. 1305(a)*). From the decree dismissing the libel the United States has appealed. In our opinion the decree should be affirmed.

The claimant Dr. Stone is a New York physician who has been licensed to practice for sixteen years and has specialized in gynecology. The package containing pessaries was sent to her by a physician in Japan for the purpose of trying them in her practice and giving her opinion as to their usefulness for contraceptive purposes. She testified that she prescribes the use of pessaries in cases where it would not be desirable for a patient to undertake a pregnancy. The accuracy and good faith of this testimony is not questioned. The New York Penal Law which makes it in general a misdemeanor to sell or give away or to advertise or offer for sale any articles for the prevention of conception excepts furnishing such articles to physicians who may in good faith prescribe their use for the cure or prevention of disease. *People v. Sanger, 222 N.Y. 192, 118 N.E. 637.* New York Penal Law (Consol. Laws, c. 40) Sec. 1145. The witnesses for both the government and the claimant testified that the use of contraceptives was in many cases necessary for the health of women and that they employed articles of the general nature of the pessaries in their practice. There was no dispute as to the truth of these statements.

Section 305(a) of the Tariff Act of 1930 (*19 U.S.C.A. 1305(a)*) provides that: 'All persons are prohibited from importing into the United States from any foreign country * * * any article whatever for the prevention of conception or for causing unlawful abortion.'

The question is whether physicians who import such articles as those involved in the present case in order to use them for the health of their patients are excepted by implication from the literal terms of the statute. Certainly they are excepted in the case of an abortive which is prescribed to save life, for section 305(a) of the Tariff Act only prohibits the importation of articles for causing 'unlawful abortion.' This was the very point decided in *Bours v. United States, 229 F. 960 (C.C.A. 7)*, where a similar statute (Cr. Code 211 (*18 U.S.C.A. 334 and note*)) declaring nonmailable 'every article or thing designed, adapted, or intended for preventing conception or producing abortion, or for any indecent or immoral use,' was held not to cover physicians using the mails in order to say that they will operate upon a patient if an examination shows the necessity of an operation to save life. And this result was reached even though the statute in forbidding the mailing of any article 'intended for * * * producing abortion' did not, as does section 305(a) of the Tariff Act, qualify the word 'abortion' by the saving adjective 'unlawful.' In *Youngs Rubber Corporation v. C. I. Lee & Co., 45 F.(2d) 103 (C.C.A. 2)*, Judge Swan, writing for this court, construed the mailing statute in the same way. In referring to the mailing of contraceptive articles bearing the plaintiff's trade-mark, he adverted to the fact that the articles might be capable of legitimate use and said, at *page 108 of 45 F.(2d)*, when discussing the incidence of the mailing statute:

'The intention to prevent a proper medical use of drugs or other articles merely because they are capable of illegal uses is not lightly to be ascribed to Congress. *Section 334* forbids also the mailing of obscene books and writings; yet it has never been thought to bar from the mails medical writings sent to or by physicians for proper purposes, though of a character which would render them highly indecent if sent broadcast to all classes of persons. * * * It would seem reasonable to give the word 'adapted' a more limited meaning than that above suggested and to construe the whole phrase 'designed, adapted or intended' as requiring an intent on the part of the sender that the article mailed * * * be used for illegal contraception or abortion or for indecent or immoral purposes.'

*739 While Judge Swan's remarks were perhaps dicta, they are in full accord with the opinion of Judge Mack in *Bours v. United States (C.C.A.) 229 F. 960*, which we have already mentioned, and were relied on by the Court of Appeals of the Sixth Circuit when construing the mailing statute in *Davis v. United States, 62 F.(2d) 473.*

Section 305(a) of the Tariff Act of 1930 (*19 U.S.C.A. 1305(a)*, as well as *title 18, section 334,* of the U.S.Code (*18 U.S.C.A. 334*), prohibiting the mailing, and title 18, section 396 of the U.S.Code (18 U.S.C.A. 396), prohibiting the importing or transporting in interstate commerce of articles 'designed, adapted, or intended for preventing conception, or producing abortion,' all originated from the so-called Comstock Act of 1873 (17 Stat. 598), which was entitled, 'An Act for the Suppression of Trade in, and Circulation of, obscene Literature and Articles of immoral Use.'

[1] Section 1 of the act of 1873 made it a crime to sell, lend or give away, 'any drug or medicine, or any article whatever, for the prevention of conception, or for causing unlawful abortion.' Section 2 prohibited sending through the mails 'any article or thing designed or intended for the prevention of conception or procuring of abortion.' Section 3 forbade the importation of 'any of the hereinbefore-mentioned articles or things, except the drugs hereinbefore-mentioned when imported in bulk, and not put up for any of the purposes before mentioned.' All the statutes we have referred to were part of a continuous scheme to suppress immoral articles and obscene literature and should so far as possible be construed together and consistently. If this be done, the articles here in question ought not to be forfeited when not intended for an immoral purpose. Such was the interpretation in the decisions of the Circuit Courts of Appeal of the Sixth and Seventh Circuits and of this court in Youngs Rubber Corporation v. I. C. Lee & Co., when construing the statute forbidding an improper use of the mails.

[2] It is argued that section 305(a) of the Tariff Act of 1930 (*19 U.S.C.A. 1305(a)* differs from the statutes prohibiting carriage by mail and in interstate commerce of articles 'intended for preventing conception or producing abortion' because in section 305(a) the adjective 'unlawful' is coupled with the word 'abortion,' but not with the words 'prevention of conception.' But in the Comstock Act, from which the others are derived, the word 'unlawful' was sometimes inserted to qualify the word 'abortion,' and sometimes omitted. It seems hard to suppose that under the second and third sections articles intended for use in procuring abortions were prohibited in all cases while, under the first section, they were only prohibited when intended for use in an 'unlawful abortion.' Nor can we see why the statute should, at least in section 1, except articles for producing abortions if used to safeguard life, and bar articles for preventing conception though employed by a physician in the practice of his profession in order to protect the health of his patients or to save them from infection.

It is true that in 1873, when the Comstock Act was passed, information now available as to the evils resulting in many cases from conception was most limited, and accordingly it is argued that the language prohibiting the sale or mailing of contraceptives should be taken literally and that Congress intended to bar the use of such articles completely. While we may assume that section 305(a) of the Tariff Act of 1930 (*19 U.S.C.A. 1305(a)*) exempts only such articles as the act of 1873 excepted, yet we are satisfied that this statute, as well as all the acts we have referred to, embraced only such articles as Congress would have denounced as immoral if it had understood all the conditions under which they were to be used. Its design, in our opinion, was not to prevent the importation, sale, or carriage by mail of things which might intelligently be employed by conscientious and competent physicians for the purpose of saving life or promoting the well being of their patients. The word 'unlawful' would make this clear as to articles for producing abortion, and the courts have read an exemption into the act covering such articles even where the word 'unlawful' is not used. The same exception should apply to articles for preventing conception. While it is true that the policy of Congress has been to forbid the use of contraceptives altogether if the only purpose of using them be to prevent conception in cases where it would not be injurious to the welfare of the patient or her offspring, it is going far beyond such a policy to hold that abortions, which destroy incipient *740 life, may be allowed in proper cases, and yet that no measures may be taken to prevent conception even though a likely result should be to require the termination of pregnancy by means of an operation. It seems unreasonable to suppose that the national scheme of legislation involves such inconsistencies and requires the complete suppression of articles, the use of which in many cases is advocated by such a weight of authority in the medical world.

The Comstock Bill, as originally introduced in the Senate, contained the words 'except on a prescription of a physician in good standing, given in good faith,' but those words were omitted from the bill as it was ultimately passed. The reason for amendment seems never to have been discussed on the floor of Congress, or in committee, and the remarks of Senator Conklin, when the bill was up for passage in final form, indicate that the scope of the measure was not well understood and that the language used was to be left largely for future interpretation. We see no ground for holding that the construction placed upon similar language in the decisions we have referred to is not applicable to the articles which the government seeks to forfeit, and common sense would seem to require a like interpretation in the case at bar.

The decree dismissing the libel is affirmed.

L. HAND, Circuit Judge (concurring).

If the decision had been left to me alone, I should have felt more strongly than my brothers the force of the Senate amendment in the original act, and of the use of the word, 'unlawful,' as it passed. There seems to me substantial reason for saying that contraceptives were meant to be forbidden, whether or not prescribed by physicians, and that no lawful use of them was contemplated. Many people have changed their minds about such matters in sixty years, but the act forbids the same conduct now as then; a statute stands until public feeling gets enough momentum to change it, which may be long after a majority would repeal it, if a poll were taken. Nevertheless, I am not prepared to dissent. I recognize that the court of the act through Congress does not tell us very much, and it is of considerable importance that the law as to importations should be the same as that as to the mails; we ought not impute differences of intention upon slight distinctions in expression. I am content therefore to accept my brothers' judgment, whatever might have been, and indeed still are, my doubts.

SOURCE: *United States v. One Package of Japanese Pessaries*, 86 F.2d 737 (2nd Cir. 1936).

DOCUMENT ANALYSIS

The 1873 Comstock Act criminalized the dissemination of obscene matter, including contraceptives, through the U.S. postal system. In 1930, The Tariff Act extended the contraceptives ban to the importation of contraceptive devices illegal as well. During the 1930s Margaret Sanger, and her National Committee for Federal Legislation on Birth Control, lobbied Congress to loosen these restrictions on birth control. When this strategy failed, Sanger ordered some pessaries (an early form of diaphragm) from a Japanese physician. A lower court ruled against the government, ruling that it could not intercept a shipment of contraceptives if it had come from a physician. Still, the U.S. government appealed, and the U.S. Federal Appeals Court affirmed the lower court's ruling.

IN HISTORY

CATHOLIC CHURCH'S STATEMENTS

The Catholic Church's position on abortion has been more inconsistent over time than many people might realize. For most of its history, the Church has subscribed to the idea that the fetus was ensouled at the time of quickening (or at about 40 days gestation). St. Augustine and others had argued that abortion prior to hominization, (ensoulment) was not homicide unless the fetus was fully formed; rather, abortion was punishable only as a sexual sin, which separated sexual union from procreation, but not as a matter of homicide. It is not until October 12, 1869, when Pope Pius IX issued his declaration "Apostolicae sedis," that abortion was outlawed from conception within the Catholic Church, and abortion became punishable by excommunication.

Following are some examples of the inconsistencies that characterize Catholic Church doctrine on abortion.

"The law does not provide that the act (abortion) pertains to homicide, for there cannot yet be said to be a live soul in a body that lacks sensation when it is not formed in flesh and so is not endowed with sense." St. Augustine, *On Exodus*, 21. 80.

"Where no homicide or no animated fetus is involved, do not punish more strictly than the sacred canons or civil legislation does," Pope Gregory XIV, *Sedes apostolica*, 1591, in overturning his predecessor's (Sixtus V) decision to impose severe penalties for abortion because of his concern over widespread prostitution in Rome.

In 1965, Vatican II, *Gaudium et Spes*, section 51, makes abortion a sin against life, not as the concealment of sexual sin, for the first time, "Human life is Sacred; from its very inception it reveals the creating hand of God."

Paul VI, *Humanae Vitae*, *Acta apostolicae sedis* 60, 481–503, asserts that all abortion should be prohibited, arguing for the essential connection between sexual union and procreation, and affirming the doctrine of immediate hominization. Cites John XXIII, "Human life is sacred; from its very inception it reveals the creating hand of God."

Document: Selection from *Margaret Sanger; An Autobiography.*
Date: Original copyright: 1938.
Where: New York: Dover Publications, Inc., 1971.
Significance: Indicates the desperation that poor women felt when faced with unplanned pregnancies and reveals the circumstances that motivated Margaret Sanger's work in contraceptive health care.

During these years in New York trained nurses were in great demand. Few people wanted to enter hospitals; they were afraid they might be "practiced" upon, and consented to go only in desperate emergencies. Sentiment was especially vehement in the matter of having babies. A woman's own bedroom, no matter how inconveniently arranged, was the usual place for her lying-in. I was not sufficiently free from domestic duties to be a general nurse, but I could ordinarily manage obstetrical cases because I was notified far enough ahead to plan my schedule. And after serving my two weeks I could get home again.

Sometimes I was summoned to small apartments occupied by young clerks, insurance salesmen, or lawyers, just starting out, most of them under thirty and whose wives were having their first or second baby. They were always eager to know the best and latest method in infant care and feeding. In particular, Jewish patients, whose lives centered around the family, welcomed advice and followed it implicitly.

But more and more my calls began to come from the Lower East Side, as though I were being magnetically drawn there by some force outside my control. I hated the wretchedness and hopelessness of the poor, and never experienced that satisfaction in working among them that so many noble women have found. My concern for my patients was now quite different from my earlier hospital attitude. I could see that much was wrong with them which did not appear in the physiological or medical diagnosis. A woman in childbirth was not merely a woman in childbirth. My expanded outlook included a view of her background, her potentialities as a human being, the kind of children she was bearing, and what was going to happen to them.

The wives of small shopkeepers were my most frequent cases, but I had carpenters, truck drivers, dishwashers, and pushcart vendors. I admired intensely the consideration most of these people had for their own. Money to pay doctor and nurse had been carefully saved months in advance—parents-in-law, grandfathers, grandmothers, all contributing.

As soon as the neighbors learned that a nurse was in the building they came in a friendly way to visit, often carrying fruit, jellies, or gefüllter fish made after a cherished recipe. It was infinitely pathetic to me that they, so poor themselves, should bring me food. Later they drifted in again with the excuse of getting the plate, and sat down for a nice talk; there was no hurry. Always back of the little gift was the question, "I am pregnant (or my daughter, or my sister is). Tell me something to keep from having another baby. We cannot afford another yet."

I tried to explain the only two methods I had ever heard of among the middle classes, both of which were invariably brushed aside as unacceptable. They were of no certain avail to the wife because they placed the burden of responsibility solely upon the husband—a burden which he seldom assumed. What she was seeking was self-protection she could herself use, and there was none.

Below this stratum of society was one in truly desperate circumstances. The men were sullen and unskilled, picking up odd jobs now and then, but more often unemployed, lounging in and out of the house at all hours of the day and night. The women seemed to slink on their way to market and were without neighborliness.

These submerged, untouched classes were beyond the scope of organized charity or religion. No labor union, no church, not even the Salvation Army reached them. They were apprehensive of everyone and rejected help of any kind, ordering all intruders to keep out; both birth and death they considered their own business. Social agents, who were just beginning to appear, were profoundly mistrusted because they pried into home and lives, asking questions about wages, how many were in the family, had any of them ever been in jail. Often two or three had been there or were now under suspicion of prostitution, shoplifting, purse snatching, petty thievery, and, in consequence, passed furtively by the big blue uniforms on the corner.

The utmost depression came over me as I approached this surreptitious region. Below Fourteenth Street I seemed to be breathing a different air, to be in another world and country where the people had habits and customs alien to anything I had ever heard about.

There were then approximately ten thousand apartments in New York into which no sun ray penetrated directly; such windows as they had opened only on a narrow court from which rose fetid odors. It was seldom cleaned, though garbage and refuse often went down into it. All these dwellings were pervaded by the foul breath of poverty, that moldy, indefinable, indescribable smell which cannot be fumigated out, sickening to me but apparently unnoticed by those who lived there. When I set to work with antiseptics, their pungent sting, at least temporarily, obscured the stench.

I remember on confinement case to which I was called by the doctor of an insurance company. I climbed up the five flights and entered the airless rooms, but the baby had come with too great speed. A boy of ten had been the only assistant. Five flights was a long way; he had wrapped the placenta in a piece of newspaper and dropped it out the window into the court.

Many families took in "borders," as they were termed, whose small contributions paid the rent. These derelicts, wanderers, alternately working and drinking, were crowded in with the children; a single room sometimes held as many as six sleepers. Little girls were accustomed to dressing and undressing in front of the men, and were often violated, occasionally by their own fathers or brothers, before they reached the age of puberty.

Pregnancy was a chronic condition among the women of this class. Suggestions as to what to do for a girl who was "in trouble" or a married woman who was "caught" passed from mouth to mouth—herb teas, turpentine, steaming, rolling downstairs, inserting slippery elm, knitting needles, shoe-hooks. When they had word of a new remedy they hurried to the drugstore, and if the clerk were inclined to be friendly he might say, "Oh, that won't help you, but here's something that may." The younger druggists usually refused to give advice because, if it were to be known, they would come under the law; midwives were even more fearful. The doomed women implored me to reveal the "secret" rich people had, offering to pay me extra to tell them; many really believed I was holding back information for money. They asked everybody and tried anything, but nothing did them any good. On Saturday nights I have seen groups of from fifty to one hundred with their shawls over their heads waiting outside the office of a five-dollar abortionist.

Each time I returned to this district, which was becoming a recurrent nightmare, I used to hear that Mrs. Cohen "had been carried to a hospital, but had never come back," or that Mrs. Kelly "had sent the children to a neighbor and put her head into the gas oven." Day after day such tales were poured into my ears—a baby born dead, great relief—the death of an older child, sorrow but again relief of a sort—the story told a thousand times of death from abortion and children going into institutions. I shuddered with horror as I listened to the details and studied the reasons back of them—destitution linked with excessive childbearing. The waste of life seemed utterly senseless. One by one worried, sad, pensive, and aging faces marshaled themselves before me in my dreams, sometimes appealingly, sometimes accusingly.

These were not merely "unfortunate conditions among the poor" such as we read about. I knew the women personally. They were living, breathing, human beings, with hopes, fears, and aspirations like my own, yet their weary, misshapen bodies, "always ailing, never failing," were destined to be thrown on the scrap heap before they were thirty-five. I could not escape from the facts of their wretchedness; neither was I able to see a way out. My own cozy and comfortable family existence was becoming a reproach to me.

Then one stifling mid-July day of 1912 I was summoned to a Grand Street tenement. My patient was a small, slight Russian Jewess, about twenty-eight years old, of the special cast of feature to which suffering lends a madonna-like expression. The cramped three-room apartment was in a sorry state of turmoil. Jake Sachs, a truck driver scarcely older than his wife, had come home to find the three children crying and her unconscious from the effects of a self-induced abortion. He had called the nearest doctor, who in turn had sent for me. Jake's earnings were trifling, and most of them had gone to keep the none-too-strong children clean and properly fed. But his wife's ingenuity had helped them to save a little, and this he was glad to spend on a nurse rather than have her go to a hospital.

The doctor and I settled ourselves to the task of fighting the septicemia. Never had I worked so fast, never so concentratedly. The sultry days and nights were melted into a torpid inferno. It did not seem possible there could be such heat, and every bit of food, ice, and drugs had to be carried up three flights of stairs.

Jake was more kind and thoughtful than many of the husbands I had encountered. He loved his children, and had always helped his wife wash and dress them. He had brought water up and carried garbage down before he left in the morning, and did as much as he could for me while he anxiously watched her progress.

After a fortnight Mrs. Sachs' recovery was in sight. Neighbors, ordinarily fatalistic as to the results of abortion, were genuinely pleased that she had survived. She smiled wanly at all who came to see her and thanked them gently, but she could not respond to their hearty congratulations. She appeared to be more despondent and anxious than she should have been, and spent too much time in meditation.

At the end of three weeks, as I was preparing to leave the fragile patient to take up her difficult life once more, she finally voiced her fears, "Another baby will finish me, I suppose?"

"It's too early to talk about that," I temporized.

But when the doctor came to make his last call, I drew him aside. "Mrs. Sachs is terribly worried about having another baby."

"She well may be," replied the doctor, and then he stood before her and said, "Any more such capers, young woman, and there'll be no need to send for me."

"I know, doctor," she replied timidly, "but," and she hesitated as though it took all her courage to say it, "what can I do to prevent it?"

The doctor was a kindly man, and he had worked hard to save her, but such incidents had become so familiar to him that he had long since lost whatever delicacy he might once have had. He laughed good-naturedly. "You want to have your cake and eat it too, do you? Well, it can't be done."

Then picking up his hat and bag to depart he said, "Tell Jake to sleep on the roof."

I glanced quickly at Mrs. Sachs. Even through my sudden tears I could see stamped on her face an expression of absolute despair. We simply looked at each other, saying no word until the door and closed behind the doctor. Then she lifted her thin, blue-veined hands and clasped them beseechingly. "He can't understand. He's only a man. But you do, don't you? Please tell me the secret, and I'll never breathe it to a soul. *Please!*"

What was I to do? I could not speak the conventionally comforting phrases which would be of no comfort. Instead, I made her as physically easy as I could and promised to come back in a few days to talk with her again. A little later, when she slept, I tiptoed away.

Night after night the wistful image of Mrs. Sachs appeared before me. I made all sorts of excuses to myself for not going back. I was busy on other cases; I really did not know what to say to her or how to convince her of my own ignorance; I was helpless to avert such monstrous atrocities. Time rolled by and I did nothing.

The telephone rang one evening three months later, and Jake Sachs' agitated voice begged me to come at once; his wife was sick again and from the same cause. For a wild moment I thought of sending someone else, but actually, of course, I hurried into my uniform, caught up my bag, and started out. All the way I longed for a subway wreck, an explosion, anything to keep me from having to enter that home again. But nothing happened, even to delay me. I turned into the dingy doorway and climbed the familiar stairs once more. The children were there, young little things.

Mrs. Sachs was in a coma and died within ten minutes. I folded her still hands across her breast, remembering how they had pleaded with me, begging so humbly for the knowledge which was her right. I drew a sheet over her pallid face. Jake was sobbing, running his hands through his hair and pulling it out like an insane person. Over and over again he wailed, "My God! My God! My God!"

I left him pacing desperately back and forth, and for hours I myself walked and walked and walked through the hushed streets. When I finally arrived home and let myself quietly in, all the household was sleeping. I looked out my window and down upon the dimly lighted city. Its pains and griefs crowded in upon me, a moving picture rolled before my eyes with photographic clearness: women writhing in travail to bring forth little babies; the babies themselves naked and hungry, wrapped in newspapers to keep them from the cold; six-year-old children with pinched, pale, wrinkled faces, old in concentrated wretchedness, pushed into gray and fetid cellars, crouching on stone floors, their small scrawny hands scuttling through rags, making lamp shades, artificial flowers; white coffins, black coffins, coffins, coffins interminably passing in never-ending succession. The scenes piled one upon another on another. I could bear it no longer.

As I stood there the darkness faded. The sun came up and threw its reflection over the house tops. It was the dawn of a new day in my life also. The doubt and questioning, the experimenting and trying, were now to be put behind me. I knew I could not go back merely to keeping people alive.

I went to bed, knowing that no matter what it might cost, I was finished with palliatives and superficial cures; I was resolved to seek out the root of evil, to do something to change the destiny of mothers whose miseries were vast as the sky.

SOURCE: Margaret Sanger, *Margaret Sanger; An Autobiography* (New York: Dover Publications, 1971), 86–92.

DOCUMENT ANALYSIS

Margaret Sanger's autobiography documents the personal experiences that lead her to a career in birth control advocacy. This particular selection tells a poignant and common story of a woman devastated by repeated pregnancies. It was these first-hand experiences that inspired Sanger to give up her practice of general nursing in favor of a focus on contraception. She spent much of her life securing funding for birth control research and expanding birth control use and literacy. This work proved very difficult. Her 1917 movie *Birth Control* was banned in New York, where she worked, and she was twice imprisoned for the distribution of birth control devices.

Still, hers is a complicated story. Various people offered support for birth control at this time in history, but they did so for a variety of reasons. For some, there was a feminist sensibility about the damage to women's health and well being from serial pregnancy. Still others worried about a rise in global population, while others expressed concern about rising birth rates among "undesirable" groups in the United States, namely the poor, recent immigrants, and people of color. Sanger herself advanced eugenics arguments at times to win middle-class, white support for her cause. Moreover, Sanger publicly disavowed the practice of abortion, focusing instead on birth control's capacity to end abortion, and thus gaining the support of more conservative Americans.

Sanger's legacy of birth control advocacy lives on today, 100 years later. Her American Birth Control Association—today's Planned Parenthood—works to expand global access to birth control.

Document: American Law Institute (ALI) Model Penal Code.
Date: 1959.
Where: Article 230.3 via the "ULA" (Uniform Laws Annotated).
Significance: The ALI offered a model abortion law, the first of its kind, in response to a growing cry for abortion law reform in the 1950s.

230.3. Abortion.

(1) Unjustified Abortion. A person who purposely and unjustifiably terminates the pregnancy of another otherwise than by a live birth commits a felony of the third degree or, where the pregnancy has continued beyond the twenty-sixth week, a felony of the second degree.

(2) Justifiable Abortion. A licensed physician is justified in terminating a pregnancy if he believes there is substantial risk that continuance of the pregnancy would gravely impair the physical or mental health of the mother or that the child would be born with grave physical or mental defect, or that the pregnancy resulted from rape, incest, or other felonious intercourse. All illicit intercourse with a girl below the age of 16 shall be deemed felonious for purposes of this subsection. Justifiable abortions shall be performed only in a licensed hospital except in case of emergency when hospital facilities are unavailable. [Additional exceptions from the requirement of hospitalization may be incorporated here to take account of situations in sparsely settled areas where hospitals are not generally accessible.]

(3) Physicians' Certificates; Presumption from Non-Compliance. No abortion shall be performed unless two physicians, one of whom may be the person performing the abortion, shall have certified in writing the circumstances which they believe to justify the abortion. Such certificate shall be submitted before the abortion to the hospital where it is to be performed and, in the case of abortion following felonious intercourse, to the prosecuting attorney or the police. Failure to comply with any of the requirements of this Subsection gives rise to a presumption that the abortion was unjustified.

(4) Self-Abortion. A woman whose pregnancy has continued beyond the twenty-sixth week commits a felony of the third degree if she purposely terminates her own pregnancy otherwise than by a live birth, or if she uses instruments, drugs or violence upon herself for that purpose. Except as justified under Subsection (2), a person who induces or knowingly aids a woman to use instruments, drugs or violence upon herself for the purpose of terminating her pregnancy otherwise than by a live birth commits a felony of the third degree whether or not the pregnancy has continued beyond the twenty-sixth week.

(5) Pretended Abortion. A person commits a felony of the third degree if, representing that it is his purpose to perform an abortion, he does an act adapted to cause abortion in a pregnant woman although the woman is in fact not pregnant, or the actor does not believe she is. A person charged with unjustified abortion under Subsection (1) or an attempt to commit that offense may be convicted thereof upon proof of conduct prohibited by this Subsection.

(6) Distribution of Abortifacients. A person who sells, offers to sell, possesses with intent to sell, advertises, or displays for sale anything specially designed to terminate a pregnancy, or held out by the actor as useful for that purpose, commits a misdemeanor, unless:

(a) the sale, offer or display is to a physician or druggist or to an intermediary in a chain of distribution to physicians or druggists; or (b) the sale is made upon prescription or order of a physician; or (c) the possession is with intent to sell as authorized in paragraphs (a) and (b); or (d) the advertising is addressed to persons named in paragraph (a) and confined to trade or professional channels not likely to reach the general public.

(7) Section Inapplicable to Prevention of Pregnancy. Nothing in this Section shall be deemed applicable to the prescription, administration or distribution of drugs or other substances for avoiding pregnancy, whether by preventing implantation of a fertilized ovum or by any other method that operates before, at or immediately after fertilization.

SOURCE: American Law Institute (ALI) Model Penal Code. Article 230.3 via the "ULA" (Uniform Laws Annotated). Copyright © 1959 by the American Law Institute. Reprinted with permission. All rights reserved.

DOCUMENT ANALYSIS

The American Law Institute (ALI), which regularly assesses best legal practices and makes recommendations for the law, issued this first model penal abortion code in response to growing concern that prevailing abortion statutes did not offer physicians enough flexibility to respond to the circumstances presented by their unhappily pregnant patients.

The model code is remarkable in several ways. First, the code affirms a long-held view that fetal life is developmental, and ascribes harsher penalties to later abortions than to early ones. Moreover, the model code sets in motion a series of causes of justifiable abortions; namely, the physical and mental health of the pregnant woman, as well as pregnancies that are the result of felonious sexual acts. Even to this day, the American public supports abortions for these reasons in far greater numbers than when an abortion is requested for economic or social reasons. Finally, the code is illustrative of a third common twentieth-century pattern in abortion litigation and adjudication: deference to physicians. Note that the law would allow an abortion only in circumstances where two physicians have agreed the procedure is justifiable; a woman's interpretation of her circumstances would not suffice.

The state of California became the first in the nation to adopt a provision similar to this model code; in 1966, then-governor Ronald Reagan signed into law an abortion provision much like the ALI version, loosening the restrictions on abortion in that state, and setting in motion a nation-wide march toward expansion of abortion access.

Document: "The Abortion Racket—What Should Be Done?"
Date: August 15, 1960.
Where: Newsweek.
Significance: This piece is notable because it is the first of its kind in a publication of such major distribution. *Newsweek's* decision to cover such a sensitive subject exposed a much wider audience to the realities of abortion provision, and may have encouraged wider activism toward policy change.

Preamble: *The Abortion Racket—What Should Be Done?* Newsweek, August 15th, 1960.

The law is clear: It is a crime to perform an abortion—"unless deemed essential to the preservation of the life of the mother." Yet, U.S. authorities estimate that this year more than

1 million abortions will be performed. And some 5,000 women may die from the bungling surgery of unskilled operators or from abortions they have induced themselves. Where does the blame lie? What should be done?

In this Special Report, NEWSWEEK MEDICINE editor Marguerite Clark explores the problem, and the efforts now being made by a growing number of doctors and lawyers in the nation to liberalize the abortion laws, put the quacks out of business, and save the lives of thousands of women.

The wan, nervous girl could see only one way out of her dilemma. A Los Angeles beauty-parlor operator had given her the telephone number of a small, inconspicuous house in the Hollywood Hills, overlooking the San Fernando Valley. The girl dialed the number and gave the password: "I want to buy a car." For identification, she gave the man on the other end of the line her first name and the last digits of her automobile license. The arrangements were quickly made. At the designated "pickup spot," a parking lot adjacent to a supermarket, the girl met two men and a woman. She presented her identification and climbed into their car. One of the men gave her pills to make her drowsy. Covered with a blanket, she dozed fitfully on the rear seat as the car wound its way through the ascending hills.

At last, the car pulled into a garage attached to the house in the Hollywood Hills. Taken inside, the girl was placed in the care of the "doctor" and his "nurse," both carefully masked and gowned (to prevent identification more than to insure sterile procedure). The abortion and post-operative rest took only 45 minutes. The girl, rid of her unwanted pregnancy, was then driven back to the Los Angeles parking lot, where she got into her own car and drove home.

This abortionist, recruiting his distressed clientele from this suburban area of vast Los Angeles, averaged four to five illegal operations a week for $500 each. Eventually, he was arrested. But, as is often the case in abortion arrests, he was not prosecuted. No one could prove that he actually had performed an abortion, for none of his victims would testify against him. Within a few months, he had moved to another house in the Hollywood Hills, and set up his illicit "practice" again.

Special Squad: The case, from the files of the Los Angeles Police Department, is not unique, but it dramatically points up the helplessness of the authorities in trying to cope with a racket that flourishes in almost every sizable city in the United States. In Los Angeles, for example, police set up a special squad in 1950 to fight the illicit abortion business. Often, this special detail will seize a lone quack, working without assistants. He may sometimes be a chiropractor, or merely a male nurse. But sometimes the abortionist is a physician, and there is nothing to prevent a physician, even one of the highest standing, from acting outside the letter of the law. If he feels the abortion law is too strict, he may diagnose and act accordingly. If he reports a "natural miscarriage," the police cannot argue with him.

Feeding on human distress which knows no social distinction, the abortion racket draws its distraught clientele from all walks—from factory girl to debutante. In Chicago, for example, the illicit practice thrives both in smart Gold Coast suites and in the dingy hovels of Negro midwives, whose operations carry a dreadful risk of infection.

In Washington, D.C., the obstetrical board of the District of Columbia Medical Society lists abortions as the second cause of maternal deaths. Toxemia of pregnancy (high blood pressure, convulsions, and coma) is the first. Of some 8,000 obstetrical admissions last year to the sprawling D.C. General Hospital, the only public hospital in the city, one in ten were abortion cases, invariably illegal. "With proper medical care, the women usually recover from the illegal attempt," said Dr. E.W. Lowe, medical director, "but sometimes they die."

What can be done to save them?

Today many M.D.'s favor liberalizing the abortion laws, which they regard as archaic. One of the most outspoken crusaders in favor of this step is Dr. Alan F. Guttmacher, the strong-faced, white-haired, 62-year-old chief of obstetrics and gynecology at New York's Mount Sinai Hospital. As chairman of the national medical committee of the Planned Parenthood Federation of America and director of the Margaret Sanger Research Bureau, Alan Guttmacher has considered the abortion problem a daily concern for 30 years.

Hippocrates Humanized: Erect in his big chair in Mount Sinai's executive office last week, wearing a benign smile, Guttmacher laid his opinions on the line: "American abortion laws are a hideous jumble of contradictions, inconsistencies, and frustrations. In the pages of the Hippocratic Oath, written about 450 B.C., we find the same contradictions and conflicts that plague us today. The Hippocratic Oath ['I will not aid a woman to procure abortion'] sanctimoniously forswears this practice. Yet we read in one of Hippocrates' case histories that when a high-priced musical entertainer came to the great seer complaining of an inconvenient pregnancy, Hippocrates suggested that she 'leap into the air seven times . . . and with such vigor, that in doing so . . . the woman lost the child.'

"I rather like that passage." Alan Guttmacher said. "It makes the Father of Medicine seem more human."

Since 1925, Dr. Guttmacher estimates he has legally performed some 150 therapeutic abortions at the hospital without a single complication. On the other hand, he says, he has "regretfully turned away thousands of women seeking abortions for which there was no legal justification under the present law."

Yet even the requirements for legal abortions in U.S. hospitals have changed drastically in the last twenty years. As late as 1940, the three chief reasons for ending pregnancy to "save the mother's life" were serious heart, lung, and kidney diseases. Today, with better techniques for treating these ailments during pregnancy, it is seldom necessary to abort the mother to save her life.

At Mount Sinai, for example, emotional illness now accounts for 40 per cent of the therapeutic abortions, but only when the patient has threatened suicide. Other cases approved by the hospital's Abortion Committee: (1) German measles in the mother during the first twelve weeks of pregnancy, when there is a chance of malformation in about 50 per cent of the children; and (2) cancer, particularly of the breast or thyroid gland, which are sensitive to the stimulating hormones of pregnancy.

Stretching the Law: Are these therapeutic operations strictly legal under the New York State laws, which stipulate that abortions may be done solely to *preserve the mother's life?*

"They are not," Guttmacher replied candidly, "not here or in any other state. The law makes hypocrites of us all." Example: In a study of California hospitals, eighteen out of 24 replied that the therapeutic operations were knowingly performed in violation of the law.

Yet most doctors feel they should stretch the abortion laws still further. "At Mount Sinai," said Dr. Guttmacher, "we do not abort mentally retarded women who can't care for their children or mothers bedridden with neurologic diseases (such as multiple sclerosis). Most important, we do not, under the law, terminate the pregnancy of victims of rape, incest, and criminal attack."

A recent case: When a 26-year-old married woman was attacked by a thug in her own home, her husband appealed to the district attorney for aid in getting a therapeutic abortion. When the DA refused, the couple borrowed a sum of money and had the abortion done by a back-room operator.

On the whole, the nation's M.D.'s disapprove of "open demand" for abortions to meet the whims of women who simply wish to avoid the responsibilities of motherhood. Yet most doctors strongly advocate reforms in the laws, which indirectly are responsible for the deaths of young mothers through surgery by unskilled abortionists.

How should the laws be changed?

Today, even the most conservative attorneys are making frank recommendations for bringing the so-called "illegal operations" out of the "back rooms." For instance, in May 1959, a Washington, D.C., meeting of the American Law Institute, a highly respected organization of judges, lawyers, and teachers, approved a proposal to extend the concept of legal abortion. In the view of the Institute, considerations such as the mother's health, the possibility that the child might be gravely defective, and unwanted pregnancies from rape or incest should be taken into account. While there was some opposition from the floor at the meeting, an effort to delete the abortion reform provision was beaten by an overwhelming voice vote. This year, the Law Institute is considering an even stronger attack on the old abortion law.

Illinois Code: In the Midwest, a joint committee of the Illinois and Chicago Bar Associations also has worked out a revised abortion code to include pregnancies from rape or incest and those in which the child may be mentally or physically defective. It is scheduled to be presented to the Illinois Legislature in 1961. Although the bill probably will be hotly debated, Stanton Ehrlich, chairman of the Illinois Bar Association's family-law section, says: "It is murder to make abortion a crime. When a child is born of rape, it is a resented child, and it will not have a happy life. And if a child will be born deformed, there is good reason why its life should be prevented."

To simplify the legal aspect of abortions, particularly for the medical profession, Dr. Guttmacher believes that one model law should be drafted and adopted by each State Legislature. To make the law uniform in all states, he feels the decision to abort should be taken out of the hands of individual hospitals, and that each community should establish a committee or board to administer the law, including an internist, an obstetrician, a social worker, a judge, and a minister.

Disdainful Doctors: In other parts of the country, the fight for less severe abortion laws is gaining ground, with help from some unexpected sources. At a session of the American Medical Association in Miami Beach in June, a lawyer and a psychiatrist addressed a group of obstetricians and gynecologists. The two were Zad Leavy, 30, Deputy District Attorney of Los Angeles, and Dr. Jerome Kummer, 39, psychiatrist of UCLA's School of Medicine. To their blunt presentation of the facts on criminal abortions, many listeners, even specialists in women's ills, reacted with shock, some with disbelief.

"Everyone knows about the country's abortion record, but no one wants to talk about it," Leavy and Kummer told their audience. "While officially, eminent physicians appear disdainful and aloof, unofficially there is evidence of considerable tolerance and acceptance of this illegality. As now constituted, the abortion law is supposed to prevent death or injury to the mother. But is society actually protecting the mother's welfare by maintaining stringent laws that drive her to the danger of illegal abortion?"

"Primarily," Leavy and Kummer emphasized, "strict religious affiliations influence the number of induced abortions. The Jewish people have the highest rate of illegal operations, the Catholics, the lowest. Yet today," the report went on to say, "there seems to be a substantial group of responsible people [favoring] cautious relaxation of abortion laws. For example, Jewish Talmudic scholars . . . would not strongly oppose broadening the laws. Nor is the

Protestant Church, for the most part, opposed to such changes. Many Protestants feel that termination of pregnancy is not a problem for the church alone, but should be handled by the doctor, the individual patient, and, if the woman wishes, her clergyman."

"The Catholic Church, on the other hand, is adamant against abortion, therapeutic or otherwise," said Zad Leavy. "In a Catholic hospital, there is no such thing as a legal abortion to save the life of the mother, or of the child."

In New York last week, a high Catholic prelate reinforced this stand: "Any direct attack on the fetus is murder," he said. "It is a violation of the Fifth Commandment—Thou shalt not kill."

Yet Leavy and Kummer, in their Miami report, urged that U.S. abortion laws be changed to include these three significant categories:

- Where termination of pregnancy is necessary to preserve the *health, both mental and physical,* of the mother;
- Where the mother is mentally deficient and where there is a probability that a congenital disease, or a malformation, will be passed on to the child;
- Where pregnancy occurs as the result of rape, incest, or moral irresponsibility of the female, either while very young or while mentally incompetent.

These are the specific issues that hundreds of other legal and medical experts are considering when they recommend new laws to take the place of the Victorian statute now in force in all the United States.

"What we really are trying to combat is the needless loss of valuable lives," a representative of abortion law reform in Illinois said recently. "One of the saddest stories I know is that of a 15-year-old pregnant schoolgirl, deserted by an older man who had seduced her. She tried in vain to get help from a reputable doctor. A week later, in Chicago's Cook County Hospital, the girl died—a victim of a quack, operating in a basement of a shabby tenement. Liberalizing our laws would have permitted us to get that poor, frightened girl into a hospital—*before*, not *after* that abortion."

Who, When, Why

Not the wanton teen-ager . . . not the naïve girl in the big city . . . but the young (between 21 and 25 years) married woman is most likely to undergo an abortion in the U.S. today. Why? She may have been forced to marry by this unwanted pregnancy. She may fear the marriage will not last, that there may be a forced separation. Or she may be the destitute mother of two or three children, unwilling and unable to face a future with another mouth to feed.

Although two out of three abortions in America involve married women, the case of the unmarried girl is more tragic, in the view of Dr. David Kushner, chairman of the District of Columbia Medical Society's subcommittee on maternal welfare. "In Washington, often it is the lonely single government girl, away from home for the first time, afloat in the city, who ends up in the abortionist's hands. It's the usual story—the immature girl who becomes pregnant by a married man."

The shocking problem of unwanted pregnancy and abortion is now spreading among teenagers. Mrs. Katherine Brownell Oettinger, chief of the Children's Bureau, U.S. Department of Health, Education, and Welfare, told NEWSWEEK: "We are so very concerned about the younger girls—both those who become illegitimate mothers and those who have abortions.

Forty per cent of all illegitimate babies are born to girls under 20. This is the group that gives us the double whammy—illegitimacy and abortion."

SOURCE: Marguerite Clark, "The Abortion Racket—What Should Be Done?" *Newsweek*, August 15, 1960, 50–52.

DOCUMENT ANALYSIS

This article exposed the inconsistencies in abortion law and practice on a national level. One of the most-read periodicals of its day, *Newsweek* brought widespread exposure to the incoherence of 1950s abortion law to a lay audience. The piece reveals some of the complexities around who sought abortion during this time, as well as the different levels of care that they might expect as a consequence of their social and economic standing. Still, one of the most revealing aspects of the article is that it underscores the point that abortion demand was common among married women.

On the eve of the women's movement, this article also points to an interesting paradox: it was not women's groups who first advocated for relaxing abortion policy, but physicians. Just as it was doctors 100 years prior who had led the movement toward policy restriction, by the mid-twentieth century, it was physicians again who advocated for change.

Further Reading

Critchlow, Donald T., ed. *The Politics of Abortion and Birth Control in Historical Perspective*. University Park, Penn.: The Pennsylvania State University, 1996.

Petchesky, Rosalind Pollack. *Abortion and Woman's Choice: The State, Sexuality, and Reproductive Freedom*, 2nd ed. Boston: Northeastern University Press, 1990.

Reagan, Leslie J. *When Abortion Was a Crime: Women, Medicine, and Law in the United States, 1867–1973*. Berkeley: University of California Press, 1997.

3

ABORTION AT A CROSSROADS: AMERICA AT MID-CENTURY

The decade before *Roe v. Wade* legalized abortion was, in many respects, a decade of dissent and social unrest. The civil rights movement was in full swing. The second wave of the women's rights movement, nascent a decade before, was fully formed by 1973. Within both movements were factions as well as disagreements about tactics and strategy. So it was with the emerging movement to liberalize abortion law.

That movement began with doctors, who bristled at the state legislators' strict imposition of abortion bans, and the inflexible language those bans contained. It would be physicians who would grapple with how to treat pregnant women, desperately ill with Rubella (or German measles), or women whose fetuses were damaged by the sedative and antinausea drug thalidomide. In general, the country's abortion laws in 1960 did not allow for abortion exceptions for the woman's health or fetal deformity, leaving physicians in the unenviable position of having to choose between abiding the law (and resigning women to their fate by refusing them abortions), or breaking the law and facing the legal consequences.

For pregnant women during the 1950s, relief from unwanted pregnancy could be granted only by hospital review boards, not by individual doctors. Most hospitals constituted these review committees to hear women's appeals, and made judgments based on a woman's rationale and psychological condition. Often these decisions were inconsistent, and at times the composition of the review boards was biased against abortion, or made up of physicians without expertise in gynecological care. As a consequence, women's primary care physicians often objected to the authority of the review boards.

Two events helped spur the physicians into action. Sherry Finkbine, a mother of four in Arizona and popular television personality, sought an abortion during her fifth pregnancy when she discovered that the tranquilizers she was taking contained thalidomide, and likely had damaged her fetus. The hospital review board that heard Finkbine's abortion request initially consented, but later retracted consent when news of the decision became public. Ultimately, Finkbine traveled to Stockholm in 1962 to receive her abortion, as many middle class women did during the mid-twentieth century when their local hospital review board denied their request.

The second episode that spurred doctors into action was a Rubella outbreak in San Francisco in the early 1960s. Rubella (or German measles), was widely understood to damage fetuses, but doctors were not permitted to perform abortions in circumstances where women were ill with the disease and likely carrying a damaged fetus. Doctors quickly mobilized

Sherri Finkbine, 30 years after her 1962 abortion, which set in motion the movement to liberalize abortion law. Getty Images.

around the inflexibility of the state law, and lobbied the California state legislature, which in 1967 became the first state to lighten its abortion restrictions. In that year, Colorado and North Carolina also liberalized their abortion restrictions, allowing teams of doctors to approve women's abortions.

By that time, the women's movement was under way. The National Organization for Women (NOW) formed in 1966 and crafted a statement on abortion at its convention the following year. This statement called for dismantling abortion laws—a position that would divide the movement into those who would liberalize, or reform, the laws to include more flexibility for doctors, and those who advocated for the repeal of abortion laws altogether.

The movement to repeal abortion laws gained some ground when Patricia Maginnis formed the California Association to Repeal Abortion Laws in 1966. By 1969, her organization grew into the National Association for the Repeal of Abortion Laws (NARAL), formed to pursue just such a course. This perspective gained ground when, in 1970, Hawaii repealed its abortion statute. Still, many more preferred the way of reform, and the number of states reforming their statutes would outnumber those that repealed.

Not all interested parties favored abortion reform. As noted in this chapter, the Catholic Church, known for softening some of its social requirements for the faithful under the Vatican II reforms, issued a restatement of its nineteenth-century prohibition on abortion, providing the early rallying call for an antiabortion movement that would become a din in the post-1973 world. This chapter documents both the emerging movements to repeal or reform abortion laws, as well as the forces resistant to change.

Document: Griswold v. Connecticut.
Date: June 7, 1965.
Where: U.S. Supreme Court.
Significance: This was the first major Supreme Court ruling establishing the constitutional right of privacy for married couples. Although the subject of this case was contraception, not abortion, it would serve as a precedent for future cases related directly to abortion.

MR. JUSTICE DOUGLAS DELIVERED THE OPINION OF THE COURT.

Appellant Griswold is Executive Director of the Planned Parenthood League of Connecticut. Appellant Buxton is a licensed physician and a professor at the Yale Medical School who served as Medical Director for the League at its Center in New Haven—a center open and operating from November 1 to November 10, 1961, when appellants were arrested. They gave information, instruction, and medical advice to married persons as to the means of preventing conception. They examined the wife and prescribed the best contraceptive device or material for her use. Fees were usually charged, although some couples were serviced free.

The statutes whose constitutionality is involved in this appeal are 53–32 and 54–196 of the General Statutes of Connecticut (1958 rev.). The former provides:

"Any person who uses any drug, medicinal article or instrument for the purpose of preventing conception shall be fined not less than fifty dollars or imprisoned not less than sixty days nor more than one year or be both fined and imprisoned."

Section 54–196 provides:

"Any person who assists, abets, counsels, causes, hires or commands another to commit any offense may be prosecuted and punished as if he were the principal offender."

The appellants were found guilty as accessories and fined $100 each, against the claim that the accessory statute as so applied violated the Fourteenth Amendment. . . .

Coming to the merits, we are met with a wide range of questions that implicate the Due Process Clause of the Fourteenth Amendment. Overtones of some arguments suggest that *Lochner v. New York*, 198 U.S. 45, should be our guide. But we decline that invitation. We do not sit as a super-legislature to determine the wisdom, need, and propriety of laws that touch economic problems, business affairs, or social conditions. This law, however, operates directly on an intimate relation of husband and wife and their physician's role in one aspect of that relation.

The association of people is not mentioned in the Constitution nor in the Bill of Rights. The right to educate a child in a school of the parents' choice—whether public or private or parochial—is also not mentioned. Nor is the right to study any particular subject or any foreign language. Yet the First Amendment has been construed to include certain of those rights.

By Pierce v. Society of Sisters, supra, the right to educate one's children as one chooses is made applicable to the States by the force of the First and Fourteenth Amendments. By Meyer v. Nebraska, supra, the same dignity is given the right to study the German language in a private school. In other words, the State may not, consistently with the spirit of the First Amendment, contract the spectrum of available knowledge . . . And so we reaffirm the principle of the Pierce and the Meyer cases.

In NAACP v. Alabama we protected the "freedom to associate and privacy in one's associations," noting that freedom of association was a peripheral First Amendment right. Disclosure of membership lists of a constitutionally valid association, we held, was invalid "as entailing the likelihood of a substantial restraint upon the exercise by petitioner's members of their right to freedom of association." Ibid. In other words, the First Amendment has a penumbra where privacy is protected from governmental intrusion. The right of "association," like the right of belief (Board of Education v. Barnette, 319 U.S. 624), is more than the right to attend a meeting; it includes the right to express one's attitudes or philosophies by membership in a group or by affiliation with it or by other lawful means. Association in that context is a form of expression of opinion; and while it is not expressly included in the First Amendment its existence is necessary in making the express guarantees fully meaningful.

The foregoing cases suggest that specific guarantees in the Bill of Rights have penumbras, formed by emanations from those guarantees that help give them life and substance. Various guarantees create zones of privacy. The right of association contained in the penumbra of the First Amendment is one, as we have seen. The Third Amendment in its prohibition against the quartering of soldiers "in any house" in time of peace without the consent of the owner is another facet of that privacy. The Fourth Amendment explicitly affirms the "right of the people to be secure in their persons, houses, papers, and effects, against unreasonable searches and seizures." The Fifth Amendment in its Self-Incrimination Clause enables the citizen to create a zone of privacy which government may not force him to surrender to his detriment. The Ninth Amendment provides: "The enumeration in the Constitution, of certain rights, shall not be construed to deny or disparage others retained by the people."

The Fourth and Fifth Amendments were described . . . as protection against all governmental invasions "of the sanctity of a man's home and the privacies of life."

We have had many controversies over these penumbral rights of "privacy and repose." These cases bear witness that the right of privacy which presses for recognition here is a legitimate one.

The present case, then, concerns a relationship lying within the zone of privacy created by several fundamental constitutional guarantees. And it concerns a law which, in forbidding the use of contraceptives rather than regulating their manufacture or sale, seeks to achieve its goals by means having a maximum destructive impact upon that relationship. Such a law cannot stand in light of the familiar principle, so often applied by this Court, that a "governmental purpose to control or prevent activities constitutionally subject to state regulation may not be achieved by means which sweep unnecessarily broadly and thereby invade the area of protected freedoms." Would we allow the police to search the sacred precincts of marital bedrooms for telltale signs of the use of contraceptives? The very idea is repulsive to the notions of privacy surrounding the marriage relationship.

We deal with a right of privacy older than the Bill of Rights—older than our political parties, older than our school system. Marriage is a coming together for better or for worse, hopefully enduring, and intimate to the degree of being sacred. It is an association that promotes a way of life, not causes; a harmony in living, not political faiths; a bilateral loyalty, not commercial or social projects. Yet it is an association for as noble a purpose as any involved in our prior decisions.

Reversed.

MR. JUSTICE GOLDBERG, WHOM THE CHIEF JUSTICE AND MR. JUSTICE BRENNAN JOIN, CONCURRING.

I agree with the Court that Connecticut's birth-control law unconstitutionally intrudes upon the right of marital privacy, and I join in its opinion and judgment. Although I have not accepted the view that "due process" as used in the Fourteenth Amendment incorporates all of the first eight Amendments, I do agree that the concept of liberty protects those personal rights that are fundamental, and is not confined to the specific terms of the Bill of Rights. My conclusion that the concept of liberty is not so restricted and that it embraces the right of marital privacy though that right is not mentioned explicitly in the Constitution is supported both by numerous decisions of this Court, referred to in the Court's opinion, and by the language and history of the Ninth Amendment. In reaching the conclusion that the right of marital privacy is protected, as being within the protected penumbra of specific guarantees of the Bill of Rights, the Court refers to the Ninth Amendment, I add these words to emphasize the relevance of that Amendment to the Court's holding.

The Court stated many years ago that the Due Process Clause protects those liberties that are "so rooted in the traditions and conscience of our people as to be ranked as fundamental."

The Ninth Amendment reads, "The enumeration in the Constitution, of certain rights, shall not be construed to deny or disparage others retained by the people." The Amendment is almost entirely the work of James Madison. It was introduced in Congress by him and passed the House and Senate with little or no debate and virtually no change in language. It was proffered to quiet expressed fears that a bill of specifically enumerated rights could not be sufficiently broad to cover all essential rights and that the specific mention of certain rights would be interpreted as a denial that others were protected.

In presenting the proposed Amendment, Madison said:

"It has been objected also against a bill of rights, that, by enumerating particular exceptions to the grant of power, it would disparage those rights which were not placed in that enumeration; and it might follow by implication, that those rights which were not singled out, were intended to be assigned into the hands of the General Government, and were consequently insecure. This is one of the most plausible arguments I have ever heard urged against the admission of a bill of rights into this system; but, I conceive, that it may be guarded against. I have attempted it, as gentlemen may see by turning to the last clause of the fourth resolution [the Ninth Amendment]."

Mr. Justice Story wrote of this argument against a bill of rights and the meaning of the Ninth Amendment:

"In regard to . . . [a] suggestion, that the affirmance of certain rights might disparage others, or might lead to argumentative implications in favor of other powers, it might be sufficient to say that such a course of reasoning could never be sustained upon any solid basis. . . . But a conclusive answer is, that such an attempt may be interdicted (as it has been) by a positive declaration in such a bill of rights that the enumeration of certain rights shall not be construed to deny or disparage others retained by the people."

He further stated, referring to the Ninth Amendment:

"This clause was manifestly introduced to prevent any perverse or ingenious misapplication of the well-known maxim, that an affirmation in particular cases implies a negation in all others; and, e converso, that a negation in particular cases implies an affirmation in all others."

These statements of Madison and Story make clear that the Framers did not intend that the first eight amendments be construed to exhaust the basic and fundamental rights which the Constitution guaranteed to the people.

To hold that a right so basic and fundamental and so deep-rooted in our society as the right of privacy in marriage may be infringed because that right is not guaranteed in so many words by the first eight amendments to the Constitution is to ignore the Ninth Amendment and to give it no effect whatsoever. Moreover, a judicial construction that this fundamental right is not protected by the Constitution because it is not mentioned in explicit terms by one of the first eight amendments or elsewhere in the Constitution would violate the Ninth Amendment, which specifically states that "[t]he enumeration in the Constitution, of certain rights, shall not be construed to deny or disparage others retained by the people. . . ."

In determining which rights are fundamental, judges are not left at large to decide cases in light of their personal and private notions. Rather, they must look to the "traditions and [collective] conscience of our people" to determine whether a principle is "so rooted [there] . . . as to be ranked as fundamental." The inquiry is whether a right involved "is of such a character that it cannot be denied without violating those 'fundamental principles of liberty and justice which lie at the base of all our civil and political institutions.' . . ."

Although the Constitution does not speak in so many words of the right of privacy in marriage, I cannot believe that it offers these fundamental rights no protection. The fact that no particular provision of the Constitution explicitly forbids the State from disrupting the traditional relation of the family—a relation as old and as fundamental as our entire civilization—surely does not show that the Government was meant to have the power to do so. Rather, as the Ninth Amendment expressly

recognizes, there are fundamental personal rights such as this one, which are protected from abridgment by the Government though not specifically mentioned in the Constitution.

The logic of the dissents would sanction federal or state legislation that seems to me even more plainly unconstitutional than the statute before us. Surely the Government, absent a showing of a compelling subordinating state interest, could not decree that all husbands and wives must be sterilized after two children have been born to them. Yet by their reasoning such an invasion of marital privacy would not be subject to constitutional challenge because, while it might be "silly," no provision of the Constitution specifically prevents the Government from curtailing the marital right to bear children and raise a family. While it may shock some of my Brethren that the Court today holds that the Constitution protects the right of marital privacy, in my view it is far more shocking to believe that the personal liberty guaranteed by the Constitution does not include protection against such totalitarian limitation of family size, which is at complete variance with our constitutional concepts. Yet, if upon a showing of a slender basis of rationality, a law outlawing voluntary birth control by married persons is valid, then, by the same reasoning, a law requiring compulsory birth control also would seem to be valid. In my view, however, both types of law would unjustifiably intrude upon rights of marital privacy which are constitutionally protected.

Mr. Justice Black, with whom Mr. Justice Stewart joins, dissenting.

I agree with my Brother STEWART'S dissenting opinion. And like him I do not to any extent whatever base my view that this Connecticut law is constitutional on a belief that the law is wise or that its policy is a good one. In order that there may be no room at all to doubt why I vote as I do, I feel constrained to add that the law is every bit as offensive to me as it is to my Brethren of the majority and my Brothers HARLAN, WHITE and GOLDBERG who, reciting reasons why it is offensive to them, hold it unconstitutional. There is no single one of the graphic and eloquent strictures and criticisms fired at the policy of this Connecticut law either by the Court's opinion or by those of my concurring Brethren to which I cannot subscribe—except their conclusion that the evil qualities they see in the law make it unconstitutional.

The Court talks about a constitutional "right of privacy" as though there is some constitutional provision or provisions forbidding any law ever to be passed which might abridge the "privacy" of individuals. But there is not. There are, of course, guarantees in certain specific constitutional provisions which are designed in part to protect privacy at certain times and places with respect to certain activities. Such, for example, is the Fourth Amendment's guarantee against "unreasonable searches and seizures." But I think it belittles that Amendment to talk about it as though it protects nothing but "privacy." To treat it that way is to give it a niggardly interpretation, not the kind of liberal reading I think any Bill of Rights provision should be given. The average man would very likely not have his feelings soothed any more by having his property seized openly than by having it seized privately and by stealth. He simply wants his property left alone. And a person can be just as much, if not more, irritated, annoyed and injured by an unceremonious public arrest by a policeman as he is by a seizure in the privacy of his office or home.

One of the most effective ways of diluting or expanding a constitutionally guaranteed right is to substitute for the crucial word or words of a constitutional guarantee another word or words, more or less flexible and more or less restricted in meaning. This fact is well illustrated by the use of the term "right of privacy" as a comprehensive substitute for the Fourth Amendment's guarantee against "unreasonable searches and seizures." "Privacy" is a broad, abstract and ambiguous concept which can easily be shrunken in meaning but which can also, on the other hand, easily be interpreted as a constitutional ban against many things other than searches and seizures. I like my privacy as well as the next one, but I am nevertheless compelled to admit that government has a right to invade it unless prohibited by some specific constitutional provision. For these reasons I cannot agree with the Court's judgment and the reasons it gives for holding this Connecticut law unconstitutional.

The due process argument which my Brothers HARLAN and WHITE adopt here is based, as their opinions indicate, on the premise that this Court is vested with power to invalidate all state laws that it considers to be arbitrary, capricious, unreasonable, or oppressive, or on this Court's belief that a particular state law under scrutiny has no "rational or justifying" purpose, or is offensive to a "sense of fairness and justice." If these formulas based on "natural justice," or others which mean the same thing, are to prevail, they require judges to determine what is or is not constitutional on the basis of their own appraisal of what laws are unwise or unnecessary. The power to make such decisions is of course that of a legislative body. Surely it has to be admitted that no provision of the Constitution specifically gives such blanket power to courts to exercise such a supervisory veto over the wisdom and value of legislative policies and to hold unconstitutional those laws which they believe unwise or dangerous.

I repeat so as not to be misunderstood that this Court does have power, which it should exercise, to hold laws unconstitutional where they are forbidden by the Federal Constitution. My point is that there is no provision of the Constitution which either expressly or impliedly vests power in this Court to sit as a supervisory agency over acts of duly constituted legislative bodies and set aside their laws because of the Court's belief that the legislative policies adopted are unreasonable, unwise, arbitrary, capricious or irrational. The adoption of such a loose, flexible, uncontrolled standard for holding laws unconstitutional, if ever it is finally achieved, will amount to a great unconstitutional shift of power to the courts which I believe and am constrained to say will be bad for the courts and worse for the country. Subjecting federal and state laws to such an unrestrained and unrestrainable judicial control as to the wisdom of legislative enactments would, I fear, jeopardize the separation of governmental powers that the Framers set up and at the same time threaten to take away much of the power of States to govern themselves which the Constitution plainly intended them to have.

I realize that many good and able men have eloquently spoken and written, sometimes in rhapsodical strains, about the duty of this Court to keep the Constitution in tune with the times. The idea is that the Constitution must be changed from time to time and that this Court is charged with a duty to make those changes. For myself, I must with all deference reject that philosophy. The Constitution makers knew the need for change and provided for it. Amendments suggested by the people's elected representatives can be submitted to the people or their selected agents for ratification. That method of change was good for our Fathers, and being somewhat old-fashioned I must add it is good enough for me. And so, I cannot rely on the Due Process Clause or the Ninth Amendment or any mysterious and uncertain natural law concept as a reason for striking down this state law. The Due Process Clause with an "arbitrary and capricious" or "shocking to the conscience" formula was liberally used by this Court to strike down economic legislation in the early decades of this century, threatening, many people thought, the tranquility and stability of the Nation. See, e.g., Lochner v. New York, 198 U.S. 45. That formula, based on subjective considerations of "natural justice," is no less dangerous when used to enforce this Court's views about personal rights than those about economic rights. I had thought that we had laid that formula, as a means for striking down state legislation, to rest once and for all.

Mr. Justice Stewart, whom Mr. Justice Black joins, dissenting.

Since 1879 Connecticut has had on its books a law which forbids the use of contraceptives by anyone. I think this is an uncommonly silly law. As a practical matter, the law is obviously unenforceable, except in the oblique context of the present case. As a philosophical matter, I believe the use of contraceptives in the relationship of marriage should be left to personal and private choice, based upon each individual's moral, ethical, and religious beliefs. As a matter of social policy, I think professional counsel about methods of birth control should be available to all, so that each individual's choice can be meaningfully made. But we are not asked in this case to say whether we think this law is unwise, or even asinine. We are asked to hold that it violates the United States Constitution. And that I cannot do.

SOURCE: *Griswold v. Connecticut.* 381 U.S. 479 (1965).

DOCUMENT ANALYSIS

Griswold v. Connecticut is a landmark case for several reasons. First is the obvious implication in hindsight, to women's reproductive rights broadly writ. What we see from the Stewart/Black dissent, however, is that the implications of *Griswold* go far beyond birth control and abortion.

Griswold changed the role of the modern court. As the dissent suggests, some view this case as a major shift in the power and authority of the Supreme Court to enter into public policy questions. The right of privacy described by the majority opinion is not explicitly delineated within the Constitution. As a consequence, the right of privacy is conveyed by the "penumbra" or shadow, of other constitutional rights that hint at, or point to, a respect for privacy. For some in the majority, constitutional suggestion of a privacy zone is enough to protect it. For the dissent, and for many critics of this decision and others, the right of privacy was questionable jurisprudence, and likely subject to years of scrutiny and debate.

Document: National Organization for Women (NOW) Bill of Rights.
Date: Adopted at the 1967 National Conference.
Where: Washington, D.C.
Significance: NOW was the first national organization to call for the repeal of abortion laws.

I. Equal Rights Constitutional Amendment

II. Enforce Law Banning Sex Discrimination in Employment

III. Maternity Leave Rights in Employment and in Social Security Benefits

IV. Tax Deduction for Home and Child Care Expenses for Working Parents

V. Child Day Care Centers

VI. Equal and Unsegregated Education

VII. Equal Job Training Opportunities and Allowances for Women in Poverty

VIII. The Right of Women to Control their Reproductive Lives

We Demand:

I. That the United States Congress immediately pass the Equal Rights Amendment to the Constitution to provide that "Equality of rights under the law shall not be denied or abridged by the United States or by any State on account of sex" and that such then be immediately ratified by the several States.

II. That equal employment opportunity be guaranteed to all women, as well as men by insisting that the Equal Employment Opportunity Commission enforce the prohibitions against sex discrimination in employment under Title VII of the Civil Rights Act of 1964 with the same vigor as it enforces the prohibitions against racial discrimination.

III. That women be protected by law to insure their rights to return to their jobs within a reasonable time after childbirth without loss of seniority or other accrued benefits and be paid maternity leave as a form of social security and/or employee benefit.

IV. Immediate revision of tax laws to permit the deduction of home and child care expenses for working parents.

V. That child care facilities be established by law on the same basis as parks, libraries and public schools adequate to the needs of children, from the pre-school years through adolescence, as a community resource to be used by all citizens from all income levels.

VI. That the right of women to be educated to their full potential equally with men be secured by Federal and State legislation, eliminating all discrimination and segregation by sex, written and unwritten, at all levels of education including college, graduate and professional schools, loans and fellowships and Federal and State training programs, such as the Job Corps.

VII. The right of women in poverty to secure job training, housing and family allowances on equal terms with men, but without prejudice to a parent's right to remain at home to care for his or her children; revision of welfare legislation and poverty programs which deny women dignity, privacy and self respect.

VIII. The right of women to control their own reproductive lives by removing from penal codes the laws limiting access to contraceptive information and devices and laws governing abortion.

SOURCE: National Organization for Women, private archives. Reproduced with permission of the National Organization for Women. The NOW Statement of Purpose and the NOW Bill of Rights are historical documents and may not reflect the current language or priorities of the organization.

DOCUMENT ANALYSIS

NOW's endorsement of abortion law repeal was a call to return to the early American response to abortion: allow women and their health care providers to determine what is medically sound and appropriate. And because NOW, as a growing national organization, took up this position (as opposed to the more moderate reform proposal sought by many), other repeal activists were emboldened to forge ahead with their demands. It is also notable that NOW's earliest documents, including its founding statement, made no mention of abortion rights. It was not until a year after its founding that the organization staked out a position on abortion policy.

Most notably, the fact that NOW agreed with repeal put momentum behind the creation of NARAL. That organization, formed two years after this statement by repeal activists in the states, would become the nation's largest political organization dedicated to reproductive freedom. And although NARAL no longer espouses a policy of repeal, it advocates for women's liberal health policy on many fronts.

IN HISTORY

CLERGY AND ABORTION: THEN AND NOW

On May 22, 1967, the *New York Times* reported on its front page that 21 rabbis and Protestant ministers in New York announced their intention to assist women seeking abortion services. The group, calling themselves the Clergymen's Consultation Service on Abortion, issued a 600-word statement announcing their decision, and calling for reform of New York State's restriction abortion law and for compassion for women with crisis pregnancies. The statement stands in stark contrast with official Catholic Church statements of that time, and is evidence of the diversity of abortion views within the faith community. Below is a brief selection from that statement:

"Therefore believing as clergymen that there are higher laws and moral obligations transcending legal codes, we believe that it is our pastoral responsibility and religious duty to give aid and assistance to all women with problem pregnancies. To that end we are establishing a Clergymen's Consultation Service on Abortion which will include referral to the best available medical advice and aid to women in need."

Document: Humanae Vitae, Encyclical of Pope Paul VI on the Regulation of Birth (footnotes omitted).
Date: July 25, 1968.
Where: St. Peter's, Rome.
Significance: Pope Paul VI issued this statement regarding human sexuality and reproduction, establishing the church's modern disagreement with the practice of abortion and setting in motion the modern prolife movement.

To His Venerable Brothers the Patriarchs, Archbishops, Bishops and other Local Ordinaries in Peace and Communion with the Apostolic See, to the Clergy and Faithful of the Whole Catholic World, and to All Men of Good Will.

Honored Brothers and Dear Sons, Health and Apostolic Benediction.

1. The transmission of human life is a most serious role in which married people collaborate freely and responsibly with God the Creator. It has always been a source of great joy to them, even though it sometimes entails many difficulties and hardships.

The fulfillment of this duty has always posed problems to the conscience of married people, but the recent course of human society and the concomitant changes have provoked new questions. The Church cannot ignore these questions, for they concern matters intimately connected with the life and happiness of human beings.

I. Problem And Competency Of The Magisterium

2. The changes that have taken place are of considerable importance and varied in nature. In the first place there is the rapid increase in population which has made many fear that world population is going to grow faster than available resources, with the consequence that many families and developing countries would be faced with greater hardships. This can easily induce public authorities to be tempted to take even harsher measures to avert this danger. There is also the fact that not only working and housing conditions but the greater demands made both in the economic and educational field pose a living situation in which it is frequently difficult these days to provide properly for a large family.

Also noteworthy is a new understanding of the dignity of woman and her place in society, of the value of conjugal love in marriage and the relationship of conjugal acts to this love.

But the most remarkable development of all is to be seen in man's stupendous progress in the domination and rational organization of the forces of nature to the point that he is endeavoring to extend this control over every aspect of his own life—over his body, over his mind and emotions, over his social life, and even over the laws that regulate the transmission of life.

New Questions

3. This new state of things gives rise to new questions. Granted the conditions of life today and taking into account the relevance of married love to the harmony and mutual fidelity of husband and wife, would it not be right to review the moral norms in force till now, especially when it is felt that these can be observed only with the gravest difficulty, sometimes only by heroic effort?

Moreover, if one were to apply here the so called principle of totality, could it not be accepted that the intention to have a less prolific but more rationally planned family might transform an action which renders natural processes infertile into a licit and provident control of birth? Could it not be admitted, in other words, that procreative finality applies to the totality of married life rather than to each single act? A further question is whether, because people are more conscious today of their responsibilities, the time has not come when the transmission of life should be regulated by their intelligence and will rather than through the specific rhythms of their own bodies.

Interpreting the Moral Law

4. This kind of question requires from the teaching authority of the Church a new and deeper reflection on the principles of the moral teaching on marriage—a teaching which is based on the natural law as illuminated and enriched by divine Revelation.

No member of the faithful could possibly deny that the Church is competent in her magisterium to interpret the natural moral law. It is in fact indisputable, as Our predecessors have many times declared, that Jesus Christ, when He communicated His divine power to Peter and the other Apostles and sent them to teach all nations His commandments, constituted them as the authentic guardians and interpreters of the whole moral law, not only, that is, of the law of the Gospel but also of the natural law. For the natural law, too, declares the will of God, and its faithful observance is necessary for men's eternal salvation.

In carrying out this mandate, the Church has always issued appropriate documents on the nature of marriage, the correct use of conjugal rights, and the duties of spouses. These documents have been more copious in recent times.

Special Studies

5. The consciousness of the same responsibility induced Us to confirm and expand the commission set up by Our predecessor Pope John XXIII, of happy memory, in March, 1963. This commission included married couples as well as many experts in the various fields pertinent to these questions. Its task was to examine views and opinions concerning married life, and especially on the correct regulation of births; and it was also to provide the teaching authority of the Church with such evidence as would enable it to give an apt reply in this matter, which not only the faithful but also the rest of the world were waiting for.

When the evidence of the experts had been received, as well as the opinions and advice of a considerable number of Our brethren in the episcopate—some of whom sent their views spontaneously, while others were requested by Us to do so—We were in a position to weigh with more precision all the aspects of this complex subject. Hence We are deeply grateful to all those concerned.

The Magisterium's Reply

6. However, the conclusions arrived at by the commission could not be considered by Us as definitive and absolutely certain, dispensing Us from the duty of examining personally this serious question. This was all the more necessary because, within the commission itself, there was not complete agreement concerning the moral norms to be proposed, and especially because certain approaches and criteria for a solution to this question had emerged which were at variance with the moral doctrine on marriage constantly taught by the magisterium of the Church.

Consequently, now that We have sifted carefully the evidence sent to Us and intently studied the whole matter, as well as prayed constantly to God, We, by virtue of the mandate entrusted to Us by Christ, intend to give Our reply to this series of grave questions.

II. Doctrinal Principles

7. The question of human procreation, like every other question which touches human life, involves more than the limited aspects specific to such disciplines as biology, psychology, demography or sociology. It is the whole man and the whole mission to which he is called that must be considered: both its natural, earthly aspects and its supernatural, eternal aspects. And since in the attempt to justify artificial methods of birth control many appeal to the demands of married love or of responsible parenthood, these two important realities of married life must be accurately defined and analyzed. This is what We mean to do, with special reference to what the Second Vatican Council taught with the highest authority in its Pastoral Constitution on the Church in the World of Today.

God's Loving Design

8. Married love particularly reveals its true nature and nobility when we realize that it takes its origin from God, who "is love," the Father "from whom every family in heaven and on earth is named."

Marriage, then, is far from being the effect of chance or the result of the blind evolution of natural forces. It is in reality the wise and provident institution of God the Creator, whose purpose was to effect in man His loving design. As a consequence, husband and wife, through that mutual gift of themselves, which is specific and exclusive to them alone, develop that union of two persons in which they perfect one another, cooperating with God in the generation and rearing of new lives.

The marriage of those who have been baptized is, in addition, invested with the dignity of a sacramental sign of grace, for it represents the union of Christ and His Church.

Married Love

9. In the light of these facts the characteristic features and exigencies of married love are clearly indicated, and it is of the highest importance to evaluate them exactly.

This love is above all fully human, a compound of sense and spirit. It is not, then, merely a question of natural instinct or emotional drive. It is also, and above all, an act of the free will, whose trust is such that it is meant not only to survive the joys and sorrows of daily life, but also to grow, so that husband and wife become in a way one heart and one soul, and together attain their human fulfillment.

It is a love which is total—that very special form of personal friendship in which husband and wife generously share everything, allowing no unreasonable exceptions and not thinking solely of their own convenience. Whoever really loves his partner loves not only for what he receives, but loves that partner for the partner's own sake, content to be able to enrich the other with the gift of himself.

Married love is also faithful and exclusive of all other, and this until death. This is how husband and wife understood it on the day on which, fully aware of what they were doing, they freely vowed themselves to one another in marriage. Though this fidelity of husband and wife sometimes presents difficulties, no one has the right to assert that it is impossible; it is, on the contrary, always honorable and meritorious. The example of countless married couples proves not only that fidelity is in accord with the nature of marriage, but also that it is the source of profound and enduring happiness.

Finally, this love is fecund. It is not confined wholly to the loving interchange of husband and wife; it also contrives to go beyond this to bring new life into being. "Marriage and conjugal love are by their nature ordained toward the procreation and education of children. Children are really the supreme gift of marriage and contribute in the highest degree to their parents' welfare."

Responsible Parenthood

10. Married love, therefore, requires of husband and wife the full awareness of their obligations in the matter of responsible parenthood, which today, rightly enough, is much insisted upon, but which at the same time should be rightly understood. Thus, we do well to consider responsible parenthood in the light of its varied legitimate and interrelated aspects.

With regard to the biological processes, responsible parenthood means an awareness of, and respect for, their proper functions. In the procreative faculty the human mind discerns biological laws that apply to the human person.

With regard to man's innate drives and emotions, responsible parenthood means that man's reason and will must exert control over them.

With regard to physical, economic, psychological and social conditions, responsible parenthood is exercised by those who prudently and generously decide to have more children, and by those who, for serious reasons and with due respect to moral precepts, decide not to have additional children for either a certain or an indefinite period of time.

Responsible parenthood, as we use the term here, has one further essential aspect of paramount importance. It concerns the objective moral order which was established by God, and of which a right conscience is the true interpreter. In a word, the exercise of responsible parenthood requires that husband and wife, keeping a right order of priorities, recognize their own duties toward God, themselves, their families and human society.

From this it follows that they are not free to act as they choose in the service of transmitting life, as if it were wholly up to them to decide what is the right course to follow. On the contrary, they are bound to ensure that what they do corresponds to the will of God the Creator. The very nature of marriage and its use makes His will clear, while the constant teaching of the Church spells it out.

Observing the Natural Law

11. The sexual activity, in which husband and wife are intimately and chastely united with one another, through which human life is transmitted, is, as the recent Council recalled, "noble and worthy." It does not, moreover, cease to be legitimate even when, for reasons independent of their will, it is foreseen to be infertile. For its natural adaptation to the expression and strengthening of the union of husband and wife is not thereby suppressed. The fact is, as experience shows, that new life is not the result of each and every act of sexual intercourse. God has wisely ordered laws of nature and the incidence of fertility in such a way that successive births are already naturally spaced through the inherent operation of these laws. The Church, nevertheless, in urging men to the observance of the precepts of the natural law, which it interprets by its constant doctrine, teaches that each and every marital act must of necessity retain its intrinsic relationship to the procreation of human life.

Union and Procreation

12. This particular doctrine, often expounded by the magisterium of the Church, is based on the inseparable connection, established by God, which man on his own initiative may not break, between the unitive significance and the procreative significance which are both inherent to the marriage act.

The reason is that the fundamental nature of the marriage act, while uniting husband and wife in the closest intimacy, also renders them capable of generating new life—and this as a result of laws written into the actual nature of man and of woman. And if each of these essential qualities, the unitive and the procreative, is preserved, the use of marriage fully retains its sense of true mutual love and its ordination to the supreme responsibility of parenthood to which man is called. We believe that our contemporaries are particularly capable of seeing that this teaching is in harmony with human reason.

Faithfulness to God's Design

13. Men rightly observe that a conjugal act imposed on one's partner without regard to his or her condition or personal and reasonable wishes in the matter, is no true act of love, and therefore offends the moral order in its particular application to the intimate relationship of husband and wife. If they further reflect, they must also recognize that an act of mutual love which impairs the capacity to transmit life which God the Creator, through specific laws, has built into it, frustrates His design which constitutes the norm of marriage, and contradicts the will of the Author of life. Hence to use this divine gift while depriving it, even if only partially, of its meaning and purpose, is equally repugnant to the nature of man and of woman,

and is consequently in opposition to the plan of God and His holy will. But to experience the gift of married love while respecting the laws of conception is to acknowledge that one is not the master of the sources of life but rather the minister of the design established by the Creator. Just as man does not have unlimited dominion over his body in general, so also, and with more particular reason, he has no such dominion over his specifically sexual faculties, for these are concerned by their very nature with the generation of life, of which God is the source. "Human life is sacred—all men must recognize that fact," Our predecessor Pope John XXIII recalled. "From its very inception it reveals the creating hand of God."

Unlawful Birth Control Methods

14. Therefore We base Our words on the first principles of a human and Christian doctrine of marriage when We are obliged once more to declare that the direct interruption of the generative process already begun and, above all, all direct abortion, even for therapeutic reasons, are to be absolutely excluded as lawful means of regulating the number of children. Equally to be condemned, as the magisterium of the Church has affirmed on many occasions, is direct sterilization, whether of the man or of the woman, whether permanent or temporary.

Similarly excluded is any action which either before, at the moment of, or after sexual intercourse, is specifically intended to prevent procreation—whether as an end or as a means.

Neither is it valid to argue, as a justification for sexual intercourse which is deliberately contraceptive, that a lesser evil is to be preferred to a greater one, or that such intercourse would merge with procreative acts of past and future to form a single entity, and so be qualified by exactly the same moral goodness as these. Though it is true that sometimes it is lawful to tolerate a lesser moral evil in order to avoid a greater evil or in order to promote a greater good," it is never lawful, even for the gravest reasons, to do evil that good may come of it— in other words, to intend directly something which of its very nature contradicts the moral order, and which must therefore be judged unworthy of man, even though the intention is to protect or promote the welfare of an individual, of a family or of society in general. Consequently, it is a serious error to think that a whole married life of otherwise normal relations can justify sexual intercourse which is deliberately contraceptive and so intrinsically wrong.

Lawful Therapeutic Means

15. On the other hand, the Church does not consider at all illicit the use of those therapeutic means necessary to cure bodily diseases, even if a foreseeable impediment to procreation should result there from—provided such impediment is not directly intended for any motive whatsoever.

Recourse to Infertile Periods

16. Now as We noted earlier (no. 3), some people today raise the objection against this particular doctrine of the Church concerning the moral laws governing marriage, that human intelligence has both the right and responsibility to control those forces of irrational nature which come within its ambit and to direct them toward ends beneficial to man. Others ask on the same point whether it is not reasonable in so many cases to use artificial birth control if by so doing the harmony and peace of a family are better served and more suitable conditions are provided for the education of children already born. To this question We must give a clear reply. The Church is the first to praise and commend the application of human intelligence to an activity in which a rational creature such as man is so closely associated with

his Creator. But she affirms that this must be done within the limits of the order of reality established by God.

If therefore there are well-grounded reasons for spacing births, arising from the physical or psychological condition of husband or wife, or from external circumstances, the Church teaches that married people may then take advantage of the natural cycles immanent in the reproductive system and engage in marital intercourse only during those times that are infertile, thus controlling birth in a way which does not in the least offend the moral principles which We have just explained.

Neither the Church nor her doctrine is inconsistent when she considers it lawful for married people to take advantage of the infertile period but condemns as always unlawful the use of means which directly prevent conception, even when the reasons given for the later practice may appear to be upright and serious. In reality, these two cases are completely different. In the former the married couple rightly use a faculty provided them by nature. In the latter they obstruct the natural development of the generative process. It cannot be denied that in each case the married couple, for acceptable reasons, are both perfectly clear in their intention to avoid children and wish to make sure that none will result. But it is equally true that it is exclusively in the former case that husband and wife are ready to abstain from intercourse during the fertile period as often as for reasonable motives the birth of another child is not desirable. And when the infertile period recurs, they use their married intimacy to express their mutual love and safeguard their fidelity toward one another. In doing this they certainly give proof of a true and authentic love.

Consequences of Artificial Methods

17. Responsible men can become more deeply convinced of the truth of the doctrine laid down by the Church on this issue if they reflect on the consequences of methods and plans for artificial birth control. Let them first consider how easily this course of action could open wide the way for marital infidelity and a general lowering of moral standards. Not much experience is needed to be fully aware of human weakness and to understand that human beings—and especially the young, who are so exposed to temptation—need incentives to keep the moral law, and it is an evil thing to make it easy for them to break that law. Another effect that gives cause for alarm is that a man who grows accustomed to the use of contraceptive methods may forget the reverence due to a woman, and, disregarding her physical and emotional equilibrium, reduce her to being a mere instrument for the satisfaction of his own desires, no longer considering her as his partner whom he should surround with care and affection.

Finally, careful consideration should be given to the danger of this power passing into the hands of those public authorities who care little for the precepts of the moral law. Who will blame a government which in its attempt to resolve the problems affecting an entire country resorts to the same measures as are regarded as lawful by married people in the solution of a particular family difficulty? Who will prevent public authorities from favoring those contraceptive methods which they consider more effective? Should they regard this as necessary, they may even impose their use on everyone. It could well happen, therefore, that when people, either individually or in family or social life, experience the inherent difficulties of the divine law and are determined to avoid them, they may give into the hands of public authorities the power to intervene in the most personal and intimate responsibility of husband and wife.

Limits to Man's Power

Consequently, unless we are willing that the responsibility of procreating life should be left to the arbitrary decision of men, we must accept that there are certain limits, beyond which it is wrong to go, to the power of man over his own body and its natural functions—limits, let it be said, which no one, whether as a private individual or as a public authority, can lawfully exceed. These limits are expressly imposed because of the reverence due to the whole human organism and its natural functions, in the light of the principles We stated earlier, and in accordance with a correct understanding of the "principle of totality" enunciated by Our predecessor Pope Pius XII.

Concern of the Church

18. It is to be anticipated that perhaps not everyone will easily accept this particular teaching. There is too much clamorous outcry against the voice of the Church, and this is intensified by modern means of communication. But it comes as no surprise to the Church that she, no less than her divine Founder, is destined to be a "sign of contradiction." She does not, because of this, evade the duty imposed on her of proclaiming humbly but firmly the entire moral law, both natural and evangelical.

Since the Church did not make either of these laws, she cannot be their arbiter—only their guardian and interpreter. It could never be right for her to declare lawful what is in fact unlawful, since that, by its very nature, is always opposed to the true good of man.

In preserving intact the whole moral law of marriage, the Church is convinced that she is contributing to the creation of a truly human civilization. She urges man not to betray his personal responsibilities by putting all his faith in technical expedients. In this way she defends the dignity of husband and wife. This course of action shows that the Church, loyal to the example and teaching of the divine Savior, is sincere and unselfish in her regard for men whom she strives to help even now during this earthly pilgrimage "to share God's life as sons of the living God, the Father of all men."

III. Pastoral Directives

19. Our words would not be an adequate expression of the thought and solicitude of the Church, Mother and Teacher of all peoples, if, after having recalled men to the observance and respect of the divine law regarding matrimony, they did not also support mankind in the honest regulation of birth amid the difficult conditions which today afflict families and peoples. The Church, in fact, cannot act differently toward men than did the Redeemer. She knows their weaknesses, she has compassion on the multitude, she welcomes sinners. But at the same time she cannot do otherwise than teach the law. For it is in fact the law of human life restored to its native truth and guided by the Spirit of God. Observing the Divine Law.

20. The teaching of the Church regarding the proper regulation of birth is a promulgation of the law of God Himself. And yet there is no doubt that to many it will appear not merely difficult but even impossible to observe. Now it is true that like all good things which are outstanding for their nobility and for the benefits which they confer on men, so this law demands from individual men and women, from families and from human society, a resolute purpose and great endurance. Indeed it cannot be observed unless God comes to their help with the grace by which the goodwill of men is sustained and strengthened. But to those who consider this matter diligently it will indeed be evident that this endurance enhances man's dignity and confers benefits on human society.

Value of Self-Discipline

21. The right and lawful ordering of birth demands, first of all, that spouses fully recognize and value the true blessings of family life and that they acquire complete mastery over themselves and their emotions. For if with the aid of reason and of free will they are to control their natural drives, there can be no doubt at all of the need for self-denial. Only then will the expression of love, essential to married life, conform to right order. This is especially clear in the practice of periodic continence. Self-discipline of this kind is a shining witness to the chastity of husband and wife and, far from being a hindrance to their love of one another, transforms it by giving it a more truly human character. And if this self-discipline does demand that they persevere in their purpose and efforts, it has at the same time the salutary effect of enabling husband and wife to develop to their personalities and to be enriched with spiritual blessings. For it brings to family life abundant fruits of tranquility and peace. It helps in solving difficulties of other kinds. It fosters in husband and wife thoughtfulness and loving consideration for one another. It helps them to repel inordinate self-love, which is the opposite of charity. It arouses in them a consciousness of their responsibilities. And finally, it confers upon parents a deeper and more effective influence in the education of their children. As their children grow up, they develop a right sense of values and achieve a serene and harmonious use of their mental and physical powers.

Promotion of Chastity

22. We take this opportunity to address those who are engaged in education and all those whose right and duty it is to provide for the common good of human society. We would call their attention to the need to create an atmosphere favorable to the growth of chastity so that true liberty may prevail over license and the norms of the moral law may be fully safeguarded.

Everything therefore in the modern means of social communication which arouses men's baser passions and encourages low moral standards, as well as every obscenity in the written word and every form of indecency on the stage and screen, should be condemned publicly and unanimously by all those who have at heart the advance of civilization and the safeguarding of the outstanding values of the human spirit. It is quite absurd to defend this kind of depravity in the name of art or culture or by pleading the liberty which may be allowed in this field by the public authorities.

Appeal to Public Authorities

23. And now We wish to speak to rulers of nations. To you most of all is committed the responsibility of safeguarding the common good. You can contribute so much to the preservation of morals. We beg of you, never allow the morals of your peoples to be undermined. The family is the primary unit in the state; do not tolerate any legislation which would introduce into the family those practices which are opposed to the natural law of God. For there are other ways by which a government can and should solve the population problem—that is to say by enacting laws which will assist families and by educating the people wisely so that the moral law and the freedom of the citizens are both safeguarded.

Seeking True Solutions

We are fully aware of the difficulties confronting the public authorities in this matter, especially in the developing countries. In fact, We had in mind the justifiable anxieties which weigh upon them when We published Our encyclical letter *Populorum Progressio*. But now We join Our voice to that of Our predecessor John XXIII of venerable memory, and We make Our own his words: "No statement of the problem and no solution to it is acceptable which does violence to man's essential dignity; those who propose such solutions base them on an utterly materialistic conception of man himself and his life. The only possible solution to this question is one which envisages the social and economic progress both of individuals and of the whole of human society, and which respects and promotes true human values." No one can, without being grossly unfair, make divine Providence responsible for what clearly seems to be the result of misguided governmental policies, of an insufficient sense of social justice, of a selfish accumulation of material goods, and finally of a culpable failure to undertake those initiatives and responsibilities which would raise the standard of living of peoples and their children. If only all governments which were able would do what some are already doing so nobly, and bestir themselves to renew their efforts and their undertakings! There must be no relaxation in the programs of mutual aid between all the branches of the great human family. Here We believe an almost limitless field lies open for the activities of the great international institutions.

To Scientists

24. Our next appeal is to men of science. These can "considerably advance the welfare of marriage and the family and also peace of conscience, if by pooling their efforts they strive to elucidate more thoroughly the conditions favorable to a proper regulation of births." It is supremely desirable, and this was also the mind of Pius XII, that medical science should by the study of natural rhythms succeed in determining a sufficiently secure basis for the chaste limitation of offspring. In this way scientists, especially those who are Catholics, will by their research establish the truth of the Church's claim that "there can be no contradiction between two divine laws—that which governs the transmitting of life and that which governs the fostering of married love."

To Christian Couples

25. And now We turn in a special way to Our own sons and daughters, to those most of all whom God calls to serve Him in the state of marriage. While the Church does indeed hand on to her children the inviolable conditions laid down by God's law, she is also the herald of salvation and through the sacraments she flings wide open the channels of grace through which man is made a new creature responding in charity and true freedom to the design of his Creator and Savior, experiencing too the sweetness of the yoke of Christ.

In humble obedience then to her voice, let Christian husbands and wives be mindful of their vocation to the Christian life, a vocation which, deriving from their Baptism, has been confirmed anew and made more explicit by the Sacrament of Matrimony. For by this sacrament they are strengthened and, one might almost say, consecrated to the faithful fulfillment of their duties. Thus will they realize to the full their calling and bear witness as becomes them, to Christ before the world. For the Lord has entrusted to them the task of making visible to men and women the holiness and joy of the law which united inseparably their love for one another and the cooperation they give to God's love, God who is the Author of human life.

We have no wish at all to pass over in silence the difficulties, at times very great, which beset the lives of Christian married couples. For them, as indeed for every one of us, "the gate is narrow and the way is hard, that leads to life." Nevertheless it is precisely the hope of that life which, like a brightly burning torch, lights up their journey, as, strong in spirit, they strive to live "sober, upright and godly lives in this world," knowing for sure that "the form of this world is passing away."

Recourse to God

For this reason husbands and wives should take up the burden appointed to them, willingly, in the strength of faith and of that hope which "does not disappoint us, because God's love has been poured into our hearts through the Holy Spirit who has been given to us. Then let them implore the help of God with unremitting prayer and, most of all, let them draw grace and charity from that unfailing fount which is the Eucharist. If, however, sin still exercises its hold over them, they are not to lose heart. Rather must they, humble and persevering, have recourse to the mercy of God, abundantly bestowed in the Sacrament of Penance. In this way, for sure, they will be able to reach that perfection of married life which the Apostle sets out in these words: "Husbands, love your wives, as Christ loved the Church. . . . Even so husbands should love their wives as their own bodies. He who loves his wife loves himself. For no man ever hates his own flesh, but nourishes and cherishes it, as Christ does the Church. . . . This is a great mystery, and I mean in reference to Christ and the Church; however, let each one of you love his wife as himself, and let the wife see that she respects her husband."

Family Apostolate

26. Among the fruits that ripen if the law of God be resolutely obeyed, the most precious is certainly this, that married couples themselves will often desire to communicate their own experience to others. Thus it comes about that in the fullness of the lay vocation will be included a novel and outstanding form of the apostolate by which, like ministering to like, married couples themselves by the leadership they offer will become apostles to other married couples. And surely among all the forms of the Christian apostolate it is hard to think of one more opportune for the present time.

To Doctors and Nurses

27. Likewise we hold in the highest esteem those doctors and members of the nursing profession who, in the exercise of their calling, endeavor to fulfill the demands of their Christian vocation before any merely human interest. Let them therefore continue constant in their resolution always to support those lines of action which accord with faith and with right reason. And let them strive to win agreement and support for these policies among their professional colleagues. Moreover, they should regard it as an essential part of their skill to make themselves fully proficient in this difficult field of medical knowledge. For then, when married couples ask for their advice, they may be in a position to give them right counsel and to point them in the proper direction. Married couples have a right to expect this much from them.

To Priests

28. And now, beloved sons, you who are priests, you who in virtue of your sacred office act as counselors and spiritual leaders both of individual men and women and of families—We turn to you filled with great confidence. For it is your principal duty—We are speaking es-

pecially to you who teach moral theology—to spell out clearly and completely the Church's teaching on marriage. In the performance of your ministry you must be the first to give an example of that sincere obedience, inward as well as outward, which is due to the magisterium of the Church. For, as you know, the pastors of the Church enjoy a special light of the Holy Spirit in teaching the truth. And this, rather than the arguments they put forward, is why you are bound to such obedience. Nor will it escape you that if men's peace of soul and the unity of the Christian people are to be preserved, then it is of the utmost importance that in moral as well as in dogmatic theology all should obey the magisterium of the Church and should speak as with one voice. Therefore We make Our own the anxious words of the great Apostle Paul and with all Our heart We renew Our appeal to you: "I appeal to you, brethren, by the name of our Lord Jesus Christ, that all of you agree and that there be no dissensions among you, but that you be united in the same mind and the same judgment."

Christian Compassion

29. Now it is an outstanding manifestation of charity toward souls to omit nothing from the saving doctrine of Christ; but this must always be joined with tolerance and charity, as Christ Himself showed in His conversations and dealings with men. For when He came, not to judge, but to save the world, was He not bitterly severe toward sin, but patient and abounding in mercy toward sinners?

Husbands and wives, therefore, when deeply distressed by reason of the difficulties of their life, must find stamped in the heart and voice of their priest the likeness of the voice and the love of our Redeemer.

So speak with full confidence, beloved sons, convinced that while the Holy Spirit of God is present to the magisterium proclaiming sound doctrine, He also illumines from within the hearts of the faithful and invites their assent. Teach married couples the necessary way of prayer and prepare them to approach more often with great faith the Sacraments of the Eucharist and of Penance. Let them never lose heart because of their weakness.

To Bishops

30. And now as We come to the end of this encyclical letter, We turn Our mind to you, reverently and lovingly, beloved and venerable brothers in the episcopate, with whom We share more closely the care of the spiritual good of the People of God. For We invite all of you, We implore you, to give a lead to your priests who assist you in the sacred ministry, and to the faithful of your dioceses, and to devote yourselves with all zeal and without delay to safeguarding the holiness of marriage, in order to guide married life to its full human and Christian perfection. Consider this mission as one of your most urgent responsibilities at the present time. As you well know, it calls for concerted pastoral action in every field of human diligence, economic, cultural and social. If simultaneous progress is made in these various fields, then the intimate life of parents and children in the family will be rendered not only more tolerable, but easier and more joyful. And life together in human society will be enriched with fraternal charity and made more stable with true peace when God's design which He conceived for the world is faithfully followed.

A Great Work

31. Venerable brothers, beloved sons, all men of good will, great indeed is the work of education, of progress and of charity to which We now summon all of you. And this We

do relying on the unshakable teaching of the Church, which teaching Peter's successor together with his brothers in the Catholic episcopate faithfully guards and interprets. And We are convinced that this truly great work will bring blessings both on the world and on the Church. For man cannot attain that true happiness for which he yearns with all the strength of his spirit, unless he keeps the laws which the Most High God has engraved in his very nature. These laws must be wisely and lovingly observed. On this great work, on all of you and especially on married couples, We implore from the God of all holiness and pity an abundance of heavenly grace as a pledge of which We gladly bestow Our apostolic blessing.

Given at St. Peters, Rome, on the 25th day of July, the feast of St. James the Apostle, in the year 1968, the sixth of Our pontificate.

SOURCE: *The Pope Speaks*, 13 (Fall, 1969), 329–46. Reprinted by permission of Liberia Editrice Vaticana.

DOCUMENT ANALYSIS

This papal encyclical was issued just as feminists were organizing to extend greater reproductive rights to women. The church's instruction, in the midst of both reform and repeal-minded movements, is a reminder that not all Americans agreed with the turn toward liberalization of abortion law. In fact, not only were many Americans unsupportive of greater abortion access, as the document suggests, not all supported the use of contraception for the prevention of unwanted pregnancy.

This papal encyclical reminded lay Catholics of their religious obligation to bear children, in wedlock, to honor God. The explicit rejection of intervention in the body's natural spacing of children, and the assertive proposition that all human life, from conception to natural death, is sacred, sparked a movement among Catholics to resist the trend toward abortion access. More importantly, in the years to come, conservative Protestant activists would join the antiabortion cause, forming their own organizations in the creation of a fully developed antiabortion social movement. That movement would not prevent the Supreme Court from extending abortion rights across the states, but by the 1970s it would create a powerful political force able to create obstacles to abortion access and provision.

Document: NARAL By-Laws and NARAL Progress Report.
Date: September *27*, 1969.
Where: Chicago, Illinois
Significance: These documents mark the beginning of a powerful movement that advocated allowing women greater control over their reproductive lives.

NARAL BY-LAWS: September 27, 1969

Article I: Name

The name of this association is NATIONAL ASSOCIATION FOR REPEAL OF ABORTION LAWS, hereinafter called NARAL. The organization is made up of individuals and autonomous organizations, free to carry out individual programs consistent with the purpose of NARAL and to resign at any time.

ARTICLE II: PURPOSE

NARAL, recognizing the basic human right of a woman to limit her own reproduction is dedicated to the elimination of all laws and practices that would compel any woman to bear a child against her will. To that end, it proposes to initiate and coordinate political, social, and legal action of individuals and groups concerned with providing safe abortions by qualified physicians for all women seeking them regardless of economic status.

NARAL NEWS, summer 1969, Vol.1, No.1

NARAL: A PROGRESS REPORT

Who we are

The National Association for Repeal of Abortion Laws was formed at the First National Conference on Abortion—Reform or Repeal? Held in February in Chicago, attended by 350 people, and sponsored by 21 organizations.

The new group became a rallying point for individuals and organizations disillusioned with the ineffectiveness of reform laws. Their position was summarized in the welcoming remarks of Dr. Lonny Myers, Department of Anesthesiology, Michael Reese Hospital, and former chairman of the Illinois Citizens for Medical Control of Abortion.

"We oppose in principle the compulsory continuance of any unwanted pregnancy. To ask me to rejoice at the prospect of a law that would compel only 90% instead of virtually 100% of women to continue unwanted pregnancies is like asking one who opposes witch burning to rejoice at a new law that allows the burning of only 90% of witches."

The substance of the repeal position as defined in Chicago has since become the Purpose of NARAL and is printed on the banner of this newsletter.

What we are

NARAL is an action organization. Our policy is:

1. Safe abortions performed by physicians should be readily available to all women on a voluntary basis regardless of economic status and without legal encumbrance; and
2. As a medical procedure, abortion should be subject only to the general laws regulating medical licensure and practice.

Our program is:

1. Assist in the formation in all states of direct political action groups dedicated to the purpose of NARAL;
2. Serve as a clearing house for activities related to NARAL's purpose;
3. Create new materials for mass distribution which tell the repeal story dramatically and succinctly;
4. Train fieldworkers to organize and stimulate legislative action;
5. Suggest direct action projects;
6. Raise funds for the above activities.

Looking ahead

The main thrust of all activities aimed at repeal of abortion laws must come through state or local organizations, and NARAL will direct its activities toward helping these groups.

Supplying fieldworkers on request and inexpensive literature for mass distribution; providing How-to-Kits on organizing repeal groups, influencing public opinion, and engineering legislative action; setting up action-oriented regional workshops and a speaker's bureau: these are some of the ideas that will be given form and direction at the fall Board Meeting.

Concurrent with these activities, NARAL will continue to press for action through the courts. We will also attempt to persuade influential individuals and national organizations (religious, professional, social service) to take a strong position favoring repeal of abortion laws.

In planning program, NARAL will carefully avoid duplication of effort and will actively seek the cooperation of other national abortion groups in meeting our common objectives.

In all activities our emphasis will be action; our objective, results.

SOURCE: NARAL archives.

DOCUMENT ANALYSIS

These two documents form the basis of NARAL, the nation's largest reproductive rights organization. As indicated by its full name, National Association for Repeal of Abortion Laws, the organization originally advocated for the *repeal* of abortion laws, not for legal *reform*. While the difference may appear slight, the causes for repeal and reform were distinct in the 1960s, and faced different political possibilities. NARAL's acronym has changed several times over the course of its history, reflecting changes in the organization's philosophy and perhaps revealing the changing tenor of American abortion politics. Today, NARAL itself does not advocate for abortion law repeal and focuses its efforts on accessible abortion as well as the prevention of unwanted pregnancy.

Document: Excerpt from *The Abortion Handbook for Responsible Women,* by Lana Clarke Phelan and Patricia Therese Maginnis.
Date: 1969.
Where: North Hollywood: Contact Books.
Significance: This handbook selection for women facing abortion review boards—cowritten by one of the founders of NARAL—reveals the power and influence those boards had over women's lives, as well as the lengths women were willing to go to get a legal, safe abortion.

With our little noses still hot on the trail of legal medical care by any means we can get it, let's sniff for a minute at the "reform" outlets for those of us who might qualify under the new "mental abnormality" clause in our few reform states.

These few states permit "legal" abortions if the pregnant woman is psychotic, an open and obvious public menace. It is easier if she has a long history of such mental disturbance, but most of us haven't such medical backgrounds. We need two psychiatrists to examine us, and certify in writing to the hospital abortion committee that we are psychotic enough to qualify under these clauses. We will get to the psychiatrists in a minute, but let's look now at the makeup of this hospital abortion committee and see how it works.

The hospital abortion committee is comprised of a cross-section of the medical staff of the hospital concerned. These committees sometimes rotate their membership. Due to the fact that women physicians have been greatly discouraged by the American Medical Association, their path to an M.D. degree has been long and thorny, and they are few in number. Practically all abortion committees are all-male in membership.

The law requires that all hospitals performing "legal" abortions be accredited. Are you impressed? Don't be. An accredited hospital is simply one with 25 beds or more. It is not necessarily a better hospital, better equipped, nor does it necessarily provide a higher level of medical care through skill and service. It is merely larger in size. You can have a heart transplant performed in a non-accredited hospital without a murmur from the medical profession or the law, as the quality of care is often far better in small, endowed private institutions.

The legal nonsense requiring that abortion surgery be performed only in accredited hospitals is deliberately misleading to the general public. It makes it far more difficult for women in smaller communities not boasting larger facilities to get into the crowded larger institutions which are usually located in cities. It also makes it more complicated to get approval from the hospital abortion committees in these large hospitals, as such hospitals are often Roman Catholic dominated, particularly in maternity sections.

However, abortion is, under normal circumstances, a non-hospital procedure. Through the first three months of pregnancy, it can and should be performed in physician's office surgeries or in smaller clinics nearby the patient's home.

Forcing this minor surgical procedure into major hospitals, already overcrowded with really ill patients, gives the public the erroneous impression that abortion is a complicated and dangerous operation, requiring great medical skill and extensive nursing care, and involving considerable recuperative time for the patient who undergoes the procedure. The only times abortion requires this kind of medical attention when the patient has developed serious complications such as infection, or hemorrhage, or is quite far along in her pregnancy before it is interrupted. Both infection and hemorrhage are by-products of simple surgery being performed illicitly by non-skilled persons, or by the patient herself. These requirements would be greatly lessened if the original abortion surgery was decently performed at an early stage by a certified medical practitioner. Very, very few U.S. women would ever require the costly extravagance of long hospitalization to abort.

Nevertheless, the law requires that all abortions be performed in these ultra-elaborate settings, with permission of many doctors, courts and hospital abortion committees. It is clear to all that such maneuvering is costly in money and time, thus pricing the surgery far beyond the ability of the impoverished woman to pay.

These extravagant fees for minimum surgical services may be splendid for the medical profession on the receiving end of this revenue. But in a nation rapidly heading for socialized medicine because of the inability of the poor to pay such padded medical bills, it will profit the suffering taxpayers to take a long, objective look at laws which permit physicians to bill them a thousand dollars for a medical service which should have been provided for not more than fifty dollars.

If the taxpayers do not resent paying this exorbitant rake-off to support religious morality laws disguised as penal codes, then good for them! We hope they will be equally generous in supporting the hundreds of thousands of state-children on welfare rolls, and promptly cease their condemnation of their reluctant mothers who tried very hard for medical relief. Remember, Mr. and Mrs. Condemning Taxpayer, your laws and your state-god made mothers of them, and each little one is now very much *yours*. Be sure and make a place for them to eat heartily from the banquet of life to which you had them summoned.

As before stated, larger hospitals are heavily dominated by Roman Catholics, specially in maternity sections, as human breeding and over breeding is a very big thing with this group. The more, the merrier in their eyes! Following their religious instruction of one hundred years ago, when their Pope declared abortion a "heavenly no-no," these physicians serve their spiritual leader before their patients. After all, what have you to offer so valuable as their heavenly property in escrow? You, dear, help to make their payments on the future, so bear down!

There are questions we need to ask . . . should a Roman Catholic physician, obviously sworn to support his Pope, be permitted to control the reproductive life of a non-Catholic woman? Should such physicians be ethically required to inform all women patients of this religious restriction in his medical practice?" Should a Roman Catholic physician be permitted to sit on a hospital abortion committee and rule on medical and surgical procedures forbidden by his religion, meanwhile carrying veto power in his hands? Would we permit such things if these physicians were vetoing blood transfusions because their religion forbade it? While most Americans heartily endorse the principle of not making a man's religion a barrier to his work and career advancements, we must make exceptions in the event a man's religion will restrict him from performing the work he has been licensed to do. When physicians refuse medical care, based not on scientific and medical facts, but purely on theological dogma, they are flagrantly guilty of malpractice. When their victims are innocently unaware of the religious restrictions of these doctors, they have every reason to think these licensed physicians will treat them in accordance with scientific knowledge and medical training. However, the devout Catholic physician was recently admonished from the Vatican to disregard his "learning and education" and told that since "his conscience could lead him astray: he must not deviate from the "pure teachings of the church," the absolute, divine truths.

So, now we have Catholic physicians practicing the "absolute and divine" medical knowledge of celibate old men in Rome, and using this guidance to deny modern care to non-Catholic American women! Such men should never be permitted to sit in judgment over the fate of a non-Catholic woman. Never. Never. Never. If they wish to practice religious medicine, let them take themselves to a monastery!

The hospital abortion committee is a completely unnecessary medical precaution, and is simply a smokescreen behind which sexual discrimination flourishes and individual doctors protect themselves against criticism by thieving this anonymous committee sanction their dereliction of duty towards their female patients. And you, Mr. and Mrs. America, pay the bills for this nonsense! So much for hospitals, let's talk about doctors and now to screen them for hang-ups which costs you time and money.

Normally, when we contract for a business or professional service, we check carefully into the background, education and personal qualifications of the person(s) with whom we contract. We would never choose anyone whose personal idiosyncrasies would restrict or prevent his business performance of the work we wished done. We apply this judgment to all contracts, whether it be construction of a building, landscaping a yard, a personal thing like marriage, or even selecting a surgeon!

A glaring exception is the surgery of abortion. Here, cowering under the cloaking blackness of superstitious taboo and ignorance, we cast aside all common sense and personal responsibility and accept the judgment of the first doctor we visit. However, it is the highest degree of responsibility for a woman and her mate to demand the legal and human right to determine their futures, and to make the most vital of human decisions, to give birth to only those infants they both want and will love and provide for through maturity. It follows then, oh, responsible ones, that we must apply some unusual methods to ferret out any peculiarities in physicians and find a non-neurotic one. Up to now, it has been a no-questions asked arrangement with him selecting you. Now we will select him!

To arm ourselves for combat, we will use their own methods and conjure ourselves up a slam-bang witch doctor image! Our omnipotent physician, just as mortal man, gets out of bed in the morning looking as if he had been buried for a week and again, just as any ordinary man, puts his pants on one leg at a time. He growls at his wife, belches in very human fashion, scratches his groin and complains that his stomach aches.

When you face this shining, bespectacled wonder of scientific accreditation behind his mammoth desk later in the morning, you will need these visions to arm you for mental combat. The wall will be lined with framed diplomas attesting to his years of medical training. These mean he sat on his royal rear a long time in some school somewhere. Usually, we are so in awe of the golden seals with which these hours of training are adorned, we dare not question the knowledge he must have in his imperious head! Yet behind the seals and splendor, you can often find a mere mortal man so full of hang ups and incorrect, unscientific notions that you wouldn't let him operate on your hangnails.

Those diplomas could have been earned so long ago that anesthesia hadn't been discovered yet.

The problem is more difficult when so few of our older physicians have managed to rise above the crippling religious and academic dogma which values fetal life, and does not value a woman's life at all. Some of these older physicians have risen above the inertia of successful "practice" and have studied through the years to upgrade their medical education. These physicians are aware of the glaring gaps between what they were taught and what women actually feel and desire in their roles as mothers. Their degree of awareness is somewhat tempered by their own attitudes towards women, that is, their personal respect for women as a sex, and the importance of woman as human being as well as a breeding animal. It is also tempered by greed for financial gain, and by fear of displeasing his peers who might feel he was "rocking the boat" if he took exception with the hundred-year old laws which are so financially profitable to his profession.

He also struggles with the old tendency of the medical profession to look down upon the doctor who practices mere female medicine. In the early part of this century, such doctors were the failures of the profession . . . the ones who couldn't make it in decent medicine. As such, he must keep his pathetic patients very much in line, and not have them bucking his authority lest his peers laugh at him for this last, most ignominious failure.

Younger physicians have the advantage of better medical training, and are much more aware of the disservice rendered a patient compelled unwillingly into motherhood. It is increasingly hard for these physicians to adjust their practice with laws which work in opposition to their training and consciences, and many of them, especially those more secure in their own masculinity, urge repeal of these degrading laws. However, even youth does not guarantee you a non-neurotic doctor, as he can be just as greedy and interested in being your personal god as his older counterpart. Watch his religion, too!

To soften these cruel charges a bit, let's remember that our man-doctor, particularly the older ones, studied from books written only by men and in schools conducted only by men and only for men. In their misguided, early efforts in the secondary field of female medicine, perhaps the authors of these books really felt they were making a humane gesture towards inferior and not-very-bright sub-human beings. Fifty years later, these doctor books still reflect this misinformation, more in the United States than they do in other countries. Yet, changes are coming about slowly, and we do not want to tear down good physicians with the bad ones. We will bear that in mind while realizing that most of them still regard us as not quite human. We'll look about a bit.

Let's conjure up another witch doctor vision!! Imagine, if you can, an erudite panel of dogs. These are the finest, most educated, brilliant, wisest dogs in the canine kingdom. This doggy panel is sitting in council to set up rules and write books of instruction on the nature and inclinations, and determine the life roles to be assigned to pussy cats. They, they wisely planned for the futures of their pussy cat subjects, and passed laws to enforce them. The resulting decisions and control procedures might represent the best thinking of the dog community, but they would have scant bearing on the needs, nature and desires of the pussy cats they controlled. There would be much trouble in Nature's kingdom, and applying this analogy to me controlling women, there is indeed trouble in Nature's kingdom of human beings.

Yet to appeal to males at this hour of trouble to relinquish these unnatural controls is roughly comparable to taking a poll of southern plantation owners as to their opinions on whether their slaves were as capable of controlling their own lives and futures as were their masters. There is tremendous ego satisfaction to physicians who refuse abortion care to women thus reducing them to sub-human, begging status.

Your physician's moods and practices

Before starting to disrobe, ask the physician outright his religious preference. If he is Catholic, or otherwise prejudiced against women as full human beings, do yourself a favor and don't waste your time and money. Perhaps you won't be able to ask this important question until the nurse has stripped you for examination. The twist to this routine is that once you are disrobed, you can count on being charged a fancy fee for what well may be unsatisfactory medical service. "Yes," he will say, "you're pregnant, but I only take care of women who want their 'babies.'" Worse yet, he may be one of the sneaky moralists who either withhold the results of your obviously positive (you're pregnant!) pregnancy test and tell you he isn't quite certain and to come back in a month or two and he'll check again. By that time, you'll be so far advanced in your pregnancy, he can be righteously indignant at your desire to terminate. He knows that the further he can get you along the road to maternity, the harder it is for you get medical relief. The aim of the doggy panel is to make you a mother, as often as possible, in any manner possible, and to deliver each conceptus alive, no matter how unwelcome. This is what he learned in his doggy books at his doggy school, and it sure hurts now when the pussy cat is in his power.

Gather your courage. Tell the nurse you wish to speak to "doctor" before disrobing. Tell him outright that you wish a pregnancy test; that you know a urine test will reveal pregnancy almost positively within six weeks after conception; that if you are pregnant, you do not plan on carrying it to term, and you wish to have him excise your uterine growth or remove it with a vacuum aspirator pump as soon as possible before your case becomes advanced.

If he dares give you the unethical disgusting routine of "You'll have to take a trip to Mexico, or Japan, England or abroad where they do 'such things,'" take your medical business elsewhere, not just your abortion business but every smitch of your gynecology business and future maternity trade. This doctor is not interested in your health and welfare and is not to be trusted. Spread the word to your friends that this doctor-type is a very neurotic fellow indeed so they can avoid him also. Don't allow him to tell you the law keeps him from practicing medicine properly. Every abortion law on the penal books would be repealed instantly if doctors didn't like it the way it is. It keeps them rich, and keeps them god. Even a god can't live very high on the hog without your money, so use the weapons at your disposal, and cut off his income and prestige.

Another thought about this obviously punitive attitude toward all women. Doctors spend many years literally buried in their doggy books with their not always correct, but demanding curricula to be mastered. He has precious little time, and less money, during this study years for normal dating or sexual adjustment with women. Lacking personal experience, and cloistered with men who share his limitations in the practical field, he often comes out of medical school and internship almost completely unequipped to deal with his own personal sex life.

These often woefully inadequate men are the same stellar citizens to whom all women are sent to consult about their marriage, sexual and personal difficulties. If you want to make your doctor blush rosy pink, ask him a straight question about your sex life. He gets all confused, drops his pencil, mumbles a lot and finally blushingly sends you to a psychiatrist, as if to indicate you are obviously in need of mental therapy if you even think of sex out loud. If you do go to his psychiatrist for this needed "guidance" you are apt to find the psychiatrist is likewise doggy trained, and in desperate need of a psychiatrist himself.

If your doctor sends you to a minister, remember these men have been trained in the most restrictive of doggy schools, and they have been firmly taught that "sex" is "sin." Therefore, if you wish to discuss human sexuality, they must translate your request into a request to talk to about sin. This is usually unrewarding, as he might as well be clicking in Hottentot, and his comments will bear scant relevance to your problem. Save your energy, and trust your instincts. You knew more about your feminine nature in your playpen than these worthies after twenty years at doggy school.

If Friend Husband is eyeing you askance at your efforts in doctor-screening about this time, perhaps he might be wondering if you have gone "feminist" on him in the hatchet-swinging, bumbershoot-poking sense of the word. Not so, fellows! Look at it this way . . . the people way!

It is a most irresponsible woman who loads her husband down with children neither of them wanted. From the physician's point of view, there is a great deal more money in delivering an infant than in doing an abortion. Further, his pediatrician partner has both "on the hook" for years to come. You will be unable to get so much as an aspirin without paying him for an office call and a prescription fee in a drugstore in which, far oftener than you suspect, the doctor holds an interest. Well, maybe you can still get an aspirin, but not for long the way things are going.

To add insult to injury, your friendly ob-gyn will tell you blandly a year-and-a-half later that it is time you "started" your next infant; that it is not good for your last infant not to have a sibling near its age; that he has noticed you seem nervous and irritable, and perhaps your maternal instincts are not being fully realized and you deep down inside desire another baby and don't quite know what is frustrating you. So your god has spoken, and you trudge home with your new instructions. You mustn't tell Friend Husband of this directive because he wouldn't understand this mysterious inner urging the ob-gyn has detected in your lady psyche, and would probably yell a lot about the grocery bills and how is he going to support all of you. It's better for you just to conveniently forget to take your pill or use your diaphragm only now and then.

Good old doc will help out when your outraged, trapped husband protests your carelessness. He will smoothly tell Friend Husband that many women psychologically reject birth control measures, and without being conscious of what they are doing, often deliberately fail to use them and thus satisfy that "secret deep inner urging" to have another baby. Got it, folks? Who is doing what to whom? Who is making the money? Look there for the one with the vested interest in making you unwilling parents. We will have mix-ups as long as doggy doctors make the vital decisions for all us kiekies, and our husbands are not even in the decision-making picture. Poor Pop, he's just the breadwinner again.

In the meanwhile, doggy logic continues to prevail through force and fear of law, egged on by money profits. At first, it may seem reasonable enough to your doggy husband. After all, he too learned in a doggy school from doggy books, and did they not teach him that being irrational is your true nature? However, he usually gets wise quicker than you do, especially when the financial shoe begins to really pinch. He doesn't mind being the superior partner in the marriage contract, but he does mind becoming an economic slave. It is reasonable to him that you should be just slightly inferior to him as a human being, as he was raised to feel that way. Yet now he finds himself in the same boat with you, chained together in the service of the state. Whatever happened to freedom?

He knows he will never see the end of the bills to pay for necessities of life for all of you; never have a really free paycheck in his life to make even a down payment on a cherished dream, the college training that would make him better able to provide for dependents; never a glimmer of hope for that lovely smelling new automobile, or a little boat or trailer, the "men's toys" that make modern life bearable for males.

Every now and then, such pressures are just too much for mere man, and he "takes off" to get away from it all, and we look sadly at each other and comment "he wasn't much good anyway." Wasn't he? Or are we being hypocrites again? So before you ladies honor your doctor above the health and welfare of your family and mate, give a little thought to what you are doing to them, and stand up to the doctor who is draining your lives of richness and joy. You might tell him he could give you something for your nerves besides pregnancy.

If you find yourself resenting this doctor directing your life and future, try transferring the honor you give the physician to the man who earns your living. We know all politicians say it is very hard to gain honor and respect in your home territory, as people seem to feel authority must rest in someone distant from you that you do not know so well. If you will take a close look at your own husband, you'll find out he's a pretty good fellow, and mighty smart in a lot of ways. Give him credit, and be a bit nicer to him.

Both of you find a modern, non-neurotic doctor whose principal concern is your health and welfare. Then if your "inner urge" still bothers you, sit down with your husband and the physician and talk about it and plan for the infant in the way all infants should be planned. You'll be glad you did . . .

Sooner or later, we have to get into this, so let's do it right now. Your physician must, as a businessman, consider his fees for taking care for you. His agile mind has already deduced that he will earn more money delivering your infant than in doing a $25 interruption of your pregnancy. We spoke of that earlier. But tying this in with his neurosis, we also recall that this man spent a lot of years sticking gold seals on his diplomas. He now needs and requires a great deal of money to uphold his status as a diploma man and to pay his dues to the American Medical Association. This is an important financial worry, and you can see it would be of much higher priority to him than the mediocre question of the "convenience" to you of having an abortion. Your "convenience" is extremely "inconvenient" to him, and his holding the trump card.

It takes a warm, liberal, loving human being type doctor to recognize the right of patients, regardless of sex, to request certain services, and then to reject these services if he has priced them beyond their financial means. The typical physician is notorious for lack of these qualities, and will be the first to tell you his profession is ultra-conservative. The American physician is part patriarch and part monarch, utilizing his magical powers to deny life or delay death, according to his whim and your ability to pay money.

If you are one of those naïve people who think the medical profession polices and regulates the conduct and practice of its members after they graduate and hang out their shingle to practice, take note. Any fraternal affiliations they have are solely designed to protect them from investigation and prosecution, limit the medical profession to those who will conform to these same ideals, enhance their income by keeping down the licensed membership, and lobby for legislation which tightens their control on the lives and pocketbooks of all Americans. If there is wrong-doing on the part of an individual doctor, and you report it to the American Medical Association, the whole profession develops an immediate sever case of myopia. They seldom find anything wrong with the conduct of any member, no matter how outrageous or unprofessional. In short, folks, you're on your own with your local doctor, so watch him.

Even though he might like the idea, today he can not order you burned at the stake, so if you displease him, he can and does take it out on you financially. Your friendly physician, if he has honored you with his services over a period of years, has compiled quite a medical history on you. You have a considerable financial investment in the knowledge he now owns, and you can't even peek at. If he points his royal finger at you in dismissal when you ask for termination of pregnancy and says, "Go away, you sinful woman. I will deliver your 'baby' but I won't do your abortion," you have two choices. Either accept his ultimatum and have your unwanted infant, or go to another doctor to seek medical remedy for your affliction.

When you go to another doctor, you start all over in laboratory tests, general physical examinations, and your entire medical history as well as you can remember. Your old doctor has been quite vague about what drugs you have been taking. "Leave it to me," he said soothingly when you asked what was wrong, or what was in a prescription, "I'm you doctor, and I know best what's good for you." Okay, but try telling this to a new doctor, and has little to start on. So he takes all the tests, etc., over and you pay the bill. When this is all done, he, too, may play god and be as fast and loose with your pocketbook and health as the first doctor. This financial lesson teaches you fast not buck the medical profession, or to question their infallible judgment as to how you and your mate must invest your time, money and actual blood and flesh in the service of his bank account. They are so concerned over your problems they usually sob all the way to the bank.

There is absolutely no latitude to extend to physicians in their grossly unethical treatment of women patients when they force them time after time through unwanted pregnancies. How dare they justify bullying them into cow-like silence when they know these patients already have far more children than they can emotionally love and physically care for? Since there is obviously this complete disinterest in the desires of the woman, no concern as to the future welfare of the new infant beyond nine-months in womb, it is hard to find possible motives for such medical behavior other than the perpetuation of power and money. Sorry about that, doc. Let's shape up. You know who's who among you. So do we . . .

Webster's Third New International Dictionary is the big book women should be forbidden to peek into. But being true daughters of Eve, one of us sneaked in during the night to look up the definition of "psychosis" so we could become one since that is sometimes necessary to get abortion medical care in the United States.

What did Webster say:

"Psychosis: A profound disorganization of mind, personality, or behavior that results from an individual's inability to tolerate the social demands of his social environment whether because of the enormity of the imposed stress or because of primary inadequacy or acquired disability of his organism esp. in regard to the central nervous system or because of disorders of perception, thinking, or affect symptoms of neurosis, or by any combination of these—distinguished from neurosis—compare INSANITY."

How about that, ladies? An hour ago we couldn't even spell "psychosis." Now we have one. Or at least we must get one or make one, and to do that we must visit two psychiatrists.

A psychiatrist is a doctor who has earned his regular medical degree and then take extensive additional training to qualify to treat mental abnormalities as his medical specialty. As he has been in school a very long time, and must have grown very wise indeed, his time is now quite valuable. You will discover this when you are charged $50 to get him to write a letter certifying you psychotic so you can get a D&C.

It boggles the mind to learn that a woman who desires to end a given pregnancy is now required by law to go in and confess psychosis bordering on complete insanity before she can obtain simple medical treatment required at some time or other by every normal woman during her childbearing years! It further bewilders us when we find psychiatrists, the very men who are most aware that this is a normal thing for women to both desire and require, are quick to endorse these "reform laws" which now channel many abortion-seeking patients into their offices and under their control as "mentally disturbed."

We suppose the "enormity of the imposed stress," as outlined by Webster, placed upon us in the form of compulsory childbearing laws might qualify all women as psychotic, insane human beings. Couldn't we just examine the facts and see if the "imposed stress" isn't the cause of the mental disorders in the woman fighting for her very existence.

There are many hazards to the legal psychosis system of getting an abortion. The route is costly in money, and time consuming. Time is quite important to you now. While physicians, lawyers and hospital boards ponder, your pregnancy marches swiftly on full speed ahead, and there is no turning back. If you are finally turned down by the religious-moralists who decide your fate, it's too late to do other than go on to unwilling motherhood, or horror that it may be, the homemade abortion that is the nightmare fate of so many fine women whose only "crime" was not wanting another child that the law and the Vatican have decreed they shall bear.

If you are going to try this medically and legally sanctioned "psychotic" escape route, be aware of this. First of all, there is nothing whatsoever mentally wrong with the average woman who wishes to terminate a given pregnancy. We have said this over and over because it is so true, yet, it is such a carefully kept secret by those who profit by making each woman think she is in some way unfeminine or abnormal when she asks for termination. Almost every woman has felt this ways, and frequently should. The "mental trauma" attributed to women who have undergone abortions is a direct result of the harassment and humiliation heaped upon them by law and ignorant society for daring to want to do a perfectly natural, normal thing. For a hundred years, terrified women have been assured that reluctance to bear an infant was a mental abnormality. Mental abnormality requires the guidance and counsel of a doctor, who was always a man, and he also assured her this was very abnormal and un-maternal on her part.

So this doctor man, who had never known what it was to be pregnant, willingly or unwillingly, and who never would feel the pain or share the labor of rearing the unwanted child dictated that the child must be born. He, instead of Nature, told her how he felt inside. If she tried to protest, to tell him he was wrong, he stormed her into silence from his lofty heights of judgment and told her that wasn't what she felt at all, and if she did, she was very unnatural . . . and women have had to put up with this nonsense for a hundred years.

From your very first visit to the legally-required psychiatrist, you both know you do not require mental care. You require a D&C, and here they are operating on your mind and pocketbook.

No witch doctor ever brewed a spell or love or death potion more lovingly than these doctors will weave your "psychosis" for you! We have learned from brainwashing techniques so successful in military encounters how intelligent people can be made to testify to almost anything, no matter how aberrant, in order to survive. As so it is with the pathetic women who must undergo this cruel and unusual brainwashing to obtain the simplest kind of medical care.

Instead of being told she can replace her pregnancy at a more convenient time for her health, or the welfare of her family, or whatever reason she has for aborting this pregnancy, she is literally hammered into silence. Regardless of her rejection of the immediate pregnancy, she must "confess" in the most primitive manner that to decide to terminate this one pregnancy, this one single ova among thousands and thousands in her body, is abnormal, and she is insane! If she isn't insane before, she may well qualify when these ding-a-lings finish with her. By the time she waits out the decision of the Hospital Abortion Committee, knowing she is almost to the "point of not return" for a safe, early abortion, there is no greater, sadder demonstration of man's inhumanity to woman that the horror she undergoes.

So, ladies, such dramatic performances can actually make you a ding-a-ling too, and in need of dubious care at $30 an hour for some time. We suggest you avoid this habit-forming activity if possible. However, it is tax-deductible.

If you succeed in putting your "psychosis" over, and get your morality clearance, and eventually your tiny surgery, be mindful of the following: (a) You have established a written, public record that you are emotionally unbalanced. (b) Even if it is phony and staged, the record does not so state and this diagnosis remains on your medical records for your lifetime. (c) You may expect life insurance policy rates to increase because of your new "suicidal" tendencies. (d) You will be denied employment and security clearance in many occupations in which "psychotic" individuals are not accepted. (e) If, heaven forbid, you should later become involved in divorce and child custody proceedings you might well lose custody of your existing children as a "mentally unstable mother."

These records are increasingly important in our rapidly-computerizing society. This few minutes of surgery could cost you a great deal more than the money presently being swindled from you by law. Think about it. Think about it. We know you will go ahead and sign such papers, as you are so terribly desperate and terrified, but at least be warned. Beware of the psychiatrist who says you will only be declared " psychotic" a little bit. The law requires that you be absolutely mentally unbalanced, and that's what he must say on his letter of recommendation. It's you that has to live with social disability, not him.

The hospital committees sometimes delay the abortion-seeking women well past three months of pregnancy while contemplating her morals. This delay causes costlier care and more surgical risks for you when you finally do get your abortion done. Their reasoning seems to be that if you undergo enough agony waiting for your approval, you will have the next child without a murmur rather than do this again. If you don't want to have a child, you should have used a contraceptive. This is a mystifying attitude on the part of physicians: that women seeking abortion care should have used contraception, and this failure, whether out of ignorance ore carelessness, or failure of the contraceptive itself, should not medically treated, but be permitted to run its course as punishment for her failure. This is hard on ladies. Most of us would give our eye teeth for a chance to do it over again, and would use contraception delightedly if it would un-pregnant us now.

We can't seem to get it across to doctors that at the same time motherhood can not be our biggest privilege and greatest punishment for stupidity and ignorance. Which is it to be, gentlemen? If women are that dull, how can you recommend them as mothers of the next generation?

Rather than dwell on the improper question as to whether it is better to use contraception than to perform a needed abortion, perhaps it would shed more light and less heat if we phrased the question more in accordance with the problem.

The question should be: "Is abortion to be withheld from a pregnant woman requesting it, and is compulsory motherhood her proper punishment if her contraceptive has failed, or she has failed to use contraception at all?"

If physicians answer "yes" to this question, why do they not apply this same punitive attitude by withholding further medical treatment from those who have taken their prescriptions improperly or not at all, or from those who have contracted lung cancer after being repeatedly warned against smoking, or from those gentlemen who report in with gonorrhea contracted while visiting a lady-of-the-evening who certainly have flaunted morality laws of somebody's church. He does not require these diseases to go their full course, but gives additional or different remedial treatment on request. Why is the unwittingly pregnant woman the victim of his morally-imposed punishment? His punishment does not teach her love, wisdom, or convert her to his code of morality. It merely makes her again face the motherhood she obviously felt unfit to undertake or she would not have been in his office. Like all slaves, she is seldom a happy servant, and her performance is something less than ideal in her shameful role. It follows then, that this physician is not concerned with the fate of the infant he delivers into her reluctant care, but is concerned with making the woman submit to his superior will, and her husband pay his unnecessary bill for the child neither of them wanted.

To add fuel to this outrage, hospital abortion committees frequently attach the requirement that a woman requesting abortion be forced to "request" a sterilization in order for the abortion to be approved. An abortion is a safe, minor operation, and when properly done, will not harm the ability of the woman to have future children at a time more to her choosing. Thus, the stipulation that she must be sterilized is obscene. Sterilization involves a tubal ligation, or tying off her Fallopian tubes. It is a major surgery, with all the attendant dangers of such surgical procedures. It is also irreversible, except at great expense in a few cases.

The poor woman, in order to be relieved of her current agony, is forced first to sign a false statement that she is insane, and using this false statement for leverage she is then forced to "request" the mayhem of sterilization, or the premature end of her reproductive life. After all, an "insane" woman must not be permitted to bear more children, and if she is insane enough not to desire children as the state and church desire she desire then that's all for her. She will learn to answer obediently when they ask the traditional questions! "Yes, sir" she will say respectfully, "I am happy over this pregnancy." Then she will go home and sob her heart out of for nine months of horror. This makes fine and loving mothers. Look all about you . . . they are everywhere, and their children are running wild in the streets, and who is to blame for the lip service given to mother love in America?

How much will we endure as decent people before we rise in fury and demand these sexually-obsessed old men get their noses out of our marriage beds, and confine themselves to things they are competent to discuss.

As we have previously stated, the payment of rather large sums of money to gynecologists and psychiatrists does not insure you will be included on the precious "abortion quota." You need not expect your money or any portion of it refunded in case you are turned down. Incidentally, the published list of women goes each calendar quarter from each accredited hospital to the state health and police departments, and to any other public agency which requests it.

Most psychiatrists ask for payment at the time of the visit because, for them, it is a "one shot" consultation. As we said, you are not in need of mental care, just a letter. They know it full well, and if you are "somebody" in the social scheme of things, they will write your nice $50 letter to the Hospital Abortion Committee and recommend your abortion since you are "psychotic" and that is the end of it. If you are not "somebody," you are good for several return visits, cash each time, as they know you will probably never get included on the approval list anyway. The precious quotas are more than filled with the "somebody" thus receiving the available "legal" abortion care.

SOURCE: Lana Clarke Phelan and Patricia Therese Maginnis, *The Abortion Handbook for Responsible Women* (North Hollywood: Contact Books, 1969), 87–110.

DOCUMENT ANALYSIS

This piece, dripping with irony and bitterness, documents what many women felt about the hospital review boards. It indicates the extent to which many women were forced to go for a legal, hospital abortion: faking psychosis. The alternatives for these women, should their hospital committee deny their request, were few. For a handful of well-off women, travel abroad was not prohibitive or logistically impossible. For many more, the only alternative was an illegal abortion.

The specter of illegal abortions was well known by women in the decades preceding *Roe v. Wade*. Thousands, possibly millions, of women died from botched abortions performed by unethical technicians. In response to the impossible choices presented by the hospital review boards, on the one hand, and the unethical illegal provider on the other, the coauthor of this pamphlet, Patricia Therese Maginnis, founded her California repeal organization that later influenced the formation of NARAL. To women like Maginnis and Phelan, reform would only continue to locate power over women with a handful of male, disapproving doctors. Repeal would return abortion control to women.

Less well known than the specter of botched abortions is the story of doctors who provided abortions safely and respectfully before they were legal. For some physicians, safe and humane abortion provision was their only response to what they considered unsafe and inhumane abortion regulations. Rather than allow women to suffer through the pain of unclean conditions and instruments, some physicians risked their careers to provide women with sterile and respectful abortions during this time.

One group of women decided to take on the abortion procedure themselves. Inspired by the simplicity of the procedure, and emboldened by self-help medical books like *Our Bodies, Our Selves*, a group of women in Chicago began an underground collective they called Jane to train women to provide abortions for each other. Eventually, 100 members of Jane provided approximately 11,000 abortions between 1969 and 1973. The lay providers of Jane inspired women to regain control of their own health care at a time when they had very little to say about the laws that governed them.

IN HISTORY

JANE

Formed in 1969 the organization known only by the innocuous name, "Jane," began referring women to underground abortion providers in Chicago who had been screened for competence and trustworthiness. Shortly thereafter, the founders of Jane discovered that one of their regular physicians was indeed not a licensed doctor. This realization inspired the organization to train lay people to perform abortions. The organization, officially titled The Abortion Counseling Service of Women's Liberation, exported its philosophy of compassionate abortion care and female empowerment to other cities in the United States. In the four years preceding *Roe v. Wade,* Jane members assisted 11,000 women in receiving safe, but illegal, abortions.

Document: Senator Maurine Neuberger's keynote address before the California Conference on Abortion.
Date: May, 1969.
Where: San Francisco, California.
Significance: This is the first major speech by a former congresswoman on the subject of abortion.

Stewart Chase once wrote an article called "Purr Words and Slur Words." Examples of the former are: Mother, moonlight, roast beef, balanced budget. Slur words include: Politician, taxes, Communist, turnip, abortion.

Recently a reporter asked me if I had long been associated with the movement to repeal abortion laws, and I told him that I hadn't. When he asked me when I had become interested, I had to stop and think because I have worked in many, many other areas in the field of health. Actually, not until the task force report on family law issued by the Citizen's Advisory Council (April, 1968) on the Status of Women got working on the abortion problem did I really begin to think about it. As Stewart Chase said about purr words and slur words, we all associate to words, and unpleasant images accumulate around a word like "abortion" that conjure up visions of illicit activities, adultery, and scenes in back rooms where those who deal in human misery ply their illegal practices.

In the report, which is quite lengthy, there is one little paragraph of two lines which states: "We are convinced that the right of a woman to determine her own reproductive life is a basic human right. Therefore, the task force recommends repeal of laws making abortion a crime."

While we were working on the report, all sorts of questions came up for discussion: whether women should have the right to manages their own property; whether or not they can lift weights; whether they should work overtime to earn premium pay, etc., but the abortion problem was the one that really attracted attention. My secretary began to phone me in Boston, saying: "We are running out of reports—we are having to have them reprinted. We have a best seller on our hands!"

A few years earlier, I had served on the Status of Women Commission, which was appointed by President Kennedy. Its Chairman was Eleanor Roosevelt, and the Assistant Chairman was Esther Peterson. Mrs. Roosevelt died before we finished out report, and Esther Peterson took over. Our studies of the laws that affect women led us to believe that it was time to talk about abortion laws, but we couldn't get our own Commission to consider such a discussion. It was said that the word "abortion" was verboten; that we couldn't get anything printed about it in government publications. Believing all this, when the task force report came to my desk, I anticipated all sorts of trouble. I expected delays and hours of debate. But not so. What had happened in that interval of a few years? Well, an educational process had been going on, organizations had been at work, and there had been a complete change in the emotional climate. The greatest dissension came, as we studied the task force report, over the proposal to amend the maximum hours law to permit women to work overtime! Very little—there was one minority report—on the abortion report. When somebody said, "Remember before, we couldn't get the government printing office to print it?" I said, "I will contact the Secretary myself." So I called up Secretary of Labor Bill Wirtz and said, "Bill, we are going to have this task force report ready soon." He said, "Fine, go ahead and print it." So here we are, in business.

Legislation conforms to the reality of the times. For instance, speed laws were liberalized to conform to what automobiles were capable of doing and improved techniques and safer roads; some states even did away with their maximum miles per hour. Divorce laws with phony residence requirements that force people to go to Mexico are being changed. Deans of women would now be burned in effigy if they tried to enforce the campus rules—in your rooms at 8:30 and lights out at ten—that I lived under when I was in college. Yet that kind of discipline didn't make me better educated than the college girls I know today. So times are changing rapidly.

The best analogy that I can think of to the repeal of abortion laws is with the repeal of prohibition. Prohibition did not work despite the fact that it was a constitutional amendment —which meant that support had been given by three-fourths of the States—and in spite of strenuous efforts by officials to enforce it. Actually, there is really more reason for controlling alcohol consumption than for controlling abortion because alcoholism is a disease that causes misery to the victim and psychological injury to his family. Lawyers and legislators say that when there is a substantial difference of opinion as to whether a criminal law is a good or not—whether it will work—then one can be sure that it is unworkable and unrealistic. And this is true of laws that prohibit abortions.

How, for instance, does one establish rape? Maybe the sexual act was perfectly agreeable to the girl until she got pregnant. In such cases, the "rape" is rarely reported to the police or even mentioned to the girls' parents unless pregnancy occurs. In many cases, according to lawyers, the use of the word "rape" is highly questionable.

Then, too, abortion is an individual problem, not a government problem. The individual is responsible for the care and upbringing of the child. True, the government will make a token effort, but oh, how little. And there is no substitute, of course, for the atmosphere of a warm home with good family relationships and a wanted child.

Before I left Boston, I thought it well to substantiate some of the things that our task force reported because, after all, almost a year had elapsed. I have close associations at the Harvard

Medical School, so I called on my friends. One is a leading obstetrician in Boston—I would almost call him a society obstetrician. I said to him, "I want to talk to you about this conference on abortion." He was great. He talked to me at great length, and he told me this story:

Recently, a daughter of a nationally-known insurance executive came in and asked for an abortion. She lives in a Boston suburb where only the so-called best people live. She goes to a good college. She is age 20. And my good friend, Dr. A. said: "What's the matter with you? You are a smart girl. Why don't you take the pill?" And she said, "Well, I did take it for a while, but I read so many articles about its side effects that I was afraid of what might happen." He said: "You didn't stop having intercourse, did you? You mean you didn't know what the side effects of that are?" Oh, he was furious with her. He cited her as one of the rich who *cannot* get an abortion on demand. Many of the rich take their daughters on an "educational" trip to Japan, and that is what the parents of this girl had to do.

I asked another doctor, "Why is the medical profession interested in the legal aspects of so-called criminal abortion?" He replied "Because medicine is shifting from a concern limited to treatment of disease to concern with health, including mental health." When I asked my obstetrician friend how to answer the question about psychosis, neurosis, and psychological damage, he replied, "I have never had a married or unmarried patient on whom I performed an abortion who wasn't damned relieved." He went on to say that abortion doesn't make a woman neurotic, but an unwanted pregnancy may.

What, I asked, would doctors like to see in an abortion law if we must have a law? He answered: One, that abortions shouldn't be done by bunglers, which—as he said—is good trade union practice as well as sound medicine. Two, to use the Model Penal Code of the American Law Institute as a basis for a new nation-wide abortion law. To it should be added a clause that would permit taking into consideration the life conditions of the mother, such as having too many children already, low income, or poor family relationships. Because, of course, a woman may be perfectly capable of bearing a fifth or sixth or seventh child, but what will bearing them do to her and to the children she already has if she hasn't the money, space, time, or energy to take proper care of them, or—even worse—doesn't want them. What is worse than an unwanted child?

Then there is the plight of the unmarried woman, especially the one who can't finance a trip to Japan, or doesn't dare tell her family. Perhaps she could marry the father of her child, but that might end in an unhappy marriage and an early divorce. Or she could go through the anguish of bearing the child and putting him up for adoption, a course of action that is far more likely to cause guilt feelings and psychological problems than an abortion early in pregnancy. Finally, she can have an abortion—if she can find a physician who will recommend an abortionist.

Any women, whether married or not, should be able to secure a safe abortion at a reasonable fee by a licensed and competent physician. Perhaps because I live right in the heart of a college community face-to-face with the facts, my outlook on this subject tends to be broad and forgiving. I was head of a house at Radcliffe and talked to a lot of girls and I understand their problems.

I believe that there is a plausible moral argument for allowing abortions. The criterion should not be a theory of whether the fetus is a human being during those early weeks of pregnancy, but the mother's desire for the child.

Catholic clergy are aware that the social evils that accompany forced pregnancy far outweigh the potential evil of destroying the fetus. Before I left for this conference I talked with Robert F. Drinan, S.J. "Father Drinan," I said, "I am going out to California to speak at a conference on abortion, and I am going to quote you." "Fine," he said. "We didn't ask the legislature to pass a law stating that it was illegal and a criminal offense to eat meat on Friday." And, in fact, Father Drinan has suggested repealing the anti-abortion laws.

At this point I must give credit to Alice Rossi of Johns Hopkins University, who presented the professional material that was so persuasive to the task force and to the Council on the Status of Women, and that gave them the fortitude, the courage, and the material and background to recommend repeal of criminal abortion laws. Alice Rossi pointed out to us 1) that the American Law Institute's Model Code leaves untouched the vast majority of women who now secure illegal abortions, and 2) that the Model Code means more committees to review abortion cases, involving among other things the loss of precious time while the committee deliberates, and increasing the probability of surgical complications. Mrs. Rossi has pointed out that the Model Code still keeps abortion under the criminal code, although this is true of no other medical procedure. The code satisfies few and discriminates against many, for it sanctions abortions in some cases while saying that abortions in all other cases are immoral.

It reminds me of the cigarette people. I am proud of the fact that I am responsible for the label on cigarette packages which says that it may be hazardous to your health to smoke. But that wasn't part of my bill. My bill called for a label that would say, "Smoking cigarettes may cause death from lung cancer and other diseases." You don't think I could get that through the Congress of the United States, do you? They just weren't willing to face up to it, because the American Tobacco Institute has the most powerful lobby that I have seen in a long time. They fought it to the bitter end. We compromised; we made a start. And for this I will ever be thankful to Robert Kennedy who stood with me on the floor of the Senate and defended even this meager token, because this was the first time the great government of the United States had ever taken a stand in this area. Others wanted such a strong-termed label that they wouldn't even vote for this bill. But when the bill that we passed expired and was up for repassage, who was there supporting the label on the cigarette package? Why, the American Tobacco Institute, because they were so afraid that we would pass a bill that would make a more frightening label mandatory.

We have only to look at the statistics in Catholic countries to know that there is a vast discrepancy between practice and doctrine. We have heard about the charter flights to London from the Continent. Where do you think these women come from? They come from France and Italy to get their abortions in London.

The laws are supposed to act as a deterrent to extramarital sex relations, but in fact they don't. Our anti-abortion laws are simply forcing people to be lawbreakers. Recently, the Supreme Court addressed itself to problems of personal freedom, holding that the Government may not interfere with personal rights which are, in many ways, less fundamental than this one.

I want to tell you this: Repeal will not come from the legislators, where the political pressures are so great, but from the courts. All legislators are subject to great fears which condition the basic processes of democracy. Thus very often politicians do not do what they want to do, but what they must (or think they must) do in order to keep their power. A member of Congress does not vote or speak without weighing the possible repercussions and recriminations of his words. If he misjudges the reaction of his constituents, he will not again be elected by them.

Because this great fear hangs over every politician, we understand and realize how in every one of us there comes a moment of rationalization. When I first went into the legislative body, I said, "I don't owe anybody anything. I have nothing to fear. I am going to speak out. I am going to say what I think on every subject." And I did. But there were times, because I knew I was going to run for reelection, that this was very difficult, and there were times when I could see what my colleagues were going through. I remember working very closely with Senator Lister Hill of Alabama for increased funds for research in cancer and other diseases. The work was successful and the budget of the National Institutes of Health went up and up. But when Senator Hill came up for reelection, he voted against the Civil Rights Law. One night I said to my husband, "What's wrong with Lister? He's been in Congress 35 years. He's an elder statesman. Why doesn't he just say, "I am sick and tired of my State of Alabama being at the bottom of everything, and I am going to quit this foolishness?" And my husband replied, "But he would be defeated in Alabama, and we need him."

So the legislator votes according to his own preference when there is no particular reason why he shouldn't. That is, when any powerful force that he is amenable to, such as the President, or a newspaper, or the Sierra Club, or the American Medical Association, has expressed an opinion that coincides with his own.

But think of him at bay: one group urging him to vote for the oil depletion allowance; the other side promising retaliation at the polls if he does. He cannot vote either way without alienating support. In such a case he usually votes to maintain the status quo. He knows the oil companies will note how he voted, and he also knows that the public forgets. Finally, he may even vote against his own conviction when he finds that to do otherwise would cost him support. For instance, some legislators voted to have no birth control information disseminated by the Agency for International Development (AID). Some, having read the report on cigarette smoking and aware that it can cause emphysema and early death, still voted for the tobacco lobby. Legislators do not lead their constituents in bringing about social change. They follow. Current abortion laws are archaic, unworkable, and discriminatory but they will remain so until pressure is brought to bear.

In conclusion, I reflect on my long activity in behalf of the status of women. Men make the laws. Do they still believe that women are their chattels? Do they subconsciously feel that women are not virtuous? Men make these laws because they believe in retribution. "Abortion is a crime and you must suffer the punishment for becoming pregnant if you are poor or unmarried or already have a large family."

Who decides when life begins? Men, who have never borne nor suckled a child. Who drew up the laws declaring that a woman has no control over the use of her own body? The inseminators. Who sees that these laws are sustained? Men. For what reasons? In their terms: for the sake of the soul, for the preservation of the family, for the good of society, the economy, the state, the wars of conquest. But whose society? Whose markets? Whose state? Whose wars? Certainly not women's.

Through thousands of years the laws that govern the lives of women have been written by men. That man should be the master of his body was never questioned. For many years men have been able to walk into a drug store in any town and buy contraceptives; but a woman—God forbid. She is a vessel to be filled, a field to be planted: such is the natural law, such is the will of God!

What we want is the right for a woman to have an abortion on request; the right to have a life in which she can bear *wanted* children. In the last analysis it is the right of a woman to decide, and is a private matter between herself and her doctor. Let's not have any more committees.

SOURCE: Senator Maurine Neuberger, "Abortion: A Political View," in *Abortion and the Unwanted Child: The California Committee on Therapeutic Abortion*, ed. C. Reiterman (New York: Springer Publishing, 1971), chapter 10, footnote omitted.

DOCUMENT ANALYSIS

Senator Neuberger's comments are remarkable for their frankness. Not only did this former U.S. senator endorse the repeal effort, she argued in this passage the moral clarity of women seeking abortion, and with honesty described the political calculations that elected officials make in deciding how far to press for abortion repeal.

Perhaps the most interesting passage from this speech is the analogy to prohibition. Prohibition was repealed largely because it was ineffective in preventing the sale and consumption of alcohol. Senator Neuberger argues here that similar prohibitions against abortion had done little to make the procedure rare. In fact, most estimates today indicate that abortion rates increased only slightly when abortion became legal nationwide in 1973. On a global scale, some of the most repressive countries in the world, with the most severe penalties for abortion, have the highest incidence of the procedure today.

It is hard to imagine a senator making such a bold cry for abortion repeal in the contemporary period. The issue has become far more politicized, and partisan, for elected officials to be as bold as Senator Neuberger was in 1969.

Document: Excerpt from Ruth Barnett, *They Weep on My Doorstep.*
Date: 1969.
Where: Beaverton, Oregon.
Significance: Ruth Barnett practiced illegal abortions in Portland, Oregon at the same time that Senator Neuberger represented Oregon. Barnett was Neuberger's constituent, and provided tens of thousands of safe but illicit abortions during her career before ultimately being tried and convicted under the state's penal code. Not one of her patients died while under her care.

So many things happen during a much-publicized trial that it is all but impossible to set them down here and it is just as well that some of these things remain unwritten.

The notoriety caused by the sensational trial brought many attendant troubles for me. It was no secret that my practice had been lucrative during World War II and the postwar years.

My income during the years of the Stewart Clinic was as much as $182,000 a year. I make no apologies for earning that kind of money. I worked hard for it and, as subsequent events have shown, I took tremendous risks for it. I paid staggering legal fees.

Furthermore, the nature of my business made me a target for both would-be extortionists and thieves. On several occasions during those years burglars entered my home and made off with large amounts of money, none of which was ever recovered.

During the trial in the spring of 1952, I received a telephone call from a trusted woman friend who received a call herself, from a stranger. She had made arrangements to meet this stranger—a woman we'll call "Mrs. X"—who offered "possible" help in my trial.

When my friend met with "Mrs. X" she was brazenly told that "Mrs. X" had control over some of the persons on my jury. "Mrs. X" was equally brazen in telling my friend that it would cost money to "fix" the jury. I told my friend, when she reported this, to go home and forget the whole thing.

Ruth Barnett, who provided roughly 40,000 illegal abortions in downtown Portland, Oregon, between 1918 and 1968. Courtesy of the Oregon Historical Society, OHS Image # ORHI62727.

The night before the case went to the jury the connivers were still at work. A man drove to my daughter's home, talked in circles for a time and then made the statement he could get me a "not guilty" verdict for $15,000. He went so far as to tell her she would have to "work fast," because he was "tired out from sitting up all last night plotting with some jurors."

My daughter was almost speechless with her indignation, but she managed to tell the man to come back in a few hours after she had talked to her husband. When the shakedown artist returned my son-in-law answered the doorbell. His remarks to the despicable character who had asked for the $15,000 were couched in language you'll never hear on your TV set. A censored version of them was:

"My mother-in-law will take what the jury decides. You may be telling the truth about controlling the jury and may not. Whichever it is, we want no part of it. Get going."

The man scooted for his car. Once inside, with the motor going, he yelled: "She'll be sorry." The only thing I've ever been sorry about was that my son-in-law hadn't booted him off the porch.

While my appeal on the misdemeanor charge was pending, the flow of distressed, frightened girls into my office continued. They came in tears usually, but left with smiles.

Most of us know what is meant by "entrapment." My lawyers have tried to explain to me, over the years, how law enforcement people can sometimes employ entrapment—the deliberate setting up of a situation to induce a person to commit a crime—but to me it is a despicable subversion of my understanding of the law.

One day, early in 1953, we were visited by a woman posing as a wronged girl in need of an abortion. With her was a male newspaper reporter posing as her brother. After the reporter handed some marked bills to the receptionist, the "patient" was escorted to a dressing room. The receptionist entered my office with the money. As she placed it on my desk, the phone rang.

I had difficulty placing the excited voice, that of a deputy sheriff whose wife I had once befriended. "Get everyone out of there, Ruth," he said. The District Attorney's going to raid you again today."

I relayed the message to the receptionist who picked up the bills and handed them to the masquerading "patient." "Take this back," said my receptionist. "And get out, quickly. There may be some trouble and we don't want you involved."

The woman refused the money, pretending not to understand. "I won't take it," she insisted. "I came here to be helped! I must be helped! Please hurry and take care of me."

"There's going to be a raid," the receptionist explained, "and we're trying to protect you. You don't want your name dragged through the courts, do you? You've got to leave quickly."

The "patient" laughed, reached insider her brassiere, and pulled out a handful of crumbled papers.

"I'm a policewoman," she announced, "and here are the warrants for everyone's arrest."

Then, she ran to a side door, opened it, and a squad of arresting officers trooped in. Once again I went to the county jail, marched up the steps to be booked and released on bail.

The District Attorney had taken no part in the second raid on my clinic. I heard later that he was sitting on a stool in a small restaurant across from the courthouse. As we were marched up the steps, he was heard to say, "There goes Ruth Barnett. I hope I get my $300 back." He meant the money the policewoman posing as "Little Sister" had tried to pay me.

I reflected, long afterward, that I had some idea how he felt about the money. The police had seized $800 of my money in the first raid on my clinic. More than 16 years later I still wonder at times whether I'll ever get that $800 back.

SOURCE: Ruth Barnett, as told to Doug Baker, *They Weep at my Doorstep* (Beaverton, Ore.: Halo Publishers, 1969), 70–72.

DOCUMENT ANALYSIS

Ruth Barnett provided 40,000 illegal abortions in downtown Portland, Oregon. Her story is legendary not because of the staggering number of procedures she performed but because it reveals the extent to which law enforcement looked the other way while she openly performed her illicit trade.

Barnett's office was located in a prominent office building on the main street of downtown Portland. For 30 years, she operated her business there, and according to her account, she helped numerous women who were attached to prominent Portland businessmen and law enforcement officers. As a result, law enforcement shielded her from the reach of the state's restrictive abortion statute.

IN HISTORY

JANE HODGSON'S ARREST

In 1970, Dr. Jane Hodgson became the only physician convicted of performing an abortion. Dr. Hodgson agreed to perform an illegal abortion in the state of Minnesota in order to challenge that state's strict abortion law, which at that time allowed abortion only to save the life of the pregnant woman. In this case. Dr. Hodgson ended the pregnancy of a mother of three, who had contracted German measles during her fourth pregnancy. Shortly after the procedure, Dr. Hodgson was arrested and later convicted. She was sentenced to 30 days in jail and a year's probation, although she served no jail time. The *Roe v. Wade* case in 1973 nullified her conviction.

Dr. Hodgson went on to become a founding fellow of the American College of Obstetrics and Gynecology, and was the lead plaintiff in a later case that challenged Minnesota's parental involvement law (*Hodgson v. Minnesota*). Dr. Hodgson died in 2006, at the age of 91.

Document: Judith Jarvis Thomson, excerpt from "A Defense of Abortion."
Date: 1971.
Where: Philosophy and Public Affairs.
Significance: Thomson's piece is the first major philosophical statement on abortion and is used by activists from different views on abortion to argue their case.

Most opposition to abortion relies on the premise that the fetus is a human being, a person, from the moment of conception. The premise is argued for, but, as I think, not well. Take, for example, the most common argument. We are asked to notice that the development of a human being from conception through birth into childhood is continuous; then it is said that to draw a line, to choose a point in this development and say "before this point the thing is not a person, after this point it is a person" is to make an arbitrary choice, a choice for which in the nature of things no good reason can be given. It is concluded that the fetus is, or anyway that we had better say it is, a person from the moment of conception. But this conclusion does not follow. Similar things might be said about the development of an acorn into an oak tree, and it does not follow that acorns are oak trees, or that we had better say they are. Arguments of this form are sometimes called "slippery slope arguments"—the phrase is perhaps self-explanatory—and it is dismaying that opponents of abortion rely on them so heavily and uncritically.

I am inclined to agree, however, that the prospects for "drawing a line" in the development of the fetus look dim. I am inclined to think also that we shall probably have to agree that the fetus has already become a human person well before birth. Indeed, it comes as a surprise when one first learns how early in its life it begins to acquire human characteristics. By the tenth week, for example, it already has a face, arms and legs, fingers and toes; it has internal organs, and brain activity is detectable. On the other hand, I think that the premise is false, that the fetus is not a person from the moment of conception. A newly fertilized ovum, a newly implanted clump of cells, is no more a person than an acorn is an oak tree. But I shall not discuss any of this. For it seems to me to be of great interest to ask what happens if, for the sake of argument, we allow the premise. How, precisely, are we supposed to get from there to the conclusion that abortion is morally impermissible? Opponents of abortion commonly spend most of their time establishing that the fetus is a person, and hardly any time explaining the step from there to the impermissibility of abortion. Perhaps they think the step too simple and obvious to require much comment. Or perhaps instead they are simply being economical in argument. Many of those who defend abortion rely on the premise that the fetus is not a person, but only a bit of tissue that will become a person at birth; and why pay out more arguments than you have to? Whatever the explanation, I suggest that the step they take is neither easy nor obvious, that it calls for closer examination than it is commonly given, and that when we do give it this closer examination we shall feel inclined to reject it.

I propose, then, that we grant that the fetus is a person from the moment of conception. How does the argument go from here? Something like this, I take it. Every person has a right to life. So the fetus has a right to life. No doubt the mother has a right to decide what shall happen in and out of her body; everyone would grant that. But surely a person's right to life is stronger and more stringent than the mother's right to decide what happens in and to her body, and so outweighs it. So the fetus may not be killed; an abortion may not be performed.

It sounds plausible. But now let me ask you to imagine this. You wake up in the morning and find yourself back to back in bed with an unconscious violinist. A famous unconscious violinist. He has been found to have a fatal kidney ailment, and the Society of Music Lovers has canvassed all the available medical records and found that you alone have the right blood type to help. They have therefore kidnapped you, and last night the violinist's circulatory system was plugged into yours, so that your kidneys can be used to extract poisons from his blood as well as your own. The director of the hospital now tells you, "Look, we're sorry the Society of Music Lovers did this to you—we would never have permitted it if we had known. But still, they did it, and the violinist now is plugged into you. To unplug you would be to kill him. But never mind, it's only for nine months. By then he will have recovered from his ailment, and can safely be unplugged from you." Is it morally incumbent on you to accede to this situation? No doubt it would be very nice of you if you did, a great kindness. But do you *have* to accede to it? What if it were not nine months, but nine years? Or longer still? What if the director of the hospital says, "Tough luck, I agree, but you've now got to stay in bed, with the violinist plugged into you, for the rest of your life. Because remember this. All persons have a right to life, and violinists are persons. Granted you have a right to decide what happens in and to your body, but a person's right to life outweighs your right to decide what happens in and to your body. So you cannot ever be unplugged from him." I imagine you would regard this as outrageous, which suggests that something really is wrong with that plausible-sounding argument I mentioned a moment ago.

In this case, of course, you were kidnapped; you didn't volunteer for the operation that plugged the violinist into your kidneys. Can those who oppose abortion on the ground I mentioned make an exception for a pregnancy due to rape? Certainly. They can say that persons have a right to life only if they didn't come into existence because of rape; or they can say that all persons have a right to life, but that some have less of a right to life than others, in particular, that those who came into existence because of rape have less. But these statements have a rather unpleasant sound. Surely the question of whether you have a right to life at all, or how much of it you have, shouldn't turn on the question of whether or not you are the product of a rape. And in fact the people who oppose abortion on the ground I mentioned do not make this distinction, and hence do not make an exception in case of rape.

SOURCE: Judith Jarvis Thomson, "A Defense of Abortion," *Philosophy and Public Affairs* 1, no. 1 (Autumn, 1971): 47–49. Reprinted with permission of Blackwell Publishing Ltd.

DOCUMENT ANALYSIS

Thompson's piece, appearing as the Supreme Court was considering the landmark *Roe v. Wade* ruling that liberalized abortion law in 1973, is one of the most cited academic writings on abortion. Best known for this selection, in which Thompson likens a pregnant woman to a famous violinist forced to share kidneys with a stranger, this article touched off a cottage industry of academic articles on the philosophical and legal principles of abortion.

Further Reading

Barnett, Ruth, as told to Doug Baker. *They Weep on My Doorstep.* Beaverton, Ore.: Halo Publishers, 1969.

Critchlow, Donald T. *Intended Consequences: Birth Control, Abortion, and the Federal Government in Modern America.* Oxford, England: Oxford University Press, 1999.

Joffe, Carole. *Doctors of Conscience: The Struggle to Provide Abortion before and after* Roe v. Wade. Boston: Beacon Press, 1995.

Kaplan, Laura. *The Story of Jane: The Legendary Underground Feminist Abortion Service.* Chicago: University of Chicago Press, 1995.

Reiterman, C. *Abortion and the Unwanted Child: The California Committee on Therapeutic Abortion.* New York: Springer Publishing, 1971.

Solinger, Rickie. *The Abortionist: A Woman Against the Law.* Berkeley: University of California Press, 1996.

4

ROE V. WADE AND ITS CRITICS

The abortion debate, which had been churning in the states for decades, made a big national splash in 1973. Although news of the Supreme Court's ruling was eclipsed briefly by the death of former President Lyndon B. Johnson, *Roe v. Wade* would become synonymous with abortion politics for a generation after the 7–2 decision was issued. Representing a single woman, then known only as Jane Roe, attorney Sarah Weddington (26 years old at the time) argued on behalf of a woman's right of privacy, and secured national protection for abortion access in 1973. Although Roe, now known to us as Norma McCorvey, never had an abortion because her state of Texas forbade abortion in all but the most dire circumstances, she too would become a national figure, surprising many by joining the antiabortion social movement in the 1980s.

The themes set into motion by *Roe v. Wade* are the subject of this chapter. For while *Roe* is synonymous today with abortion, it is also associated with a wide range of perspectives: fear of court expansion, questions about the reach of federal government, social movements for and against abortion access, and the lack of true equality for American women. This decision galvanized a uniquely wide range of criticisms from across the political spectrum, while simultaneously fulfilling the abortion reform movement's goal of national abortion policy change. And while Americans may not agree on the value of this ruling, they would likely agree that in some ways, the ruling raised more questions than it settled and became a landmark case in American jurisprudence.

Prochoice advocates demanding protection for abortion rights. Getty Images.

Document: Excerpt from *Roe v. Wade,* footnotes omitted.
Date: January 22, 1973.
Where: U.S. Supreme Court.
Significance: This decision extended the privacy right to abortion, including a woman's decision to end a pregnancy in the arena of a constitutionally protected zone of privacy. The case balances the woman's privacy right to against a state's emerging interest in its future citizens, creating a compromise that would allow abortions in the first half of pregnancy with few restrictions while opening the door to late-term restrictions.

MR. JUSTICE BLACKMUN delivered the opinion of the Court.

This Texas federal appeal and its Georgia companion, *Doe v. Bolton, post,* p. 179, present constitutional challenges to state criminal abortion legislation. The Texas statutes under attack here are typical of those that have been in effect in many States for approximately a century. The Georgia statutes, in contrast, have a modern cast, and are a legislative product that, to an extent at least, obviously reflects the influences of recent attitudinal change, of advancing medical knowledge and techniques, and of new thinking about an old issue.

We forthwith acknowledge our awareness of the sensitive and emotional nature of the abortion controversy, of the vigorous opposing views, even among physicians, and of the deep and seemingly absolute convictions that the subject inspires. One's philosophy, one's experiences, one's exposure to the raw edges of human existence, one's religious training, one's attitudes toward life and family and their values, and the moral standards one establishes and seeks to observe, are all likely to influence and to color one's thinking and conclusions about abortion.

In addition, population growth, pollution, poverty, and racial overtones tend to complicate and not to simplify the problem.

Our task, of course, is to resolve the issue by constitutional measurement, free of emotion and of predilection. We seek earnestly to do this, and, because we do, we have inquired into, and in this opinion place some emphasis upon, medical and medical-legal history and what that history reveals about man's attitudes toward the abortion procedure over the centuries. We bear in mind, too, Mr. Justice Holmes' admonition in his now-vindicated dissent in *Lochner v. New York,* 198 U.S. 45, 76 (1905):

[The Constitution] is made for people of fundamentally differing views, and the accident of our finding certain opinions natural and familiar or novel and even shocking ought not to conclude our judgment upon the question whether statutes embodying them conflict with the Constitution of the United States.

The Texas statutes that concern us here are Arts. 1191–1194 and 1196 of the State's Penal Code. These make it a crime to "procure an abortion," as therein defined, or to attempt one, except with respect to "an abortion procured or attempted by medical advice for the purpose of saving the life of the mother." Similar statutes are in existence in a majority of the States.

Texas first enacted a criminal abortion statute in 1854. . . . This was soon modified into language that has remained substantially unchanged to the present time. . . . The final article in each of these compilations provided the same exception, as does the present Article 1196, for an abortion by "medical advice for the purpose of saving the life of the mother."

II

Jane Roe, a single woman who was residing in Dallas County, Texas, instituted this federal action in March 1970 against the District Attorney of the county. She sought a declaratory judgment that the Texas criminal abortion statutes were unconstitutional on their face, and an injunction restraining the defendant from enforcing the statutes.

Roe alleged that she was unmarried and pregnant; that she wished to terminate her pregnancy by an abortion "performed by a competent, licensed physician, under safe, clinical conditions"; that she was unable to get a "legal" abortion in Texas because her life did not appear to be threatened by the continuation of her pregnancy; and that she could not afford to travel to another jurisdiction in order to secure a legal abortion under safe conditions. She claimed that the Texas statutes were unconstitutionally vague and that they abridged her right of personal privacy, protected by the First, Fourth, Fifth, Ninth, and Fourteenth Amendments. By an amendment to her complaint, Roe purported to sue "on behalf of herself and all other women" similarly situated.

James Hubert Hallford, a licensed physician, sought and was granted leave to intervene in Roe's action. In his complaint, he alleged that he had been arrested previously for violations of the Texas abortion statutes, and that two such prosecutions were pending against him. He described conditions of patients who came to him seeking abortions, and he claimed that for many cases he, as a physician, was unable to determine whether they fell within or outside the exception recognized by Article 1196. He alleged that, as a consequence, the statutes were vague and uncertain, in violation of the Fourteenth Amendment, and that they violated his own and his patients' rights to privacy in the doctor-patient relationship and his own right to practice medicine, rights he claimed were guaranteed by the First, Fourth, Fifth, Ninth, and Fourteenth Amendments.

John and Mary Doe, a married couple, filed a companion complaint to that of Roe. They also named the District Attorney as defendant, claimed like constitutional deprivations, and sought declaratory and injunctive relief. The Does alleged that they were a childless couple; that Mrs. Doe was suffering from a "neural-chemical" disorder; that her physician had "advised her to avoid pregnancy until such time as her condition has materially improved" (although a pregnancy at the present time would not present "a serious risk" to her life); that, pursuant to medical advice, she had discontinued use of birth control pills; and that, if she should become pregnant, she would want to terminate the pregnancy by an abortion performed by a competent, licensed physician under safe, clinical conditions. By an amendment to their complaint, the Does purported to sue "on behalf of themselves and all couples similarly situated."

The two actions were consolidated and heard together by a duly convened three-judge district court. The suits thus presented the situations of the pregnant single woman, the childless couple, with the wife not pregnant, and the licensed practicing physician, all joining in the attack on the Texas criminal abortion statutes. Upon the filing of affidavits, motions were made for dismissal and for summary judgment. The court held that Roe and members of her class, and Dr. Hallford, had standing to sue and presented justiciable controversies, but that the Does had failed to allege facts sufficient to state a present controversy, and did not have standing. It concluded that, with respect to the requests for a declaratory judgment, abstention was not warranted. On the merits, the District Court held that the fundamental right of single women and married persons to choose whether to have children is protected by the Ninth Amendment, through the Fourteenth Amendment, and that the Texas criminal abortion statutes were void on their face because they were both unconstitutionally vague and constituted an overbroad infringement of the plaintiffs' Ninth Amendment rights. The court then held that abstention was warranted with respect to the requests for an injunction. It therefore dismissed the Does' complaint, declared the abortion statutes void, and dismissed the application for injunctive relief. 314 F. Supp. 1217, 1225 (ND Tex.1970).

The plaintiffs Roe and Doe and the intervenor Hallford, pursuant to 28 U.S.C. § 1253 have appealed to this Court from that part of the District Court's judgment denying the injunction. The defendant District Attorney has purported to cross-appeal, pursuant to the same statute, from the court's grant of declaratory relief to Roe and Hallford. Both sides also have taken protective appeals to the United States Court of Appeals for the Fifth Circuit. That court ordered the appeals held in abeyance pending decision here. We postponed decision on jurisdiction to the hearing on the merits. 402 U.S. 941 (1971)

It might have been preferable if the defendant, pursuant to our Rule 20, had presented to us a petition for certiorari before judgment in the Court of Appeals with respect to the granting of the plaintiffs' prayer for declaratory relief. Our decisions in *Mitchell v. Donovan*, 398 U.S. 427 (1970), and *Gunn v. University Committee*, 399 U.S. 383 (1970), are to the effect that § 1253 does not authorize an appeal to this Court from the grant or denial of declaratory relief alone. We conclude, nevertheless, that those decisions do not foreclose our review of both the injunctive and the declaratory aspects of a case of this kind when it is properly here, as this one is, on appeal under 1253 from specific denial of injunctive relief, and the arguments as to both aspects are necessarily identical. . . . It would be destructive of time and energy for all concerned were we to rule otherwise . . .

IV

We are next confronted with issues of justiciability, standing, and abstention. Have Roe and the Does established that "personal stake in the outcome of the controversy," *Baker v. Carr*, 369 U.S. 186, 204 (1962), that insures that the dispute sought to be adjudicated will be presented in an adversary context and in a form historically viewed as capable of judicial resolution, And what effect did the pendency of criminal abortion charges against Dr. Hallford in state court have upon the propriety of the federal court's granting relief to him as a plaintiff-intervenor?

A. *Jane Roe*. Despite the use of the pseudonym, no suggestion is made that Roe is a fictitious person. For purposes of her case, we accept as true, and as established, her existence; her pregnant state, as of the inception of her suit in March 1970 and as late as May 21 of that year when she filed an alias affidavit with the District Court; and her inability to obtain a legal abortion in Texas.

Viewing Roe's case as of the time of its filing and thereafter until as late a May, there can be little dispute that it then presented a case or controversy and that, wholly apart from the class aspects, she, as a pregnant single woman thwarted by the Texas criminal abortion laws, had standing to challenge those statutes. . . . Indeed, we do not read the appellee's brief as really asserting anything to the contrary. The "logical nexus between the status asserted and the claim sought to be adjudicated," . . . and the necessary degree of contentiousness, . . . are both present.

The appellee notes, however, that the record does not disclose that Roe was pregnant at the time of the District Court hearing on May 22, 1970, or on the following June 17 when the court's opinion and judgment were filed. And he suggests that Roe's case must now be moot because she and all other members of her class are no longer subject to any 1970 pregnancy.

The usual rule in federal cases is that an actual controversy must exist at stages of appellate or certiorari review, and not simply at the date the action is initiated. . . .

But when, as here, pregnancy is a significant fact in the litigation, the normal 266-day human gestation period is so short that the pregnancy will come to term before the usual appellate process is complete. If that termination makes a case moot, pregnancy litigation seldom will survive much beyond the trial stage, and appellate review will be effectively denied. Our law should not be that rigid. Pregnancy often comes more than once to the same woman, and in the general population, if man is to survive, it will always be with us. Pregnancy provides a classic justification for a conclusion of nonmootness. It truly could be "capable of repetition, yet evading review." . . .

We, therefore, agree with the District Court that Jane Roe had standing to undertake this litigation, that she presented a justiciable controversy, and that the termination of her 1970 pregnancy has not rendered her case moot.

B. *Dr. Hallford.* The doctor's position is different. He entered Roe's litigation as a plaintiff-intervenor, alleging in his complaint that he:

> [I]n the past has been arrested for violating the Texas Abortion Laws and at the present time stands charged by indictment with violating said laws in the Criminal District Court of Dallas County, Texas to-wit: (1) The State of Texas vs. James H. Hallford, No. C-69–5307-IH, and (2) The State of Texas vs. James H. Hallford, No. C-692524-H. In both cases, the defendant is charged with abortion. . . .

In his application for leave to intervene, the doctor made like representations as to the abortion charges pending in the state court. These representations were also repeated in the affidavit he executed and filed in support of his motion for summary judgment.

Dr. Hallford is, therefore, in the position of seeking, in a federal court, declaratory and injunctive relief with respect to the same statutes under which he stands charged in criminal prosecutions simultaneously pending in state court. Although he stated that he has been arrested in the past for violating the State's abortion laws, he makes no allegation of any substantial and immediate threat to any federally protected right that cannot be asserted in his defense against the state prosecutions. Neither is there any allegation of harassment or bad faith prosecution. In order to escape the rule articulated in the cases cited in the next paragraph of this opinion that, absent harassment and bad faith, a defendant in a pending state criminal case cannot affirmatively challenge in federal court the statutes under which the State is prosecuting him, Dr. Hallford seeks to distinguish his status as a present state defendant from his status as a "potential future defendant," and to assert only the latter for standing purposes here.

We see no merit in that distinction. Our decision in *Samuels v. Mackell,* 401 U.S. 66 (1971), compels the conclusion that the District Court erred when it granted declaratory relief to Dr. Hallford instead of refraining from so doing. The court, of course, was correct in refusing to grant injunctive relief to the doctor. . . . We note, in passing, that *Younger* and its companion cases were decided after the three-judge District Court decision in this case.

Dr. Hallford's complaint in intervention, therefore, is to be dismissed. He is remitted to his defenses in the state criminal proceedings against him. We reverse the judgment of the District Court insofar as it granted Dr. Hallford relief and failed to dismiss his complaint in intervention.

C. *The Does*. In view of our ruling as to Roe's standing in her case, the issue of the Does' standing in their case has little significance. The claims they assert are essentially the same as those of Roe, and they attack the same statutes. Nevertheless, we briefly note the Does' posture.

Their pleadings present them as a childless married couple, the woman not being pregnant, who have no desire to have children at this time because of their having received medical advice that Mrs. Doe should avoid pregnancy, and for "other highly personal reasons." But they "fear . . . they may face the prospect of becoming parents." And if pregnancy ensues, they "would want to terminate" it by an abortion. They assert an inability to obtain an abortion legally in Texas and, consequently, the prospect of obtaining an illegal abortion there or of going outside Texas to some place where the procedure could be obtained legally and competently.

We thus have as plaintiffs a married couple who have, as their asserted immediate and present injury, only an alleged "detrimental effect upon [their] marital happiness" because they are forced to "the choice of refraining from normal sexual relations or of endangering Mary Doe's health through a possible pregnancy." Their claim is that, sometime in the future, Mrs. Doe might become pregnant because of possible failure of contraceptive measures, and, at that time in the future, she might want an abortion that might then be illegal under the Texas statutes.

This very phrasing of the Does' position reveals its speculative character. Their alleged injury rests on possible future contraceptive failure, possible future pregnancy, possible future unpreparedness for parenthood, and possible future impairment of health. Any one or more of these several possibilities may not take place, and all may not combine. In the Does' estimation, these possibilities might have some real or imagined impact upon their marital happiness. But we are not prepared to say that the bare allegation of so indirect an injury is sufficient to present an actual case or controversy. . . . The Does' claim falls far short of those resolved otherwise in the cases that the Does urge upon us . . .

The Does therefore are not appropriate plaintiffs in this litigation. Their complaint was properly dismissed by the District Court, and we affirm that dismissal.

V

The principal thrust of appellant's attack on the Texas statutes is that they improperly invade a right, said to be possessed by the pregnant woman, to choose to terminate her pregnancy. Appellant would discover this right in the concept of personal "liberty" embodied in the Fourteenth Amendment's Due Process Clause; or in personal, marital, familial, and sexual privacy said to be protected by the Bill of Rights or its penumbras, *see Griswold v. Connecticut*, 381 U.S. 479 (1965); *Eisenstadt v. Baird*, 405 U.S. 438 (1972); *id.* at 460 (WHITE, J., concurring in result); or among those rights reserved to the people by the Ninth Amendment, *Griswold v. Connecticut*, 381 U.S. at 486 (Goldberg, J., concurring). Before addressing this claim, we feel it desirable briefly to survey, in several aspects, the history of abortion, for such insight as that history may afford us, and then to examine the state purposes and interests behind the criminal abortion laws.

VI

It perhaps is not generally appreciated that the restrictive criminal abortion laws in effect in a majority of States today are of relatively recent vintage. Those laws, generally proscribing abortion or its attempt at any time during pregnancy except when necessary to preserve the pregnant woman's life, are not of ancient or even of common law origin. Instead, they derive from statutory changes effected, for the most part, in the latter half of the 19th century.

1. *Ancient attitudes.* These are not capable of precise determination. We are told that, at the time of the Persian Empire, abortifacients were known, and that criminal abortions were severely punished. We are also told, however, that abortion was practiced in Greek times as well as in the Roman Era, and that "it was resorted to without scruple." The Ephesian, Soranos, often described as the greatest of the ancient gynecologists, appears to have been generally opposed to Rome's prevailing free-abortion practices. He found it necessary to think first of the life of the mother, and he resorted to abortion when, upon this standard, he felt the procedure advisable. Greek and Roman law afforded little protection to the unborn. If abortion was prosecuted in some places, it seems to have been based on a concept of a violation of the father's right to his offspring. Ancient religion did not bar abortion.

2. *The HippocraticOath.* What then of the famous Oath that has stood so long as the ethical guide of the medical profession and that bears the name of the great Greek (460(?)–377(?) B.C.), who has been described as the Father of Medicine, the "wisest and the greatest practitioner of his art," and the "most important and most complete medical personality of antiquity," who dominated the medical schools of his time, and who typified the sum of the medical knowledge of the past? The Oath varies somewhat according to the particular translation, but in any translation the content is clear: I will give no deadly medicine to anyone if asked, nor suggest any such counsel; and in like manner, I will not give to a woman a pessary to produce abortion, or I will neither give a deadly drug to anybody if asked for it, nor will I make a suggestion to this effect. Similarly, I will not give to a woman an abortive remedy. Although the Oath is not mentioned in any of the principal briefs in this case or in *Doe v. Bolton, post,* p. 179, it represents the apex of the development of strict ethical concepts in medicine, and its influence endures to this day. Why did not the authority of Hippocrates dissuade abortion practice in his time and that of Rome? The late Dr. Edelstein provides us with a theory: The Oath was not uncontested even in Hippocrates' day; only the Pythagorean school of philosophers frowned upon the related act of suicide. Most Greek thinkers, on the other hand, commended abortion, at least prior to viability. See Plato, Republic, V, 461; Aristotle, Politics, VII, 1335b 25. For the Pythagoreans, however, it was a matter of dogma. For them, the embryo was animate from the moment of conception, and abortion meant destruction of a living being. The abortion clause of the Oath, therefore, "echoes Pythagorean doctrines," and "[i]n no other stratum of Greek opinion were such views held or proposed in the same spirit of uncompromising austerity." Dr. Edelstein then concludes that the Oath originated in a group representing only a small segment of Greek opinion, and that it certainly was not accepted by all ancient physicians. He points out that medical writings down to Galen (A.D. 130–200) "give evidence of the violation of almost every one of its injunctions." But with the end of antiquity, a decided change took place. Resistance against suicide and against abortion became common. The Oath came to be popular. The emerging teachings of Christianity were in agreement with the Pythagorean ethic. The Oath "became the nucleus of all medical ethics," and "was applauded as the embodiment of truth." Thus, suggests Dr. Edelstein, it is "a Pythagorean manifesto, and not the expression of an absolute standard of medical conduct." This, it seems to us, is a satisfactory and acceptable explanation of the Hippocratic Oath's apparent rigidity. It enables us to understand, in historical context, a long-accepted and revered statement of medical ethics.

3. The common law. It is undisputed that, at common law, abortion performed before "quickening" —the first recognizable movement of the fetus *in utero,* appearing usually from the 16th to the

18th week of pregnancy—was not an indictable offense. The absence of a common law crime for pre-quickening abortion appears to have developed from a confluence of earlier philosophical, theological, and civil and canon law concepts of when life begins. These disciplines variously approached the question in terms of the point at which the embryo or fetus became "formed" or recognizably human, or in terms of when a "person" came into being, that is, infused with a "soul" or "animated." A loose consensus evolved in early English law that these events occurred at some point between conception and live birth. This was "mediate animation." Although Christian theology and the canon law came to fix the point of animation at 40 days for a male and 80 days for a female, a view that persisted until the 19th century, there was otherwise little agreement about the precise time of formation or animation. There was agreement, however, that, prior to this point, the fetus was to be regarded as part of the mother, and its destruction, therefore, was not homicide. Due to continued uncertainty about the precise time when animation occurred, to the lack of any empirical basis for the 40–80-day view, and perhaps to Aquinas' definition of movement as one of the two first principles of life, Bracton focused upon quickening as the critical point. The significance of quickening was echoed by later common law scholars, and found its way into the received common law in this country. Whether abortion of a quick fetus was a felony at common law, or even a lesser crime, is still disputed. Bracton, writing early in the 13th century, thought it homicide. But the later and predominant view, following the great common law scholars, has been that it was, at most, a lesser offense. In a frequently cited passage, Coke took the position that abortion of a woman "quick with childe" is "a great misprision, and no murder." Blackstone followed, saying that, while abortion after quickening had once been considered manslaughter (though not murder), "modern law" took a less severe view. A recent review of the common law precedents argues, however, that those precedents contradict Coke, and that even post-quickening abortion was never established as a common law crime. This is of some importance, because, while most American courts ruled, in holding or dictum, that abortion of an unquickened fetus was not criminal under their received common law, others followed Coke in stating that abortion of a quick fetus was a "misprision," a term they translated to mean "misdemeanor." That their reliance on Coke on this aspect of the law was uncritical and, apparently in all the reported cases, dictum (due probably to the paucity of common law prosecutions for post-quickening abortion), makes it now appear doubtful that abortion was ever firmly established as a common law crime even with respect to the destruction of a quick fetus.

4. *The English statutory law.* England's first criminal abortion statute, Lord Ellenborough's Act, 43 Geo. 3, c. 58, came in 1803. It made abortion of a quick fetus, § 1, a capital crime, but, in § 2, it provided lesser penalties for the felony of abortion before quickening, and thus preserved the "quickening" distinction. This contrast was continued in the general revision of 1828, 9 Geo. 4, c. 31, § 13. It disappeared, however, together with the death penalty, in 1837, 7 Will. 4 & 1 Vict., c. 85. § 6, and did not reappear in the Offenses Against the Person Act of 1861, 24 & 25 Vict., c. 100, § 59, that formed the core of English anti-abortion law until the liberalizing reforms of 1967. In 1929, the Infant Life (Preservation) Act, 19 & 20 Geo. 5, c. 34, came into being. Its emphasis was upon the destruction of "the life of a child capable of being born alive." It made a willful act performed with the necessary intent a felony. It contained a proviso that one was not to be found guilty of the offense unless it is proved that the act which caused the death of the child was not done in good faith for the purpose only of preserving the life of the mother. A seemingly notable development in the English law was the case of *Rex v. Bourne*, [1939] 1 K.B. 687. This case apparently answered in the affirmative the question whether an abortion necessary to preserve the life of the pregnant woman was excepted from the criminal penalties of the 1861 Act. In his instructions to the jury, Judge Macnaghten referred to the 1929 Act, and observed that that Act related to "the case where a child is killed by a willful act at the time when it is being delivered in the ordinary course of nature." *Id.* at 691. He concluded that the 1861 Act's use of the word "unlawfully," imported the same meaning expressed by the

specific proviso in the 1929 Act, even though there was no mention of preserving the mother's life in the 1861 Act. He then construed the phrase "preserving the life of the mother" broadly, that is, "in a reasonable sense," to include a serious and permanent threat to the mother's health, and instructed the jury to acquit Dr. Bourne if it found he had acted in a good faith belief that the abortion was necessary for this purpose. *Id.* at 693–694. The jury did acquit. Recently, Parliament enacted a new abortion law. This is the Abortion Act of 1967, 15 & 16 Eliz. 2, c. 87. The Act permits a licensed physician to perform an abortion where two other licensed physicians agree (a) that the continuance of the pregnancy would involve risk to the life of the pregnant woman, or of injury to the physical or mental health of the pregnant woman or any existing children of her family, greater than if the pregnancy were terminated, or (b) that there is a substantial risk that, if the child were born it would suffer from such physical or mental abnormalities as to be seriously handicapped. The Act also provides that, in making this determination, "account may be taken of the pregnant woman's actual or reasonably foreseeable environment." It also permits a physician, without the concurrence of others, to terminate a pregnancy where he is of the good faith opinion that the abortion "is immediately necessary to save the life or to prevent grave permanent injury to the physical or mental health of the pregnant woman."

5. *TheAmerican law.* In this country, the law in effect in all but a few States until mid-19th century was the preexisting English common law. Connecticut, the first State to enact abortion legislation, adopted in 1821 that part of Lord Ellenborough's Act that related to a woman "quick with child." The death penalty was not imposed. Abortion before quickening was made a crime in that State only in 1860. In 1828, New York enacted legislation that, in two respects, was to serve as a model for early anti-abortion statutes. First, while barring destruction of an unquickened fetus as well as a quick fetus, it made the former only a misdemeanor, but the latter second-degree manslaughter. Second, it incorporated a concept of therapeutic abortion by providing that an abortion was excused if it shall have been necessary to preserve the life of such mother, or shall have been advised by two physicians to be necessary for such purpose. By 1840, when Texas had received the common law, only eight American States had statutes dealing with abortion. It was not until after the War Between the States that legislation began generally to replace the common law. Most of these initial statutes dealt severely with abortion after quickening, but were lenient with it before quickening. Most punished attempts equally with completed abortions. While many statutes included the exception for an abortion thought by one or more physicians to be necessary to save the mother's life, that provision soon disappeared, and the typical law required that the procedure actually be necessary for that purpose. Gradually, in the middle and late 19th century, the quickening distinction disappeared from the statutory law of most States and the degree of the offense and the penalties were increased. By the end of the 1950's, a large majority of the jurisdictions banned abortion, however and whenever performed, unless done to save or preserve the life of the mother. The exceptions, Alabama and the District of Columbia, permitted abortion to preserve the mother's health. Three States permitted abortions that were not "unlawfully" performed or that were not "without lawful justification," leaving interpretation of those standards to the courts. In the past several years, however, a trend toward liberalization of abortion statutes has resulted in adoption, by about one-third of the States, of less stringent laws, most of them patterned after the ALI Model Penal Code, § 230.3, set forth as Appendix B to the opinion in *Doe v. Bolton, post,* p. 205. It is thus apparent that, at common law, at the time of the adoption of our Constitution, and throughout the major portion of the 19th century, abortion was viewed with less disfavor than under most American statutes currently in effect. Phrasing it another way, a woman enjoyed a substantially broader right to terminate a pregnancy than she does in most States today. At least with respect to the early stage of pregnancy, and very possibly without such a limitation, the opportunity to make this choice was present in this country well into the 19th century. Even later, the law continued for some time to treat less punitively an abortion procured in early pregnancy.

6. *The position of theAmerican Medical Association.* The anti-abortion mood prevalent in this country in the late 19th century was shared by the medical profession. Indeed, the attitude of the profession may have played a significant role in the enactment of stringent criminal abortion legislation during that period. An AMA Committee on Criminal Abortion was appointed in May, 1857. It presented its report, 12 Trans. of the Am.Med.Assn. 778 (1859), to the Twelfth Annual Meeting. That report observed that the Committee had been appointed to investigate criminal abortion "with a view to its general suppression." It deplored abortion and its frequency and it listed three causes of "this general demoralization": The first of these causes is a widespread popular ignorance of the true character of the crime—a belief, even among mothers themselves, that the foetus is not alive till after the period of quickening. The second of the agents alluded to is the fact that the profession themselves are frequently supposed careless of foetal life. . . . The third reason of the frightful extent of this crime is found in the grave defects of our laws, both common and statute, as regards the independent and actual existence of the child before birth, as a living being. These errors, which are sufficient in most instances to prevent conviction, are based, and only based, upon mistaken and exploded medical dogmas. With strange inconsistency, the law fully acknowledges the foetus *in utero* and its inherent rights, for civil purposes; while personally and as criminally affected, it fails to recognize it, and to its life as yet denies all protection. *Id.* at 776. The Committee then offered, and the Association adopted, resolutions protesting "against such unwarrantable destruction of human life," calling upon state legislatures to revise their abortion laws, and requesting the cooperation of state medical societies "in pressing the subject." *Id.* at 28, 78. In 1871, a long and vivid report was submitted by the Committee on Criminal Abortion. It ended with the observation, We had to deal with human life. In a matter of less importance, we could entertain no compromise. An honest judge on the bench would call things by their proper names. We could do no less. 22 Trans. of the Am.Med.Assn. 268 (1871). It proffered resolutions, adopted by the Association, *id.* at 38–39, recommending, among other things, that it be unlawful and unprofessional for any physician to induce abortion or premature labor without the concurrent opinion of at least one respectable consulting physician, and then always with a view to the safety of the child—if that be possible, and calling the attention of the clergy of all denominations to the perverted views of morality entertained by a large class of females—aye, and men also, on this important question. Except for periodic condemnation of the criminal abortionist, no further formal AMA action took place until 1967. In that year, the Committee on Human Reproduction urged the adoption of a stated policy of opposition to induced abortion except when there is "documented medical evidence" of a threat to the health or life of the mother, or that the child "may be born with incapacitating physical deformity or mental deficiency," or that a pregnancy "resulting from legally established statutory or forcible rape or incest may constitute a threat to the mental or physical health of the patient," two other physicians "chosen because of their recognized professional competence have examined the patient and have concurred in writing," and the procedure "is performed in a hospital accredited by the Joint Commission on Accreditation of Hospitals." The providing of medical information by physicians to state legislatures in their consideration of legislation regarding therapeutic abortion was "to be considered consistent with the principles of ethics of the American Medical Association." This recommendation was adopted by the House of Delegates. Proceedings of the AMA House of Delegates 40–51 (June 1967). In 1970, after the introduction of a variety of proposed resolutions and of a report from its Board of Trustees, a reference committee noted "polarization of the medical profession on this controversial issue"; division among those who had testified; a difference of opinion among AMA councils and committees; "the remarkable shift in testimony" in six months, felt to be influenced "by the rapid changes in state laws and by the judicial decisions which tend to make abortion more freely available;" and a feeling "that this trend will continue." On June 25, 1970, the House of Delegates adopted preambles and most of the resolutions proposed by the reference committee. The preambles emphasized "the best interests of the patient," "sound clinical judgment," and "informed patient consent," in contrast to "mere acquiescence to

the patient's demand." The resolutions asserted that abortion is a medical procedure that should be performed by a licensed physician in an accredited hospital only after consultation with two other physicians and in conformity with state law, and that no party to the procedure should be required to violate personally held moral principles. Proceedings of the AMA House of Delegates 220 (June 1970). The AMA Judicial Council rendered a complementary opinion.

7.   *The position of the American Public Health Association.* In October, 1970, the Executive Board of the APHA adopted Standards for Abortion Services. These were five in number:

a.   Rapid and simple abortion referral must be readily available through state and local public health departments, medical societies, or other nonprofit organizations.

b.   An important function of counseling should be to simplify and expedite the provision of abortion services; it should not delay the obtaining of these services.

c.   Psychiatric consultation should not be mandatory. As in the case of other specialized medical services, psychiatric consultation should be sought for definite indications, and not on a routine basis.

d.   A wide range of individuals from appropriately trained, sympathetic volunteers to highly skilled physicians may qualify as abortion counselors.

e.   Contraception and/or sterilization should be discussed with each abortion patient. Recommended Standards for Abortion Services, 61 Am.J.Pub.Health 396 (1971). Among factors pertinent to life and health risks associated with abortion were three that "are recognized as important":

a.   the skill of the physician,

b.   the environment in which the abortion is performed, and above all

c.   the duration of pregnancy, as determined by uterine size and confirmed by menstrual history. *Id.* at 397. It was said that "a well equipped hospital" offers more protection to cope with unforeseen difficulties than an office or clinic without such resources. . . . The factor of gestational age is of overriding importance. Thus, it was recommended that abortions in the second trimester and early abortions in the presence of existing medical complications be performed in hospitals as inpatient procedures. For pregnancies in the first trimester, abortion in the hospital with or without overnight stay "is probably the safest practice." An abortion in an extramural facility, however, is an acceptable alternative "provided arrangements exist in advance to admit patients promptly if unforeseen complications develop." Standards for an abortion facility were listed. It was said that, at present, abortions should be performed by physicians or osteopaths who are licensed to practice and who have "adequate training." *Id.* at 398.

8.   *The position of the American Bar Association.* At its meeting in February, 1972, the ABA House of Delegates approved, with 17 opposing votes, the Uniform Abortion Act that had been drafted and approved the preceding August by the Conference of Commissioners on Uniform State Laws. 58 A.B.A.J. 380 (1972). We set forth the Act in full in the margin. The Opinion of the Court Conference has appended an enlightening Prefatory Note.

VII

Three reasons have been advanced to explain historically the enactment of criminal abortion laws in the 19th century and to justify their continued existence.

It has been argued occasionally that these laws were the product of a Victorian social concern to discourage illicit sexual conduct. Texas, however, does not advance this justification in the present case, and it appears that no court or commentator has taken the argument seriously. The appellants and *amici* contend, moreover, that this is not a proper state purpose, at all and suggest that, if it were, the Texas statutes are overbroad in protecting it, since the law fails to distinguish between married and unwed mothers.

A second reason is concerned with abortion as a medical procedure. When most criminal abortion laws were first enacted, the procedure was a hazardous one for the woman. This was particularly true prior to the development of antisepsis. Antiseptic techniques, of course, were based on discoveries by Lister, Pasteur, and others first announced in 1867, but were not generally accepted and employed until about the turn of the century. Abortion mortality was high. Even after 1900, and perhaps until as late as the development of antibiotics in the 1940's, standard modern techniques such as dilation and curettage were not nearly so safe as they are today. Thus, it has been argued that a State's real concern in enacting a criminal abortion law was to protect the pregnant woman, that is, to restrain her from submitting to a procedure that placed her life in serious jeopardy.

Modern medical techniques have altered this situation. Appellants and various *amici* refer to medical data indicating that abortion in early pregnancy, that is, prior to the end of the first trimester, although not without its risk, is now relatively safe. Mortality rates for women undergoing early abortions, where the procedure is legal, appear to be as low as or lower than the rates for normal childbirth. Consequently, any interest of the State in protecting the woman from an inherently hazardous procedure, except when it would be equally dangerous for her to forgo it, has largely disappeared. Of course, important state interests in the areas of health and medical standards do remain. The State has a legitimate interest in seeing to it that abortion, like any other medical procedure, is performed under circumstances that insure maximum safety for the patient. This interest obviously extends at least to the performing physician and his staff, to the facilities involved, to the availability of after-care, and to adequate provision for any complication or emergency that might arise. The prevalence of high mortality rates at illegal "abortion mills" strengthens, rather than weakens, the State's interest in regulating the conditions under which abortions are performed. Moreover, the risk to the woman increases as her pregnancy continues. Thus, the State retains a definite interest in protecting the woman's own health and safety when an abortion is proposed at a late stage of pregnancy.

The third reason is the State's interest—some phrase it in terms of duty—in protecting prenatal life. Some of the argument for this justification rests on the theory that a new human life is present from the moment of conception. The State's interest and general obligation to protect life then extends, it is argued, to prenatal life. Only when the life of the pregnant mother herself is at stake, balanced against the life she carries within her, should the interest of the embryo or fetus not prevail. Logically, of course, a legitimate state interest in this area need not stand or fall on acceptance of the belief that life begins at conception or at some other point prior to live birth. In assessing the State's interest, recognition may be given to the less rigid claim that as long as at least potential life is involved, the State may assert interests beyond the protection of the pregnant woman alone.

Parties challenging state abortion laws have sharply disputed in some courts the contention that a purpose of these laws, when enacted, was to protect prenatal life. Pointing to the absence of legislative history to support the contention, they claim that most state laws were designed solely to protect the woman. Because medical advances have lessened this concern, at least with respect to abortion in early pregnancy, they argue that with respect to such abortions the laws can no longer be justified by any state interest. There is some scholarly support for this view of original purpose. The few state courts called upon to interpret their laws in the late 19th and early 20th centuries did focus on the State's interest in protecting the woman's health, rather than in preserving the embryo and fetus. Proponents of this view point out that in many States, including Texas, by statute or judicial interpretation, the pregnant woman herself could not be prosecuted for self-abortion or for cooperating in an abortion performed upon her by another. They claim that adoption of the "quickening" distinction through received common law and state statutes tacitly recognizes the greater health hazards inherent in late abortion and impliedly repudiates the theory that life begins at conception.

It is with these interests, and the eight to be attached to them, that this case is concerned.

VIII

The Constitution does not explicitly mention any right of privacy. In a line of decisions, however, going back perhaps as far as *Union Pacific R. Co. v. Botsford*, 141 U.S. 250, 251 (1891), the Court has recognized that a right of personal privacy, or a guarantee of certain areas or zones of privacy, does exist under the Constitution. In varying contexts, the Court or individual Justices have, indeed, found at least the roots of that right in the First Amendment, *Stanley v. Georgia*, 394 U.S. 557, 564 (1969); in the Fourth and Fifth Amendments, *Terry v. Ohio*, 392 U.S. 1, 8–9 (1968), *Katz v. United States*, 389 U.S. 347, 350 (1967), *Boyd v. United States*, 116 U.S. 616 (1886), *see Olmstead v. United States*, 277 U.S. 438, 478 (1928) (Brandeis, J., dissenting); in the penumbras of the Bill of Rights, *Griswold v. Connecticut*, 381 U.S. at 484–485; in the Ninth Amendment, *id.* at 486 (Goldberg, J., concurring); or in the concept of liberty guaranteed by the first section of the Fourteenth Amendment, *see Meyer v. Nebraska*, 262 U.S. 390, 399 (1923). These decisions make it clear that only personal rights that can be deemed "fundamental" or "implicit in the concept of ordered liberty," *Palko v. Connecticut*, 302 U.S. 319, 325 (1937), are included in this guarantee of personal privacy. They also make it clear that the right has some extension to activities relating to marriage, *Loving v. Virginia*, 388 U.S. 1, 12 (1967); procreation, *Skinner v. Oklahoma*, 316 U.S. 535, 541–542 (1942); contraception, *Eisenstadt v. Baird*, 405 U.S. at 453–454; *id.* at 460, 463–465 [p153] (WHITE, J., concurring in result); family relationships, *Prince v. Massachusetts*, 321 U.S. 158, 166 (1944); and childrearing and education, *Pierce v. Society of Sisters*, 268 U.S. 510, 535 (1925), *Meyer v. Nebraska, supra.*

This right of privacy, whether it be founded in the Fourteenth Amendment's concept of personal liberty and restrictions upon state action, as we feel it is, or, as the District Court determined, in the Ninth Amendment's reservation of rights to the people, is broad enough to encompass a woman's decision whether or not to terminate her pregnancy. The detriment that the State would impose upon the pregnant woman by denying this choice altogether is apparent. Specific and direct harm medically diagnosable even in early pregnancy may be involved. Maternity, or additional offspring, may force upon the woman a distressful life and future. Psychological harm may be imminent. Mental and physical health may be taxed by child care. There is also the distress, for all concerned, associated with the unwanted child, and there is the problem of bringing a child into a family already unable, psychologically and otherwise, to care for it. In other cases, as in this one, the additional difficulties and continuing stigma of unwed motherhood may be involved. All these are factors the woman and her responsible physician necessarily will consider in consultation.

On the basis of elements such as these, appellant and some *amici* argue that the woman's right is absolute and that she is entitled to terminate her pregnancy at whatever time, in whatever way, and for whatever reason she alone chooses. With this we do not agree. Appellant's arguments that Texas either has no valid interest at all in regulating the abortion decision, or no interest strong enough to support any limitation upon the woman's sole determination, are unpersuasive. The Court's decisions recognizing a right of privacy also acknowledge that some state regulation in areas protected by that right is appropriate. As noted above, a State may properly assert important interests in safeguarding health, in maintaining medical standards, and in protecting potential life. At some point in pregnancy, these respective interests become sufficiently compelling to sustain regulation of the factors that govern the abortion decision. The privacy right involved, therefore, cannot be said to be absolute. In fact, it is not clear to us that the claim asserted by some *amici* that one has an unlimited right to do with one's body as one pleases bears a close relationship to the right of privacy previously articulated in the Court's decisions. The Court has refused to recognize an unlimited right of this kind in the past. *Jacobson v. Massachusetts*, 197 U.S. 11 (1905) (vaccination); *Buck v. Bell*, 274 U.S. 200 (1927) (sterilization).

We, therefore, conclude that the right of personal privacy includes the abortion decision, but that this right is not unqualified, and must be considered against important state interests in regulation.

We note that those federal and state courts that have recently considered abortion law challenges have reached the same conclusion. A majority, in addition to the District Court in the present case, have held state laws unconstitutional, at least in part, because of vagueness or because of overbreadth and abridgment of rights. . .

Others have sustained state statutes. . . . .

Although the results are divided, most of these courts have agreed that the right of privacy, however based, is broad enough to cover the abortion decision; that the right, nonetheless, is not absolute, and is subject to some limitations; and that, at some point, the state interests as to protection of health, medical standards, and prenatal life, become dominant. We agree with this approach. . . .

In the recent abortion cases cited above, courts have recognized these principles. Those striking down state laws have generally scrutinized the State's interests in protecting health and potential life, and have concluded that neither interest justified broad limitations on the reasons for which a physician and his pregnant patient might decide that she should have an abortion in the early stages of pregnancy. Courts sustaining state laws have held that the State's determinations to protect health or prenatal life are dominant and constitutionally justifiable.

IX

The District Court held that the appellee failed to meet his burden of demonstrating that the Texas statute's infringement upon Roe's rights was necessary to support a compelling state interest, and that, although the appellee presented "several compelling justifications for state presence in the area of abortions," the statutes outstripped these justifications and swept "far beyond any areas of compelling state interest." 314 F.Supp. at 1222–1223. Appellant and appellee both contest that holding. Appellant, as has been indicated, claims an absolute right that bars any state imposition of criminal penalties in the area. Appellee argues that the State's determination to recognize and protect prenatal life from and after conception constitutes a compelling state interest. As noted above, we do not agree fully with either formulation.

A. The appellee and certain *amici* argue that the fetus is a "person" within the language and meaning of the Fourteenth Amendment. In support of this, they outline at length and in detail the well known facts of fetal development. If this suggestion of personhood is established, the appellant's case, of course, collapses, for the fetus' right to life would then be guaranteed specifically by the Amendment. The appellant conceded as much on reargument. On the other hand, the appellee conceded on reargument that no case could be cited that holds that a fetus is a person within the meaning of the Fourteenth Amendment.

The Constitution does not define "person" in so many words. Section 1 of the Fourteenth Amendment contains three references to "person." The first, in defining "citizens," speaks of "persons born or naturalized in the United States." The word also appears both in the Due Process Clause and in the Equal Protection Clause. "Person" is used in other places in the Constitution: in the listing of qualifications for Representatives and Senators, Art. I, § 2, cl. 2, and § 3, cl. 3; in the Apportionment Clause, Art. I, § 2, cl. 3; in the Migration and Importation provision, Art. I, § 9, cl. 1; in the Emolument Clause, Art. I, § 9, cl. 8; in the Electors provisions, Art. II, § 1, cl. 2, and the superseded cl. 3; in the provision outlining qualifications for the office of President, Art. II, § 1, cl. 5; in the Extradition provisions, Art. IV, § 2, cl. 2, and the superseded Fugitive Slave Clause 3; and in the Fifth, Twelfth, and Twenty-second Amendments, as well as in §§ 2 and 3 of the Fourteenth Amendment. But in nearly all these instances, the use of the word is such that it has application only post-natally. None indicates, with any assurance, that it has any possible pre-natal application.

All this, together with our observation, *supra,* that, throughout the major portion of the 19th century, prevailing legal abortion practices were far freer than they are today, persuades us that the word "person," as used in the Fourteenth Amendment, does not include the unborn. This is in accord with the results reached in those few cases where the issue has been squarely presented. . . . inferentially is to the same effect, for we there would not have indulged in statutory interpretation favorable to abortion in specified circumstances if the necessary consequence was the termination of life entitled to Fourteenth Amendment protection.

This conclusion, however, does not of itself fully answer the contentions raised by Texas, and we pass on to other considerations.

B. The pregnant woman cannot be isolated in her privacy. She carries an embryo and, later, a fetus, if one accepts the medical definitions of the developing young in the human uterus. See Dorland's Illustrated Medical Dictionary 478–479, 547 (24th ed.1965). The situation therefore is inherently different from marital intimacy, or bedroom possession of obscene material, or marriage, or procreation, or education, with which Eisenstadt and Griswold, Stanley, Loving, Skinner, and Pierce and Meyer were respectively concerned. As we have intimated above, it is reasonable and appropriate for a State to decide that, at some point in time another interest, that of health of the mother or that of potential human life, becomes significantly involved. The woman's privacy is no longer sole and any right of privacy she possesses must be measured accordingly.

Texas urges that, apart from the Fourteenth Amendment, life begins at conception and is present throughout pregnancy, and that, therefore, the State has a compelling interest in protecting that life from and after conception. We need not resolve the difficult question of when life begins. When those trained in the respective disciplines of medicine, philosophy, and theology are unable to arrive at any consensus, the judiciary, at this point in the development of man's knowledge, is not in a position to speculate as to the answer.

It should be sufficient to note briefly the wide divergence of thinking on this most sensitive and difficult question. There has always been strong support for the view that life does not begin until live birth. This was the belief of the Stoics. It appears to be the predominant, though not the unanimous, attitude of the Jewish faith. It may be taken to represent also the position of a large segment of the Protestant community, insofar as that can be ascertained; organized groups that have taken a formal position on the abortion issue have generally regarded abortion as a matter for the conscience of the individual and her family. As we have noted, the common law found greater significance in quickening. Physician and their scientific colleagues have regarded that event with less interest and have tended to focus either upon conception, upon live birth, or upon the interim point at which the fetus becomes "viable," that is, potentially able to live outside the mother's womb, albeit with artificial aid. Viability is usually placed at about seven months (28 weeks) but may occur earlier, even at 24 weeks. The Aristotelian theory of "mediate animation," that held sway throughout the Middle Ages and the Renaissance in Europe, continued to be official Roman Catholic dogma until the 19th century, despite opposition to this "ensoulment" theory from those in the Church who would recognize the existence of life from the moment of conception. The latter is now, of course, the official belief of the Catholic Church. As one brief *amicus* discloses, this is a view strongly held by many non-Catholics as well, and by many physicians. Substantial problems for precise definition of this view are posed, however, by new embryological data that purport to indicate that conception is a "process" over time, rather than an event, and by new medical techniques such as menstrual extraction, the "morning-after" pill, implantation of embryos, artificial insemination, and even artificial wombs.

In areas other than criminal abortion, the law has been reluctant to endorse any theory that life, as we recognize it, begins before live birth, or to accord legal rights to the unborn except in narrowly defined situations and except when the rights are contingent upon live birth. For example, the traditional rule of tort law denied recovery for prenatal injuries even though the child was born alive. That rule has been changed in almost every jurisdiction. In most States, recovery is said to be permitted only if the fetus was viable, or at least quick, when the injuries were sustained, though few courts have squarely so held. In a recent development, generally opposed by the commentators, some States permit the parents of a stillborn child to maintain an action for wrongful death because of prenatal injuries. Such an action, however, would appear to be one to vindicate the parents' interest and is thus consistent with the view that the fetus, at most, represents only the potentiality of life. Similarly, unborn children have been recognized as acquiring rights or interests by way of inheritance or other devolution of property, and have been represented by guardians *ad litem*. Perfection of the interests involved, again, has generally been contingent upon live birth. In short, the unborn have never been recognized in the law as persons in the whole sense.

X

In view of all this, we do not agree that, by adopting one theory of life, Texas may override the rights of the pregnant woman that are at stake. We repeat, however, that the State does have an important and legitimate interest in preserving and protecting the health of the pregnant woman, whether she be a resident of the State or a nonresident who seeks medical consultation and treatment there, and that it has still *another* important and legitimate interest in protecting the potentiality of human life. These interests are separate and distinct.

Each grows in substantiality as the woman approaches term and, at a point during pregnancy, each becomes "compelling."

With respect to the State's important and legitimate interest in the health of the mother, the "compelling" point, in the light of present medical knowledge, is at approximately the end of the first trimester. This is so because of the now-established medical fact, referred to above at 149, that, until the end of the first trimester mortality in abortion may be less than mortality in normal childbirth. It follows that, from and after this point, a State may regulate the abortion procedure to the extent that the regulation reasonably relates to the preservation and protection of maternal health. Examples of permissible state regulation in this area are requirements as to the qualifications of the person who is to perform the abortion; as to the licensure of that person; as to the facility in which the procedure is to be performed, that is, whether it must be a hospital or may be a clinic or some other place of less-than-hospital status; as to the licensing of the facility; and the like.

This means, on the other hand, that, for the period of pregnancy prior to this "compelling" point, the attending physician, in consultation with his patient, is free to determine, without regulation by the State, that, in his medical judgment, the patient's pregnancy should be terminated. If that decision is reached, the judgment may be effectuated by an abortion free of interference by the State.

With respect to the State's important and legitimate interest in potential life, the "compelling" point is at viability. This is so because the fetus then presumably has the capability of meaningful life outside the mother's womb. State regulation protective of fetal life after viability thus has both logical and biological justifications. If the State is interested in protecting fetal life after viability, it may go so far as to proscribe abortion during that period, except when it is necessary to preserve the life or health of the mother.

Measured against these standards, Art. 1196 of the Texas Penal Code, in restricting legal abortions to those "procured or attempted by medical advice for the purpose of saving the life of the mother," sweeps too broadly. The statute makes no distinction between abortions performed early in pregnancy and those performed later, and it limits to a single reason, "saving" the mother's life, the legal justification for the procedure. The statute, therefore, cannot survive the constitutional attack made upon it here.

This conclusion makes it unnecessary for us to consider the additional challenge to the Texas statute asserted on grounds of vagueness. *See United States v. Vuitch*, 402 U.S. at 67–72.

XI

To summarize and to repeat:

1. A state criminal abortion statute of the current Texas type, that excepts from criminality only a lifesaving procedure on behalf of the mother, without regard to pregnancy stage and without recognition of the other interests involved, is violative of the Due Process Clause of the Fourteenth Amendment.

    (a) For the stage prior to approximately the end of the first trimester, the abortion decision and its effectuation must be left to the medical judgment of the pregnant woman's attending physician.

    (b) For the stage subsequent to approximately the end of the first trimester, the State, in promoting its interest in the health of the mother, may, if it chooses, regulate the abortion procedure in ways that are reasonably related to maternal health.

(c) For the stage subsequent to viability, the State in promoting its interest in the potentiality of human life may, if it chooses, regulate, and even proscribe, abortion except where it is necessary, in appropriate medical judgment, for the preservation of the life or health of the mother.

2. The State may define the term "physician," as it has been employed in the preceding paragraphs of this Part XI of this opinion, to mean only a physician currently licensed by the State, and may proscribe any abortion by a person who is not a physician as so defined.

In *Doe v. Bolton, post,* p. 179, procedural requirements contained in one of the modern abortion statutes are considered. That opinion and this one, of course, are to be read together.

This holding, we feel, is consistent with the relative weights of the respective interests involved, with the lessons and examples of medical and legal history, with the lenity of the common law, and with the demands of the profound problems of the present day. The decision leaves the State free to place increasing restrictions on abortion as the period of pregnancy lengthens, so long as those restrictions are tailored to the recognized state interests. The decision vindicates the right of the physician to administer medical treatment according to his professional judgment up to the points where important state interests provide compelling justifications for intervention. Up to those points, the abortion decision in all its aspects is inherently, and primarily, a medical decision, and basic responsibility for it must rest with the physician. If an individual practitioner abuses the privilege of exercising proper medical judgment, the usual remedies, judicial and intra-professional, are available.

XII

Our conclusion that Art. 1196 is unconstitutional means, of course, that the Texas abortion statutes, as a unit, must fall. The exception of Art. 1196 cannot be struck down separately, for then the State would be left with a statute proscribing all abortion procedures no matter how medically urgent the case.

Although the District Court granted appellant Roe declaratory relief, it stopped short of issuing an injunction against enforcement of the Texas statutes. The Court has recognized that different considerations enter into a federal court's decision as to declaratory relief, on the one hand, and injunctive relief, on the other. . . We are not dealing with a statute that, on its face, appears to abridge free expression, an area of particular concern under *Dombrowski* and refined in *Younger v. Harris,* 401 U.S. at 50.

We find it unnecessary to decide whether the District Court erred in withholding injunctive relief, for we assume the Texas prosecutorial authorities will give full credence to this decision that the present criminal abortion statutes of that State are unconstitutional.

The judgment of the District Court as to intervenor Hallford is reversed, and Dr. Hallford's complaint in intervention is dismissed. In all other respects, the judgment of the District Court is affirmed. Costs are allowed to the appellee.

It is so ordered.

MR. JUSTICE STEWART, concurring.

In 1963, this Court, in *Ferguson v. Skrupa,* 372 U.S. 726, purported to sound the death knell for the doctrine of substantive due process, a doctrine under which many state laws had in the past been held to violate the Fourteenth Amendment. As Mr. Justice Black's opinion for the Court in *Skrupa* put it:

We have returned to the original constitutional proposition that courts do not substitute their social and economic beliefs for the judgment of legislative bodies, who are elected to pass laws. *Id.* at 730.

Barely two years later, in *Griswold v. Connecticut*, 381 U.S. 479, the Court held a Connecticut birth control law unconstitutional. In view of what had been so recently said in *Skrupa*, the Court's opinion in *Griswold* understandably did its best to avoid reliance on the Due Process Clause of the Fourteenth Amendment as the ground for decision. Yet the Connecticut law did not violate any provision of the Bill of Rights, nor any other specific provision of the Constitution. So it was clear to me then, and it is equally clear to me now, that the *Griswold* decision can be rationally understood only as a holding that the Connecticut statute substantively invaded the "liberty" that is protected by the Due Process Clause of the Fourteenth Amendment. As so understood, *Griswold* stands as one in a long line of pre-*Skrupa* cases decided under the doctrine of substantive due process, and I now accept it as such.

"In a Constitution for a free people, there can be no doubt that the meaning of 'liberty' must be broad indeed." *Board of Regents v. Roth*, 408 U.S. 564, 572. The Constitution nowhere mentions a specific right of personal choice in matters of marriage and family life, but the "liberty" protected by the Due Process Clause of the Fourteenth Amendment covers more than those freedoms explicitly named in the Bill of Rights. . .

As Mr. Justice Harlan once wrote:

> [T]he full scope of the liberty guaranteed by the Due Process Clause cannot be found in or limited by the precise terms of the specific guarantees elsewhere provided in the Constitution. This "liberty" is not a series of isolated points pricked out in terms of the taking of property; the freedom of speech, press, and religion; the right to keep and bear arms; the freedom from unreasonable searches and seizures; and so on. It is a rational continuum which, broadly speaking, includes a freedom from all substantial arbitrary impositions and purposeless restraints . . . and which also recognizes, what a reasonable and sensitive judgment must, that certain interests require particularly careful scrutiny of the state needs asserted to justify their abridgment.

Poe v. Ullman, 367 U.S. 497, 543 (opinion dissenting from dismissal of appeal) (citations omitted). In the words of Mr. Justice Frankfurter,

> Great concepts like . . . "liberty" . . . were purposely left to gather meaning from experience. For they relate to the whole domain of social and economic fact, and the statesmen who founded this Nation knew too well that only a stagnant society remains unchanged. *National Mutual Ins. Co. v. Tidewater Transfer Co.*, 337 U.S. 582, 646 (dissenting opinion).

Several decisions of this Court make clear that freedom of personal choice in matters of marriage and family life is one of the liberties protected by the Due Process Clause of the Fourteenth Amendment . . . As recently as last Term, in *Eisenstadt v. Baird,* 405 U.S. 438, 453, we recognized the right of the *individual,* married or single, to be free from unwarranted governmental intrusion into matters so fundamentally affecting a person as the decision whether to bear or beget a child.

That right necessarily includes the right of a woman to decide whether or not to terminate her pregnancy.

Certainly the interests of a woman in giving of her physical and emotional self during pregnancy and the interests that will be affected throughout her life by the birth and raising of a child are of a far greater degree of significance and personal intimacy than the right to send a child to private school protected in *Pierce v. Society of Sisters*, 268 U.S. 510 (1925), or the right to teach a foreign language protected in *Meyer v. Nebraska*, 262 U.S. 390 (1923).

Abele v. Markle, 351 F.Supp. 224, 227 (Conn.1972).

Clearly, therefore, the Court today is correct in holding that the right asserted by Jane Roe is embraced within the personal liberty protected by the Due Process Clause of the Fourteenth Amendment.

It is evident that the Texas abortion statute infringes that right directly. Indeed, it is difficult to imagine a more complete abridgment of a constitutional freedom than that worked by the inflexible criminal statute now in force in Texas. The question then becomes whether the state interests advanced to justify this abridgment can survive the "particularly careful scrutiny" that the Fourteenth Amendment here requires.

The asserted state interests are protection of the health and safety of the pregnant woman, and protection of the potential future human life within her. These are legitimate objectives, amply sufficient to permit a State to regulate abortions as it does other surgical procedures, and perhaps sufficient to permit a State to regulate abortions more stringently, or even to prohibit them in the late stages of pregnancy. But such legislation is not before us, and I think the Court today has thoroughly demonstrated that these state interests cannot constitutionally support the broad abridgment of personal liberty worked by the existing Texas law. Accordingly, I join the Court's opinion holding that that law is invalid under the Due Process Clause of the Fourteenth Amendment.

MR. JUSTICE REHNQUIST, dissenting.

The Court's opinion brings to the decision of this troubling question both extensive historical fact and a wealth of legal scholarship. While the opinion thus commands my respect, I find myself nonetheless in fundamental disagreement with those parts of it that invalidate the Texas statute in question, and therefore dissent.

The Court's opinion decides that a State may impose virtually no restriction on the performance of abortions during the first trimester of pregnancy. Our previous decisions indicate that a necessary predicate for such an opinion is a plaintiff who was in her first trimester of pregnancy at some time during the pendency of her lawsuit. While a party may vindicate his own constitutional rights, he may not seek vindication for the rights of others. *Moose Lodge v. Irvis*, 407 U.S. 163 (1972); *Sierra, Club v. Morton*, 405 U.S. 727 (1972). The Court's statement of facts in this case makes clear, however, that the record in no way indicates the presence of such a plaintiff. We know only that plaintiff Roe at the time of filing her complaint was a pregnant woman; for aught that appears in this record, she may have been in her last trimester of pregnancy as of the date the complaint was filed.

Nothing in the Court's opinion indicates that Texas might not constitutionally apply its proscription of abortion as written to a woman in that stage of pregnancy. Nonetheless, the Court uses her complaint against the Texas statute as a fulcrum for deciding that States may impose virtually no restrictions on medical abortions performed during the first trimester of pregnancy. In deciding such a hypothetical lawsuit, the Court departs from the longstanding admonition that it should never "formulate a rule of constitutional law broader than is required by the precise facts to which it is to be applied." *Liverpool, New York & Philadelphia S.S. Co. v. Commissioners of Emigration*, 113 U.S. 33, 39 (1885). *See also Ashwander v. TVA*, 297 U.S. 288, 345 (1936) (Brandeis, J., concurring).

II

Even if there were a plaintiff in this case capable of litigating the issue which the Court decides, I would reach a conclusion opposite to that reached by the Court. I have difficulty in concluding, as the Court does, that the right of "privacy" is involved in this case. Texas, by the statute here challenged, bars the performance of a medical abortion by a licensed physician on a plaintiff such as Roe. A transaction resulting in an operation such as this is not "private" in the ordinary usage of that word. Nor is the "privacy" that the Court finds here even a distant relative of the freedom from searches and seizures protected by the Fourth Amendment to the Constitution, which the Court has referred to as embodying a right to privacy. *Katz v. United States*, 389 U.S. 347 (1967).

If the Court means by the term "privacy" no more than that the claim of a person to be free from unwanted state regulation of consensual transactions may be a form of "liberty" protected by the Fourteenth Amendment, there is no doubt that similar claims have been upheld in our earlier decisions on the basis of that liberty. I agree with the statement of MR. JUSTICE STEWART in his concurring opinion that the "liberty," against deprivation of which without due process the Fourteenth Amendment protects, embraces more than the rights found in the Bill of Rights. But that liberty is not guaranteed absolutely against deprivation, only against deprivation without due process of law. The test traditionally applied in the area of social and economic legislation is whether or not a law such as that challenged has a rational relation to a valid state objective. *Williamson v. Lee Optical Co.*, 348 U.S. 483, 491 (1955). The Due Process Clause of the Fourteenth Amendment undoubtedly does place a limit, albeit a broad one, on legislative power to enact laws such as this. If the Texas statute were to prohibit an abortion even where the mother's life is in jeopardy, I have little doubt that such a statute would lack a rational relation to a valid state objective under the test stated in *Williamson, supra*. But the Court's sweeping invalidation of any restrictions on abortion during the first trimester is impossible to justify under that standard, and the conscious weighing of competing factors that the Court's opinion apparently substitutes for the established test is far more appropriate to a legislative judgment than to a judicial one.

The Court eschews the history of the Fourteenth Amendment in its reliance on the "compelling state interest" test. *See Weber v. Aetna Casualty & Surety Co.*, 406 U.S. 164, 179 (1972) (dissenting opinion). But the Court adds a new wrinkle to this test by transposing it from the legal considerations associated with the Equal Protection Clause of the Fourteenth Amendment to this case arising under the Due Process Clause of the Fourteenth Amendment. Unless I misapprehend the consequences of this transplanting of the "compelling state interest test," the Court's opinion will accomplish the seemingly impossible feat of leaving this area of the law more confused than it found it.

While the Court's opinion quotes from the dissent of Mr. Justice Holmes in *Lochner v. New York*, 198 U.S. 45, 74 (1905), the result it reaches is more closely attuned to the majority opinion of Mr. Justice Peckham in that case. As in *Lochner* and similar cases applying substantive due process standards to economic and social welfare legislation, the adoption of the compelling state interest standard will inevitably require this Court to examine the legislative policies and pass on the wisdom of these policies in the very process of deciding whether a particular state interest put forward may or may not be "compelling." The decision here to break pregnancy into three distinct terms and to outline the permissible restrictions the State may impose in each one, for example, partakes more of judicial legislation than it does of a determination of the intent of the drafters of the Fourteenth Amendment.

The fact that a majority of the States reflecting, after all, the majority sentiment in those States, have had restrictions on abortions for at least a century is a strong indication, it seems to me, that the asserted right to an abortion is not "so rooted in the traditions and conscience of our people as to be ranked as fundamental," *Snyder v. Massachusetts*, 291 U.S. 97, 105 (1934). Even today, when society's views on abortion are changing, the very existence of the debate is evidence that the "right" to an abortion is not so universally accepted as the appellant would have us believe.

To reach its result, the Court necessarily has had to find within the scope of the Fourteenth Amendment a right that was apparently completely unknown to the drafters of the Amendment. As early as 1821, the first state law dealing directly with abortion was enacted by the Connecticut Legislature. Conn.Stat., Tit. 22, §§ 14, 16. By the time of the adoption of the Fourteenth Amendment in 1868, there were at least 36 laws enacted by state or territorial legislatures limiting abortion. While many States have amended or updated their laws, 21 of the laws on the books in 1868 remain in effect today. Indeed, the Texas statute struck down today was, as the majority notes, first enacted in 1857, and "has remained substantially unchanged to the present time." *Ante* at 119.

There apparently was no question concerning the validity of this provision or of any of the other state statutes when the Fourteenth Amendment was adopted. The only conclusion possible from this history is that the drafters did not intend to have the Fourteenth Amendment withdraw from the States the power to legislate with respect to this matter.

III

Even if one were to agree that the case that the Court decides were here, and that the enunciation of the substantive constitutional law in the Court's opinion were proper, the actual disposition of the case by the Court is still difficult to justify. The Texas statute is struck down *in toto*, even though the Court apparently concedes that, at later periods of pregnancy Texas might impose these self-same statutory limitations on abortion. My understanding of past practice is that a statute found to be invalid as applied to a particular plaintiff, but not unconstitutional as a whole, is not simply "struck down" but is, instead, declared unconstitutional as applied to the fact situation before the Court. *Yick Wo v. Hopkins*, 118 U.S. 356 118 U.S. 356 (1886); 118 U.S. 356 (1886); *Street v. New York*, 394 U.S. 576 (1969).

For all of the foregoing reasons, I respectfully dissent.

SOURCE: Roe v. Wade, 410 U.S. 113 (1973).

DOCUMENT ANALYSIS

The *Roe v. Wade* decision represents an American landmark both in terms of women's rights and in terms of judicial history. The decision is sweeping in its scope, and had the immediate effect of nullifying nearly every state abortion law in the country. For this reason, some heralded the ruling as a major achievement for women's advancement while others decried it a departure from the conventional role of the Supreme Court.

Justice Blackmun's majority opinion reaches widely through Western social history to make the argument that abortion has been practiced commonly across time and across societies. His venture into medical and religious history is an effort to search for definitive social practices and norms around abortion; in the end, the justice argues that neither medical nor religious institutions have settled on unanimous answers to the major questions of life. As a consequence, the justice turns to the U.S. Constitution for guidance in the case. Finding no overt protection there of unborn, or "potential" citizens, the majority concludes that the state restricting abortion has no compelling interest in doing so, at least not until the pregnancy is near its conclusion, and a citizen is imminent.

On the other side of this equation, Justice Blackmun argues that the U.S. Constitution is so infused with privacy protections that the right to end a pregnancy must be included there; he adds, too, the argument that recent decisions around privacy and pregnancy support the outcome in *Roe.* So the majority creates the *trimester system* of abortion policy, weighting the woman's interests in controlling her fate heavily in the beginning stages of pregnancy, and acknowledging increasing legitimacy of the state's interest in the pregnancy by the final trimester.

Justice Stewart adds his own statement to support the notion that liberty's reach goes well beyond the Bill of Rights. Justice Rehnquist, on the other hand, disagrees with much of the Court's decision, and lays out a powerful dissent that foreshadows the documents that follow in this book.

Rehnquist's dissent first points out the obvious fact that Jane Roe is no longer pregnant when her case is heard. He argues that American jurisprudence does not have a history of allowing a plaintiff to make a claim once her personal injury has past. Allowing this type of class action suit opens the court to a new role, and expands its reach in a way that many critics of *Roe* dislike.

Beyond this procedural objection, Justice Rehnquist also disapproves of the substantive reasoning offered by the majority. The trimester system, he says, is more like a legislative judgment than a judicial one. Furthermore, in his view, the majority did not give sufficient weight to the state's interest in fetal life.

These themes (the court's expansion over the states, its increasingly legislative approach, and the substantive balance struck in favor of women's rights) form the basis for many objections to *Roe v. Wade,* and set the agenda of the antiabortion movement borne of this decision. Threads of Justice Rehnquist's dissent are evident in the following documents and become a dominant view on the Court some years later when Rehnquist becomes Chief Justice and is joined on the Court by new, like-minded justices.

Roe might be seen as a rather moderate decision. While sweeping in its impact on state statutes and on court authority, the decision did not extend abortion rights as far as it might have. For instance, the majority might have extended a blanket "right to abortion" based on the penumbras of privacy, or some other, more rigorous location in the Constitution such as the equal protection clause of the Fourteenth Amendment. What is more, Justice Blackmun mentions at several points that the majority is not extending abortion "on demand," but rather, is creating a model that balances state interest in fetal life against a woman's freedom. Justice Blackmun is clear that physicians—not individual women—would be the arbiters of women's abortion decisions; in this way, the decision does more for physician freedoms than for women's.

In hindsight, the most powerful aspect of the decision is the protection of women's health; more than any other aspect of *Roe,* the view that a woman's health should guide policymakers in their con-

Norma McCorvey, known as "Jane Roe," now an abortion opponent. Getty Images.

sideration of abortion restrictions would withstand the test of future scrutiny until, in 2007, the Court backed away from this principle (see chapter 7).

IN HISTORY

DEATHS FROM ILLEGAL ABORTIONS

Scholars have struggled to confirm the number of women who perished as a consequence of illegal abortions. Many barriers to precise data exist. The reluctance of women themselves to seek medical intervention following a botched abortion, the shame of family members who sought to hide their loved one's actions, and uneven coding and reporting by medical facilities all make perfect accounting of abortion fatalities impossible.

Still, based on the best information we have, deaths from illegal abortions in the United States before 1973 number in the thousands per year. In the post–*Roe v. Wade* era, the number of maternal fatalities from abortions have plummeted to approximately 10 per year.

Document: Excerpt from John Hart Ely, "The Wages of Crying Wolf: A Comment on *Roe v. Wade.*"
Date: April, 1973.
Where: The Yale Law Journal.
Significance: Professor Ely's scathing criticism of *Roe v. Wade*, published shortly after the decision was issued, articulated more fully some of Justice Rehnquist's concerns in his dissenting opinion, and would frame much of the anti-*Roe* rhetoric for years to come.

In *Roe v. Wade*, decided January 22, 1973, the Supreme Court—Justice Blackmun speaking for everyone but Justices White and Rehnquist—held unconstitutional Texas's (and virtually every other state's) criminal abortion statute. The broad outlines of its argument are difficult to make out. . . .

A number of fairly standard criticisms can be made of *Roe*. A plausible narrower basis of decision, that of vagueness, is brushed aside in the rush toward a broader ground. The opinion strikes the reader initially as a sort of guidebook, addressing questions not before the Court and drawing lines with an apparent precision one generally associates with a commissioner's regulations. On closer examination, however, the precision proves largely illusory. Confusing signals are emitted, particularly with respect to the nature of the doctor's responsibilities and the permissible scope of health regulations after the first trimester. The Court seems, moreover, to get carried away on the subject of remedies: Even assuming the case can be made for an unusually protected constitutional right to an abortion, it hardly seems necessary to have banned during the first trimester *all* state regulation of the conditions under which abortions can be performed.

By terming such criticisms "standard", I do not mean to suggest they are unimportant, for they are not. But if they were all that was wrong with *Roe*, it would not merit special comment.

Let us not underestimate what is at stake: having an unwanted child can go a long way toward ruining a woman's life. And at bottom *Roe* signals the Court's judgment that this result cannot be justified by any good that anti-abortion legislation accomplishes. This surely is an understandable conclusion—indeed it is on with which I agree—but ordinarily the court claims no mandate to second-guess legislative balances, at least not when the Constitution has designed neither of the values in conflict as entitled to special protection. But even assuming it would be a good idea for the Court to assume this function, *Roe* seems a curious place to have begun. Laws prohibiting the use of "soft" drugs or, even more obviously, homosexual acts between consenting adults can stunt "the preferred life styles" of those against whom enforcement is threatened in very serious ways. It is clear such acts harm no one besides the participants, and indeed the case that the participants are harmed is a rather shaky one. Yet such laws survive, on the theory that there exists a societal consensus that the behavior involved is revolting or at any rate immoral. Of course the consensus is not universal but it is sufficient, and this is what is counted crucial, to get the laws passed and keep them on the books. Whether anti-abortion legislation cramps the life style of an unwilling mother more significantly than anti-homosexuality legislation cramps the life style of a homosexual is a close question. But even granting that it does, the *other* side of the balance looks very different. For there is more than simple societal revulsion to support legislation restricting abortion: Abortion ends (or if it makes a difference, prevents) the life of a human being other than the one making the choice.

The Court's response here is simply not adequate. It agrees, indeed it holds, that after the point of viability (a concept it failed to note will become even less clear than it is now as the technology of birth continues to develop) the interest in protecting the fetus is compelling. Exactly why that is the magic moment is not made clear: viability, as the Court defines it, is achieved some six to twelve weeks after quickening. (Quickening is the point at which the fetus begins discernibly to move independently of the mother and the point that has historically been deemed crucial—to the extent *any* point between conception and birth has been focused on.) But no, it is *viability* that is constitutionally critical: the Court's defense seems to mistake a definition for a syllogism.

With respect to the State's important and legitimate interest in potential life, the "compelling" point is at viability. This is so because the fetus then the presumably has the capacity of meaningful life outside the mother's womb.

With regard to why the state cannot consider this "important and legitimate interest" prior to viability, the opinion is even less satisfactory. The discussion begins sensibly enough: the interest asserted is not necessarily tied to the question whether the fetus is "alive," for whether or not one calls it a living being, it is an entity with the potential for (and indeed the likelihood of) life. But all of arguable relevance that follows are arguments that fetuses (a) are not recognized as "persons in the whole sense" by legal doctrine generally and (b) are not "persons" protected by the Fourteenth Amendment.

To the extent they are not entirely inconclusive, the bodies of doctrine to which the Court adverts respecting the protection of fetuses under general legal and doctrine tend to undercut rather than support its conclusion. And the argument that fetuses (unlike, say, corporations) are not "persons" under the Fourteenth Amendment fares little better. The Court notes that most constitutional clauses using the word "persons"—such as the one outlining the qualifications for the Presidency—appear to have been drafted with postnatal beings in mind. (It might have added that most of them were plainly drafted with *adults* in mind, but I suppose that wouldn't have helped.). . . .

The canons of construction employed here are perhaps most intriguing when they are contrasted with those invoked to derive the constitutional right to an abortion. But in any event, the argument that fetuses lack constitutional rights is simply irrelevant. For it has never been held or even asserted that the state interest needed to justify forcing a person to refrain from an activity, *whether or not that activity is constitutionally protected*, must implicate either the life or the constitutional rights of another person. Dogs are not "persons in the whole sense" nor have they constitutional rights, but that does not mean the state cannot prohibit killing them: It does not even mean the state cannot prohibit killing them in the exercise of the First Amendment right of political protest. Come to think of it, draft cards aren't persons either.

Thus even assuming the Court ought generally to get into the business of second-guessing legislative balances; it has picked a strange case with which to begin. Its purported evaluation of the balance that produced anti-abortion legislation simply does not meet the issue: that the life plans of the mother must, not simply may, prevail over the state's desire to protect the fetus simply does not follow from the judgment that the fetus is not a person. Beyond all that, however, the Court has no business getting into that business.

Were I a legislator I would vote for a statute very much like the one the Court ends up drafting. I hope this reaction reflects more than the psychological phenomenon that keeps bombardiers sane—the fact that it is somehow easier to "terminate" those you cannot see—and am inclined to think it does: that the mother, unlike the unborn child, has begun to imagine a future for herself strikes me as morally quite significant. But God knows I'm not *happy* with that resolution. Abortion is too much like infanticide on the one hand, and too much like contraception on the other, to leave one comfortable with any answer; and the moral issue it poses is as fiendish as any philosopher's hypothetical. . . .

Compared with men, very few women sit in our legislatures, a fact I believe should bear some relevance—even without an Equal Rights Amendment—to the appropriate standard of review for our legislation that favors men over women. But *no* fetuses sit in our legislatures. Of course they have their champions, but so have women. The two interests have clashed repeatedly in the political arena, and had continued to do so up to the date of the opinion, generating quite a wide variety of accommodations. By the Court's lights virtually all of the legislative accommodations had unduly favored fetuses; by its definition of victory women had lost. Yet in every legislative balance one of the competing interests loses to some extent; indeed usually, as here, they both do. On some occasions the Constitution throws its weight on the side of one of them, indicating the balance must be restruck. And on others—and this is Justice Stone's suggestion—it is at least arguable that, constitutional directive or not, the Court should throw *its* weight on the side of a minority demanding in court more that it was able to achieve politically. But even assuming this suggestion can be given principled content, it was clearly intended and should be reserved for those interests which, *as compared with the interests to which they have been subordinated*, constitute minorities unusually incapable of protecting themselves. Compared with men, women may constitute such a "minority"; compared with the unborn, they do not. I'm not sure I'd know a discrete and insular minority if I saw one, but confronted with a multiple choice question requiring me to designate (a) women or (b) fetuses as one, I'd expect no credit for the former answer.

Of course a woman's freedom to choose an abortion is part of the "liberty" the Fourteenth Amendment says shall not be denied without due process of law, as indeed is anyone's freedom to do what he wants. But "due process" generally guarantees only that the inhibition be procedurally fair and that it have some "rational" connection—though plausible is probably a better word—with a permissible governmental goal. What is unusual about *Roe* is that the liberty involved is accorded a far more stringent protection, so protection is more stringent, I think it is fair to say, than that the present Court accords more freedom of the press explicitly guaranteed by the First Amendment. What is frightening about *Roe* is that this super protected right is not inferable from the language of the Constitution, the framers' thinking respecting the specific problem at issue, any general value derivable from the provisions they included, or the nation's governmental structure. Nor is it explainable in terms of the unusual political impotence of the group politically protected vis-à-vis the interest that legislatively prevailed over it. And that, I believe—the predictable early reaction to *Roe* not withstanding ("more of the same Warren-type activism")—is a charge that can responsibly be leveled at no other decision of the past twenty years. At times the inferences the Court has drawn from the values the Constitution marks for special protection have been controversial, even shaky, but never before has its sense of an obligation to draw one been so obviously lacking.

SOURCE: John Hart Ely, "The Wages of Crying Wolf: A Comment on *Roe v. Wade." The Yale Law Journal* 82 (1973): 920–49. Reprinted by permission of The Yale Law Journal Company and William S. Hein Company.

DOCUMENT ANALYSIS

Professor Ely delivered a considerable criticism of *Roe* in his article, and one that has become famous in abortion policy circles. The critique touches on at least two key themes that subsequently become part of the antiabortion movement's rhetoric and some later Supreme Court decisions.

The first of those themes is the emphasis on changing technologies. Ely argues that the Blackmun opinion hangs on the tenuous line of fetal viability. Arguing for a balance between the state's interest in emerging citizen life (the fetus) and the women's inherent interest in her privacy right to control her fertility, the majority settles on the point of viability as the tipping point between these countervailing weights. Before viability, legal deference goes to the woman; but after it, the state's interest may become compelling enough to justify restrictions, with a woman's health considerations in mind. Ely reminds his reader that the line of viability is not bright: it can vary by the individual fetus and hinges often on contemporary technological diagnostics and intervention techniques. So, for Ely, basing the privacy right on such a precarious marker at mid-pregnancy—and one that will surely change with advances in technology—makes a weak constitutional justification.

Ancillary to this point is Ely's concern that Justice Blackmun draws too bright a line between the interests on either side of viability. The majority opinion gives short shrift, contends Ely, to a view that the state might have *some* interest in fetal life before viability, which, for Ely, appears too stark a view and unworkable in policy terms.

But perhaps the most devastating critique Ely offers of the *Roe* ruling pertains to its constitutional grounding. As Blackmun himself acknowledges, the *Roe* decision maintains that privacy is observed in the corners of the Constitution, its "penumbras." That is to say that the right of privacy is not delineated in the Constitution; in fact, the phrase does not exist there. Blackmun and his colleagues argue that privacy exists within the shadows of the Constitution, so thoroughly a piece of American governance that it did not require mention in our founding document. For Ely, and others after him opposed to *Roe*, this is a damning observation that the right of privacy hangs on a constitutional thread.

Document: The Hyde Amendment.
Date: June 24, 1976.
Where: U.S. House of Representatives.
Significance: The Hyde Amendment ended most federal funding for abortion and was a direct result of the backlash to *Roe v. Wade.*

Mr. HYDE. Mr. Chairman, I offer an amendment.

The Clerk read as follows:

Amendment offered by Mr. Hyde: On page 36, after line 9, add the following new section: "Sec. 209. None of the fund appropriated under this Act shall be used to pay for abortions or to promote or encourage abortions."

Mr. HYDE. Mr. Chairman, this amendment may stimulate a lot of debate—but it need not—because I believe most Members know how they will vote on this issue.

Nevertheless, there are those of us who believe it is to the everlasting shame of this country that in 1973 approximately 800,000 legal abortions were performed in this country—as so it is fair to assume that this year over a million human lives will be destroyed because they are inconvenient to someone.

The unborn child facing an abortion can best be classified as a member of the innocently inconvenient and since the pernicious doctrine that some lives are more important than others seems to be persuasive with the pro-abortion forces, we who seek to protect that most defenseless and innocent of human lives—the unborn—seek to inhibit the use of Federal funds to pay for and thus encourage abortion as an answer to the human and compelling problem of an unwanted child.

We are all exercised at the wanton killing of the porpoise, the baby seal. We urge big game hunters to save the tiger, but we somehow turn away at the specter of a million human beings being violently destroyed because this great society does not want them.

And make no mistake, an abortion is violent.

I think in the final analysis, you must determine whether or not the unborn person is human. If you think it is animal or vegetable then, of course, it is disposable like an empty beer can to be crushed and thrown out with the rest of the trash.

But medicine, biology, embryology, say that growing living organism is not animal or vegetable or mineral—but it is a human life.

And if you believe that human life is deserving of due process of law—of equal protection of the laws—then you cannot in logic and conscience help fund the execution of these innocent defenseless human lives.

If we are to order our lives by the precepts of animal husbandry, then I guess abortion is an acceptable answer. If we human beings are not of a higher order than animals then let us save our pretentious aspirations for a better and more just world and recognize this is an anthill we inhabit and there are no such things as ideals or justice of morality.

Once conception has occurred an new and unique genetic package has been created, not a potential human being, but a human being with potential. For 9 months the mother provides nourishment and shelter, and birth is no substantial change, it is merely a change of address.

We are told that bringing an unwanted child into the world is an obscene act. Unwanted by whom? Is it too subtle a notion to understand it is more important to be a loving person than to be one who is loved. We need more people who are capable of projecting love.

We hear the claim that the poor are denied a right available to other women if we do not use tax money to fund abortions.

Well, make a list of all the things society denies poor women and let them make the choice of what we will give them.

Don't say "poor woman, go destroy your young, and we will pay for it."

An innocent, defenseless human life, in a caring and human society deserves better than to be flushed down a toilet or burned in an incinerator.

The promise of America is that life is not just for the privileged, the planned, or the perfect.

SOURCE: *Congressional Record*, House of Representatives, June 24, 1976, 20410.

DOCUMENT ANALYSIS

Representative Henry Hyde (R-IL) became a symbol of the antiabortion movement as a consequence of this speech. Not surprisingly, the fact of federal support for abortion arose as the first target of the antiabortion movement after *Roe*. Those who objected to the practice of abortion were especially motivated to end federal support of the procedure. Much like antiwar protesters who view Defense Department dollars as a morally repugnant use of their taxes, antiabortion activists sought the elimination of federal abortion support.

Between 1973 and 1977, when the Hyde Amendment was first implemented, close to one million abortions were subsidized by the federal government through Medicaid. With the Hyde Amendment, that support ended, and the Supreme Court upheld the Hyde funding ban in 1980 with its *Harris v. McRae* decision (448 U.S. 297). The Hyde Amendment has been in effect ever since, although the number and kind of exceptions to the ban has varied slightly. At its passage, the only exception to the ban was to save the woman's life. At some points, rape and incest victims have been eligible to seek federal support to end their pregnancies, but since 2001 the Hyde Amendment ban has reverted to its original restriction: only women whose lives would be ended through continued pregnancy are afforded federal abortion support. The result is that only a handful of abortions annually are subsidized by the American taxpayer.

IN HISTORY

COST AND NUMBER OF FEDERALLY FUNDED ABORTIONS

Between 1973 and 1976, the federal government funded abortions for poor women who qualified for Medicaid medical benefits, which provides health care for low-income Americans. In 1976, the last year that benefits extended to abortion services, the United States spent approximately $45 million to pay for roughly 300,000 abortions. With the Hyde Amendment's implementation in 1977, federal abortion funding was virtually eliminated in all but a handful of cases.

Document: Excerpt from "Privacy v. Equality: Beyond *Roe v. Wade."*
Date: 1983.
Where: Originally a conference address, law professor Catharine A. MacKinnon ultimately published this piece in her book *Feminism Unmodified: Discourses on Life and Law.*
Significance: MacKinnon's piece is characteristic of the critiques of *Roe* coming from the left end of the ideological spectrum. While many of the detractors were levying conservative complaints similar to John Hart Ely's, MacKinnon's criticism represents the position held by many feminists that *Roe* simply had not gone far enough in protecting women's rights, and served to imbue the abortion rights movement with intellectual insight and fresh perspective.

Most women who seek abortions became pregnant while having sexual intercourse with men. Most did not mean or wish to conceive. In contrast to this fact of women's experience, which converges sexuality with reproduction with gender, the abortion debate has centered on separating control over sexuality from control over reproduction, and on separating both from gender and the life options of the sexes. Liberals have supported the availability of the abortion choice as if the woman just happened on the fetus. The political right, imagining that the intercourse preceding the conception is usually voluntary, urges abstinence, as if sex were up to women, while defending male authority, specifically including a wife's duty to submit to sex. Continuing with this logic, many opponents of state funding of abortions, such as supporters of some versions of the Hyde Amendment, would permit funding of abortions when pregnancy results from rape or incest. They make *exceptions* for those special occasions during which they presume women did *not* control sex. From all this I deduce that abortion's proponents and opponents share a tacit assumption that women significantly do control sex.

Feminist investigations suggest otherwise. Sexual intercourse, still the most common cause of pregnancy, cannot simply be presumed coequally determined. Feminism has found that women feel compelled to preserve the appearance—which, acted upon, becomes the reality—of male direction of sexual expression, as if male initiative itself were what we want, as if it were that which turns us on. Men enforce this. It is much of what men want in a woman. It is what pornography eroticizes and prostitutes provide. Rape—that is, intercourse with force that is recognized as force—is adjudicated not according to the power and force that the man wields, but according to the indices of intimacy between the parties. The more intimate you are with your accused rapist, the less likely the court is to deem that what happened to you was rape. Often indices of intimacy include intercourse itself. If "no" can be taken as "yes" how free can "yes" be?

Under these conditions, women often do not use birth control because of its social meaning, a meaning we did not create. Using contraception means acknowledging and planning the possibility of intercourse, accepting one's sexual availability, and appearing non-spontaneous. It means appearing available to male incursions. A good user of contraception can be presumed sexually available and among other consequences, raped with relative impunity. (If you think this isn't true, you should consider rape cases in which the fact that a woman had a diaphragm in is taken as an indication that what happened to her was intercourse, not rape. "Why did you leave your diaphragm in?") From studies of abortion clinics, women who repeatedly seek abortions (and now I'm looking at the repeat offenders high on the list of the right's villains, their best case for opposing abortion as female irresponsibility), when asked why, say something like, "The sex just happened." Like every night for two and a half years. I wonder if a woman can be presumed to control access to her sexuality if she feels unable to interrupt intercourse to inset a diaphragm, or worse, cannot even want to, aware that she risks a pregnancy she knows she does not want. Do you think she would stop the man for any other reason, such as the real taboo—lack of desire? If she would not, how is sex, hence its consequences, meaningfully voluntarily for women? Norms of sexual rhythm and romance that are felt interrupted by women's needs are constructed against women's interests. Sex doesn't look a whole lot like freedom when it appears normatively less costly for women to risk an undesired, often painful traumatic, dangerous, sometimes illegal and potentially life-threatening procedure than to protect themselves in advance. Yet abortion policy has never been explicitly approached in the context of how women get pregnant, that is, as a consequence of intercourse under conditions of gender inequality; that is, as an issue of forced sex.

Now, law. In 1973 *Roe v. Wade* found that a statute that made criminal all abortions except those to save the life of the mother violated the constitutional right to privacy. The privacy right had been previously created as a constitutional principle in a case that decriminalized the prescription and use of contraceptives. Note that courts use the privacy rubric to connect contraception with abortion through privacy in the same way that I just did through sexuality. In *Roe* that right to privacy was found "broad enough to encompass a woman's decision whether or not to terminate her pregnancy." In 1977 three justices observed, "In the abortion contest, we have held that the right to privacy shields the woman from undue state intrusion in and external scrutiny of her very personal choice."

In 1981 the Supreme Court in *Harris v. McRae* decides that the right to privacy did not mean that federal Medicaid programs had to fund medically necessary abortions. Privacy, the Court had said, was guaranteed for a woman's *decision* whether or not to terminate her pregnancy." The Court then permitted the government to support one decision and not another: to fund continuing conceptions and not to fund discontinuing them. Asserting that decisional privacy was nevertheless constitutionally intact, the Court states that "although the government may not place obstacles in the path of a woman's exercise of her freedom of choice, it need not remove those not of its own creation." It is apparently a very short step from that which the government has a duty *not* to intervene in to that which it has *no* duty to intervene in.

The idea of privacy, if regarded as the outer edge of the limitations on government, embodies, I think, a tension between the preclusion of public exposure or governmental intrusion, on the one hand, and autonomy in the sense of protecting personal self-action on the other. This is a tension, not just two facets of one whole right. In the liberal state this tension is resolved by demarking the threshold of the state at its permissible extent of penetration into a domain that is considered free by definition: the private sphere. It is by this move that the state secures to individuals what has been called "autonomy or control over the intimacies of personal identity." The state does this by centering its self restraint on body and home, especially bedroom. By staying out of marriage and the family, prominently meaning sexuality —that is to say, heterosexuality—from contraception through pornography to the abortion decision, the law of privacy proposes to guarantee individual bodily integrity, personal exercise of moral intelligence and freedom of intimacy. But if one asks whether *women's* rights to these values have been guaranteed, it appears that the law of privacy works to translate traditional social values into rhetoric of individual rights as a means of subordinating those rights to specific social imperatives. In feminist terms, I am arguing that the logic of *Roe* consummated in *Harris* translates the ideology of the private sphere into the individual woman's collective needs to the imperatives of male supremacy.

This is my retrospective on *Roe v. Wade*. Reproduction is sexual, men control sexuality and the state supports the interest of men as a group. *Roe* does not contradict this. So why was abortion legalized? Why were women even imagined to have such a right as privacy? It is not an accusation of bad faith to answer that the interests of men as a social group converged with the definition of justice embodied in law in what I call the male point of view. The way the male point of view constructs a social even or legal need will be the way that social even or legal need is framed by state policy. For example, to the extent that possession is the point of sex, illegal rape will be sex with a woman who is not yours unless the act makes her yours. If part of the kick of pornography involves eroticizing the putatively prohibited, illegal pornography—obscenity—will be prohibited enough to keep pornography desirable without ever making it truly illegitimate or unavailable. If, from the male standpoint, male is the implicit definition of human, maleness will be the implicit standard by which sex equality is measured in discrimination law. In parallel terms, abortion's availability frames, and is framed by, the conditions men work out among themselves to grant legitimacy to women to control the reproductive consequences of intercourse.

Since Freud, the social problem posed by sexuality has been perceived as the problem of the innate desire for sexual pleasure being by the constraints of civilization. In this context, the inequality of the sexes arises as an issue only in women's repressive socialization to passivity and coolness (so-called frigidity), in women's so-called desexualization, and in the disparate consequences of biology, that is, pregnancy. Who defines what is sexual, what sexuality therefore is, to whom what stimuli are erotic and why, and who defines the conditions under which sexuality is expressed—these issues are not even available to be considered. "Civilization's" answer to these questions fuses women's reproductivity with our attributed sexuality in its definition of what a woman is. We are defined as woman by the uses to which men put us. In this context it becomes clear why the struggle for reproductive freedom has never included a woman's right to refuse sex. In this notion of sexual liberation, the equality issue has been framed as a struggle for women to have sex with men on the same terms as men: "without consequences." In this sense the abortion right has been sought as freedom from the reproductive consequences of sexual expression, with sexuality defined as centered heterosexual genital intercourse. It is as if biological organisms, rather than social relations, reproduced the species. But if your concern is not how people is not how more people can get more sex, but who defines sexuality—pleasure and violation both—then the abortion right is situated within a very different problematic: the social and political problematic of the inequality of the sexes. As Susan Sontag said, "Sex itself is not liberating for women. Neither is more sex . . . The question is, what sexuality shall women be liberated to enjoy?" To address this requires reformulating the problems of sexuality from the repression of drives by civilization to the oppression of women by men.

Arguments for abortion under the rubric of feminism have rested upon the right to control one's own body—gender neutral. I think that argument has been appealing for the same reasons it is inadequate: socially, women's bodies have not been ours; we have not controlled their meanings and destinies. Feminists tried to assert that control without risking pursuit of the idea that something more might be at stake than our bodies, something closer to a net of relations which we are (at present inescapably) gendered. Some feminists have noticed that our right to decide has become merged with the right of on overwhelmingly male profession's right not to have its professional judgment second-guessed by the government. But most abortion advocates argue in rigidly and rigorously gender neutral terms.

Thus, for instance, Judith Jarvis Thomson's argument that an abducted woman had no obligation to be a celebrated violinist's life support system meant that women have no obligation to support a fetus. The parallel seems misframed. No woman who needs an abortion—no woman period—is valued, no potential a woman's life might hold is cherished, like a gender-neutral famous violinist's unencumbered possibilities. The problems of gender are thus underlined here rather than solved, or even addressed, Too, the underlying recognition in the parallel of the origin of the problem in rape—the origin in force, in abduction, that gives the hypothetical much of its moral weight—would confine abortions to instances in which force is recognized as force, like rape or incest. The applicability of this to the normal case of abortion is neither embraced nor disavowed, although the parallel was meant to apply to the normal case, as is abortion policy usually. This parable is constructed precisely to begin the debate after sex occurred, yet even it requires discussion of intercourse in relation to rape in relation to conception, in order to make sense. Because this issue has been studiously avoided in the abortion contest, the unequal basis on which woman's personhood is being constructed is obscured.

In the context of sexual critique of gender inequality, abortion promises to women sex with men on the same reproductive terms as men have sex with women. So long as women do not control access to our sexuality, abortions facilitates women's heterosexual availability. In other words, under conditions of gender inequality, sexual liberation in this sense does not free women; it frees male sexual aggression. The availability of abortion removes the one remaining legitimized reason that women have had for refusing sex besides the headache. As Andrea Dworkin put it, analyzing male ideology on abortion, "Getting laid was at stake." The Playboy Foundation has supported abortion rights from day one; it continues to, even with shrinking disposable funds, on a level of priority comparable to that of its opposition to censorship.

Privacy doctrine is an ideal vehicle for this process, The liberal ideal of the private—and privacy as an ideal has been formulated in liberal terms—holds that, so long as the public does not interfere, autonomous individuals interact freely and equally. Conceptually, this private is hermetic. It *means* that which is inaccessible to, unaccountable to, unconstructed by anything beyond itself. By definition, it is not part of or conditioned by anything systematic or outside of it. It is personal, intimate, autonomous, particular, individual, the original source and final outpost of the self, gender neutral. It is in short, defined by everything that feminism reveals women have never been allowed to be or have, and everything that women have been equated with and defined in terms of *men's* ability to have. To complain in public of inequality within it contradicts the liberal definition of the private. In this view, no act of the state contributes to—hence should properly participate in—shaping the internal alignments of the private or distributing its internal forces. Its inviolability by the state, framed as an individual right, presupposes that the private is not already an arm of the state. In this scheme, intimacy is implicitly thought to guarantee symmetry of power. Injuries arise in violating the private sphere, not within and by and because of it.

In private, consent tends to be presumed. It is true that a showing of coercion voids this presumption. But the problem is getting anything private to be perceived as coercive. Why one would allow force in private—the "why doesn't she leave" question asked of battered women—is a question given its urgency by the social meaning of the private as a sphere of choice. But for women the measure of the intimacy has been the measure of the oppression. This is why feminism has had to explode the private. This is why feminism has seen the personal as the political. In this sense, there is no private, either normatively or empirically. Feminism confronts the fact that women have no privacy to lose or guarantee. We are not inviolable. Our sexuality is not only violable, it is—hence, we are—seen *in* and *as* our violation. To confront the fact that we have no privacy is to confront the intimate degradation of women as the public order.

In this light a right to privacy looks like an injury got up as a gift. Freedom from public intervention coexists uneasily with any right that requires social preconditions to be meaningfully delivered. For example, if inequality is socially pervasive and enforced, equality will require intervention, not abdication, to be meaningful. But the right to privacy is not thought to require social change. It is not even thought to require any social preconditions, other than nonintervention by the public. The point of this for the abortion cases is not that indigency—which was the specific barrier to effective choice in *Harris*—is well within the public power to remedy, nor that the state is exempt in issues of the distribution of wealth. The point is rather that *Roe v. Wade* presumes that government nonintervention into the private sphere promotes a woman's freedom of choice. When the alternative is jail, there is much to be said for this argument. But the Harris result sustains the ultimate meaning of privacy in *Roe:* women are guaranteed by the public no more than what we can get in private—that is, what we can extract through our intimate associations with men. Women with privileges get rights.

So women got abortion as a private privilege, not as a public right. We got control over reproduction that is controlled by "a man or The Man," an individual man or the doctors or the government. Abortion was not decriminalized; it was legalized. In *Roe* the government set the stage for the conditions under which women gain access to this right. Virtually every ounce of control that women won out of this legalization has gone directly into the hands of men—husbands, doctors, or fathers—or is now in the process of attempts to reclaim it through regulation. Thus surely, must be what is meant by reform.

It is not inconsistent, then that framed as a privacy right, a woman's decision to abort would have no claim on public support and would genuinely not be seen as burdened by that deprivation. Privacy conceived as a right against public intervention and disclosure is the opposite of the relief that *Harris* sought for welfare women. State intervention would have provided a choice women did *not* have in private. The women in *Harris*, women whose sexual refusal has counted for particularly little, needed something to make their privacy effective. The logic of the Court's response resembles the logic by which women are supposed to consent to sex. Preclude the alternatives than call the sole remaining option "her choice." The point is that the alternatives are precluded *prior* to the reach of the chosen legal doctrine. The are precluded by conditions of sex, race and class—the very conditions the privacy frame not only leaves tacit but exists to *guarantee.*

When the law of privacy restricts intrusions into intimacy, it bars change in control over that intimacy. The existing distribution of power and resources within the private sphere will be precisely what the law of privacy exists to protect. It is probably not coincidence that the very things feminism regards as central to the subjection of women—the very place, the body; the very relations, heterosexual; the very activities, intercourse and reproduction; and the very feelings, intimate—form the core of what is covered by privacy doctrine. From this perspective, the legal concept of privacy can and has shielded the place of battery, marital rape and women's exploited labor, has preserved the central institutions whereby women are *deprived* of identity, autonomy, control and self definition; and has protected the primary activity through which male supremacy is expressed and enforced. Just as pornography is legally protected as individual freedom of expression—without questioning whose freedom and whose expression and at whose expense—abstract privacy protects abstract autonomy, without inquiring into whose freedom of action is being sanctioned at whose expense.

To fail to recognize the meaning of the private on the ideology and reality of women's subordination by seeking protection behind a right *to* that privacy is to cut women off from collective verification and state support in the same act. I think this has a lot to do with why we can't organize women on the abortion issue. When women are segregated in private, separated from each other, one at a time, a right to that privacy isolates us at once from each other and from public recourse. This right to privacy is a right of men "to be let alone" to oppress women one at a time. It embodies and reflects the private sphere's existing definition of woman hood. This is an instance of liberalism called feminism, liberalism applied to the woman as if we *are* persons, gender neutral. It is at once an ideological division that lies about a woman's shared experience and that mystifies the unity among the spheres of woman's violation. It is a very material division that keeps the private beyond public redress and depoliticizes women's subjection within it. It keeps some men out of the bedrooms of other men.

SOURCE: Catharine A. MacKinnon, *Feminism Unmodified: Discourses on Life and Law* (Cambridge, Mass.: Harvard University Press, 1987), 94–102. Copyright © 1987 by the President and Fellows of Harvard College.

DOCUMENT ANALYSIS

This article, typical of Catharine MacKinnon's work, takes aim at the very assumptions built into her subject. This legal scholar's view is that *Roe v. Wade* is flawed fundamentally, although her logic differs considerably from Professor John Hart Ely's. For MacKinnon, the ruling was intrinsically gendered, and as such, is limited in its ability to transform women's reproductive lives.

MacKinnon argues that women do not control their sexual lives, and that the presumption in *Roe*, as well as among its detractors, is that women in fact do control their intimate relationships. For MacKinnon, the private sphere is a space dominated by men, and constraining the decision to the private realm (i.e., the decision to choose abortion) is a far cry short of full, public rights.

As seen in the Hyde Amendment, the *Roe* decision only extended to women a right to choose abortion, not a right to procure one. As historian Rickie Solinger has articulated in the book *Beggars and Choosers*, *Roe v. Wade*, and the Hyde Amendment in its wake, separated women into "beggars" (those without resources to procure abortion), and "choosers" (those with resources). And because poverty is disproportionately prevalent among women of color, the ban on federal financing allowed under *Roe* would further divide women by race.

MacKinnon's position has implications for the abortion rights movement. That movement has embraced the concept of choice, and in MacKinnon's view, that framework is fundamentally flawed because it joins abortion-access advocates with antiabortion forces in the belief that women can and do choose the conditions of their intimate relationships. And as the chapters that follow this one indicate, the concept of choice would have limited impact on expanding abortion options for women, making MacKinnon's words of 1983 almost prescient.

Further Reading

Balkin, Jack M., ed. *What* Roe v. Wade *Should Have Said: The Nation's Top Legal Experts Rewrite America's Most Controversial Decision*. New York: New York University Press, 2005.

Faux, Marian. Roe v. Wade: *The Untold Story of the Landmark Supreme Court Decision That Made Abortion Legal*. New York: Macmillan Publishing Company, 1988.

Garrow, David J. *Liberty and Sexuality: The Right to Privacy and the Making of* Roe v. Wade. New York: Macmillan Publishing Company, 1994.

Hull, N.E.H., and Peter Charles Hoffer. Roe v. Wade: *The Abortion Rights Controversy in American History*. Lawrence: University Press of Kansas, 2001.

McCorvey, Norma, with Andy Meisler. *I am Roe: My Life*, Roe v. Wade, *and Freedom of Choice*. New York: HarperCollins Publishers, 1994.

Solinger, Rickie. *Beggars and Choosers: How the Politics of Choice Shapes Adoption, Abortion, and Welfare in the United States*. New York: Hill and Wang, 2001.

Solinger, Rickie. *Wake Up Little Susie: Single Pregnancy and Race Before* Roe v. Wade. New York: Routledge, 1992.

Weddington, Sarah. *A Question of Choice*. New York: Putnam's, 1992.

5

THE PARTIES COLLIDE

The opposition to *Roe v. Wade* gained little legislative ground in the 1970s. Beyond the significant exception of eliminating public funds for abortion, the movement to undermine the landmark protection of abortion struggled to gain a foothold in government. By the 1980s, however, the political winds began to shift, and the antiabortion organizations felt new cause for hope.

In the immediate aftermath of *Roe*, neither abortion supporters nor abortion opponents had a real presence in either political party. The two major parties remained aloof from abortion policy until *Roe v. Wade* forced the issue into the national limelight. In fact, from the vantage point of twenty-first-century America, it is surprising how little difference there was between the two major political parties in the immediate aftermath of the ruling. In the 1976 presidential election, there was only minimal discussion of abortion, and the two major candidates each struck a moderate tone. But by 1980s, the parties had begun to shift.

For their part, the Republicans had been on the forefront of women's progress for decades. The first to support the Equal Rights Amendment (ERA), the Party of Lincoln made a difficult decision in 1980 when it chose to abandon its 40-year commitment to the ERA, exchanging it in the party platform for a statement opposing abortion. Having been the minority party for some time, the Republicans decided to join forces with the emerging anti-abortion, profamily movement, and in doing so, left behind its commitment to progressive women's issues. Still, the 1980 platform left room for dissent within party ranks; party strategist Lee Atwater's "big tent" philosophy yielded a moderate stance.

Democrats also embraced moderation. In a tepid statement, the 1980 Democratic party platform walked a cautious line, observing differences of opinion within the party's ranks, while indicating support for the Supreme Court's decision. All of this moderation would evaporate four years later.

From 1984 onward, the two major parties in America chose increasingly polarized abortion positions. These statements set in motion a partisan element to abortion policy that had been largely absent from pre-*Roe* abortion policy debates. The next generation of Americans would come to associate the two parties with their distinct abortion positions, and over time new voters would gravitate to the parties based on their abortion stance.

The antiabortion position articulated by the Republican Party's platform calls for one specific objective that would change abortion policy fundamentally, taking policy further and further from the *Roe* decision as the years passed. First articulated in 1984 and then confirmed with each passing presidential platform, the Republicans promised to remake the judiciary by nominating only antiabortion justices. Understanding that abortion policy is often resolved in the courts, this strategy would deliver quick results, as seen in the Supreme Court decision included in this chapter. Between 1989 and 1992, the Supreme Court, with its new Republican, antiabortion appointments, would undermine *Roe* in significant and lasting ways, leaving the Clinton administration—beginning in 1993—with the task of unraveling 12 years of antiabortion advances.

Document: Republican and Democratic Party abortion platform statements.
Date: 1984.
Where: Democratic National Committee; Republican National Committee.
Significance: These statements crystallized the two parties' distinct approaches to abortion policy and set the terms of the policy debate for the end of the twentieth century.

Democratic Party Platform of 1984

The Democratic Party recognizes reproductive freedom as a fundamental human right. We therefore oppose government interference in the reproductive decisions of Americans, especially government interference which denies poor Americans their right to privacy by funding or advocating one or a limited number of reproductive choices only. We fully recognize the religious and ethical concern which many Americans have about abortion. But we also recognize the belief of many Americans that a woman has a right to choose whether and when to have a child. The Democratic Party supports the 1973 Supreme Court decision on abortion rights as the law of land and opposes any constitutional amendment to restrict or overturn that decision. We deplore violence and harassment against health providers and women seeking services, and will work to end such acts. We support a local family planning and family life education programs and medical research aimed at reducing the need for abortion.

Republican Party Platform of 1984

The unborn child has a fundamental individual right to life which cannot be infringed. We therefore reaffirm our support for a human life amendment to the Constitution, and we endorse legislation to make clear that the Fourteenth Amendment's protections apply to unborn children. We oppose the use of public revenues for abortion and will eliminate funding for organizations which advocate or support abortion. We commend the efforts of those individuals and religious and private organizations that are providing positive alternatives to abortion by meeting the physical, emotional, and financial needs of pregnant women and offering adoption services where needed.

We applaud President Reagan's fine record of judicial appointments, and we reaffirm our support for the appointment of judges at all levels of the judiciary who respect traditional family values and the sanctity of innocent human life.

SOURCE: Democratic and Republican National Committees, http://www.presidency_ucsb.edu/plat forms.php.

DOCUMENT ANALYSIS

The perspectives articulated in the 1984 abortion platform planks reflected the emerging two social-movement perspectives on abortion and solidified the public discourse on abortion policy. For their part, Republicans asserted a "fundamental right to life" for the fetus, turning *Roe v. Wade* on its head. And despite some Republicans' deep objection to sustained federal intervention in abortion policy, the plank also asserts the parties' intention to effect policy change through judicial nominations. Because of the party's recent objections to federal authority in other social policy arenas (civil rights most clearly), this willingness to invoke the federal government to deal with social policy would create a lasting tension within Republican Party ranks.

On the other side of the issue, Democrats invoked much of the language of the prochoice movement in their statement, fully embracing that movement's goals and followers into the party. The objective of privacy would remain fixed in proabortion rights circles for decades to come, even while that rhetoric allowed opponents to use that same argument to deny public funds for a "private" decision. Framing abortion as a "choice" would become a strategic liability by the twenty-first century, as many Americans would "choose" not to use public dollars for such a private and morally debatable decision. Additionally, the call for freedom from government intrusion in the arena of reproductive decision-making would also make it easier to keep government out of abortion provision or financial support. Having cast abortion as a private matter, the abortion rights forces would face increasing objections to any public assistance—whether that assistance be monetary, or in terms of personnel and public buildings.

IN HISTORY

GLOBAL GAG RULE

Abortion politics began to seep into international politics during the Reagan administration. For example, in 1984 President Reagan instituted the first "global gag rule," withholding federal funds from family planning agencies that provide abortion services or information abroad. President Clinton lifted the rule in 1993, and President George W. Bush reinstated the ban once more in 2001.

Document: Ruth Bader Ginsburg, "Some Thoughts on Autonomy and Equality in Relation to *Roe v. Wade.*"
Date: 1985.
Where: North Carolina Law Review.
Significance: This statement by the nation's second woman on the U.S. Supreme Court indicates the opportunities and limits within the abortion landmark.

These remarks contrast two related areas of constitutional adjudication: gender-based classification and reproductive autonomy. In both areas, the Burger Court, in contrast to the Warren Court, has been uncommonly active. The two areas are intimately related in this practical sense: the law's response to questions subsumed under these headings bears pervasively on the situation of women in society. Inevitably, the shape of the law on gender-based classification and reproductive autonomy indicates and influences the opportunity women will have to participate as men's full partners in the nation's social, political, and economic life. Doctrine in the two areas, however, has evolved in discrete compartments. The High Court has analyzed classification by gender under an equal protection/sex discrimination rubric; it has treated reproductive autonomy under a substantive due process/personal autonomy headline not expressly linked to discrimination against women. The Court's gender classification decisions overturning state and federal legislation, in the main, have not provoked large controversy; the Court's initial 1973 abortion decision, *Roe v. Wade*, on the other hand, became and remains a storm center. *Roe v. Wade* sparked public opposition and academic criticism, in part, I believe, because the Court ventured too far in the change it ordered and presented an incomplete justification for its action. I will attempt to explain these twin perspectives on *Roe* later in this Essay. Preliminarily, I will relate why an invitation to speak at Chapel Hill on any topic relating to constitutional law led me to think about gender-based classification coupled with *Roe* and its aftermath. In 1971, just before the Supreme Court's turning-point gender-classification decision in *Reed v. Reed*, and over a year before *Roe v. Wade*, I visited a neighboring institution to participate in a conference on women and the law. I spoke then of the utility of litigation attacking official line-drawing by sex. My comments focused on the chance in the 1970s that courts, through constitutional adjudication, would aid in evening out the rights, responsibilities, and opportunities of women and men. I did not mention the abortion cases then on the dockets of several lower courts—I was not at that time or any other time thereafter personally engaged in reproductive-autonomy litigation. Nonetheless, the most heated questions I received concerned abortion. The questions were pressed by black men. The suggestion, not thinly veiled, was that legislative reform and litigation regarding abortion might have less to do with individual autonomy or discrimination against women than with restricting population growth among oppressed minorities. The strong word "genocide" was uttered more than once. It is a notable irony that, as constitutional law in this domain has unfolded, women who are not poor have achieved access to abortion with relative ease; for poor women, however, a group in which minorities are disproportionately represented, access to abortion is not markedly different from what it was in pre-*Roe* days. I will summarize first the Supreme Court's performance in cases challenging explicit gender-based classification—a development that has encountered no significant backlash—and then turn to the far more turbulent reproductive autonomy area. The Warren Court uncabined the equal protection guarantee in diverse settings, but line drawing by sex was a quarter in which no change occurred in the 1950s and 1960s. From the 1860s until 1971, the record remained unbroken: the Supreme Court rejected virtually every effort to overturn sexbased classification by law. Without offense to the Constitution, for example, women could be kept off juries and could be barred from occupations ranging from lawyer to bartender. In the 1970s overt sex-based classification fell prey to the Burger Court's intervention. Men could not be preferred to women for estate administration purposes, the Court declared in the pivotal *Reed v. Reed* decision. Married women in the military could not be denied fringe benefits—family housing and health care allowances—accorded married men in military service, the High Court held in *Frontiero v. Richardson*. Social security benefits, welfare assistance, and workers' compensation secured by a male's employment must be secured, to the same extent, by a female's employment the Supreme Court ruled in a progression of cases: *Weinberger v. Wiesenfeld, Califano v. Goldfarb, Califano v. Westcott*, and *Wengler v. Druggists Mutual Insurance Co.* Girls are entitled to the same parental support as boys, the Supreme Court stated in *Stanton v. Stanton*. Evidencing its neutrality, the Court declared in

Craig v. Boren that boys must be permitted to buy 3.2 percent beer at the same age as girls and, in *Orr v. Orr*, that alimony could not be retained as a one-way street: a state could compel able men to make payments to women in need only if it also held women of means accountable for payments to men unable to fend for themselves. Louisiana's rule, derived from Napoleon's Civil Code, designating husband head and master of the household, was held in *Kirchberg v. Feenstra* to be offensive to the evolving sex equality principle. However sensible—and noncontroversial—these results, the decisions had a spectacular aspect. The race cases that trooped before the Warren Court could be viewed as moving the federal judiciary onto the course set by the Reconstruction Congress a century earlier in the post-Civil War amendments. No similar foundation, set deliberately by actors in the political arena, can account for the Burger Court sex discrimination. Perhaps for that reason, the Court has proceeded cautiously. It has taken no giant step. In its most recent decision, *Mississippi University for Women v. Hogan*, the High Court recognized the right of men to a nursing school education at an institution maintained by the state for women only. But it earlier had declined to condemn a state property tax advantage reserved for widows, a state statutory rape law penalizing males but not females, and draft registration limited to males. It has formally reserved judgment on the question whether, absent ratification of an equal rights amendment, sex, like race, should rank as a suspect classification.

The Court's gender-based classification precedent impelled acknowledgment of a middle-tier equal protection standard of review, a level of judicial scrutiny demanding more than minimal rationality but less than a near-perfect fit between legislative ends and means. This movement away from the empty-cupboard interpretation of the equal protection principle in relation to sex equality claims largely trailed and mirrored changing patterns in society—most conspicuously, the emergence of the two-career family. The Court's decisions provoked no outraged opposition in legislative chambers. On the contrary, in a key area in which the Court rejected claims of impermissible sex-based classification, Congress indicated a different view, one more sensitive to discrimination against women. The area, significantly in view of the Court's approach to reproductive choice, was pregnancy. In 1974 the Court decided an issue pressed by pregnant school teachers forced to terminate their employment, or take unpaid maternity leave, months before the anticipated birth date. Policies singling out pregnant women for disadvantageous treatment discriminated invidiously on the basis of sex, the teachers argued. The Court bypassed that argument; instead, the Court rested its decision holding mandatory maternity leaves unconstitutional on due process/conclusive presumption reasoning. Some weeks later, the Court held that a state-operated disability income protection plan could exclude normal pregnancy without offense to the equal protection principle. In a statutory setting as well, under Title VII, the Court later ruled, as it earlier had held in a constitutional context, that women unable to work due to pregnancy or childbirth could be excluded from disability coverage. The classifications in these disability cases, according to the Court, were not gender-based on their face, and were not shown to have any sex-discriminatory effect. All "nonpregnant persons," women along with men, the Court pointed out, were treated alike. With respect to Title VII, Congress prospectively overruled the Court in 1978. It amended the statute to state explicitly that classification on the basis of sex includes classification on the basis of pregnancy. That congressional definition is not controlling in constitutional adjudication, but it might stimulate the Court one day to revise its position that regulation governing "pregnant persons" is not sex-based. *Roe v. Wade*, in contrast to decisions involving explicit male/female classification, has occasioned searing criticism of the Court, over a decade of demonstrations, a stream of vituperative mail addressed to Justice Blackmun (the author of the opinion), annual proposals for overruling *Roe* by constitutional amendment, and a variety of measures in Congress and state legislatures to contain or curtail the decision. In 1973, when *Roe* issued, abortion law was in a state of change across the nation. There was a distinct trend in the states, noted by the Court, "toward liberalization of abortion statutes." Several states had adopted the American Law Institute's Model Penal Code approach setting out grounds on which abortion could be justified at any stage of pregnancy; most significantly, the Code included as a permissible ground preservation of the woman's physical or mental health. Four states—New York, Washington, Alaska, and Hawaii—permitted physicians to perform first-trimester abortions with virtually no restrictions. This movement in legislative arenas bore some resemblance to the law revision activity that eventually swept through the states establishing no-fault divorce as the national pattern. The Texas law at issue in *Roe* made it a crime to "procure an abortion" except "by medical advice for the purpose of saving the life of the mother." It was the most extreme prohibition extant. The Court had in close view two pathmarking opinions on reproductive autonomy: first, a 1965 precedent, *Griswold v. Connecticut,* holding inconsistent with personal privacy, somehow sheltered by due process, a state ban on the use of contraceptives even by married couples; second, a 1972 decision, *Eisenstadt v. Baird,* extending *Griswold* to strike down a state prohibition on sales of contraceptives except to married persons by prescription. The Court had already decided *Reed v. Reed,* recognizing the arbitrariness in the 1970s of a once traditional gender-based classification, but it did not further pursue that avenue in *Roe.* The decision in *Roe* appeared to be a stunning victory for the plaintiffs. The Court declared that a woman, guided by the medical judgment of her physician, had a "fundamental" right to abort a pregnancy, a right the Court anchored to a concept of personal autonomy derived from the due process guarantee. The Court then proceeded to define with precision the state regulation of abortion henceforth permissible. The rulings in *Roe,* and in a companion case decided the same day, *Doe v. Bolton,* were stunning in this sense: they called into question the criminal abortion statutes of every state, even those with the least restrictive provisions. *Roe* announced a trimester approach Professor Archibald Cox has described as "read[ing] like a set of hospital rules and regulations." During the first trimester, "the abortion decision and its effectuation must be left to the medical judgment of the pregnant woman's attending physician"; in the next, roughly three-month stage, the state may, if it chooses, require other measures protective of the woman's health. During the final months, "the stage subsequent to viability," the state also may concern itself with an emerging interest, the "potentiality of human life"; at that stage, the state "may, if it chooses, regulate, and even proscribe, abortion except where it is necessary, in appropriate medical judgment, for the preservation of the life or health of the mother." Justice O'Connor, ten years after *Roe,* described the trimester approach as "on a collision course with itself." Advances in medical technology would continue to move *forward* the point at which regulation could be justified as protective of a woman's health, and to move *backward* the point of viability, when the state could proscribe abortions unnecessary to preserve the patient's life or health. The approach, she thought, impelled legislatures to remain *au courant* with changing medical practices and called upon courts to examine legislative judgments, not as jurists applying "neutral principles," but as "science review boards." I earlier observed that, in my judgment, *Roe* ventured too far in the change it ordered. The sweep and detail of the opinion stimulated the mobilization of a right-to-life movement and an attendant reaction in Congress and state legislatures. In place of the trend "toward liberalization of abortion statutes" noted in *Roe,* legislatures adopted measures aimed at minimizing the impact of the 1973 rulings, including notification and consent requirements, prescriptions for the protection of fetal life, and bans on public expenditures for poor women's abortions. Professor Paul Freund explained where he thought the Court went astray in *Roe,* and I agree with his statement. The Court properly invalidated the Texas proscription, he indicated, because "[a] law that absolutely made criminal all kinds and forms of abortion could not stand up; it is not a reasonable accommodation of interests." If *Roe* had left off at that point and not adopted what Professor Freund called a "medical approach," physicians might have been less pleased with the decision, but the legislative trend might have continued in the direction in which it was headed in the early 1970s. "[S]ome of the bitter debate on the issue might have been averted," Professor Freund believed; "[t]he animus against the Court might at least have been diverted to the legislative halls." Overall, he thought that the *Roe* distinctions turning on trimesters and viability of the fetus illustrated a troublesome tendency of the modern Supreme Court under Chief Justices Burger and Warren "to specify by a kind of legislative code the one alternative pattern that will satisfy the Constitution." I commented at the outset that I believe the Court presented an incomplete justification for its action. Academic criticism of *Roe,* charging the Court with reading its own values into the due process clause, might have been less pointed had the Court placed the woman alone, rather than the woman tied to her physician, at the center of its attention. Professor Karst's commentary is indicative of the perspective not developed in the High Court's opinion: he solidly linked abortion prohibitions with discrimination against women. The issue in *Roe,* he wrote, deeply touched and concerned "women's position in society in relation to men." It is not a sufficient answer to charge it all to women's anatomy—a natural, not man-made, phenomenon. Society, not anatomy, "places a greater stigma on unmarried women who become pregnant than on the men who father their children." Society expects, but nature does not command, that "women take the major responsibility . . . for child care" and that they will stay with their children, bearing nurture and support burdens alone, when fathers deny paternity or otherwise refuse to provide care or financial support for unwanted offspring. I do not pretend that, if the Court had added a distinct sex discrimination theme to its medically oriented opinion, the storm *Roe* generated would have been less furious. I appreciate the intense divisions of opinion on the moral question and recognize that abortion today cannot fairly be described as nothing more than birth control delayed. The conflict, however, is not simply one between a fetus' interests and a woman's interests, narrowly conceived, nor is the overriding issue state versus private control of a woman's body for a span of nine months. Also in the balance is a woman's autonomous charge of her full life's course—as Professor Karst put it, her ability to stand in relation to man, society, and the state as an independent, self-sustaining, equal citizen. On several occasions since *Roe* the Court has confronted legislative responses to the decision. With the notable exception of the public funding cases, the Court typically has applied *Roe* to overturn or limit efforts to impede access to abortion. I will not survey in the brief compass of this Essay the Court's series of opinions addressing: regulation of the abortion decisionmaking process; specifications regarding personnel, facilities, and medical procedures; and parental notification and consent requirements in the case of minors. Instead, I will simply highlight the Court's statement last year reaffirming *Roe*'s "basic principle that a woman has a fundamental right to make the highly personal choice whether or not to terminate her pregnancy." In *City of Akron v. Akron Center for Reproductive Health, Inc.,* the Court acknowledged arguments it continues to hear that *Roe* "erred in interpreting the Constitution." Nonetheless, the Court declared it would adhere to *Roe* because "*stare decisis,* while perhaps never entirely persuasive on a constitutional question, is a doctrine that demands respect in a society governed by the rule of law." I turn, finally, to the plight of the woman who lacks resources to finance privately implementation of her personal choice to terminate her pregnancy. The hostile reaction to *Roe* has trained largely on her. Some observers speculated that the seven-two judgment in *Roe* was motivated at least in part by pragmatic considerations—population control concerns, the specter of coat hanger abortions, and concerns about unwanted children born to impoverished women. I recalled earlier the view that the demand for open access to abortions had as its real purpose suppressing minorities. In a set of 1977 decisions, however, the Court upheld state denial of medical expense reimbursement or hospital facilities for abortions sought by indigent women. Moreover, in a 1980 decision, *Harris v. McRae*, the Court found no constitutional infirmity in the Hyde Amendment, which excluded even medically necessary abortions from Medicaid coverage. After these decisions, the Court was accused of sensitivity only to the Justices' own social milieu—"of creating a middle-class right to abortion." The argument for constitutionally mandated public assistance to effectuate the poor woman's choice ran along these lines. Accepting that our Constitution's Bill of Rights places restraints, not affirmative obligations, on government, counsel for the impoverished women stressed that childbirth was publicly subsidized. As long as the government paid for childbirth, the argument proceeded, public funding could not be denied for abortion, often a safer and always a far less expensive course, short and long run. By paying for childbirth but not abortion, the complainants maintained, government increased spending and intruded upon or steered a choice *Roe* had ranked as a woman's "fundamental" right. The Court responded that, like other individual rights secured by the Constitution, the right to abortion is indeed a negative right. Government could not intervene by blocking a woman's utilization of her own resources to effectuate her decision. It could not "'impose its will by force of law.'" But *Roe* did not demand government neutrality, the Court reasoned; it left room for substantive government control to this extent: Action "deemed in the public interest"—in this instance, protection of the potential life of the fetus—could be promoted by encouraging childbirth in preference to abortion. Financial need alone, under the Court's jurisprudence, does not identify a class of persons whose complaints of disadvantageous treatment attract close scrutiny. Generally, constitutional claims to government benefits on behalf of the poor have prevailed only when tied to another bark—a right to travel interstate, discrimination because of out-of-wedlock birth, or gender-based discrimination. If the Court had acknowledged a woman's equality aspect, not simply a patient-physician autonomy constitutional dimension to the abortion issue, a majority perhaps might have seen the public assistance cases as instances in which, borrowing a phrase from Justice Stevens, the sovereign had violated its "duty to govern impartially." I have tried to discuss some features of constitutional adjudication concerning sex equality, in relation to the autonomy and equal-regard values involved in cases on abortion. I have done so tentatively and with trepidation. *Roe v. Wade* is a decision I approached gingerly in prior comment; until now I have limited my remarks to a brief description of what others have said. While I claim no original contribution, I have endeavored here to state my own reflections and concerns. *Roe,* I believe, would have been more acceptable as a judicial decision if it had not gone beyond a ruling on the extreme statute before the Court. The political process was moving in the early 1970s, not swiftly enough for advocates of quick, complete change, but majoritarian institutions were listening and acting. Heavy-handed judicial intervention was difficult to justify and appears to have provoked, not resolved, conflict. The public funding of abortion decisions appear incongruous following so soon after the intrepid 1973 rulings. The Court did not adequately explain why the "fundamental" choice principle and trimester approach embraced in *Roe* did not bar the sovereign, at least at the previability stage of pregnancy, from taking sides. Overall, the Court's *Roe* positions in weakened, I believe, by the opinion's concentration on a medically approved autonomy idea, to the exclusion of a constitutionally based sex-equality perspective. I understand the view that for political reasons the reproductive autonomy controversy should be isolated from the general debate on equal rights, responsibilities, and opportunities for women and men. I expect, however, that organized and determined opposing efforts to inform and persuade the public on the abortion issue will continue through the 1980s. In that process there will be opportunities for elaborating in public forums the equal-regard conception of women's claims to reproductive choice uncoerced and unsteered by government.

SOURCE: Ruth Bader Ginsburg, "Some Thoughts on Autonomy and Equality in Relation to *Roe v. Wade*." *North Carolina Law Review* 375 (January 1985): 63 (footnotes omitted). Reprinted with permission of Justice Ruth Bader Ginsburg.

DOCUMENT ANALYSIS

Ruth Bader Ginsburg's perspective is notable both for its content as well as its timing. Before her tenure on the Supreme Court, Judge Ginsburg worked on sex discrimination cases, although, as she reports here, not on abortion-related cases. Her unique perspective as an advocate for women's equality is valuable in its own right, and significant because it is offered just as *Roe* is unraveling and before she is appointed to the Supreme Court.

Ginsburg maintains that the weakness of *Roe* lies in the Court's overreach into legislating medical procedures and in its theoretical underpinnings. Her argument that the Court ventured too far into abortion policy through the trimester system is consistent with the views of many abortion opponents of that era, but for her articulates a concern that the Court's reach may be the very cause of the antiabortion backlash of the 1980s. Had the Court simply ruled the Texas statute unconstitutional, and left the rest of the states to their reform paths, she argues that the social movement reaction to the decision could have been truncated.

In justifying its ruling, Ginsburg also argues the Court made a mistake. There, she argues the Court did not go far enough: the decision weights fetal and state interests against the women's autonomy rights, but misses the larger question of how fertility control relates to women's overall place in society. For Ginsburg, this misstep is equally problematic, and creates an opportunity for legislatures to deny abortion funding rather than view funding as necessary for all women to fully exercise this right of self-actualization. A sex-equality justification for overturning the Texas statute would have put women on firm footing constitutionally, while the balancing act constructed by *Roe* made women vulnerable to changes in technology and public sympathy for abortion rights.

Ginsburg's views on abortion jurisprudence would gain far greater attention when President Clinton nominated her to the Supreme Court in 1993. At her Senate confirmation hearings, Ginsburg acknowledged her support for the right of privacy but refused to fully articulate her view on many controversial subjects, including abortion. After a smooth 96–3 Senate vote confirming her position on the Court, Ginsburg assumed that role on August 10, 1993, where she has voted consistently to uphold abortion rights.

Document: Excerpt from *Webster v. Reproductive Health Services.*

Date: July 3, 1989.

Where: U.S. Supreme Court.

Significance: Webster marks a significant turning point in the Court's abortion rulings. Chief Justice Rehnquist, who announced the ruling, was in the dissent in *Roe v. Wade.* Now in the majority, his view of expanded authority of states to regulate abortion had gained ground by 1989.

CHIEF JUSTICE REHNQUIST announced the judgment of the Court and delivered the opinion of the Court with respect to Parts I, II-A, II-B, and II-C, and an opinion with respect to Parts II-D and III, in which JUSTICE WHITE and JUSTICE KENNEDY join.

This appeal concerns the constitutionality of a Missouri statute regulating the performance of abortions. The United States Court of Appeals for the Eighth Circuit struck down several provisions of the statute on the ground that they violated this Court's decision in *Roe v. Wade,* 410 U.S. 113 (1973), and cases following it. We noted probable jurisdiction, 488 U.S. 1003 (1989), and now reverse.

I

In June, 1986, the Governor of Missouri signed into law Missouri Senate Committee Substitute for House Bill No. 1596 (hereinafter Act or statute), which amended existing state law concerning unborn children and abortions. The Act consisted of 20 provisions, 5 of which are now before the Court. The first provision, or preamble, contains "findings" by the state legislature that "[t]he life of each human being begins at conception," and that "unborn children have protectable interests in life, health, and wellbeing." Mo.Rev. Stat. §§ 1.205.1(1), (2) (1986).

William and Karen Bell, parents of Becky Bell, an Indiana teen who died from an illegal abortion. Getty Images.

The Act further requires that all Missouri laws be interpreted to provide unborn children with the same rights enjoyed by other persons, subject to the Federal Constitution and this Court's precedents. § 1.205.2. Among its other provisions, the Act requires that, prior to performing an abortion on any woman whom a physician has reason to believe is 20 or more weeks pregnant, the physician ascertain whether the fetus is viable by performing

> such medical examinations and tests as are necessary to make a finding of the gestational age, weight, and lung maturity of the unborn child.

§ 188. 029. The Act also prohibits the use of public employees and facilities to perform or assist abortions not necessary to save the mother's life, and it prohibits the use of public funds, employees, or facilities for the purpose of "encouraging or counseling" a woman to have an abortion not necessary to save her life. §§ 188.205, 188.210, 188.215.

In July, 1986, five health professionals employed by the State and two nonprofit corporations brought this class action in the United States District Court for the Western District of Missouri to challenge the constitutionality of the Missouri statute. Plaintiffs, appellees in this Court, sought declaratory and injunctive relief on the ground that certain statutory provisions violated the First, Fourth, Ninth, and Fourteenth Amendments to the Federal Constitution. App. A9. They asserted violations of various rights, including the "privacy rights of pregnant women seeking abortions"; the "woman's right to an abortion"; the "righ[t] to privacy in the physician-patient relationship"; the physician's "righ[t] to practice medicine"; the pregnant woman's "right to life due to inherent risks involved in childbirth"; and the woman's right to "receive . . . adequate medical advice and treatment" concerning abortions. *Id.* at A17-A19.

Plaintiffs filed this suit on their own behalf and on behalf of the entire class consisting of facilities and Missouri licensed physicians or other health care professionals offering abortion services or pregnancy counseling and on behalf of the entire class of pregnant females seeking abortion services or pregnancy counseling within the State of Missouri.

Id. at A13. The two nonprofit corporations are Reproductive Health Services, which offers family planning and gynecological services to the public, including abortion services up to 22 weeks "gestational age," and Planned Parenthood of Kansas City, which provides abortion services up to 14 weeks gestational age. *Id.* at A9-A10. The individual plaintiffs are three physicians, one nurse, and a social worker. All are "public employees" at "public facilities" in Missouri, and they are paid for their services with "public funds," as those terms are defined by § 188.200. The individual plaintiffs, within the scope of their public employment, encourage and counsel pregnant women to have nontherapeutic abortions. To of the physicians perform abortions. App. A54-A55.

Several weeks after the complaint was filed, the District Court temporarily restrained enforcement of several provisions of the Act. Following a 3-day trial in December, 1986, the District Court declared seven provisions of the Act unconstitutional and enjoined their enforcement. 662 F.Supp. 407 (WD Mo.1987). These provisions included the preamble, § 1.205; the "informed consent" provision, which required physicians to inform the pregnant woman of certain facts before performing an abortion, § 188.039; the requirement that post-16-week abortions be performed only in hospitals, § 188.025; the mandated tests to determine viability, § 188.029; and the prohibition on the use of public funds, employees, and facilities to perform or assist nontherapeutic abortions, and the restrictions on the use of public funds, employees, and facilities to encourage or counsel women to have such abortions, §§ 188.205, 188.210, 188.215. *Id.* at 430.

The Court of Appeals for the Eighth Circuit affirmed, with one exception not relevant to this appeal. 851 F.2d 1071 (1988). The Court of Appeals determined that Missouri's declaration that life begins at conception was "simply an impermissible state adoption of a theory of when life begins to justify its abortion regulations." *Id.* at 1076. Relying on *Colautti v. Franklin,* 439 U.S. 379, 388–389 (1979), it further held that the requirement that physicians perform viability tests was an unconstitutional legislative intrusion on a matter of medical skill and judgment. 851 F.2d at 1074–1075. The Court of Appeals invalidated Missouri's prohibition on the use of public facilities and employees to perform or assist abortions not necessary to save the mother's life. *Id.* at 1081–1083. It distinguished our decisions in *Harris v. McRae,* 448 U.S. 297 (1980), and *Maher v. Roe,* 432 U.S. 464 (1977), on the ground that

> "[t]here is a fundamental difference between providing direct funding to effect the abortion decision and allowing staff physicians to perform abortions at an existing publicly owned hospital."

851 F.2d at 1081, quoting *Nyberg v. City of Virginia,* 667 F.2d 754, 758 (CA8 1982), *appeal dism'd,* 462 U.S. 1125 (1983). The Court of Appeals struck down the provision prohibiting the use of public funds for "encouraging or counseling" women to have nontherapeutic abortions, for the reason that this provision was both overly vague and inconsistent with the right to an abortion enunciated in *Roe v. Wade.* 851 F.2d at 1077–1080. The court also invalidated the hospitalization requirement for 16-week abortions, *id.* at 1073–1074, and the prohibition on the use of public employees and facilities for abortion counseling, *id.* at 1077–1080, but the State has not appealed those parts of the judgment below. *See* Juris. Statement I-II.

II

Decision of this case requires us to address four sections of the Missouri Act: (a) the preamble; (b) the prohibition on the use of public facilities or employees to perform abortions; (c) the prohibition on public funding of abortion counseling; and (d) the requirement that physicians conduct viability tests prior to performing abortions. We address these *seriatim.*

A

The Act's preamble, as noted, sets forth "findings" by the Missouri legislature that "[t]he life of each human being begins at conception," and that "[u]nborn children have protectable interests in life, health, and wellbeing." Mo.Rev.Stat. §§ 1.205.1(1), (2) (1986). The Act then mandates that state laws be interpreted to provide unborn children with "all the rights, privileges, and immunities available to other persons, citizens, and residents of this state," subject to the Constitution and this Court's precedents. § 1.205.2. In invalidating the preamble, the Court of Appeals relied on this Court's dictum that "'a State may not adopt one theory of when life begins to justify its regulation of abortions.'" 851 F.2d at 1075–1076, quoting *Akron v. Akron Center for Reproductive Health, Inc.,* 462 U.S. 416, 444 (1983), in turn citing *Roe v. Wade,* 410 U.S. at 159–162. It rejected Missouri's claim that the preamble was "abortion-neutral," and "merely determine[d] when life begins in a nonabortion context, a traditional state prerogative." 851 F.2d at 1076. The court thought that "[t]he only plausible inference" from the fact that "every remaining section of the bill save one regulates the performance of abortions" was that "the state intended its abortion regulations to be understood against the backdrop of its theory of life." *Ibid.*

The State contends that the preamble itself is precatory, and imposes no substantive restrictions on abortions, and that appellees therefore do not have standing to challenge it. Brief for Appellants 21–24. Appellees, on the other hand, insist that the preamble is an operative part of the Act intended to guide the interpretation of other provisions of the Act. Brief for Appellees 19–23. They maintain, for example, that the preamble's definition of life may prevent physicians in public hospitals from dispensing certain forms of contraceptives, such as the intrauterine device. *Id.* at 22.

In our view, the Court of Appeals misconceived the meaning of the *Akron* dictum, which was only that a State could not "justify" an abortion regulation otherwise invalid under *Roe v. Wade* on the ground that it embodied the State's view about when life begins. Certainly the preamble does not, by its terms, regulate abortion or any other aspect of appellees' medical practice. The Court has emphasized that *Roe v. Wade* "implies no limitation on the authority of a State to make a value judgment favoring childbirth over abortion." *Maher v. Roe*, 432 U.S. at 474. The preamble can be read simply to express that sort of value judgment.

We think the extent to which the preamble's language might be used to interpret other state statutes or regulations is something that only the courts of Missouri can definitively decide. State law has offered protections to unborn children in tort and probate law, *see Roe v. Wade, supra,* at 161–162, and § 1.205.2 can be interpreted to do no more than that. What we have, then, is much the same situation that the Court confronted in *Alabama State Federation of Labor v. McAdory,* 325 U.S. 450 (1945). As in that case:

We are thus invited to pass upon the constitutional validity of a state statute which has not yet been applied or threatened to be applied by the state courts to petitioners or others in the manner anticipated. Lacking any authoritative construction of the statute by the state courts, without which no constitutional question arises, and lacking the authority to give such a controlling construction ourselves, and with a record which presents no concrete set of facts to which the statute is to be applied, the case is plainly not one to be disposed of by the declaratory judgment procedure.

Id. at 460. It will be time enough for federal courts to address the meaning of the preamble should it be applied to restrict the activities of appellees in some concrete way. Until then, this Court is not empowered to decide . . . abstract propositions, or to declare, for the government of future cases, principles or rules of law which cannot affect the result a to the thing in issue in the case before it.

. . . We therefore need not pass on the constitutionality of the Act's preamble.

B

Section 188.210 provides that

[i]t shall be unlawful for any public employee within the scope of his employment to perform or assist an abortion, not necessary to save the life of the mother,

while § 188.215 makes it

unlawful for any public facility to be used for the purpose of performing or assisting an abortion not necessary to save the life of the mother.

The Court of Appeals held that these provisions contravened this Court's abortion decisions. 851 F.2d at 1082–1083. We take the contrary view.

As we said earlier this Term in *DeShaney v. Winnebago County Dept. of Social Services*, 489 U.S. 189, 196 (1989):

> [O]ur cases have recognized that the Due Process Clauses generally confer no affirmative right to governmental aid, even where such aid may be necessary to secure life, liberty, or property interests of which the government itself may not deprive the individual.

In *Maher v. Roe, supra*, the Court upheld a Connecticut welfare regulation under which Medicaid recipients received payments for medical services related to childbirth, but not for nontherapeutic abortions. The Court rejected the claim that this unequal subsidization of childbirth and abortion was impermissible under *Roe v. Wade*. As the Court put it: The Connecticut regulation before us is different in kind from the laws invalidated in our previous abortion decisions. The Connecticut regulation places no obstacles—absolute or otherwise—in the pregnant woman's path to an abortion. An indigent woman who desires an abortion suffers no disadvantage as a consequence of Connecticut's decision to fund childbirth; she continues as before to be dependent on private sources for the service she desires. The State may have made childbirth a more attractive alternative, thereby influencing the woman's decision, but it has imposed no restriction on access to abortions that was not already there. The indigency that may make it difficult—and in some cases, perhaps, impossible—for some women to have abortions is neither created nor in any way affected by the Connecticut regulation.

432 U.S. at 474. Relying on *Maher*, the Court in *Poelker v. Doe*, 432 U.S. 519, 521 (1977), held that the city of St. Louis committed no constitutional violation . . . in electing, as a policy choice, to provide publicly financed hospital services for childbirth without providing corresponding services for nontherapeutic abortions.

More recently, in *Harris v. McRae*, 448 U.S. 297 (1980), the Court upheld "the most restrictive version of the Hyde Amendment," *id*. at 325, n. 27, which withheld from States federal funds under the Medicaid program to reimburse the costs of abortions, "'except where the life of the mother would be endangered if the fetus were carried to term.'" *Ibid*. (quoting Pub.L. 94–439, § 209, 90 Stat. 1434). As in *Maher* and *Poelker*, the Court required only a showing that Congress' authorization of "reimbursement for medically necessary services generally, but not for certain medically necessary abortions" was rationally related to the legitimate governmental goal of encouraging childbirth. 448 U.S. at 325.

The Court of Appeals distinguished these cases on the ground that [t]o prevent access to a public facility does more than demonstrate a political choice in favor of childbirth; it clearly narrows, and in some cases forecloses, the availability of abortion to women.

851 F.2d at 1081. The court reasoned that the ban on the use of public facilities could prevent a woman's chosen doctor from performing an abortion because of his unprivileged status at other hospitals or because a private hospital adopted a similar anti-abortion stance.

Ibid. It also thought that "[s]uch a rule could increase the cost of obtaining an abortion and delay the timing of it as well." *Ibid*.

We think that this analysis is much like that which we rejected in *Maher*, *Poelker*, and *McRae*. As in those cases, the State's decision here to use public facilities and staff to encourage childbirth over abortion "places no governmental obstacle in the path of a woman who chooses to terminate her pregnancy." *McRae*, 448 U.S. at 315. Just as Congress' refusal to fund abortions in *McRae* left an indigent woman with at least the same range of choice in deciding whether to obtain a medically necessary abortion as she would have had if Congress had chosen to subsidize no health care costs at all,

id. at 317, Missouri's refusal to allow public employees to perform abortions in public hospitals leaves a pregnant woman with the same choices as if the State had chosen not to operate any public hospitals at all. The challenged provisions only restrict a woman's ability to obtain an abortion to the extent that she chooses to use a physician affiliated with a public hospital. This circumstance is more easily remedied, and thus considerably less burdensome, than indigency, which "may make it difficult—and in some cases, perhaps, impossible—for some women to have abortions" without public funding. *Maher*, 432 U.S. at 474. Having held that the State's refusal to fund abortions does not violate *Roe v. Wade*, it strains logic to reach a contrary result for the use of public facilities and employees. If the State may "make a value judgment favoring childbirth over abortion and . . . implement that judgment by the allocation of public funds," *Maher, supra*, at 474, surely it may do so through the allocation of other public resources, such as hospitals and medical staff.

The Court of Appeals sought to distinguish our cases on the additional ground that "[t]he evidence here showed that all of the public facility's costs in providing abortion services are recouped when the patient pays." 851 F.2d at 1083. Absent any expenditure of public funds, the court thought that Missouri was "expressing" more than "its preference for childbirth over abortions," but rather was creating an "obstacle to exercise of the right to choose an abortion [that could not] stand absent a compelling state interest." *Ibid.* We disagree.

"Constitutional concerns are greatest," we said in *Maher, supra*, at 476, when the State attempts to impose its will by the force of law; the State's power to encourage actions deemed to be in the public interest is necessarily far broader.

Nothing in the Constitution requires States to enter or remain in the business of performing abortions. Nor, as appellees suggest, do private physicians and their patients have some kind of constitutional right of access to public facilities for the performance of abortions. Brief for Appellees 46–47. Indeed, if the State does recoup all of its costs in performing abortions, and no state subsidy, direct or indirect, is available, it is difficult to see how any procreational choice is burdened by the State's ban on the use of its facilities or employees for performing abortions.

Maher, Poelker, and *McRae* all support the view that the State need not commit any resources to facilitating abortions, even if it can turn a profit by doing so. In *Poelker*, the suit was filed by an indigent who could not afford to pay for an abortion, but the ban on the performance of nontherapeutic abortions in city-owned hospitals applied whether or not the pregnant woman could pay. 432 U.S. at 520; *id.* at 524 (BRENNAN, J., dissenting). The Court emphasized that the mayor's decision to prohibit abortions in city hospitals was "subject to public debate and approval or disapproval at the polls," and that the Constitution does not forbid a State or city, pursuant to democratic processes, from expressing a preference for normal childbirth, as St. Louis has done.

Id. at 521. Thus we uphold the Act's restrictions on the use of public employees and facilities for the performance or assistance of nontherapeutic abortions.

C

The Missouri Act contains three provisions relating to "encouraging or counseling a woman to have an abortion not necessary to save her life." Section 188.205 states that no public funds can be used for this purpose; § 188.210 states that public employees cannot, within the scope of their employment, engage in such speech; and § 188.215 forbids such speech in public facilities. The Court of Appeals did not consider § 188.205 separately from §§ 188.210 and 188.215. It held that all three of these provisions were unconstitutionally vague, and that the ban on using public funds, employees, and facilities to encourage or counsel a woman to have an abortion is an unacceptable infringement of the woman's fourteenth amendment right to choose an abortion after receiving the medical information necessary to exercise the right knowingly and intelligently. 851 F.2d at 1079.

Missouri has chosen only to appeal the Court of Appeals' invalidation of the public funding provision, § 188.205. *See* Juris. Statement I-II. A threshold question is whether this provision reaches primary conduct, or whether it is simply an instruction to the State's fiscal officers not to allocate funds for abortion counseling. We accept, for purposes of decision, the State's claim that § 188.205 "is not directed at the conduct of any physician or health care provider, private or public," but "is directed solely at those persons responsible for expending public funds." Brief for Appellants 43.

Appellees contend that they are not "adversely" affected under the State's interpretation of § 188.205, and therefore that there is no longer a case or controversy before us on this question. Brief for Appellees 31–32. Plaintiffs are masters of their complaints, and remain so at the appellate stage of a litigation. *See Caterpillar Inc. v. Williams*, 482 U.S. 386, 398–399 (1987). A majority of the Court agrees with appellees that the controversy over § 188.205 is now moot, because appellees' argument amounts to a decision to no longer seek a declaratory judgment that § 188.205 is unconstitutional and accompanying declarative relief. *See Deakins v. Monaghan*, 484 U.S. 193, 199–201 (1988); *United States v. Munsingwear, Inc.*, 340 U.S. 36, 39–40 (1950). We accordingly direct the Court of Appeals to vacate the judgment of the District Court with instructions to dismiss the relevant part of the complaint. *Deakins*, 484 U.S. at 200.

Because this [dispute] was rendered moot in part by [appellees'] willingness permanently to withdraw their equitable claims from their federal action, a dismissal with prejudice is indicated.

Ibid.

D

Section 188.029 of the Missouri Act provides:

Before a physician performs an abortion on a woman he has reason to believe is carrying an unborn child of twenty or more weeks gestational age, the physician shall first determine if the unborn child is viable by using and exercising that degree of care, skill, and proficiency commonly exercised by the ordinarily skillful, careful, and prudent physician engaged in similar practice under the same or similar conditions. In making this determination of viability, the physician shall perform or cause to be performed such medical examinations and tests as are necessary to make a finding of the gestational age, weight, and lung maturity of the unborn child and shall enter such findings and determination of viability in the medical record of the mother.

As with the preamble, the parties disagree over the meaning of this statutory provision. The State emphasizes the language of the first sentence, which speaks in terms of the physician's determination of viability being made by the standards of ordinary skill in the medical profession. Brief for Appellants 32–35. Appellees stress the language of the second sentence, which prescribes such "tests as are necessary" to make a finding of gestational age, fetal weight, and lung maturity. Brief for Appellees 26–30.

The Court of Appeals read § 188.029 as requiring that, after 20 weeks, "doctors *must* perform tests to find gestational age, fetal weight and lung maturity." 851 F.2d at 1075, n. 5. The court indicated that the tests needed to determine fetal weight at 20 weeks are "unreliable and inaccurate," and would add $125 to $250 to the cost of an abortion. *Ibid*. It also stated that amniocentesis, the only method available to determine lung maturity, is contrary to accepted medical practice until 28–30 weeks of gestation, expensive, and imposes significant health risks for both the pregnant woman and the fetus.

Ibid.

We must first determine the meaning of § 188.029 under Missouri law. Our usual practice is to defer to the lower court's construction of a state statute, but we believe the Court of Appeals has "fallen into plain error" in this case . . .

"In expounding a statute, we must not be guided by a single sentence or member of a sentence, but look to the provisions of the whole law, and to its object and policy." . . . The Court of Appeals' interpretation also runs "afoul of the well-established principle that statutes will be interpreted to avoid constitutional difficulties." *Frisby, supra*, at 483.

We think the viability testing provision makes sense only if the second sentence is read to require only those tests that are useful to making subsidiary findings as to viability. If we construe this provision to require a physician to perform those tests needed to make the three specified findings *in all circumstances*, including when the physician's reasonable professional judgment indicates that the tests would be irrelevant to determining viability or even dangerous to the mother and the fetus, the second sentence of § 188.029 would conflict with the first sentence's *requirement* that a physician apply his reasonable professional skill and judgment. It would also be incongruous to read this provision, especially the word "necessary," to require the performance of tests irrelevant to the expressed statutory purpose of determining viability. It thus seems clear to us that the Court of Appeals' construction of § 188.029 violates well-accepted canons of statutory interpretation used in the Missouri courts, *see State ex rel. Stern Brothers & Co. v. Stilley*, 337 S.W.2d 934, 939 (Mo.1960) ("The basic rule of statutory construction is to first seek the legislative intention, and to effectuate it if possible, and the law favors constructions which harmonize with reason, and which tend to avoid unjust, absurd, unreasonable or confiscatory results, or oppression"); *Bell v. Mid-Century Ins. Co.*, 750 S.W.2d 708, 710 (Mo.App.1988) ("Interpreting the phrase literally would produce an absurd result, which the Legislature is strongly presumed not to have intended"), which JUSTICE BLACKMUN ignores. Post at 545–546.

The viability testing provision of the Missouri Act is concerned with promoting the State's interest in potential human life, rather than in maternal health. Section 188.029 creates what is essentially a presumption of viability at 20 weeks, which the physician must rebut with tests indicating that the fetus is not viable prior to performing an abortion. It also directs the physician's determination as to viability by specifying consideration, if feasible, of gestational age, fetal weight, and lung capacity. The District Court found that "the medical evidence is uncontradicted that a 20-week fetus is *not* viable," and that "23 ½ to 24 weeks gestation is the earliest point in pregnancy where a reasonable possibility of viability exists."

662 F.Supp. at 420. But it also found that there may be a 4-week error in estimating gestational age, *id.* at 421, which supports testing at 20 weeks.

In *Roe v. Wade,* the Court recognized that the State has "important and legitimate" interests in protecting maternal health and in the potentiality of human life. 410 U.S. at 162. During the second trimester, the State "may, if it chooses, regulate the abortion procedure in ways that are reasonably related to maternal health." *Id.* at 164. After viability, when the State's interest in potential human life was held to become compelling, the State may, if it chooses, regulate, and even proscribe, abortion except where it is necessary, in appropriate medical judgment, for the preservation of the life or health of the mother.

Id. at 165.

In *Colautti v. Franklin,* 439 U.S. 379 (1979), upon which appellees rely, the Court held that a Pennsylvania statute regulating the standard of care to be used by a physician performing an abortion of a possibly viable fetus was void for vagueness. *Id.* at 390–401. But in the course of reaching that conclusion, the Court reaffirmed its earlier statement in *Planned Parenthood of Central Mo. v. Danforth,* 428 U.S. 52, 64 (1976), that "the determination of whether a particular fetus is viable is, and must be, a matter for the judgment of the responsible attending physician."

439 U.S. at 396. JUSTICE BLACKMUN, *post* at 545, n. 6, ignores he statement in *Colautti* that neither the legislature nor the courts may proclaim one of the elements entering into the ascertainment of viability—be it weeks of gestation or fetal weight or any other single factor—as the determinant of when the State has a compelling interest in the life or health of the fetus.

439 U.S. at 388–389. To the extent that § 188.029 regulates the method for determining viability, it undoubtedly does superimpose state regulation on the medical determination whether a particular fetus is viable. The Court of Appeals and the District Court thought it unconstitutional for this reason. 851 F.2d at 1074–1075; 662 F.Supp. at 423. To the extent that the viability tests increase the cost of what are in fact second-trimester abortions, their validity may also be questioned under *Akron,* 462 U.S. at 434–435, where the Court held that a requirement that second-trimester abortions must be performed in hospitals was invalid because it substantially increased the expense of those procedures.

We think that the doubt cast upon the Missouri statute by these cases is not so much a flaw in the statute as it is a reflection of the fact that the rigid trimester analysis of the course of a pregnancy enunciated in *Roe* has resulted in subsequent cases like *Colautti* and *Akron* making constitutional law in this area a virtual Procrustean bed. Statutes specifying elements of informed consent to be provided abortion patients, for example, were invalidated if they were thought to "structur[e] . . . the dialogue between the woman and her physician." *Thornburgh v. American College of Obstetricians and Gynecologists,* 476 U.S. 747, 763 (1986). As the dissenters in *Thornburgh* pointed out, such a statute would have been sustained under any traditional standard of judicial review, *id.* at 802 (WHITE, J., dissenting), or for any other surgical procedure except abortion. *Id.* at 783 (Burger, C.J., dissenting).

Stare decisis is a cornerstone of our legal system, but it has less power in constitutional cases, where, save for constitutional amendments, this Court is the only body able to make needed changes. *See United States v. Scott,* 437 U.S. 82, 101 (1978). We have not refrained from reconsideration of a prior construction of the Constitution that has proved "unsound in principle and unworkable in practice." . . . We think the *Roe* trimester framework falls into that category.

In the first place, the rigid *Roe* framework is hardly consistent with the notion of a Constitution cast in general terms, as ours is, and usually speaking in general principles, as ours does. The key elements of the *Roe* framework—trimesters and viability—are not found in the text of the Constitution, or in any place else one would expect to find a constitutional principle. Since the bounds of the inquiry are essentially indeterminate, the result has been a web of legal rules that have become increasingly intricate, resembling a code of regulations rather than a body of constitutional doctrine. AS JUSTICE WHITE has put it, the trimester framework has left this Court to serve as the country's "*ex officio* medical board with powers to approve or disapprove medical and operative practices and standards throughout the United States." *Planned Parenthood of Central Mo. v. Danforth*, 428 U.S. at 99 (opinion concurring in part and dissenting in part). Cf. *Garcia, supra*, at 547.

In the second place, we do not see why the State's interest in protecting potential human life should come into existence only at the point of viability, and that there should therefore be a rigid line allowing state regulation after viability but prohibiting it before viability. The dissenters in *Thornburgh*, writing in the context of the *Roe* trimester analysis, would have recognized this fact by positing against the "fundamental right" recognized in *Roe* the State's "compelling interest" in protecting potential human life throughout pregnancy. "[T]he State's interest, if compelling after viability, is equally compelling before viability." *Thornburgh*, 476 U.S. at 795 (WHITE, J., dissenting); *see id.* at 828 (O'CONNOR, J., dissenting) ("State has compelling interests in ensuring maternal health and in protecting potential human life, and these interests exist 'throughout pregnancy'") (citation omitted).

The tests that § 188.029 requires the physician to perform are designed to determine viability. The State here has chosen viability as the point at which its interest in potential human life must be safeguarded. *See* Mo.Rev.Stat. § 188.030 (1986) ("No abortion of a viable unborn child shall be performed unless necessary to preserve the life or health of the woman"). It is true that the tests in question increase the expense of abortion, and regulate the discretion of the physician in determining the viability of the fetus. Since the tests will undoubtedly show in many cases that the fetus is not viable, the tests will have been performed for what were, in fact, second-trimester abortions. But we are satisfied that the requirement of these tests permissibly furthers the State's interest in protecting potential human life, and we therefore believe § 188.029 to be constitutional.

JUSTICE BLACKMUN takes us to task for our failure to join in a "great issues" debate as to whether the Constitution includes an "unenumerated" general right to privacy as recognized in cases such as *Griswold v. Connecticut*, 381 U.S. 479 (1965), and *Roe*. But *Griswold v. Connecticut*, unlike *Roe*, did not purport to adopt a whole framework, complete with detailed rules and distinctions, to govern the cases in which the asserted liberty interest would apply. As such, it was far different from the opinion, if not the holding, of *Roe v. Wade*, which sought to establish a constitutional framework for judging state regulation of abortion during the entire term of pregnancy. That framework sought to deal with areas of medical practice traditionally subject to state regulation, and it sought to balance once and for all by reference only to the calendar the claims of the State to protect the fetus as a form of human life against the claims of a woman to decide for herself whether or not to abort a fetus she was carrying. The experience of the Court in applying *Roe v. Wade* in later cases, *see supra* at 518, n. 15, suggests to us that there is wisdom in not unnecessarily attempting to elaborate the abstract differences between a "fundamental right" to abortion, as the Court described it in *Akron*, 462 U.S. at 420, n. 1, a "limited fundamental constitutional right," which JUSTICE BLACKMUN today treats *Roe* as having established, *post* at 555, or a liberty interest protected by the Due Process Clause, which we believe it to be. The Missouri testing requirement here is reasonably designed to ensure that abortions are not performed where the fetus is viable—an end which all concede is legitimate—and that is sufficient to sustain its constitutionality.

JUSTICE BLACKMUN also accuses us, *inter alia,* of cowardice and illegitimacy in dealing with "the most politically divisive domestic legal issue of our time." *Post* at 559. There is no doubt that our holding today will allow some governmental regulation of abortion that would have been prohibited under the language of cases such as *Colautti v. Franklin*, 439 U.S. 379 (1979), and *Akron v. Akron Center for Reproductive Health, Inc., supra*. But the goal of constitutional adjudication is surely not to remove inexorably "politically divisive" issues from the ambit of the legislative process, whereby the people through their elected representatives deal with matters of concern to them. The goal of constitutional adjudication is to hold true the balance between that which the Constitution puts beyond the reach of the democratic process and that which it does not. We think we have done that today. JUSTICE BLACKMUN's suggestion, post at 538, 557–558, that legislative bodies, in a Nation where more than half of our population is women, will treat our decision today as an invitation to enact abortion regulation reminiscent of the dark ages not only misreads our views but does scant justice to those who serve in such bodies and the people who elect them.

III

Both appellants and the United States as *Amicus Curiae* have urged that we overrule our decision in *Roe v. Wade*. Brief for Appellants 12–18; Brief for United States as *Amicus Curiae* 8–24. The facts of the present case, however, differ from those at issue in *Roe*. Here, Missouri has determined that viability is the point at which its interest in potential human life must be safeguarded. In *Roe*, on the other hand, the Texas statute criminalized the performance of *all* abortions, except when the mother's life was at stake. 410 U.S. at 117–118. This case therefore affords us no occasion to revisit the holding of *Roe*, which was that the Texas statute unconstitutionally infringed the right to an abortion derived from the Due Process Clause, *id.* at 164, and we leave it undisturbed. To the extent indicated in our opinion, we would modify and narrow *Roe* and succeeding cases.

Because none of the challenged provisions of the Missouri Act properly before us conflict with the Constitution, the judgment of the Court of Appeals is *Reversed*.

JUSTICE O'CONNOR, concurring in part and concurring in the judgment.

I concur in Parts I, II-A, II-B, and II-C of the Court's opinion.

I

Nothing in the record before us or the opinions below indicates that subsections 1(1) and 1(2) of the preamble to Missouri's abortion regulation statute will affect a woman's decision to have an abortion. JUSTICE STEVENS, following appellees, *see* Brief for Appellees 22, suggests that the preamble may also "interfer[e] with contraceptive choices," *post* at 492 U.S. 564"]564, because certain contraceptive devices act on a female ovum after it has been fertilized by a male sperm. The Missouri Act defines "conception" as "the fertilization of the ovum of a female by a sperm of a male," Mo.Rev.Stat. § 188.015(3) (1986), and invests "unborn children" with "protectable interests in life, health, and wellbeing," § 1.205.1(2), from "the moment of conception. . . ." § 1.205.3. JUSTICE STEVENS asserts that any possible interference with a woman's right to use such postfertilization contraceptive devices would be unconstitutional under 564, because certain contraceptive devices act on a female ovum after it has been fertilized by a male sperm. The Missouri Act defines "conception" as "the fertilization of the ovum of a female by a sperm of a male," Mo.Rev.Stat. § 188.015(3) (1986), and invests "unborn children" with "protectable interests in life, health, and wellbeing," § 1.205.1(2), from "the moment of conception. . . . "§ 1.205.3. JUSTICE STEVENS asserts that any possible interference with a woman's right to use such postfertilization contraceptive devices would be unconstitutional under *Griswold v. Connecticut,* 381 U.S. 479 (1965), and our subsequent contraception cases. *Post* at 564–566. Similarly, certain *amici* suggest that the Missouri Act's preamble may prohibit the developing technology of *in vitro* fertilization, a technique used to aid couples otherwise unable to bear children in which a number of ova are removed from the woman and fertilized by male sperm. This process often produces excess fertilized ova ("unborn children" under the Missouri Act's definition) that are discarded, rather than reinserted into the woman's uterus. Brief for Association of Reproductive Health Professionals *et al.* as *Amici Curiae* 38. It may be correct that the use of post-fertilization contraceptive devices is constitutionally protected by *Griswold* and its progeny, but, as with a woman's abortion decision, nothing in the record or the opinions below indicates that the preamble will affect a woman's decision to practice contraception. For that matter, nothing in appellees' original complaint, App. 8–21, or their motion *in limine* to limit testimony and evidence on their challenge to the preamble, *id.* at 57–59, indicates that appellees sought to enjoin potential violations of *Griswold.* Neither is there any indication of the possibility that the preamble might be applied to prohibit the performance of *in vitro* fertilization. I agree with the Court, therefore, that all of these intimations of unconstitutionality are simply too hypothetical to support the use of declaratory judgment procedures and injunctive remedies in this case.

Similarly, it seems to me to follow directly from our previous decisions concerning state or federal funding of abortions, *Harris v. McRae,* 448 U.S. 297 448 U.S. 297 (1980), 448 U.S. 297 (1980), *Maher v. Roe,* 432 U.S. 464 432 U.S. 464 (1977), and 432 U.S. 464 (1977), and *Poelker v. Doe,* 432 U.S. 519 (1977), that appellees' facial challenge to the constitutionality of Missouri's ban on the utilization of public facilities and the participation of public employees in the performance of abortions not necessary to save the life of the mother, Mo.Rev.Stat. §§ 188.210, 188.215 (1986), cannot succeed. Given Missouri's definition of "public facility" as any public institution, public facility, public equipment, or any physical asset owned, leased, or controlled by this state or any agency or political subdivisions thereof, § 188.200(2), there may be conceivable applications of the ban on the use of public facilities that would be unconstitutional. Appellees and *amici* suggest that the State could try to enforce the ban against private hospitals using public water and sewage lines, or against private hospitals leasing state-owned equipment or state land. *See* Brief for Appellees 49–50; Brief for National Association of Public Hospitals as *Amicus Curiae* 9–12. Whether some or all of these or other applications of § 188.215 would be constitutional need not be decided here. *Maher, Poelker,* and *McRae* stand for the proposition that some quite straightforward applications of the Missouri ban on the use of public facilities for performing abortions would be constitutional, and that is enough to defeat appellees' assertion that the ban is facially unconstitutional.

A facial challenge to a legislative Act is, of course, the most difficult challenge to mount successfully, since the challenger must establish that no set of circumstances exists under which the Act would be valid. The fact that the [relevant statute] might operate unconstitutionally under some conceivable set of circumstances is insufficient to render it wholly invalid, since we have not recognized an "overbreadth" doctrine outside the limited context of the First Amendment.

United States v. Salerno, 481 U.S. 739, 745 (1987).

I also agree with the Court that, under the interpretation of § 188.205 urged by the State and adopted by the Court, there is no longer a case or controversy before us over the constitutionality of that provision. I would note, however, that this interpretation of § 188.205 is not binding on the Supreme Court of Missouri which has the final word on the meaning of that State's statutes. *Virginia v. American Booksellers Assn., Inc.*, 484 U.S. 383, 395 (1988); *O'Brien v. Skinner*, 414 U.S. 524, 531 (1974). Should it happen that § 188.205, as ultimately interpreted by the Missouri Supreme Court, does prohibit publicly employed health professionals from giving specific medical advice to pregnant women, the vacation and dismissal of the complaint that has become moot "clears the path for future relitigation of the issues between the parties," should subsequent events rekindle their controversy.

. . . Unless such events make their appearance and give rise to relitigation, I agree that we and all federal courts are without jurisdiction to hear the merits of this moot dispute.

II

In its interpretation of Missouri's "determination of viability" provision, Mo.Rev.Stat. § 188.029 (1986), *see ante* at 513–521, the plurality has proceeded in a manner unnecessary to deciding the question at hand. I agree with the plurality that it was plain error for the Court of Appeals to interpret the second sentence of § 188.029 as meaning that "doctors *must* perform tests to find gestational age, fetal weight and lung maturity." 851 F.2d at 1075, n. 5 (emphasis in original). When read together with the first sentence of § 188.029—which requires a physician to determine if the unborn child is viable by using and exercising that degree of care, skill, and proficiency commonly exercised by the ordinary skillful, careful, and prudent physician engaged in similar practice under the same or similar conditions—it would be contradictory nonsense to read the second sentence as requiring a physician to perform viability examinations and tests in situations where it would be careless and imprudent to do so. The plurality is quite correct: the viability testing provision makes sense only if the second sentence is read to require only those tests that are useful to making subsidiary findings as to viability, *ante* at 514, and, I would add, only those examinations and tests that it would not be imprudent or careless to perform in the particular medical situation before the physician.

Unlike the plurality, I do not understand these viability testing requirements to conflict with any of the Court's past decisions concerning state regulation of abortion. Therefore, there is no necessity to accept the State's invitation to reexamine the constitutional validity of *Roe v. Wade*, 410 U.S. 113 (1973). Where there is no need to decide a constitutional question, it is a venerable principle of this Court's adjudicatory processes not to do so, for "[t]he Court will not 'anticipate a question of constitutional law in advance of the necessity of deciding it.'" . . . Neither will it generally "formulate a rule of constitutional law broader than is required by the precise facts to which it is to be applied." 297 U.S. at 347. Quite simply, "[i]t is not the habit of the court to decide questions of a constitutional nature unless absolutely necessary to a decision of the case." *Burton v. United States*, 196 U.S. 283, 295 (1905). The Court today has accepted the State's every interpretation of its abortion statute, and has upheld, under our existing precedents, every provision of that statute which is properly before us. Precisely for this reason, reconsideration of *Roe* falls not into any "good-cause exception" to this "fundamental rule of judicial restraint. . . . " *Three Affiliated Tribes of Fort Berthold Reservation v. Wold Engineering, P. C.*, 467 U.S. 138, 157 (1984). *See post* at 532–533 (SCALIA, J., concurring in part and concurring in judgment). When the constitutional invalidity of a

State's abortion statute actually turns on the constitutional validity of *Roe v. Wade*, there will be time enough to reexamine *Roe*. And to do so carefully.

In assessing § 188.029, it is especially important to recognize that appellees did not appeal the District Court's ruling that the first sentence of § 188.029 is constitutional. 662 F.Supp. at 420–422. There is, accordingly, no dispute between the parties before us over the constitutionality of the "presumption of viability at 20 weeks," *ante* at 492 U.S. 515"]515, created by the first sentence of § 188.029. If anything might arguably conflict with the Court's previous decisions concerning the determination of viability, I would think it is the introduction of this presumption. The plurality, *see ante* at 515, refers to a passage from 515, created by the first sentence of § 188.029. If anything might arguably conflict with the Court's previous decisions concerning the determination of viability, I would think it is the introduction of this presumption. The plurality, see ante at 515, refers to a passage from *Planned Parenthood of Central Mo. v. Danforth*, 428 U.S. 52, 64 (1976):

The time when viability is achieved may vary with each pregnancy, and the determination of whether a particular fetus is viable is, and must be, a matter for the judgment of the responsible attending physician.

The 20-week presumption of viability in the first sentence of § 188.029, it could be argued (though, I would think, unsuccessfully), restricts "the judgment of the responsible attending physician," by imposing on that physician the burden of overcoming the presumption. This presumption may be a "superimpos[ition] [of] state regulation on the medical determination whether a particular fetus is viable," *ante* at 517, but, if so, it is a restriction on the physician's judgment that is not before us. As the plurality properly interprets the second sentence of § 188.029, it does nothing more than delineate means by which the unchallenged 20-week presumption of viability may be overcome if those means are useful in doing so and can be prudently employed. Contrary to the plurality's suggestion, *see ante* at 517, the District Court did not think the second sentence of § 188.029 unconstitutional for this reason. Rather, both the District Court and the Court of Appeals thought the second sentence to be unconstitutional precisely because they interpreted that sentence to impose state regulation on the determination of viability that it does not impose.

Appellees suggest that the interpretation of § 188. 029 urged by the State may "virtually eliminat[e] the constitutional issue in this case." Brief for Appellees 30. Appellees therefore propose that we should abstain from deciding that provision's constitutionality "in order to allow the state courts to render the saving construction the State has proposed." *Ibid*. Where the lower court has so clearly fallen into error, I do not think abstention is necessary or prudent. Accordingly, I consider the constitutionality of the second sentence of § 188.029, as interpreted by the State, to determine whether the constitutional issue is actually eliminated.

I do not think the second sentence of § 188.029, as interpreted by the Court, imposes a degree of state regulation on the medical determination of viability that in any way conflicts with prior decisions of this Court. As the plurality recognizes, the requirement that, where not imprudent, physicians perform examinations and tests useful to making subsidiary findings to determine viability "promot[es] the State's interest in potential human life, rather than in maternal health." *Ante* at 515. No decision of this Court has held that the State may not directly promote its interest in potential life when viability is possible. Quite the contrary. In *Thornburgh v. American College of Obstetricians and Gynecologists*, 476 U.S. 747 (1986), the Court considered a constitutional challenge to a Pennsylvania statute requiring that a second physician be present during an abortion performed "when viability is possible." *Id*. at 769–770. For guidance, the Court looked to the earlier decision in *Planned Parenthood*

Assn. of Kansas City, Mo., Inc. v. Ashcroft, 462 U.S. 476 (1983), upholding a Missouri statute requiring the presence of a second physician during an abortion performed after viability. *Id.* at 482–486 (opinion of Powell, J.); *id.* at 505 (O'CONNOR, J., concurring in judgment in part and dissenting in part). The *Thornburgh* majority struck down the Pennsylvania statute merely because the statute had no exception for emergency situations, and not because it found a constitutional difference between the State's promotion of its interest in potential life when viability is possible and when viability is certain. 476 U.S. at 770–771. Despite the clear recognition by the *Thornburgh* majority that the Pennsylvania and Missouri statutes differed in this respect, there is no hint in the opinion of the *Thornburgh* Court that the State's interest in potential life differs depending on whether it seeks to further that interest postviability or when viability is possible. Thus, all nine Members of the *Thornburgh* Court appear to have agreed that it is not constitutionally impermissible for the State to enact regulations designed to protect the State's interest in potential life when viability is possible. *See id.* at 811 (WHITE, J., dissenting); *id.* at 832 (O'CONNOR, J., dissenting). That is exactly what Missouri has done in § 188.029.

Similarly, the basis for reliance by the District Court and the Court of Appeals below on *Colautti v. Franklin*, 439 U.S. 379 (1979), disappears when § 188.029 is properly interpreted. In *Colautti*, the Court observed: Because this point [of viability] may differ with each pregnancy, neither the legislature nor the courts may proclaim one of the elements entering into the ascertainment of viability—be it weeks of gestation or fetal weight or any other single factor—as the determinant of when the State has a compelling interest in the life or health of the fetus. Viability is the critical point.

Id. at 388–389. The courts below, on the interpretation of § 188.029 rejected here, found the second sentence of that provision at odds with this passage from *Colautti*. *See* 851 F.2d at 1074; 662 F.Supp. at 423. On this Court's interpretation of § 188.029, it is clear that Missouri has not substituted any of the "elements entering into the ascertainment of viability" as "the determinant of when the State has a compelling interest in the life or health of the fetus." All the second sentence of § 188.029 does is to require, when not imprudent, the performance of "those tests that are useful to making *subsidiary* findings as to viability." *Ante* at 514 (emphasis added). Thus, consistent with *Colautti*, viability remains the "critical point" under § 188.029.

Finally, and rather half-heartedly, the plurality suggests that the marginal increase in the cost of an abortion created by Missouri's viability testing provision may make § 188.029, even as interpreted, suspect under this Court's decision in *Akron v. Akron Center for Reproductive Health, Inc.*, 462 U.S. 416, 434–439 (1983), striking down a second-trimester hospitalization requirement. *See ante* at 517. I dissented from the Court's opinion in *Akron* because it was my view that, even apart from *Roe*'s trimester framework, which I continue to consider problematic, *see Thornburgh, supra*, at 828 (dissenting opinion), the *Akron* majority had distorted and misapplied its own standard for evaluating state regulation of abortion which the Court had applied with fair consistency in the past: that, previability, "a regulation imposed on a lawful abortion is not unconstitutional unless it unduly burdens the right to seek an abortion." *Akron, supra*, at 453 (dissenting opinion) (internal quotations omitted).

It is clear to me that requiring the performance of examinations and tests useful to determining whether a fetus is viable, when viability is possible, and when it would not be medically imprudent to do so, does not impose an undue burden on a woman's abortion decision. On this ground alone, I would reject the suggestion that § 188.029 as interpreted is unconstitutional. More to the point, however, just as I see no conflict between § 188.029 and

Colautti or any decision of this Court concerning a State's ability to give effect to its interest in potential life, I see no conflict between § 188.029 and the Court's opinion in *Akron*. The second-trimester hospitalization requirement struck down in *Akron* imposed, in the majority's view, "a heavy, and unnecessary, burden," 462 U.S. at 438, more than doubling the cost of "women's access to a relatively inexpensive, otherwise accessible, and safe abortion procedure." *Ibid.*; *see also id.* at 434. By contrast, the cost of examinations and tests that could usefully and prudently be performed when a woman is 20–24 weeks pregnant to determine whether the fetus is viable would only marginally, if at all, increase the cost of an abortion. *See* Brief for American Association of Prolife Obstetricians and Gynecologists *et al.* as *Amici Curiae* 3 ("At twenty weeks gestation, an ultrasound examination to determine gestational age is standard medical practice. It is routinely provided by the plaintiff clinics. An ultrasound examination can effectively provide all three designated findings of sec. 188.029"); *id.* at 22 ("A finding of fetal weight can be obtained from the same ultrasound test used to determine gestational age"); *id.* at 25 ("There are a number of different methods in standard medical practice to determine fetal lung maturity at twenty or more weeks gestation. The most simple and most obvious is by inference. It is well known that fetal lungs do not mature until 33–34 weeks gestation. . . . If an assessment of the gestational age indicates that the child is less than thirty-three weeks, a general finding can be made that the fetal lungs are not mature. This finding can then be used by the physician in making his determination of viability under section 188.029"); *cf.* Brief for American Medical Association *et al.* as *Amici Curiae* 42 (no suggestion that fetal weight and gestational age cannot be determined from the same sonogram); *id.* at 43 (another clinical test for gestational age and, by inference, fetal weight and lung maturity, is an accurate report of the last menstrual period), citing Smith, Frey, & Johnson, Assessing Gestational Age, 33 Am.Fam.Physician 215, 219–220 (1986).

Moreover, the examinations and tests required by § 188.029 are to be performed when viability is possible. This feature of § 188.029 distinguishes it from the second-trimester hospitalization requirement struck down by the *Akron* majority. As the Court recognized in *Thornburgh*, the State's compelling interest in potential life postviability renders its interest in determining the critical point of viability equally compelling. *See supra* at 527–528. Under the Court's precedents, the same cannot be said for the *Akron* second-trimester hospitalization requirement. As I understand the Court's opinion in Akron, therefore, the plurality's suggestion today that *Akron* casts doubt on the validity of § 188.029, even as the Court has interpreted it, is without foundation, and cannot provide a basis for reevaluating *Roe*. Accordingly, because the Court of Appeals misinterpreted § 188.029, and because, properly interpreted, § 188.029 is not inconsistent with any of this Court's prior precedents, I would reverse the decision of the Court of Appeals.

In sum, I concur in Parts I, II-A, II-B, and II-C of the Court's opinion and concur in the judgment as to Part II-D.

JUSTICE SCALIA, concurring in part and concurring in the judgment.

I join Parts I, II-A, II-B, and II-C of the opinion of the Court. As to Part II-D, I share JUSTICE BLACKMUN's view, *post* at 556, that it effectively would overrule *Roe v. Wade*, 410 U.S. 113 (1973). I think that should be done, but would do it more explicitly. Since today we contrive to avoid doing it, and indeed to avoid almost any decision of national import, I need not set forth my reasons, some of which have been well recited in dissents of my colleagues in other cases. . . .

The outcome of today's case will doubtless be heralded as a triumph of judicial statesmanship. It is not that, unless it is statesmanlike needlessly to prolong this Court's self-awarded sovereignty over a field where it has little proper business, since the answers to most of the cruel questions posed are political, and not juridical—a sovereignty which therefore quite properly, but to the great damage of the Court, makes it the object of the sort of organized public pressure that political institutions in a democracy ought to receive.

JUSTICE O'CONNOR's assertion, *ante* at 526, that a "'fundamental rule of judicial restraint'" requires us to avoid reconsidering *Roe,* cannot be taken seriously. By finessing *Roe* we do not, as she suggests, *ante* at 526, adhere to the strict and venerable rule that we should avoid "'decid[ing] questions of a constitutional nature.'" We have not disposed of this case on some statutory or procedural ground, but have decided, and could not avoid deciding, whether the Missouri statute meets the requirements of the United States Constitution. The only choice available is whether, in deciding that constitutional question, we should use *Roe v. Wade* as the benchmark, or something else. What is involved, therefore, is not the rule of avoiding constitutional issues where possible, but the quite separate principle that we will not "'formulate a rule of constitutional law broader than is required by the precise facts to which it is to be applied.'" *Ante* at 526. The latter is a sound general principle, but one often departed from when good reason exists. Just this Term, for example, in an opinion authored by JUSTICE O'CONNOR, despite the fact that we had already held a racially based setaside unconstitutional because unsupported by evidence of identified discrimination, which was all that was needed to decide the case, we went on to outline the criteria for properly tailoring race-based remedies in cases where such evidence is present. *Richmond v. J. A. Croson Co.,* 488 U.S. 469, 506–508 (1989). Also this Term, in an opinion joined by JUSTICE O'CONNOR, we announced the constitutional rule that deprivation of the right to confer with counsel during trial violates the Sixth Amendment even if no prejudice can be shown, despite our finding that there had been no such deprivation on the facts before us—which was all that was needed to decide that case. *Perry v. Leeke,* 488 U.S. 272, 278–280 (1989); *see id.* at 285 (KENNEDY, J., concurring in part). I have not identified with certainty the first instance of our deciding a case on broader constitutional grounds than absolutely necessary, but it is assuredly no later than *Marbury v. Madison,* 1 Cranch 137 (1803), where we held that mandamus could constitutionally issue against the Secretary of State, although that was unnecessary given our holding that the law authorizing issuance of the mandamus by this Court was unconstitutional.

The Court has often spoken more broadly than needed in precisely the fashion at issue here, announcing a new rule of constitutional law when it could have reached the identical result by applying the rule thereby displaced. To describe two recent opinions that JUSTICE O'CONNOR joined: In *Daniels v. Williams,* 474 U.S. 327 (1986), we overruled our prior holding that a "deprivation" of liberty or property could occur through negligent governmental acts, ignoring the availability of the alternative constitutional ground that, even if a deprivation had occurred, the State's postdeprivation remedies satisfied due process, *see id.* at 340–343 (STEVENS, J., concurring in judgment). In *Illinois v. Gates,* 462 U.S. 213 (1983), we replaced the preexisting "two-pronged" constitutional test for probable cause with a totality-of-the-circumstances approach, ignoring the concurrence's argument that the same outcome could have been reached under the old test, *see id.* at 267–272 (WHITE, J., concurring in judgment). It is rare, of course, that the Court goes out of its way to *acknowledge* that its judgment could have been reached under the old constitutional rule, making its adoption of the new one unnecessary to the decision, but even such explicit acknowledgment is not unheard of. . . . It would be wrong, in any decision, to ignore the reality that our policy not to "formulate a rule of constitutional law broader than is required by the precise facts" has a frequently applied good-cause exception. But it seems particularly perverse to convert the policy into an absolute in the present case, in order to place beyond reach the inexpressibly "broader than was required by the precise facts" structure established by *Roe v. Wade*. The real question, then, is whether there are valid reasons to go beyond the most stingy possible holding today. It seems to me there are not only valid but compelling ones. Ordinarily, speaking no more broadly than is absolutely required avoids throwing settled law into confusion; doing so today preserves a chaos that is evident to anyone who can read and count. Alone sufficient to justify a broad holding is the fact that our retaining control, through *Roe,* of what I believe to be, and many of our citizens recognize to be, a political issue, continuously distorts the public perception of the role of this Court. We can now look forward to at least another Term with carts full of mail from the public, and streets full of demonstrators, urging us—their unelected and life-tenured judges who have been awarded those extraordinary, undemocratic characteristics precisely in order that we might follow the law despite the popular will—to follow the popular will. Indeed, I expect we can look forward to even more of that than before, given our indecisive decision today. And if these reasons for taking the unexceptional course of reaching a broader holding are not enough, then consider the nature of the constitutional question we avoid: in most cases, we do no harm by not speaking more broadly than the decision requires. Anyone affected by the conduct that the avoided holding would have prohibited will be able to challenge it himself and have his day in court to make the argument. Not so with respect to the harm that many States believed, pre-*Roe,* and many may continue to believe, is caused by largely unrestricted abortion. That will continue to occur if the States have the constitutional power to prohibit it, and would do so, but we skillfully avoid telling them so. Perhaps those abortions cannot constitutionally be proscribed. That is surely an arguable question, the question that reconsideration of *Roe v. Wade* entails. But what is not at all arguable, it seems to me, is that we should decide now, and not insist that we be run into a corner before we grudgingly yield up our judgment. The only sound reason for the latter course is to prevent a change in the law—but to think that desirable begs the question to be decided.

It was an arguable question today whether § 188.029 of the Missouri law contravened this Court's understanding of *Roe v. Wade,* and I would have examined *Roe* rather than examining the contravention. Given the Court's newly contracted abstemiousness, what will it take, one must wonder, to permit us to reach that fundamental question? The result of our vote today is that we will not reconsider that prior opinion, even if most of the Justices think it is wrong, unless we have before us a statute that in fact contradicts it—and even then (under our newly discovered "no broader than necessary" requirement) only minor problematical aspects of *Roe* will be reconsidered, unless one expects state legislatures to adopt provisions whose compliance with *Roe* cannot even be argued with a straight face. It thus appears that the mansion of constitutionalized abortion law, constructed overnight in *Roe v. Wade,* must be disassembled doorjamb by doorjamb, and never entirely brought down, no matter how wrong it may be. Of the four courses we might have chosen today—to reaffirm *Roe,* to overrule it explicitly, to overrule it *sub silentio,* or to avoid the question—the last is the least responsible. On the question of the constitutionality of § 188.029, I concur in the judgment of the Court and strongly dissent from the manner in which it has been reached.

* That question, compared with the question whether we should reconsider and reverse Roe, is hardly worth a footnote, but I think JUSTICE O'CONNOR answers that incorrectly as well. In Roe v. Wade, 410 U.S. 113, 165–166 (1973), we said that the physician [has

the right] to administer medical treatment according to his professional judgment up to the points where important state interests provide compelling justifications for intervention.

We have subsequently made clear that it is also a matter of medical judgment when viability (one of those points) is reached.

The time when viability is achieved may vary with each pregnancy, and the determination of whether a particular fetus is viable is, and must be, a matter for the judgment of the responsible attending physician.

Planned Parenthood of Central Mo. v. Danforth, 428 U.S. 52, 64 (1976). Section 188.029 conflicts with the purpose, and hence the fair import, of this principle, because it will sometimes require a physician to perform tests that he would not otherwise have performed to determine whether a fetus is viable. It is therefore a legislative imposition on the judgment of the physician, and one that increases the cost of an abortion.

JUSTICE O'CONNOR would nevertheless uphold the law because it "does not impose an undue burden on a woman's abortion decision." *Ante* at 492 U.S. 530 530. This conclusion is supported by the observation that the required tests impose only a marginal cost on the abortion procedure, far less of an increase than the cost-doubling hospitalization requirement invalidated in 530. This conclusion is supported by the observation that the required tests impose only a marginal cost on the abortion procedure, far less of an increase than the cost-doubling hospitalization requirement invalidated in *Akron v. Akron Center for Reproductive Health, Inc.*, 462 U.S. 416 (1983). *See ante* at 530–531. The fact that the challenged regulation is less costly than what we struck down in *Akron* tells us only that we cannot decide the present case on the basis of that earlier decision. It does not tell us whether the present requirement is an "undue burden," and I know of no basis for determining that this particular burden (or any other for that matter) is "due." One could with equal justification conclude that it is not. To avoid the question of *Roe v. Wade's* validity, with the attendant costs that this will have for the Court and for the principles of self-governance, on the basis of a standard that offers "no guide but the Court's own discretion," *Baldwin v. Missouri*, 281 U.S. 586, 595 (1930) (Holmes, J., dissenting), merely adds to the irrationality of what we do today.

Similarly irrational is the new concept that JUSTICE O'CONNOR introduces into the law in order to achieve her result, the notion of a State's "interest in potential life when viability is possible." Ante at 528. Since "viability" means the mere possibility (not the certainty) of survivability outside the womb, "possible viability" must mean the possibility of a possibility of survivability outside the womb. Perhaps our next opinion will expand the third trimester into the second even further, by approving state action designed to take account of "the chance of possible viability."

JUSTICE BLACKMUN, with whom JUSTICE BRENNAN and JUSTICE MARSHALL join, concurring in part and dissenting in part.

Today, *Roe v. Wade*, 410 U.S. 113 (1973), and the fundamental constitutional right of women to decide whether to terminate a pregnancy, survive, but are not secure. Although the Court extricates itself from this case without making a single, even incremental, change in the law of abortion, the plurality and JUSTICE SCALIA would overrule *Roe* (the first silently, the other explicitly) and would return to the States virtually unfettered authority to control the quintessentially intimate, personal, and life-directing decision whether to carry a fetus to term. Although today, no less than yesterday, the Constitution and the decisions of this Court prohibit a State from enacting laws that inhibit women from the meaningful exercise of that right, a plurality of this Court implicitly invites every state legislature to enact more and more restrictive abortion regulations in order to provoke more and more test cases, in the hope that, sometime down the line, the Court will return the law of procreative freedom to the severe limitations that generally prevailed in this country before January 22, 1973. Never in my memory has a plurality announced a judgment of this Court that so foments disregard for the law and for our standing decisions.

Nor in my memory has a plurality gone about its business in such a deceptive fashion. At every level of its review, from its effort to read the real meaning out of the Missouri statute to its intended evisceration of precedents and its deafening silence about the constitutional protections that it would jettison, the plurality obscures the portent of its analysis. With feigned restraint, the plurality announces that its analysis leaves *Roe* "undisturbed," albeit "modif[ied] and narrow[ed]." *Ante* at 521. But this disclaimer is totally meaningless. The plurality opinion is filled with winks, and nods, and knowing glances to those who would do away with *Roe* explicitly, but turns a stone face to anyone in search of what the plurality conceives as the scope of a woman's right under the Due Process Clause to terminate a pregnancy free from the coercive and brooding influence of the State. The simple truth is that *Roe* would not survive the plurality's analysis, and that the plurality provides no substitute for *Roe*'s protective umbrella.

I fear for the future. I fear for the liberty and equality of the millions of women who have lived and come of age in the 16 years since Roe was decided. I fear for the integrity of, and public esteem for, this Court. I dissent.

I

THE CHIEF JUSTICE parades through the four challenged sections of the Missouri statute *seriatim*. I shall not do this, but shall relegate most of my comments as to those sections to the margin. Although I disagree with the Court's consideration of §§ 1.205, 188.210, and 188.215, and am especially disturbed by its misapplication of our past decisions in upholding Missouri's ban on the performance of abortions at "public facilities," its discussion of these provisions is merely prologue to the plurality's consideration of the statute's viability testing requirement, § 188.029—the only section of the Missouri statute that the plurality construes as implicating *Roe* itself. There, tucked away at the end of its opinion, the plurality suggests a radical reversal of the law of abortion; and there, primarily, I direct my attention.

In the plurality's view, the viability testing provision imposes a burden on second-trimester abortions as a way of furthering the State's interest in protecting the potential life of the fetus. Since, under the *Roe* framework, the State may not fully regulate abortion in the interest of potential life (as opposed to maternal health) until the third trimester, the plurality finds it necessary, in order to save the Missouri testing provision, to throw out *Roe's* trimester framework. *Ante* at 518–520. In flat contradiction to *Roe*, 410 U.S. at 163, the plurality concludes that the State's interest in potential life is compelling before viability, and upholds the testing provision because it "permissibly furthers" that state interest. *Ante* at 519.

A

At the outset, I note that, in its haste to limit abortion rights, the plurality compounds the errors of its analysis by needlessly reaching out to address constitutional questions that are not actually presented. The conflict between § 188.029 and *Roe's* trimester framework, which purportedly drives the plurality to reconsider our past decisions, is a contrived conflict: the product of an aggressive misreading of the viability testing requirement and a needlessly wooden application of the *Roe* framework.

The plurality's reading of § 188.029 is irreconcilable with the plain language of the statute, and is in derogation of this Court's settled view that "'district courts and courts of appeals are better schooled in and more able to interpret the laws of their respective States'" . . . Abruptly setting aside the construction of § 188.029 adopted by both the District Court and Court of Appeals as "plain error," the plurality reads the viability testing provision as requiring only that, before a physician may perform an abortion on a woman whom he believes to be carrying a fetus of 20 or more weeks gestational age, the doctor must determine whether the fetus is viable and, as part of that exercise, must, to the extent feasible and consistent with sound medical practice, conduct tests necessary to make findings of gestational age, weight, and lung maturity. *Ante* at 514–517. But the plurality's reading of the provision, according to which the statute requires the physician to perform tests only in order to determine *viability*, ignores the statutory language explicitly directing that the physician *shall* perform or cause to be performed such medical examinations and tests as are *necessary to make a finding of the gestational age, weight, and lung maturity* of the unborn child and *shall* enter such findings in the mother's medical record. § 188.029 (emphasis added). The statute's plain language requires the physician to undertake whatever tests are necessary to determine gestational age, weight, and lung maturity, regardless of whether these tests are necessary to a finding of viability, and regardless of whether the tests subject the pregnant woman or the fetus to additional health risks or add substantially to the cost of an abortion.

Had the plurality read the statute as written, it would have had no cause to reconsider the *Roe* framework. As properly construed, the viability testing provision does not pass constitutional muster under even a rational basis standard, the least restrictive level of review applied by this Court. *See Williamson v. Lee Optical Co.*, 348 U.S. 483 (1955). By mandating tests to determine fetal weight and lung maturity for every fetus thought to be more than 20 weeks gestational age, the statute requires physicians to undertake procedures, such as amniocentesis, that, in the situation presented, have no medical justification, impose significant additional health risks on both the pregnant woman and the fetus, and bear no rational relation to the State's interest in protecting fetal life. As written, § 188.029 is an arbitrary imposition of discomfort, risk, and expense, furthering no discernible interest except to make the procurement of an abortion as arduous and difficult as possible. Thus, were it not for the plurality's tortured effort to avoid the plain import of § 188.029, it could have struck down the testing provision as patently irrational irrespective of the *Roe* framework.

The plurality eschews this straightforward resolution in the hope of precipitating a constitutional crisis. Far from avoiding constitutional difficulty, the plurality attempts to engineer a dramatic retrenchment in our jurisprudence by exaggerating the conflict between its untenable construction of § 188.029 and the *Roe* trimester framework.

No one contests that, under the *Roe* framework, the State, in order to promote its interest in potential human life, may regulate and even proscribe nontherapeutic abortions once the fetus becomes viable. *Roe*, 410 U.S. at 164–165. If, as the plurality appears to hold, the testing provision simply requires a physician to use appropriate and medically sound tests to determine whether the fetus is actually viable when the estimated gestational age is greater than 20 weeks (and therefore within what the District Court found to be the margin of error for viability, *ante* at 515–516), then I see little or no conflict with *Roe*. Nothing in *Roe*, or any of its progeny, holds that a State may not effectuate its compelling interest in the potential life of a viable fetus by seeking to ensure that no viable fetus is mistakenly aborted because of the inherent lack of precision in estimates of gestational age. A requirement that a physician make a finding of viability, one way or the other, for every fetus that falls within the range of possible viability does no more than preserve the State's recognized authority. Although, as the plurality correctly points out, such a testing requirement would have the effect of imposing additional costs on second-trimester abortions where the tests indicated that the fetus was not viable, these costs would be merely incidental to, and a necessary accommodation of, the State's unquestioned right to prohibit nontherapeutic abortions after the point of viability. In short, the testing provision, as construed by the plurality, is consistent with the *Roe* framework, and could be upheld effortlessly under current doctrine.

How ironic it is, then, and disingenuous, that the plurality scolds the Court of Appeals for adopting a construction of the statute that fails to avoid constitutional difficulties. *Ante* at 514, 515. By distorting the statute, the plurality manages to avoid invalidating the testing provision on what should have been noncontroversial constitutional grounds; having done so, however, the plurality rushes headlong into a much deeper constitutional thicket, brushing past an obvious basis for upholding § 188.029 in search of a pretext for scuttling the trimester framework. Evidently, from the plurality's perspective, the real problem with the Court of Appeals' construction of § 188.029 is not that it raised a constitutional difficulty, but that it raised the wrong constitutional difficulty—one not implicating *Roe*. The plurality has remedied that, traditional canons of construction and judicial forbearance notwithstanding.

B

Having set up the conflict between § 188.029 and the *Roe* trimester framework, the plurality summarily discards *Roe*'s analytic core as "'unsound in principle and unworkable in practice.'" . . . This is so, the plurality claims, because the key elements of the framework do not appear in the text of the Constitution, because the framework more closely resembles a regulatory code than a body of constitutional doctrine, and because, under the framework, the State's interest in potential human life is considered compelling only after viability, when, in fact, that interest is equally compelling throughout pregnancy. *Ante* at 519–520. The plurality does not bother to explain these alleged flaws in *Roe*. Bald assertion masquerades as reasoning. The object, quite clearly, is not to persuade, but to prevail.

The plurality opinion is far more remarkable for the arguments that it does not advance than for those that it does. The plurality does not even mention, much less join, the true jurisprudential debate underlying this case: whether the Constitution includes an "unenumerated" general right to privacy as recognized in many of our decisions, most notably *Griswold v. Connecticut,* 381 U.S. 479 (1965), and *Roe,* and, more specifically, whether, and to what extent, such a right to privacy extends to matters of childbearing and family life, including abortion. . . These are questions of unsurpassed significance in this Court's interpretation of the Constitution, and mark the battleground upon which this case was fought by the parties, by the Solicitor General as *amicus* on behalf of petitioners, and by an unprecedented number of *amici*. On these grounds, abandoned by the plurality, the Court should decide this case.

But rather than arguing that the text of the Constitution makes no mention of the right to privacy, the plurality complains that the critical elements of the *Roe* framework—trimesters and viability—do not appear in the Constitution, and are, therefore, somehow inconsistent with a Constitution cast in general terms. *Ante* at 518–519. Were this a true concern, we would have to abandon most of our constitutional jurisprudence. As the plurality well knows, or should know, the "critical elements" of countless constitutional doctrines nowhere appear in the Constitution's text. The Constitution makes no mention, for example, of the First Amendment's "actual malice" standard for proving certain libels, *see New York Times Co.*

v. Sullivan, 376 U.S. 254 (1964), or of the standard for determining when speech is obscene. *See Miller v. California*, 413 U.S. 15 (1973). Similarly, the Constitution makes no mention of the rational basis test, or the specific verbal formulations of intermediate and strict scrutiny by which this Court evaluates claims under the Equal Protection Clause. The reason is simple. Like the *Roe* framework, these tests or standards are not, and do not purport to be, rights protected by the Constitution. Rather, they are judge-made methods for evaluating and measuring the strength and scope of constitutional rights or for balancing the constitutional rights of individuals against the competing interests of government.

With respect to the *Roe* framework, the general constitutional principle, indeed the fundamental constitutional right, for which it was developed is the right to privacy, *see, e.g., Griswold v. Connecticut*, 381 U.S. 479"]381 U.S. 479 (1965), a species of "liberty" protected by the Due Process Clause, which under our past decisions safeguards the right of women to exercise some control over their own role in procreation. As we recently reaffirmed in 381 U.S. 479 (1965), a species of "liberty" protected by the Due Process Clause, which under our past decisions safeguards the right of women to exercise some control over their own role in procreation. As we recently reaffirmed in *Thornburgh v. American College of Obstetricians and Gynecologists*, 476 U.S. 747 (1986), few decisions are "more basic to individual dignity and autonomy" or more appropriate to that "certain private sphere of individual liberty" that the Constitution reserves from the intrusive reach of government than the right to make the uniquely personal, intimate, and self-defining decision whether to end a pregnancy. *Id.* at 772. It is this general principle, the "'moral fact that a person belongs to himself and not others nor to society as a whole,'" *id.* at 777, n. 5 (STEVENS, J., concurring), quoting Fried, Correspondence, 6 Phil. & Pub.Aff. 288–289 (1977), that is found in the Constitution. *See Roe*, 410 U.S. at 152–153. The trimester framework simply defines and limits that right to privacy in the abortion context to accommodate, not destroy, a State's legitimate interest in protecting the health of pregnant women and in preserving potential human life. Id. at 154–162. Fashioning such accommodations between individual rights and the legitimate interests of government, establishing benchmarks and standards with which to evaluate the competing claims of individuals and government, lies at the very heart of constitutional adjudication. To the extent that the trimester framework is useful in this enterprise, it is not only consistent with constitutional interpretation, but necessary to the wise and just exercise of this Court's paramount authority to define the scope of constitutional rights.

The plurality next alleges that the result of the trimester framework has "been a web of legal rules that have become increasingly intricate, resembling a code of regulations, rather than a body of constitutional doctrine." *Ante* at 518. Again, if this were a true and genuine concern, we would have to abandon vast areas of our constitutional jurisprudence. The plurality complains that, under the trimester framework, the Court has distinguished between a city ordinance requiring that second-trimester abortions be performed in clinics and a state law requiring that these abortions be performed in hospitals, or between laws requiring that certain information be furnished to a woman by a physician or his assistant and those requiring that such information be furnished by the physician exclusively. . . . Are these distinctions any finer, or more "regulatory," than the distinctions we have often drawn in our First Amendment jurisprudence, where, for example, we have held that a "release time" program permitting public school students to leave school grounds during school hours to receive religious instruction does not violate the Establishment Clause, even though a release time program permitting religious instruction on school grounds does violate the Clause? . . . Our Fourth Amendment jurisprudence recognizes factual distinctions no less intricate. Just this

Term, for example, we held that, while an aerial observation from a helicopter hovering at 400 feet does not violate any reasonable expectation of privacy, such an expectation of privacy would be violated by a helicopter observation from an unusually low altitude. *Florida v. Riley*, 488 U.S. 445, 451 (1989) (O'CONNOR, J., concurring in judgment). Similarly, in a Sixth Amendment case, the Court held that, although an overnight ban on attorney-client communication violated the constitutionally guaranteed right to counsel, *Geders v. United States*, 425 U.S. 80 (1976), that right was not violated when a trial judge separated a defendant from his lawyer during a 15-minute recess after the defendant's direct testimony. *Perry v. Leeke*, 488 U.S. 272 (1989).

That numerous constitutional doctrines result in narrow differentiations between similar circumstances does not mean that this Court has abandoned adjudication in favor of regulation. Rather, these careful distinctions reflect the process of constitutional adjudication itself, which is often highly fact-specific, requiring such determinations as whether state laws are "unduly burdensome" or "reasonable" or bear a "rational" or "necessary" relation to asserted state interests. In a recent due process case, THE CHIEF JUSTICE wrote for the Court:

[M]any branches of the law abound in nice distinctions that may be troublesome but have been thought nonetheless necessary:

I do not think we need trouble ourselves with the thought that my view depends upon differences of degree. The whole law does so as soon as it is civilized.

These "differences of degree" fully account for our holdings in *Simopoulos*, *supra*, and *Akron*, *supra*. Those decisions rest on this Court's reasoned and accurate judgment that hospitalization and doctor counseling requirements unduly burdened the right of women to terminate a pregnancy, and were not rationally related to the State's asserted interest in the health of pregnant women, while Virginia's substantially less restrictive regulations were not unduly burdensome and did rationally serve the State's interest. That the Court exercised its best judgment in evaluating these markedly different statutory schemes no more established the Court as an "'*ex officio* medical board,'" *ante* at 519, quoting *Planned Parenthood of Central Mo. v. Danforth*, 428 U.S. 52, 99 (1976) (opinion of WHITE, J., concurring in part and dissenting in part), than our decisions involving religion in the public schools establish the Court as a national school board, or our decisions concerning prison regulations establish the Court as a bureau of prisons. *See Thornburgh v. Abbott*, 490 U.S. 401 (1989) (adopting different standard of First Amendment review for incoming, as opposed to outgoing, prison mail). If, in delicate and complicated areas of constitutional law, our legal judgments "have become increasingly intricate," *ante* at 518, it is not, as the plurality contends, because we have overstepped our judicial role. Quite the opposite: the rules are intricate because we have remained conscientious in our duty to do justice carefully, especially when fundamental rights rise or fall with our decisions.

Finally, the plurality asserts that the trimester framework cannot stand because the State's interest in potential life is compelling throughout pregnancy, not merely after viability. *Ante* at 519. The opinion contains not one word of rationale for its view of the State's interest. This "it is so because we say so" jurisprudence constitutes nothing other than an attempted exercise of brute force; reason, much less persuasion, has no place.

In answering the plurality's claim that the State's interest in the fetus is uniform and compelling throughout pregnancy, I cannot improve upon what JUSTICE STEVENS has written:

I should think it obvious that the State's interest in the protection of an embryo—even if that interest is defined as "protecting those who will be citizens" . . .—increases progressively and dramatically as the organism's capacity to feel pain, to experience pleasure, to survive, and to react to its surroundings increases day by day. The development of a fetus—and pregnancy itself—are not static conditions, and the assertion that the government's interest is static simply ignores this reality. . . . [U]nless the religious view that a fetus is a "person" is adopted . . . there is a fundamental and well-recognized difference between a fetus and a human being; indeed, if there is not such a difference, the permissibility of terminating the life of a fetus could scarcely be left to the will of the state legislatures. And if distinctions may be drawn between a fetus and a human being in terms of the state interest in their protection—even though the fetus represents one of "those who will be citizens"—it seems to me quite odd to argue that distinctions may not also be drawn between the state interest in protecting the freshly fertilized egg and the state interest in protecting the 9-month-gestated, fully sentient fetus on the eve of birth. Recognition of this distinction is supported not only by logic, but also by history and by our shared experiences.

Thornburgh, 476 U.S. at 778–779 (footnote omitted). *See also Roe,* 410 U.S. at 129–147.

For my own part, I remain convinced, as six other Members of this Court 16 years ago were convinced, that the *Roe* framework, and the viability standard in particular, fairly, sensibly, and effectively functions to safeguard the constitutional liberties of pregnant women while recognizing and accommodating the State's interest in potential human life. The viability line reflects the biological facts and truths of fetal development; it marks that threshold moment prior to which a fetus cannot survive separate from the woman and cannot reasonably and objectively be regarded as a subject of rights or interests distinct from, or paramount to, those of the pregnant woman. At the same time, the viability standard takes account of the undeniable fact that, as the fetus evolves into its postnatal form, and as it loses its dependence on the uterine environment, the State's interest in the fetus' potential human life, and in fostering a regard for human life in general, becomes compelling. As a practical matter, because viability follows "quickening"—the point at which a woman feels movement in her womb—and because viability occurs no earlier than 23 weeks gestational age, it establishes an easily applicable standard for regulating abortion while providing a pregnant woman ample time to exercise her fundamental right with her responsible physician to terminate her pregnancy. Although I have stated previously for a majority of this Court that "[c]onstitutional rights do not always have easily ascertainable boundaries," to seek and establish those boundaries remains the special responsibility of this Court. *Thornburgh,* 476 U.S. at 771. In *Roe,* we discharged that responsibility as logic and science compelled. The plurality today advances not one reasonable argument as to why our judgment in that case was wrong and should be abandoned.

C

Having contrived an opportunity to reconsider the *Roe* framework, and then having discarded that framework, the plurality finds the testing provision unobjectionable because it "permissibly furthers the State's interest in protecting potential human life." *Ante* at 519–520. This newly minted standard is circular, and totally meaningless. Whether a challenged abortion regulation "permissibly furthers" a legitimate state interest is the question that courts must answer in abortion cases, not the standard for courts to apply. In keeping with the rest of its opinion, the plurality makes no attempt to explain or to justify its new standard, either in the abstract or as applied in this case. Nor could it. The "permissibly furthers" standard has no independent meaning, and consists of nothing other than what a majority of this Court may believe at any given moment in any given case. The plurality's novel test appears to be nothing more than a dressed-up version of rational basis review, this Court's most lenient level of scrutiny. One thing is clear, however: were the plurality's "permissibly furthers" standard adopted by the Court, for all practical purposes, *Roe* would be overruled.

The "permissibly furthers" standard completely disregards the irreducible minimum of *Roe*: the Court's recognition that a woman has a limited fundamental constitutional right to decide whether to terminate a pregnancy. That right receives no meaningful recognition in the plurality's written opinion. Since, in the plurality's view, the State's interest in potential life is compelling as of the moment of conception, and is therefore served only if abortion is abolished, every hindrance to a woman's ability to obtain an abortion must be "permissible." Indeed, the more severe the hindrance, the more effectively (and permissibly) the State's interest would be furthered. A tax on abortions or a criminal prohibition would both satisfy the plurality's standard. So, for that matter, would a requirement that a pregnant woman memorize and recite today's plurality opinion before seeking an abortion.

The plurality pretends that *Roe* survives, explaining that the facts of this case differ from those in *Roe*: here, Missouri has chosen to assert its interest in potential life only at the point of viability, whereas, in *Roe*, Texas had asserted that interest from the point of conception, criminalizing all abortions except where the life of the mother was at stake. *Ante* at 521. This, of course, is a distinction without a difference. The plurality repudiates every principle for which *Roe* stands; in good conscience, it cannot possibly believe that *Roe* lies "undisturbed" merely because this case does not call upon the Court to reconsider the Texas statute or one like it. If the Constitution permits a State to enact any statute that reasonably furthers its interest in potential life, and if that interest arises as of conception, why would the Texas statute fail to pass muster? One suspects that the plurality agrees. It is impossible to read the plurality opinion, and especially its final paragraph, without recognizing its implicit invitation to every State to enact more and more restrictive abortion laws, and to assert their interest in potential life as of the moment of conception. All these laws will satisfy the plurality's nonscrutiny until, sometime, a new regime of old dissenters and new appointees will declare what the plurality intends: that *Roe* is no longer good law.

D

Thus, "not with a bang, but a whimper," the plurality discards a landmark case of the last generation and casts into darkness the hopes and visions of every woman in this country who had come to believe that the Constitution guaranteed her the right to exercise some control over her unique ability to bear children. The plurality does so either oblivious or insensitive to the fact that millions of women, and their families, have ordered their lives around the right to reproductive choice, and that this right has become vital to the full participation of women in the economic and political walks of American life. The plurality would clear the way once again for government to force upon women the physical labor and specific and direct medical and psychological harms that may accompany carrying a fetus to term. The plurality would clear the way again for the State to conscript a woman's body and to force upon her a "distressful life and future." *Roe*, 410 U.S. at 153.

The result, as we know from experience, *see* Cates & Rochat, Illegal Abortions in the United States: 1972–1974, 8 Family Planning Perspectives 86, 92 (1976), would be that, every year, hundreds of thousands of women, in desperation, would defy the law and place their health and safety in the unclean and unsympathetic hands of back-alley abortionists, or they would attempt to perform abortions upon themselves, with disastrous results. Every year, many women, especially poor and minority women, would die or suffer debilitating physical trauma, all in the name of enforced morality or religious dictates or lack of compassion, as it may be.

Of the aspirations and settled understandings of American women, of the inevitable and brutal consequences of what it is doing, the tough-approach plurality utters not a word. This silence is callous. It is also profoundly destructive of this Court as an institution. To overturn a constitutional decision is a rare and grave undertaking. To overturn a constitutional decision that secured a fundamental personal liberty to millions of persons would be unprecedented in our 200 years of constitutional history. . . This requirement of justification applies with unique force where, as here, the Court's abrogation of precedent would destroy people's firm belief, based on past decisions of this Court, that they possess an unabridgeable right to undertake certain conduct.

As discussed at perhaps too great length above, the plurality makes no serious attempt to carry "the heavy burden of persuading . . . that changes in society or in the law dictate" the abandonment of *Roe* and its numerous progeny, *Vasquez,* 474 U.S. at 266, much less the greater burden of explaining the abrogation of a fundamental personal freedom. Instead, the plurality pretends that it leaves *Roe* standing, and refuses even to discuss the real issue underlying this case: whether the Constitution includes an unenumerated right to privacy that encompasses a woman's right to decide whether to terminate a pregnancy. To the extent that the plurality does criticize the *Roe* framework, these criticisms are pure *ipse dixit*.

This comes at a cost. The doctrine of *stare decisis* permits society to presume that bedrock principles are founded in the law, rather than in the proclivities of individuals, and thereby contributes to the integrity of our constitutional system of government, both in appearance and in fact.

474 U.S. at 265–266. Today's decision involves the most politically divisive domestic legal issue of our time. By refusing to explain or to justify its proposed revolutionary revision in the law of abortion, and by refusing to abide not only by our precedents, but also by our canons for reconsidering those precedents, the plurality invites charges of cowardice and illegitimacy to our door. I cannot say that these would be undeserved.

II

For today, at least, the law of abortion stands undisturbed. For today, the women of this Nation still retain the liberty to control their destinies. But the signs are evident and very ominous, and a chill wind blows.

JUSTICE STEVENS, concurring in part and dissenting in part.

Having joined Part II-C of the Court's opinion, I shall not comment on § 188.205 of the Missouri statute. With respect to the challenged portions of §§ 188.210 and 188.215, I agree with JUSTICE BLACKMUN, *ante* at 539–541, n. 1 (concurring in part and dissenting in part), that the record identifies a sufficient number of unconstitutional applications to support the Court of Appeals' judgment invalidating those provisions. The reasons why I would also affirm that court's invalidation of § 188.029, the viability testing provision, and §§ 1.205.1(1), (2) of the preamble, require separate explanation.

I

It seems to me that in Part II-D of its opinion, the plurality strains to place a construction on § 188.029 that enables it to conclude: "[W]e would modify and narrow *Roe* and succeeding cases," *ante* at 521. That statement is ill-advised, because there is no need to modify even slightly the holdings of prior cases in order to uphold § 188.029. For the most plausible non-literal construction, as both JUSTICE BLACKMUN, *ante* at 542–544 (concurring in part and dissenting in part), and JUSTICE O'CONNOR, *ante* at 525–531 (concurring in part and concurring in judgment), have demonstrated, is constitutional and entirely consistent with our precedents.

I am unable to accept JUSTICE O'CONNOR's construction of the second sentence in § 188.029, however, because I believe it is foreclosed by two controlling principles of statutory interpretation. First, it is our settled practice to accept the interpretation of state law in which the District Court and the Court of Appeals have concurred even if an examination of the state law issue without such guidance might have justified a different conclusion.

Bishop v. Wood, 426 U.S. 341, 346 (1976). Second,

[t]he fact that a particular application of the clear terms of a statute might be unconstitutional does not provide us with a justification for ignoring the plain meaning of the statute.

Public Citizen v. Department of Justice, 491 U.S. 440, 481 (1989) (KENNEDY, J., concurring in judgment). In this case, I agree with the Court of Appeals, 851 F.2d 1071, 1074–1075 (CA8 1988), and the District Court, 662 F.Supp. 407, 423 (WD Mo.1987), that the meaning of the second sentence of § 188.029 is too plain to be ignored. The sentence twice uses the mandatory term "shall," and contains no qualifying language. If it is implicitly limited to tests that are useful in determining viability, it adds nothing to the requirement imposed by the preceding sentence.

My interpretation of the plain language is supported by the structure of the statute as a whole, particularly the preamble, which "finds" that life "begins at conception" and further commands that state laws shall be construed to provide the maximum protection to "the unborn child at every stage of development." Mo.Rev.Stat. §§ 1.205.1(1), 1.205.2 (1986). I agree with the District Court that "[o]bviously, the purpose of this law is to protect the potential life of the fetus, rather than to safeguard maternal health." 662 F.Supp. at 420. A literal reading of the statute tends to accomplish that goal. Thus it is not "incongruous," *ante* at 515, to assume that the Missouri Legislature was trying to protect the potential human life of nonviable fetuses by making the abortion decision more costly. On the contrary, I am satisfied that the Court of Appeals, as well as the District Court, correctly concluded that the Missouri Legislature meant exactly what it said in the second sentence of § 188.029. I am also satisfied, for the reasons stated by JUSTICE BLACKMUN, that the testing provision is manifestly unconstitutional under *Williamson v. Lee Optical Co.*, 348 U.S. 483 (1955)," irrespective of the *Roe v. Wade*, 410 U.S. 113 (1973),] framework." *Ante* at 544 (concurring in part and dissenting in part).

II

The Missouri statute defines "conception" as "the fertilization of the ovum of a female by a sperm of a male," Mo.Rev.Stat. § 188.015(3) (1986), even though standard medical texts equate "conception" with implantation in the uterus, occurring about six days after fertilization. Missouri's declaration therefore implies regulation not only of previability abortions, but also of common forms of contraception such as the IUD and the morning-after pill. Because the preamble, read in context, threatens serious encroachments upon the liberty of the pregnant woman and the health professional, I am persuaded that these plaintiffs, appellees before us, have standing to challenge its constitutionality. *Accord,* 851 F.2d at 1075–1076.

To the extent that the Missouri statute interferes with contraceptive choices, I have no doubt that it is unconstitutional under the Court's holdings in *Griswold v. Connecticut,* 381 U.S. 479 (1965); *Eisenstadt v. Baird,* 405 U.S. 438 (1972); and *Carey v. Population Services International,* 431 U.S. 678 (1977). The place of *Griswold* in the mosaic of decisions defining a woman's liberty interest was accurately stated by Justice Stewart in his concurring opinion in *Roe v. Wade,* 410 U.S. 113, 167–170 (1973):

[I]n *Griswold v. Connecticut,* 381 U.S. 479, the Court held a Connecticut birth control law unconstitutional. In view of what had been so recently said in *[Ferguson v.] Skrupa,* [372 U.S. 726 (1963),] the Court's opinion in *Griswold* understandably did its best to avoid reliance on the Due Process Clause of the Fourteenth Amendment as the ground for decision. Yet the Connecticut law did not violate any provision of the Bill of Rights, nor any other specific provision of the Constitution. So it was clear to me then, and it is equally clear to me now, that the *Griswold* decision can be rationally understood only as a holding that the Connecticut statute substantively invaded the "liberty" that is protected by the Due Process Clause of the Fourteenth Amendment. As so understood, *Griswold* stands as one in a long line of pre-*Skrupa* cases decided under the doctrine of substantive due process, and I now accept it as such. Several decisions of this Court make clear that freedom of personal choice in matters of marriage and family life is one of the liberties protected by the Due Process Clause of the Fourteenth Amendment. . . . As recently as last Term, in *Eisenstadt v. Baird,* 405 U.S. 438, 453, we recognized the right of the *individual,* married or single, to be free from unwarranted governmental intrusion into matters so fundamentally affecting a person as the decision whether to bear or beget a child. That right necessarily includes the right of a woman to decide whether or not to terminate her pregnancy. Certainly the interests of a woman in giving of her physical and emotional self during pregnancy and the interests that will be affected throughout her life by the birth and raising of a child are of a far greater degree of significance and personal intimacy than the right to send a child to private school protected in *Pierce v. Society of Sisters,* 268 U.S. 510"]268 U.S. 510 (1925), or the right to teach a foreign language protected in 268 U.S. 510 (1925), or the right to teach a foreign language protected in *Meyer v. Nebraska,* 262 U.S. 390 (1923).

Abele v. Markle, 351 F.Supp. 224, 227 (Conn.1972).

Clearly, therefore, the Court today is correct in holding that the right asserted by Jane Roe is embraced within the personal liberty protected by the Due Process Clause of the Fourteenth Amendment.

(Emphasis in original; footnotes omitted.)

One might argue that the *Griswold* holding applies to devices "preventing conception," 381 U.S. at 480—that is, fertilization—but not to those preventing implantation, and therefore, that *Griswold* does not protect a woman's choice to use an IUD or take a morning-after pill. There is unquestionably a theological basis for such an argument, just as there was unquestionably a theological basis for the Connecticut statute that the Court invalidated in *Griswold.* Our jurisprudence, however, has consistently required a secular basis for valid legislation. *See, e.g., Stone v. Graham,* 449 U.S. 39, 40 (1980) (per curiam). Because I am not aware of any secular basis for differentiating between contraceptive procedures that are effective immediately before and those that are effective immediately after fertilization, I believe it inescapably follows that the preamble to the Missouri statute is invalid under *Griswold* and its progeny.

Indeed, I am persuaded that the absence of any secular purpose for the legislative declarations that life begins at conception and that conception occurs at fertilization makes the relevant portion of the preamble invalid under the Establishment Clause of the First Amendment to the Federal Constitution. This conclusion does not, and could not, rest on the fact that the statement happens to coincide with the tenets of certain religions, *see McGowan v. Maryland,* 366 U.S. 420, 442 (1961); *Harris v. McRae,* 448 U.S. 297, 319–320 (1980), or on the fact that the legislators who voted to enact it may have been motivated by religious considerations, *see Washington v. Davis,* 426 U.S. 229, 253 (1976) (STEVENS, J., concurring). Rather, it rests on the fact that the preamble, an unequivocal endorsement of a religious tenet of some, but by no means all, Christian faiths, serves no identifiable secular purpose. That fact alone compels a conclusion that the statute violates the Establishment Clause. *Wallace v. Jaffree,* 472 U.S. 38, 56 (1985).

My concern can best be explained by reference to the position on this issue that was widely accepted by the leaders of the Roman Catholic Church for many years. The position is summarized in a report, entitled "Catholic Teaching On Abortion," prepared by the Congressional Research Service of the Library of Congress. It states in part:

The disagreement over the status of the unformed as against the formed fetus was crucial for Christian teaching on the soul. It was widely held that the soul was not present until the formation of the fetus 40 or 80 days after conception, for males and females respectively. Thus, abortion of the "unformed" or "inanimate" fetus (from *anima,* soul) was something less than true homicide, rather a form of anticipatory or quasi-homicide. This view received its definitive treatment in St. Thomas Aquinas, and became for a time the dominant interpretation m the Latin Church. For St. Thomas, as for mediaeval Christendom generally, there is a lapse of time—approximately 40 to 80 days—after conception and before the soul's infusion. . . .

For St. Thomas, "seed and what is not seed is determined by sensation and movement." What is destroyed in abortion of the unformed fetus is seed, not man. This distinction received its most careful analysis in St. Thomas. It was the general belief of Christendom, reflected, for example, in the Council of Trent (1545–1563), which restricted penalties for homicide to abortion of an animated fetus only.

C. Whittier, Catholic Teaching on Abortion: Its Origin and Later Development (1981), reprinted in Brief for Americans United for Separation of Church and State as *Amicus Curiae* 13a, 17a (quoting *In octo libros politicorum* 7.12, attributed to St. Thomas Aquinas). If the views of St. Thomas were held as widely today as they were in the Middle Ages, and if a state legislature were to enact a statute prefaced with a "finding" that female life begins 80 days after conception and male life begins 40 days after conception, I have no doubt that this Court would promptly conclude that such an endorsement of a particular religious tenet is violative of the Establishment Clause.

In my opinion the difference between that hypothetical statute and Missouri's preamble reflects nothing more than a difference in theological doctrine. The preamble to the Missouri statute endorses the theological position that there is the same secular interest in preserving the life of a fetus during the first 40 or 80 days of pregnancy as there is after viability—indeed, after the time when the fetus has become a "person" with legal rights protected by the

Constitution. To sustain that position as a matter of law, I believe Missouri has the burden of identifying the secular interests that differentiate the first 40 days of pregnancy from the period immediately before or after fertilization when, as *Griswold* and related cases establish, the Constitution allows the use of contraceptive procedures to prevent potential life from developing into full personhood. Focusing our attention on the first several weeks of pregnancy is especially appropriate, because that is the period when the vast majority of abortions are actually performed.

As a secular matter, there is an obvious difference between the state interest in protecting the freshly fertilized egg and the state interest in protecting a 9-month-gestated, fully sentient fetus on the eve of birth. There can be no interest in protecting the newly fertilized egg from physical pain or mental anguish, because the capacity for such suffering does not yet exist; respecting a developed fetus, however, that interest is valid. In fact, if one prescinds the theological concept of ensoulment—or one accepts St. Thomas Aquinas' view that ensoulment does not occur for at least 40 days—a State has no greater secular interest in protecting the potential life of an embryo that is still "seed" than in protecting the potential life of a sperm or an unfertilized ovum.

There have been times in history when military and economic interests would have been served by an increase in population. No one argues today, however, that Missouri can assert a societal interest in increasing its population as its secular reason for fostering potential life. Indeed, our national policy, as reflected in legislation the Court upheld last Term, is to prevent the potential life that is produced by "pregnancy and childbirth among unmarried adolescents." *Bowen v. Kendrick*, 487 U.S. 589, 593 (1988); *accord, id.* at 602. If the secular analysis were based on a strict balancing of fiscal costs and benefits, the economic costs of unlimited childbearing would outweigh those of abortion. There is, of course, an important and unquestionably valid secular interest in "protecting a young pregnant woman from the consequences of an incorrect decision," *Planned Parenthood of Central Mo. v. Danforth*, 428 U.S. 52, 102 (1976) (STEVENS, J., concurring in part and dissenting in part). Although that interest is served by a requirement that the woman receive medical and, in appropriate circumstances, parental, advice, it does not justify the state legislature's official endorsement of the theological tenet embodied in §§ 1.205.1(1), (2).

The State's suggestion that the "finding" in the preamble to its abortion statute is, in effect, an amendment to its tort, property, and criminal laws is not persuasive. The Court of Appeals concluded that the preamble "is simply an impermissible state adoption of a theory of when life begins to justify its abortion regulations." 851 F.2d at 1076. Supporting that construction is the state constitutional prohibition against legislative enactments pertaining to more than one subject matter. Mo.Const., Art. 3, § 23. *See In re Ray*, 83 B.R. 670 (Bkrtcy Ct., ED Mo.1988); *Berry v. Majestic Milling Co.*, 223 S.W. 738 (Mo.1920). Moreover, none of the tort, property, or criminal law cases cited by the State was either based on or buttressed by a theological answer to the question of when life begins. Rather, the Missouri courts, as well as a number of other state courts, had already concluded that a "fetus is a 'person,' 'minor,' or 'minor child' within the meaning of their particular wrongful death statutes." *O'Grady v. Brown*, 654 S.W.2d 904, 910 (Mo.1983) (en banc).

Bolstering my conclusion that the preamble violates the First Amendment is the fact that the intensely divisive character of much of the national debate over the abortion issue reflects the deeply held religious convictions of many participants in the debate. The Missouri Legislature may not inject its endorsement of a particular religious tradition into this debate, for "[t]he Establishment Clause does not allow public bodies to foment such disagreement."

See County of Allegheny v. American Civil Liberties Union, Greater Pittsburgh Chapter, post at 651 (STEVENS, J., concurring in part and dissenting in part).

In my opinion, the preamble to the Missouri statute is unconstitutional for two reasons. To the extent that it has substantive impact on the freedom to use contraceptive procedures, it is inconsistent with the central holding in *Griswold*. To the extent that it merely makes "legislative findings without operative effect," as the State argues, Brief for Appellants 22, it violates the Establishment Clause of the First Amendment. Contrary to the theological "finding" of the Missouri Legislature, a woman's constitutionally protected liberty encompasses the right to act on her own belief that—to paraphrase St. Thomas Aquinas—until a seed has acquired the powers of sensation and movement, the life of a human being has not yet begun.

SOURCE: *Webster v. Reproductive Health Services*, 492 U.S. 490 (1989) (footnotes omitted).

DOCUMENT ANALYSIS

The *Webster* decision, in hindsight, appears like a major turning point in abortion constitutional law. At the time it was issued, just before Independence Day in 1989, all sides in the abortion controversy claimed victory. On the one hand, *Roe v. Wade* was left standing— something that surprised and exulted many abortion rights advocates. On the other hand, the decision was a retraction from *Roe's* holding that abortion is part of a fundamental right of privacy. In allowing new state abortion restrictions to stand, the Court was also affirming the views of antiabortion forces. In upholding all four aspects of the Missouri abortion law (the preamble stating that life begins at conception, the ban on use of public facilities and employees for abortion procedures, the ban on use of public funds, and the implementation of viability tests for mid-pregnancy abortions), the Court embraced a new era of abortion restriction while refusing to follow Justice Scalia's advice and overturn *Roe v. Wade* altogether.

The real impact of the decision would become evident the following year. In 1990, several hundred abortion restrictions were considered in state legislatures across the country. Clearly, antiabortion activists and legislators viewed *Webster* as a new opportunity to advance their interests through state governments. From waiting periods and counseling requirements to public facilities bans, the states pushed for new limitations on abortion access as a consequence of this decision.

While the decision fell short of overturning *Roe*, *Webster* did chip away at one core element of the earlier landmark: the trimester system. Justice Blackmun and the majority created the trimester system in order to balance the interests of the state in fetal life against a woman's privacy right. Still, to the plurality in *Webster*, that balancing act became impracticable in light of technological advances that created both earlier fetal viability and later abortion procedure safety for women. Beyond its perceived impracticability, the plurality in *Webster* also argued that the trimester system did not allow antiabortion states to fully assert their interest in fetal life.

Webster also provides us with a window into future abortion rulings. Justice O'Connor, writing separately from Chief Justice Rehnquist, does so in order to advance her theory of *undue burden*. For O'Connor, and later a majority of the Court, the standard of abortion as a part of privacy right erects too high a hurdle for states choosing to limit abortion access. Rather, O'Connor argues for a new, lower threshold for states to justify abortion barriers: the undue burden standard. Under this rubric, the state would be able to assert its right to regulate abortion so long as that assertion does not create an undue burden on women. What that standard means would be more fully articulated in the years to come.

In part, this development was a reflection of the ruling's vagueness: while the decision came one vote short of overturning *Roe v. Wade*, it had clearly undermined that decision. What would become of *Roe*? How many more restrictions would now be acceptable to the Court? And would the Court—given the right opportunity—eventually overturn *Roe* altogether? The restrictions debated, and in some cases enacted, in the post-*Webster* environment were created to test these and other questions. The answers would become more clear three years later, in another landmark abortion ruling.

Document: Paul Hill, "Why Shoot an Abortionist?"
Date: 1994.
Where: Florida State Prison, Starke, FL.
Significance: This statement and others like it are indicative of the mounting abortion violence common in the 1980s and 1990s and indicate the extent to which a few extreme abortion protesters were willing to take their movement.

Paul Hill, convicted of the murder of a physician and his assistant, at an interview in 2003, one day before his execution in Florida. Getty Images.

When I first appeared on *Donahue*, I asked the audience to suspend judgment as to whether the action had been wise, but I took the position that Griffin's killing of Dr. Gunn was justified. I later realized, however, that using the force necessary to defend the unborn gives credibility, urgency, and direction to the pro-life movement which it has lacked and which it needs in order to prevail.

I realized that using force to stop abortion is the same means that God has used to stop similar atrocities throughout history. In the book of Esther, for instance, Ahasuerus, king of Persia, passed a law in 473 B.C. allowing the Persians to kill their Jewish neighbors. But the Jews did not passively submit; their uses of defensive force prevented a calamity of immense proportions.

In much the same way, when abortion was first legalized in our nation, if the people had resisted this atrocity with the means necessary it would have saved millions of children from a bloody death. It is not unwise or unspiritual, thus, to use the means that God has appointed for keeping His commandments; rather it is presumptuous to neglect these means and expect Him to work apart from them.

I realized that a large number of very important things would be accomplished by my shooting another abortionist in Pensacola.

- This would put the pro-life rhetoric about defending born and unborn children equally into practice.
- It would bear witness to the full humanity of the unborn as nothing else could.
- It would also open the people's eyes to the enormous consequences of abortion—not only for the unborn, but also for the government that had sanctioned it and for those who are required to resist it.

- This would convict millions of people of their past neglect and spur many to future obedience.
- I also realized that this would help to force people to decide whether they would join the battle in defense of abortionists or side with their intended victims.
- *But most importantly,* I realized that this would uphold the truth of the Gospel at the precise point of Satan's current attack (the abortionist's knife). While most Christians firmly profess the duty to defend *born* children with force (which is not being disputed by the government) most of these professors have neglected the duty to similarly defend the *unborn.* They are steady everywhere on the battlefield except where the battle currently rages. I was certain that if I took my stand at this point, others would join with me, and the Lord would eventually bring about a great victory.

SOURCE: Paul Hill, "Why Shoot an Abortionist?" (1994), available at: http://armyofgod.com/PHill onepage.html. Reprinted with permission.

DOCUMENT ANALYSIS

Paul Hill was a former Presbyterian minister. He was convicted of murdering Dr. John Britton and his bodyguard James Barrett, and seriously injuring June Barrett, on July 29, 1994, and was subsequently sentenced to death. The first abortion protester executed for murdering a physician, Hill died by lethal injection in 2003.

Hill's view that abortion opposition requires and justifies violence represents an extreme, but minority, view within the antiabortion movement. Although a minority, the impact of this fringe element within the movement is serious. Abortion activists were responsible for a wave of clinic violence starting in the 1980s and peaking in the early 1990s. Facing this wave of violence, Congress passed legislation in 1994 called the Freedom of Access to Clinic Entrances, which elevated clinic-blockade violence to a federal offense. As a consequence, much of the violence associated with the 1980s and 1990s has abated.

Although clinic violence has subsided somewhat, the specter of that violence is widely cited as a reason for the decline of abortion availability in recent years. Fewer physicians are willing to risk their personal safety to perform the procedure—an effect that violent protesters no doubt intended. As the number of providers declines, abortion inevitably becomes harder to procure.

IN HISTORY

NUMBER OF ABORTION PROVIDERS, 1992–2000

As a consequence of abortion clinic violence and other abortion restrictions, the number of abortion providers declined 24 percent from 1992 to 2000, leaving 87 percent of all U.S. counties without a single abortion provider at the beginning of the twenty-first century.

Further Reading

Bachiochi, Erika, ed. *The Cost of "Choice": Women Evaluate the Impact of Abortion*. San Francisco: Encounter Books, 2004.

Doan, Alesha E. *Opposition & Intimidation: The Abortion Wars and Strategies of Political Harassment*. Ann Arbor: University of Michigan Press, 2007.

Glendon, Mary Ann. *Abortion and Divorce in Western Law: American Failures, European Challenges*. Cambridge, Mass.: Harvard University Press, 1987.

Gorney, Cynthia. *Articles of Faith: A Frontline History of the Abortion Wars*. New York: Simon and Schuster, 1998.

McKeegan, Michelle. *Abortion Politics: Mutiny in the Ranks of the Right*. New York: The Free Press, 1992.

Risen, James, and Judy L. Thomas. *Wrath of Angels: The American Abortion War*. New York: Basic Books, 1998.

Terry, Randall A. *Operation Rescue*. Springdale, Penn.: Whitaker House, 1988.

6

THE PENDULUM SWINGS AGAIN

By the 1990s, abortion politics had intensified in our nation's capitol. A hundred years before, abortion debates on a national level proved the exception rather than the rule. By the 1990s, both major political parties were entrenched in their abortion policy preferences despite there being wide appreciation for moderate abortion solutions among rank-and-file voters. Growing increasingly polarized, the party's divergent positions allowed for national abortion politics to reach passionate, new levels.

Adding to the intensification of abortion politics on the national landscape was the increased levels of clinic violence. As the Clinton administration assumed power in 1993, the Democrats began to look for ways to not only roll back conservative abortion policy from the Reagan and Bush years but also to extend greater protection to clinic workers and patients. Paul Hill's murder of an abortion provider in 1993 created such a catalyst for change that many Republicans joined Democratic ranks to pass legislation dealing specifically with clinic violence.

Throughout this time, the Republican view of abortion policy gained a foothold despite a unified Democratic government in 1993 and 1994. The Supreme Court had been remade by 1992 as a consequence of the Republicans' commitment to appointing abortion foes to the bench, and the Reagan and Bush years saw five openings on the Court, as well as the elevation of Nixon appointee William Rehnquist to Chief Justice. This created a real opportunity for Republicans, working with the antiabortion movement leaders, to deliver on their promise of an antiabortion Court.

Toward the end of the twentieth century, elected Democrats were under increasing pressure to reconsider their abortion policy preferences. Although public opinion has supported moderate abortion rights consistently over the past 35 years, the momentum of prolife organization and Court-led policy change creates waves within Democratic ranks. And while President Clinton was able to advance clinic violence legislation during his years of unified government, his ability to effect prochoice goals was stymied by the midterm election of 1994, which delivered congressional control to conservative Republicans for the first time in 40 years.

From 1995 until the end of his presidency, Bill Clinton was barely able to stem the tide of anti-abortion reform, and then only with the veto pen.

Document: Planned Parenthood of Southeastern Pennsylvania v. Robert P. Casey, et al.
Date: October 21, 1991.

Where: United States Court of Appeals, Third Circuit.

Significance: This opinion gives a window into then-Judge Samuel A. Alito's judicial views of abortion and foreshadowed his later role as Supreme Court Justice. Alito was confirmed to the Supreme Court 16 years after the following opinion, having been nominated by President George W. Bush.

ALITO, Circuit Judge, concurring in part and dissenting in part.

I concur in the court's judgment except insofar as it holds that 18 Pa.Cons.Stat.Ann. § 3209 (Supp.1991) (spousal notice) is unconstitutional. I also join all of the court's opinion except for the portions concerning Section 3209 and those interpreting Justice O'Connor's opinion in *Hodgson v. Minnesota*, 497 U.S. 417, 110 S.Ct. 2926, 2949–51, 111 L.Ed.2d 344 (1990), to mean that the two-parent notification requirement without judicial bypass imposed an "undue burden" and was thus required to satisfy strict scrutiny.

*720 I.

As the court suggests, the crux of this case concerns the identification of the constitutional standard that the lower courts must now apply in cases involving laws regulating abortion. For the reasons carefully explained in the court's opinion, I agree that *Webster v. Reproductive Health Services*, 492 U.S. 490, 109 S.Ct. 3040, 106 L.Ed.2d 410 (1989), and Hodgson changed the law that we are bound to apply and that the test set out in Justice O'Connor's opinions now represents the governing legal standard.

My disagreement with the majority regarding a single provision of the Pennsylvania Abortion Control Act, 18 Pa.Cons.Stat.Ann. § 3201 et seq. (1983 & Supp.1991), results from disagreement about the portion of Justice O'Connor's two-part test that must be applied to this provision. Under that test, as the majority explains, a law that imposes an "undue burden" must serve a "compelling" state interest. By contrast, a law that does not impose an "undue burden" must simply be "rationally" or "reasonably" related to a "legitimate" state interest. The majority holds that Section 3209 constitutes an undue burden. The majority therefore applies the first prong of the two-part test and strikes down Section 3209 on the ground that it does not serve a "compelling" interest. I do not believe that Section 3209 has been shown to impose an undue burden as that term is used in the relevant Supreme Court opinions; I therefore apply the second prong of the two-part test; and I conclude that Section 3209 is constitutional because it is "rationally related" to a "legitimate" state interest.

Although the majority and I apply different prongs of this two-part test, I see no indication that we disagree concerning the conclusion produced when either prong is applied to Section 3209. If the majority is correct that Section 3209 must satisfy heightened scrutiny, I agree that its constitutionality is doubtful. Similarly, I do not interpret the majority opinion to mean that Section 3209 cannot satisfy the rational relationship test. Indeed, the majority acknowledges that Section 3209 serves a "legitimate" interest. See majority opin. at 715, 716. Thus, my major disagreement with the majority concerns the question whether Section 3209 imposes an "undue burden," and I will therefore turn to that question.

II.

A. Justice O'Connor has explained the meaning of the term "undue burden" in several abortion opinions. In *Akron v. Akron Center for Reproductive Health*, 462 U.S. at 464, 103 S.Ct. at 2510 (O'Connor, J., dissenting), she wrote that "an 'undue burden' has been found for the most part in situations involving absolute obstacles or severe limitations on the abortion decision." She noted that laws held unconstitutional in prior cases involved statutes that "criminalized all abortions except those necessary to save the life of the mother," inhibited "'the vast majority of abortions after the first 12 weeks,' "or gave the parents of a pregnant minor an absolute veto power over the abortion decision. Id. (emphasis in original; citations omitted). She suggested that an "undue burden" would not be created by "a state regulation [that] may 'inhibit' abortions to some degree." Id. She also suggested that there is no undue burden unless a measure has the effect of "substantially limiting access." Id. at 463, 103 S.Ct. at 2509, quoting *Carey v. Population Services International*, 431 U.S. 678, 688, 97 S.Ct. 2010, 2017, 52 L.Ed.2d 675 (1977) (emphasis added in Justice O'Connor's opinion).

Justice O'Connor reiterated the same analysis in *Thornburgh v. American College of Obstetricians and Gynecologists*, 476 U.S. 747, 106 S.Ct. 2169 (1986). She wrote (id. at 828, 106 S.Ct. at 2214 (O'Connor, J., dissenting), quoting *Akron*, 462 U.S. at 464, 103 S.Ct. at 2510 (O'Connor, J., dissenting):

An undue burden would generally be found "in situations involving absolute obstacles or severe limitations on the abortion decision," not wherever a state regulation "may 'inhibit' abortions to some degree."

*721 She also criticized the majority for taking an approach under which "the mere possibility that some women will be less likely to choose to have an abortion by virtue of the presence of a particular state regulation suffices to invalidate it." Id. 476 U.S. at 829, 106 S.Ct. at 2214 (emphasis added).

Justice O'Connor's application of the undue burden test in several cases further illustrates the meaning of this test. In Hodgson, 110 S.Ct. at 2950–51, Justice O'Connor found that no undue burden was imposed by a law requiring notice to both parents or judicial authorization before a minor could obtain an abortion. Justice O'Connor reached this conclusion despite statistics adduced by Justice Marshall to show that mandatory parental notice may inhibit a significant percentage of minors from obtaining abortions (id. at 2953–54) (Marshall, J., dissenting) and despite the district court's finding, noted in Justice Marshall's dissent, that the judicial bypass option "so daunted" some minors that they felt compelled to carry to term (id. at 2959, quoting 648 F.Supp. at 763).

Justice O'Connor has also suggested on more than one occasion that no undue burden was created by the statute upheld in *H.L. v. Matheson*, 450 U.S. 398, 101 S.Ct. 1164, 67 L.Ed.2d 388 (1981), which required parental notice prior to any abortion on an unemancipated minor. Instead, she has stated that this statute merely inhibited abortions to "some degree." Thornburgh, 476 U.S. at 828, 106 S.Ct. at 2214 (O'Connor, J., dissenting); Akron, 462 U.S. at 464, 103 S.Ct. at 2510 (O'Connor, J., dissenting). In dissent in Matheson, Justice Marshall argued that the statute would result in substantial interference with abortions sought by minors. He wrote (450 U.S. at 398, 101 S.Ct. at 1164) (Marshall, J., dissenting) that "the minor may confront physical or emotional abuse, withdrawal of financial support or actual obstruction of the abortion decision." These harms are almost identical to those that the majority in this case attributes to Section 3209. See majority opin. at 711–12. See also *Planned Parenthood Association v. Ashcroft*, 462 U.S. 476, 505, 103 S.Ct. 2517, 2532, 76 L.Ed.2d 733 (1983) (O'Connor concurring and dissenting) (statute requiring parental consent or judicial authorization "imposes no undue burden").

Finally, Justice O'Connor has concluded that regulations that simply increase the cost of abortions, including regulations that may double the cost, do not create an "undue burden."

See Akron, 462 U.S. at 434–35, 103 S.Ct. at 2494–95 (maj. op.); at 466–67, 103 S.Ct. at 2511–12 (O'Connor, J., dissenting). Justice O'Connor reached this conclusion even though it seems clear that such increased costs may well deter some women.

Taken together, Justice O'Connor's opinions reveal that an undue burden does not exist unless a law (a) prohibits abortion or gives another person the authority to veto an abortion or (b) has the practical effect of imposing "severe limitations," rather than simply inhibiting abortions "'to some degree'" or inhibiting "some women." Thornburgh, 476 U.S. at 828, 829, 106 S.Ct. at 2213, 2214 (O'Connor, J., dissenting), quoting Akron, 462 U.S. at 464, 103 S.Ct. at 2510 (O'Connor, J., dissenting). Furthermore, Justice O'Connor's opinions disclose that the practical effect of a law will not amount to an undue burden unless the effect is greater than the burden imposed on minors seeking abortions in Hodgson or Matheson or the burden created by the regulations in Akron that appreciably increased costs. Since the laws at issue in those cases had inhibiting effects that almost certainly were substantial enough to dissuade some women from obtaining abortions, it appears clear that an undue burden may not be established simply by showing that a law will have a heavy impact on a few women but that instead a broader inhibiting effect must be shown.

In this case, the plaintiffs, who made a facial attack on Section 3209, did not prove that this provision would impose an undue burden. Section 3209 does not create an "absolute obstacle" or give a husband "veto power." Rather, this provision merely requires a married woman desiring an abortion to certify that she has notified her husband or to claim one of the statutory exceptions.

The plaintiffs also failed to carry their burden of proving that Section 3209 if enforced would have the kind of broad practical impact needed to establish an "undue burden" under the opinions discussed above. Clearly the plaintiffs did not substantiate the impact of Section 3209 with the degree of analytical rigor that should be demanded before striking down a state statute. Cf. Akron, 462 U.S. at 463, 103 S.Ct. at 2510 (O'Connor, J., dissenting) (citation omitted) (courts should exercise "'deliberate restraint' "before finding an undue burden "'in view of the respect that properly should be accorded legislative judgments'"); id. at 465, 103 S.Ct. at 2511.

At the outset, it is apparent that two factors imposed a low ceiling on any showing that the plaintiffs could have made. First, as the district court found, the "vast majority" of married women voluntarily inform their husbands before seeking an abortion. Planned Parenthood v. Casey, 744 F.Supp. 1323, 1360 (E.D.Pa.1990). Indeed, in the trial testimony on which the district court relied, the plaintiffs' witness stated that in her experience 95% of married women notify their husbands. App. at 701. Second, the overwhelming majority of abortions are sought by unmarried women. Thus, it is immediately apparent that Section 3209 cannot affect more than about 5% of married women seeking abortions or an even smaller percentage of all women desiring abortions.

The plaintiffs failed to show even roughly how many of the women in this small group would actually be adversely affected by Section 3209. As previously noted, Section 3209 contains four significant exceptions. These exceptions apply if a woman certifies that she has not notified her husband because she believes that (1) he is not the father of the child, (2) he cannot be found after diligent effort, (3) the pregnancy is the result of a spousal sexual assault that has been reported to the authorities, or (4) she has reason to believe that notification is likely to result in the infliction of bodily injury upon her. If Section 3209 were allowed to take effect, it seems safe to assume that some percentage of the married women seeking abortions without notifying their husbands would qualify for and invoke these exceptions. The record, however, is devoid of evidence showing how many women could or could not invoke an exception.

Of the potentially affected women who could not invoke an exception, it seems safe to assume that some percentage, despite an initial inclination not to tell their husbands, would notify their husbands without suffering substantial ill effects. Again, however, the record lacks evidence showing how many women would or would not fall into this category. Thus, the plaintiffs did not even roughly substantiate how many women might be inhibited from obtaining an abortion or otherwise harmed by Section 3209. At best, the record shows that Section 3209 would inhibit abortions "'to some degree'" or that "some women [would] be less likely to choose to have an abortion by virtue of the presence" of Section 3209. Thornburgh, 476 U.S. at 828, 106 S.Ct. at 2214 (O'Connor, J., dissenting), quoting Akron, 462 U.S. at 464, 103 S.Ct. at 2510 (O'Connor, J., dissenting). And even with respect to these women, the plaintiffs did not show that the impact of Section 3209 would be any greater or any different from the impact of the notice requirement upheld in Matheson. Consequently, the plaintiffs failed to prove that Section 3209 would impose an undue burden.

Second, the plaintiffs offered testimony that the exceptions in Section 3209 would not cover a case in which a woman did not want to notify her husband for fear that he would retaliate in some way other than the infliction of bodily injury upon her, such as by subjecting her to psychological abuse or abusing their children (see 744 F.Supp. at 1360–62). The plaintiffs, however, do not appear to have offered any evidence showing how many (or indeed that any actual women) would be affected by this asserted imperfection in the statute.

Third, the plaintiffs introduced general evidence about the problem of spouse abuse (see 744 F.Supp. at 1361). They offered widely varying statistics concerning the dimensions of the problem, as well as evidence that battering occurs in all socioeconomic groups and is sometimes fatal. This proof, while documenting the existence of a broad national problem, provides no basis for any estimate of what is relevant here—the impact of Section 3209.

Fourth, the plaintiffs offered evidence that "mere notification of pregnancy is frequently a flashpoint for battering" (see 744 F.Supp. at 1361). This proof indicates when violence is likely to occur in an abusive marriage but provides no basis for determining how many women would be adversely affected by Section 3209.

Finally, the plaintiffs offered the opinion of one of their witnesses that most battered women would be psychologically incapable of taking advantage of Section 3209's fourth exception, i.e., the exception for cases in which the woman has reason to fear that notification will lead to the infliction of bodily harm upon her (see 744 F.Supp. at 1363). However, the plaintiffs failed to show how many of the women potentially affected by Section 3209 (married women seeking abortions without notifying their husbands) are victims of battering. Thus, the opinion offered by their expert, even if taken at face value, merely describes the likely behavior of most of the women in a group of unknown size. Clearly, then, this evidence does not show how many women would be inhibited or otherwise harmed by Section 3209. I cannot believe that a state statute may be held facially unconstitutional simply because one expert testifies that in her opinion the provision would harm a completely unknown number of women.

Needless to say, the plight of any women, no matter how few, who may suffer physical abuse or other harm as a result of this provision is a matter of grave concern. It is apparent that the Pennsylvania legislature considered this problem and attempted to prevent Section 3209 from causing adverse effects by adopting the four exceptions noted above. Whether the legislature's approach represents sound public policy is not a question for us to decide. Our task here is simply to decide whether Section 3209 meets constitutional standards. The first step in this analysis is to determine whether Section 3209 has been shown to create an undue burden under Supreme Court precedent, and for the reasons just explained it seems clear that an undue burden has not been established.

B. This conclusion is not undermined (and may indeed be supported) by the portion of Justice O'Connor's opinion in Hodgson regarding the constitutionality of the two-parent notice requirement without judicial bypass. The majority in this case interprets Justice O'Connor's opinion to mean that this requirement imposed an undue burden and did not serve a "compelling" interest. Majority opin. at 696. I interpret Justice O'Connor's opinion differently. I do not read her opinion to mean that the two-parent notice requirement without judicial bypass constituted an undue burden. Rather, I interpret her opinion to mean that this requirement was unconstitutional because it was not reasonably related to a legitimate state interest. Thus, I do not believe that her opinion (or the Court's holding) supports the majority's conclusion in the present case that the spousal notification requirement in Section 3209 imposes an undue burden.

In Hodgson, Justice Stevens wrote the lead opinion discussing the unconstitutionality of the two-parent notification requirement without judicial bypass, and Justice O'Connor joined most of Justice Stevens' opinion (see 110 S.Ct. at 2949 (O'Connor, J., concurring)). Thus, in interpreting Justice O'Connor's position, it is helpful to begin with the relevant portions of Justice Stevens' opinion.

Two portions of Justice Stevens' opinion, Parts III and VII, are most important for present purposes. In Part III, Justice Stevens discussed the applicable constitutional standard. Nowhere in this portion of his opinion (or indeed in any portion of his opinion) did Justice Stevens make reference to "strict," "exacting," or "heightened" scrutiny or any of the terminology associated with that level of review. Instead, he concluded that the statute failed to satisfy even the least demanding standard of review. He wrote (110 S.Ct. at 2937): "Under any analysis, the . . . statute cannot be sustained if the obstacles it imposes are not reasonably related to legitimate state interests."

In Part VII of his opinion, Justice Stevens explained (id. at 2945) why the two-parent notice requirement did not "reasonably further any legitimate state interest." Thus it seems clear that Justice Stevens' opinion concluded that the two-parent notice requirement without judicial bypass was unconstitutional because it failed some variant of the rational relationship test.

In my view, Justice O'Connor's opinion in Hodgson did not subject this requirement to a more exacting level of scrutiny. Although Justice O'Connor did not join Part III of Justice Stevens' opinion (in which he discussed the general constitutional standard that he applied), Justice O'Connor wrote as follows (110 S.Ct. at 2949–50 emphasis added):

> It has been my understanding in this area that "[i]f the particular regulation does not 'unduly burde[n]' the fundamental right, . . . then our evaluation of that regulation is limited to our determination that the regulation rationally relates to a legitimate state purpose.". . . . It is with that understanding that I agree with Justice Stevens' statement "that the statute cannot be sustained if the obstacles it imposes are not reasonably related to legitimate state interests."

I interpret this to mean that Justice O'Connor agreed with Justice Stevens that the challenged statute should be judged under the rational relationship test. I do not think that she would have expressed general agreement with Justice Stevens' statement of the governing legal standard if she believed that the statute imposed an undue burden and was thus required to satisfy an entirely different legal standard. I also do not think that she would have concluded that the statute created an undue burden without explaining the basis for that conclusion. Moreover, Justice O'Connor joined Part VII of Justice Stevens' opinion, in which, as previously noted, Justice Stevens concluded that the two-parent notice requirement without judicial bypass was not "reasonably" related to any "legitimate interest." I do not think that Justice O'Connor would have joined this portion of Justice Stevens' opinion if her position regarding the constitutionality of the provision was based on a fundamentally different analysis. Thus, I conclude that Justice O'Connor found the two-parent notice statute unconstitutional under the rational relationship test. This must mean either (a) that she did not believe that this requirement constituted an undue burden or (b) that she did not find it necessary to reach that question because she believed that the requirement could not even pass the rational relationship test. In either event, her position in no way undermines my conclusion that Section 3209 has not been shown to create an undue burden.

III.

Since Section 3209 has not been proven to impose an undue burden, it must serve a "legitimate" (but not necessarily a "compelling") state interest. The majority acknowledges that this provision serves a "legitimate" interest, namely, the state's interest in furthering the husband's interest in the fetus. See majority opin. at 715, 716. I agree with this conclusion, and I do not think that this point requires extended discussion.

The Supreme Court has held that a man has a fundamental interest in preserving his ability to father a child. *Skinner v. Oklahoma*, 316 U.S. 535, 541, 62 S.Ct. 1110, 1113, 86 L.Ed. 1655 (1942). The Court's opinions also seem to establish that a husband who is willing to participate in raising a child has a fundamental interest in the child's welfare . . . It follows that a husband has a "legitimate" interest in the welfare of a fetus he has conceived with his wife.

To be sure, the Supreme Court held in *Planned Parenthood of Missouri v. Danforth*, 428 U.S. 52, 67–72, 96 S.Ct. 2831, 2840–43, 49 L.Ed.2d 788 (1976), that a potential father may not be given the legal authority to veto an abortion, and thus the Court apparently held that the potential father's interest was not "compelling." But the Court did not question the legitimacy of this interest. On the contrary, the Court wrote (id. at 69, 96 S.Ct. at 2841 (emphasis added)): "We are not unaware of the deep and proper concern and interest that a devoted and protective husband has in his wife's pregnancy and in the growth and development of the fetus she is carrying." See also id. at 93, 96 S.Ct. at 2852 (White, J., dissenting) ("A father's interest in having a child—perhaps his only child—may be unmatched by any other interest in his life"). Since a "deep and proper . . . interest" appears indistinguishable from a "legitimate" interest, it seems clear that a husband has a "legitimate" interest in the fate of the fetus.

This interest may be legitimately furthered by state legislation. "[S]tatutory regulation of domestic relations [is] an area that has long been regarded as a virtually exclusive province of the States." *Sosna v. Iowa*, 419 U.S. 393, 404, 95 S.Ct. 553, 560, 42 L.Ed.2d 532 (1975) . . . Accordingly, Pennsylvania has a legitimate interest in furthering the husband's interest in the fate of the fetus, as the majority in this case acknowledges.

IV.

The remaining question is whether Section 3209 is "rationally" or "reasonably" related to this interest. Under the rational relationship test, which developed in equal protection cases, "legislation carries with it a presumption of rationality that can only be overcome by a clear showing of arbitrariness and irrationality." Hodel v. Indiana, 452 U.S. 314, 331–32, 101 S.Ct. 2376, 2386–87, 69 L.Ed.2d 40 (1981). This test does not permit the invalidation of legislation simply because it is "deemed unwise or unartfully drawn." U.S. Railroad Retirement Board v. Fritz, 449 U.S. 166, 175, 101 S.Ct. 453, 459, 66 L.Ed.2d 368 (1981). Legislation does not violate this test simply because it produces some adverse effects. . . . As the Court wrote in Dandridge v. Williams, 397 U.S. 471, 485–86, 90 S.Ct. 1153, 1161–62, 25 L.Ed.2d 491 (1970):

"The problems of government are practical ones and may justify, if they do not require, rough accommodations—illogical, it may be, and unscientific." Metropolis Theatre Co. v. City of Chicago, 228 U.S. 61, 68- 70 [33 S.Ct. 441, 443, 57 L.Ed. 730 (1913)]. . . . . . [The rational-basis standard] is true to the principle that the Fourteenth Amendment gives the federal courts no power to impose upon the States their views of what constitutes wise economic or social policy.

See also Dallas v. Stanglin, 490 U.S. 19, 25–27, 109 S.Ct. 1591, 1595–96, 104 L.Ed.2d 18 (1989); Cleburne v. Cleburne Living Center, Inc., 473 U.S. 432, 439–40, 105 S.Ct. 3249, 3253–54, 87 L.Ed.2d 313 (1985). Rather, "those challenging the legislative judgment must convince the Court that the legislative facts on which the classification is apparently based could not reasonably be conceived to be true by the governmental decisionmaker." Vance v. Bradley, 440 U.S. 93, 111, 99 S.Ct. 939, 949, 59 L.Ed.2d 171 (1979). See also Hancock Industries v. Schaeffer, 811 F.2d 225, 238 (3d Cir.1987).

Even assuming that the rational relationship test is more demanding in the present context than in most equal protection cases, that test is satisfied here. The Pennsylvania legislature could have rationally believed that some married women are initially inclined to obtain an abortion without their husbands' knowledge because of perceived problems—such as economic constraints, future plans, or the husbands' previously expressed opposition—that may be obviated by discussion prior to the abortion. In addition, the legislature could have reasonably concluded that Section 3209 would lead to such discussion and thereby properly further a husband's interests in the fetus in a sufficient percentage of the affected cases to justify enactment of this measure. Although the plaintiffs and supporting amici argue that Section 3209 will do little if any good and will produce appreciable adverse effects, the Pennsylvania legislature presumably decided that the law on balance would be beneficial. We have no authority to overrule that legislative judgment even if we deem it "unwise" or worse. U.S. Railroad Retirement Board v. Fritz, 449 U.S. at 175, 101 S.Ct. at 459. "We should not forget that 'legislatures are ultimate guardians of the liberty and welfare of the people in quite as great a degree as the courts.'" Akron v. Akron Center For Reproductive Health, 462 U.S. at 465, 103 S.Ct. at 2511 (O'Connor, J., dissenting), quoting Missouri, K. & T.R. Co. v. May, 194 U.S. 267, 270, 24 S.Ct. 638, 639, 48 L.Ed. 971 (1904). Clearly, the plaintiffs have not shown that "the legislative facts on which [the statute] is apparently based could not reasonably be conceived to be true by the governmental decisionmaker." *727 Vance v. Bradley, 440 U.S. at 111, 99 S.Ct. at 949. Thus, Section 3209 is rationally related to a legitimate state interest and may not be invalidated under the Supreme Court's abortion precedents.

SOURCE: *Planned Parenthood of Southeastern Pennsylvania v. Robert P. Casey, et al. 947 F.2d 682, 60 USLW 2276 (1991).*

DOCUMENT ANALYSIS

Judge Alito's dissent in this decision does offer insight into his views on liberty, abortion rights, and women. But perhaps most importantly, the opinion sheds light on now-Justice Alito's interpretation of the *undue burden* standard created by his Supreme Court predecessor, Justice Sandra Day O'Connor, and how he would apply that standard to abortion limitations.

Justice O'Connor's undue burden standard was fully articulated in her 1992 opinion in *Planned Parenthood v. Casey* (see the following document) when the high Court reviewed this lower court's ruling. In using this standard in his dissent, Judge Alito was interpreting past reference to undue burden in O'Connor's dissenting opinions of previous cases. Thus, he did not have the benefit of O'Connor's more elaborate description of 1992.

What Alito did have, however, was Supreme Court precedent. In 1976, the Supreme Court issued its *Planned Parenthood of Central Missouri v. Danforth* decision (428 U.S. 52). In that ruling, the justices considered a Missouri law that would have required a husband's consent to his wife's abortion. Based on the higher standard of abortion as a fundamental right, the Court argued that husband consent requirements were unconstitutional.

Pennsylvania's statute required notification, not consent, of the prospective father prior to abortion. This distinction, combined with Alito's interpretation of O'Connor's emerging undue burden standard, led the judge to approve the husband notification provision in Pennsylvania law. Judge Alito simply did not find compelling the argument that spousal notification could endanger certain women who had reason to fear domestic violence. And while the Supreme Court agreed with Alito's colleagues that even under undue burden, a husband notification requirement fails to meet constitutional muster, Alito's perspective likely has followed him to his new post at the Supreme Court.

Document: Justice O'Connor's plurality opinion from *Planned Parenthood of Southeastern Pennsylvania v. Casey* (footnotes omitted).
Date: June 29, 1992.
Where: U.S. Supreme Court.
Significance: Casey is most notable for answering some of the questions raised three years earlier in *Webster*. The case clarifies the Court's position about abortion through the creation of a new standard for abortion restrictions: the

Antiabortion protestors praying outside the U.S. Supreme Court building during the 2005 "March for Life," an annual protest marking the anniversary of the *Roe v. Wade* ruling. Getty Images.

undue burden standard. Using this new standard Justice O'Connor and the Court do not agree with Judge Alito that husband notification is constitutionally acceptable.

Liberty finds no refuge in a jurisprudence of doubt. Yet 19 years after our holding that the Constitution protects a woman's right to terminate her pregnancy in its early stages, *Roe v. Wade*, 410 U.S. 113 (1973), that definition of liberty is still questioned. Joining the respondents as *amicus curiae*, the United States, as it has done in five other cases in the last decade, again asks us to overrule *Roe* . . .

At issue in these cases are five provisions of the Pennsylvania Abortion Control Act of 1982 as amended in 1988 and 1989. . . . The Act requires that a woman seeking an abortion give her informed consent prior to the abortion procedure, and specifies that she be provided with certain information at least 24 hours before the abortion is performed. For a minor to obtain an abortion, the Act requires the informed consent of one of her parents, but provides for a judicial bypass option if the minor does not wish to or cannot obtain a parent's consent. Another provision of the Act requires that, unless certain exceptions apply, a married woman seeking an abortion must sign a statement indicating that she has notified her husband of her intended abortion. The Act exempts compliance with these three requirements in the event of a "medical emergency," which is defined in the Act. In addition to the above provisions regulating the performance of abortions, the Act imposes certain reporting requirements on facilities that provide abortion services. Before any of these provisions took effect, the petitioners, who are five abortion clinics and one physician representing himself as well as a class of physicians who provide abortion services, brought this suit seeking declaratory and injunctive relief. Each provision was challenged as unconstitutional on its face. The District Court entered a preliminary injunction against the enforcement of the regulations, and, after a 3 day bench trial, held all the provisions at issue here unconstitutional, entering a permanent injunction against Pennsylvania's enforcement of them. 744 F.Supp. 1323 (ED Pa. 1990). The Court of Appeals for the Third Circuit affirmed in part and reversed in part, upholding all of the regulations except for the husband notification requirement. 947 F. 2d 682 (1991). We granted certiorari. 502 U.S. ____ (1992).

The Court of Appeals found it necessary to follow an elaborate course of reasoning even to identify the first premise to use to determine whether the statute enacted by Pennsylvania meets constitutional standards. . . And at oral argument in this Court, the attorney for the parties challenging the statute took the position that none of the enactments can be upheld without overruling *Roe v. Wade*. Tr. of Oral Arg. 5–6. We disagree with that analysis; but we acknowledge that our decisions after *Roe* cast doubt upon the meaning and reach of its holding. Further, the Chief Justice admits that he would overrule the central holding of *Roe* and adopt the rational relationship test as the sole criterion of constitutionality. . . State and federal courts as well as legislatures throughout the Union must have guidance as they seek to address this subject in conformance with the Constitution. Given these premises, we find it imperative to review once more the principles that define the rights of the woman and the legitimate authority of the State respecting the termination of pregnancies by abortion procedures.

After considering the fundamental constitutional questions resolved by *Roe*, principles of institutional integrity, and the rule of *stare decisis*, we are led to conclude this: the essential holding of *Roe v. Wade* should be retained and once again reaffirmed.

It must be stated at the outset and with clarity that *Roe*'s essential holding, the holding we reaffirm, has three parts. First is a recognition of the right of the woman to choose to have an abortion before viability and to obtain it without undue interference from the State. Before viability, the State's interests are not strong enough to support a prohibition of abortion or the imposition of a substantial obstacle to the woman's effective right to elect the procedure. Second is a confirmation of the State's power to restrict abortions after fetal viability, if the law contains exceptions for pregnancies which endanger a woman's life or health. And third is the principle that the State has legitimate interests from the outset of the pregnancy in protecting the health of the woman and the life of the fetus that may become a child. These principles do not contradict one another; and we adhere to each.

Constitutional protection of the woman's decision to terminate her pregnancy derives from the Due Process Clause of the Fourteenth Amendment. It declares that no State shall "deprive any person of life, liberty, or property, without due process of law." The controlling word in the case before us is "liberty." Although a literal reading of the Clause might suggest that it governs only the procedures by which a State may deprive persons of liberty . . . the Clause has been understood to contain a substantive component as well, one "barring certain government actions regardless of the fairness of the procedures used to implement them." *Daniels v. Williams*, 474 U.S. 327, 331 (1986). As Justice Brandeis (joined by Justice Holmes) observed, "[d]espite arguments to the contrary which had seemed to me persuasive, it is settled that the due process clause of the Fourteenth Amendment applies to matters of substantive law as well as to matters of procedure. Thus all fundamental rights comprised within the term liberty are protected by the Federal Constitution from invasion by the States." . . .

The most familiar of the substantive liberties protected by the Fourteenth Amendment are those recognized by the Bill of Rights. We have held that the Due Process Clause of the Fourteenth Amendment incorporates most of the Bill of Rights against the States. . . It is tempting, as a means of curbing the discretion of federal judges, to suppose that liberty encompasses no more than those rights already guaranteed to the individual against federal interference by the express provisions of the first eight amendments to the Constitution. . . . But of course this Court has never accepted that view. It is also tempting, for the same reason, to suppose that the Due Process Clause protects only those practices, defined at the most specific level, that were protected against government interference by other rules of law when the Fourteenth Amendment was ratified. . . But such a view would be inconsistent with our law. It is a promise of the Constitution that there is a realm of personal liberty which the government may not enter. We have vindicated this principle before . . .

The inescapable fact is that adjudication of substantive due process claims may call upon the Court in interpreting the Constitution to exercise that same capacity which by tradition courts always have exercised: reasoned judgment. Its boundaries are not susceptible of expression as a simple rule. That does not mean we are free to invalidate state policy choices with which we disagree; yet neither does it permit us to shrink from the duties of our office . . .

Men and women of good conscience can disagree, and we suppose some always shall disagree, about the profound moral and spiritual implications of terminating a pregnancy, even in its earliest stage. Some of us as individuals find abortion offensive to our most basic principles of morality, but that cannot control our decision. Our obligation is to define the liberty of all, not to mandate our own moral code. The underlying constitutional issue is whether the State can resolve these philosophic questions in such a definitive way that a woman lacks all choice in the matter, except perhaps in those rare circumstances in which the pregnancy is itself a danger to her own life or health, or is the result of rape or incest.

It is conventional constitutional doctrine that where reasonable people disagree the government can adopt one position or the other. . . That theorem, however, assumes a state of affairs in which the choice does not intrude upon a protected liberty. Thus, while some people might disagree about whether or not the flag should be saluted, or disagree about the proposition that it may not be defiled, we have ruled that a State may not compel or enforce one view or the other . . .

Our law affords constitutional protection to personal decisions relating to marriage, procreation, contraception, family relationships, child rearing, and education. *Carey v. Population Services International*, 431 U.S., at 685. Our cases recognize "the right of the *individual*, married or single, to be free from unwarranted governmental intrusion into matters so fundamentally affecting a person as the decision whether to bear or beget a child." *Eisenstadt v. Baird, supra*, at 453 (emphasis in original). Our precedents "have respected the private realm of family life which the state cannot enter." *Prince v. Massachusetts*, 321 U.S. 158, 166 (1944). These matters, involving the most intimate and personal choices a person may make in a lifetime, choices central to personal dignity and autonomy, are central to the liberty protected by the Fourteenth Amendment. At the heart of liberty is the right to define one's own concept of existence, of meaning, of the universe, and of the mystery of human life. Beliefs about these matters could not define the attributes of personhood were they formed under compulsion of the State.

These considerations begin our analysis of the woman's interest in terminating her pregnancy but cannot end it, for this reason: though the abortion decision may originate within the zone of conscience and belief, it is more than a philosophic exercise. Abortion is a unique act. It is an act fraught with consequences for others: for the woman who must live with the implications of her decision; for the persons who perform and assist in the procedure; for the spouse, family, and society which must confront the knowledge that these procedures exist, procedures some deem nothing short of an act of violence against innocent human life; and, depending on one's beliefs, for the life or potential life that is aborted. Though abortion is conduct, it does not follow that the State is entitled to proscribe it in all instances. That is because the liberty of the woman is at stake in a sense unique to the human condition and so unique to the law. The mother who carries a child to full term is subject to anxieties, to physical constraints, to pain that only she must bear. That these sacrifices have from the beginning of the human race been endured by woman with a pride that ennobles her in the eyes of others and gives to the infant a bond of love cannot alone be grounds for the State to insist she make the sacrifice. Her suffering is too intimate and personal for the State to insist, without more, upon its own vision of the woman's role, however dominant that vision has been in the course of our history and our culture. The destiny of the woman must be shaped to a large extent on her own conception of her spiritual imperatives and her place in society.

It should be recognized, moreover, that in some critical respects the abortion decision is of the same character as the decision to use contraception, to which *Griswold v. Connecticut*, *Eisenstadt v. Baird*, and *Carey v. Population Services International*, afford constitutional protection. We have no doubt as to the correctness of those decisions. They support the reasoning in *Roe* relating to the woman's liberty because they involve personal decisions concerning not only the meaning of procreation but also human responsibility and respect for it. As with abortion, reasonable people will have differences of opinion about these matters. One view is based on such reverence for the wonder of creation that any pregnancy ought to be welcomed and carried to full term no matter how difficult it will be to provide for the child and ensure its well being. Another is that the inability to provide for the nurture and care of the infant is a cruelty to the child and an anguish to the parent. These are intimate views with infinite variations, and their deep, personal character underlay our decisions in *Griswold*, *Eisenstadt*, and *Carey*. The same concerns are present when the woman confronts the reality that, perhaps despite her attempts to avoid it, she has become pregnant.

It was this dimension of personal liberty that *Roe* sought to protect, and its holding invoked the reasoning and the tradition of the precedents we have discussed, granting protection to substantive liberties of the person. *Roe* was, of course, an extension of those cases and, as the decision itself indicated, the separate States could act in some degree to further their own legitimate interests in protecting pre-natal life. The extent to which the legislatures of the States might act to outweigh the interests of the woman in choosing to terminate her pregnancy was a subject of debate both in *Roe* itself and in decisions following it.

While we appreciate the weight of the arguments made on behalf of the State in the case before us, arguments which in their ultimate formulation conclude that *Roe* should be overruled, the reservations any of us may have in reaffirming the central holding of *Roe* are outweighed by the explication of individual liberty we have given combined with the force of *stare decisis*. We turn now to that doctrine . . .

Even when the decision to overrule a prior case is not, as in the rare, latter instance, virtually foreordained, it is common wisdom that the rule of *stare decisis* is not an "inexorable command," and certainly it is not such in every constitutional case. . . Rather, when this Court reexamines a prior holding, its judgment is customarily informed by a series of prudential and pragmatic considerations designed to test the consistency of overruling a prior decision with the ideal of the rule of law, and to gauge the respective costs of reaffirming and overruling a prior case. Thus, for example, we may ask whether the rule has proved to be intolerable simply in defying practical workability, *Swift & Co. v. Wickham*, 382 U.S. 111, 116 (1965); whether the rule is subject to a kind of reliance that would lend a special hardship to the consequences of overruling and add inequity to the cost of repudiation, *e. g.*, *United States v. Title Ins. & Trust Co.*, 265 U.S. 472, 486 (1924); whether related principles of law have so far developed as to have left the old rule no more than a remnant of abandoned doctrine, see *Patterson v. McLean Credit Union*, 491 U.S. 164, 173–174 (1989); or whether facts have so changed or come to be seen so differently, as to have robbed the old rule of significant application or justification, *e.g.*, *Burnet, supra*, at 412 (Brandeis, J., dissenting).

So in this case we may inquire whether *Roe*'s central rule has been found unworkable; whether the rule's limitation on state power could be removed without serious inequity to those who have relied upon it or significant damage to the stability of the society governed by the rule in question; whether the law's growth in the intervening years has left *Roe*'s central rule a doctrinal anachronism discounted by society; and whether *Roe*'s premises of fact have so far changed in the ensuing two decades as to render its central holding somehow irrelevant or unjustifiable in dealing with the issue it addressed.

Although *Roe* has engendered opposition, it has in no sense proven "unworkable," see *Garcia v. San Antonio Metropolitan Transit Authority*, 469 U.S. 528, 546 (1985), representing as it does a simple limitation beyond which a state law is unenforceable. While *Roe* has, of course, required judicial assessment of state laws affecting the exercise of the choice guaranteed against government infringement, and although the need for such review will remain as a consequence of today's decision, the required determinations fall within judicial competence.

The inquiry into reliance counts the cost of a rule's repudiation as it would fall on those who have relied reasonably on the rule's continued application. Since the classic case for weighing reliance heavily in favor of following the earlier rule occurs in the commercial context . . . where advance planning of great precision is most obviously a necessity, it is no cause for surprise that some would find no reliance worthy of consideration in support of *Roe*.

While neither respondents nor their *amici* in so many words deny that the abortion right invites some reliance prior to its actual exercise, one can readily imagine an argument stressing the dissimilarity of this case to one involving property or contract. Abortion is customarily chosen as an unplanned response to the consequence of unplanned activity or to the failure of conventional birth control, and except on the assumption that no intercourse would have occurred but for *Roe*'s holding, such behavior may appear to justify no reliance claim. Even if reliance could be claimed on that unrealistic assumption, the argument might run, any reliance interest would be *de minimis*. This argument would be premised on the hypothesis that reproductive planning could take virtually immediate account of any sudden restoration of state authority to ban abortions.

To eliminate the issue of reliance that easily, however, one would need to limit cognizable reliance to specific instances of sexual activity. But to do this would be simply to refuse to face the fact that for two decades of economic and social developments, people have organized intimate relationships and made choices that define their views of themselves and their places in society, in reliance on the availability of abortion in the event that contraception should fail. The ability of women to participate equally in the economic and social life of the Nation has been facilitated by their ability to control their reproductive lives. . . The Constitution serves human values, and while the effect of reliance on *Roe* cannot be exactly measured, neither can the certain cost of overruling *Roe* for people who have ordered their thinking and living around that case be dismissed.

No evolution of legal principle has left *Roe*'s doctrinal footings weaker than they were in 1973. No development of constitutional law since the case was decided has implicitly or explicitly left *Roe* behind as a mere survivor of obsolete constitutional thinking.

It will be recognized, of course, that *Roe* stands at an intersection of two lines of decisions, but in whichever doctrinal category one reads the case, the result for present purposes will be the same. The *Roe* Court itself placed its holding in the succession of cases most prominently exemplified by *Griswold v. Connecticut*, 381 U.S. 479 (1965), see *Roe*, 410 U.S., at 152–153. When it is so seen, *Roe* is clearly in no jeopardy, since subsequent constitutional developments have neither disturbed, nor do they threaten to diminish, the scope of recognized protection accorded to the liberty relating to intimate relationships, the family, and decisions about whether or not to beget or bear a child . . .

Roe, however, may be seen not only as an exemplar of *Griswold* liberty but as a rule (whether or not mistaken) of personal autonomy and bodily integrity, with doctrinal affinity to cases recognizing limits on governmental power to mandate medical treatment or to bar its rejection. If so, our cases since *Roe* accord with *Roe*'s view that a State's interest in the protection of life falls short of justifying any plenary override of individual liberty claims . . .

Finally, one could classify *Roe* as *sui generis*. If the case is so viewed, then there clearly has been no erosion of its central determination. The original holding resting on the concurrence of seven Members of the Court in 1973 was expressly affirmed by a majority of six in 1983, see *Akron v. Akron Center for Reproductive Health, Inc.*, 462 U.S. 416 (1983) (*Akron I*), and by a majority of five in 1986 , see *Thornburgh v. American College of Obstetricians and Gynecologists*, 476 U.S. 747 (1986), expressing adherence to the constitutional ruling despite legislative efforts in some States to test its limits. More recently, in *Webster v. Reproductive Health Services*, 492 U.S. 490 (1989), although two of the present authors questioned the trimester framework in a way consistent with our judgment today, see *id.*, at 518 (Rehnquist C. J., joined by White, and Kennedy, JJ.); *id.*, at 529 (O'Connor, J., concurring in part and concurring in judgment), a majority of the Court either decided to reaffirm or declined to address the constitutional validity of the central holding of *Roe*. See *Webster*, 492 U.S., at 521 (Rehnquist, C. J., joined by White and Kennedy, JJ.); *id.*, at 525–526 (O'Connor, J., concurring in part and concurring in judgment); *id.*, at 537, 553 (Blackmun, J., joined by Brennan and Marshall, JJ., concurring in part and dissenting in part); *id.*, at 561–563 (Stevens, J., concurring in part and dissenting in part).

Nor will courts building upon *Roe* be likely to hand down erroneous decisions as a consequence. Even on the assumption that the central holding of *Roe* was in error, that error would go only to the strength of the state interest in fetal protection, not to the recognition afforded by the Constitution to the woman's liberty. The latter aspect of the decision fits comfortably within the framework of the Court's prior decisions . . .

The soundness of this prong of the *Roe* analysis is apparent from a consideration of the alternative. If indeed the woman's interest in deciding whether to bear and beget a child had not been recognized as in *Roe*, the State might as readily restrict a woman's right to choose to carry a pregnancy to term as to terminate it, to further asserted state interests in population control, or eugenics, for example. Yet *Roe* has been sensibly relied upon to counter any such suggestions. . . . In any event, because *Roe's* scope is confined by the fact of its concern with postconception potential life, a concern otherwise likely to be implicated only by some forms of contraception protected independently under *Griswold* and later cases, any error in *Roe* is unlikely to have serious ramifications in future cases.

We have seen how time has overtaken some of *Roe's* factual assumptions: advances in maternal health care allow for abortions safe to the mother later in pregnancy than was true in 1973, see *Akron I*, *supra*, at 429, n. 11, and advances in neonatal care have advanced viability to a point somewhat earlier. Compare *Roe*, 410 U.S., at 160, with *Webster*, *supra*, at 515–516 (opinion of Rehnquist, C. J.); see *Akron I*, *supra*, at 457, and n. 5 (O'Connor, J., dissenting). But these facts go only to the scheme of time limits on the realization of competing interests, and the divergences from the factual premises of 1973 have no bearing on the validity of *Roe's* central holding, that viability marks the earliest point at which the State's interest in fetal life is constitutionally adequate to justify a legislative ban on nontherapeutic abortions. The soundness or unsoundness of that constitutional judgment in no sense turns on whether viability occurs at approximately 28 weeks, as was usual at the time of *Roe*, at 23 to 24 weeks, as it sometimes does today, or at some moment even slightly earlier in pregnancy, as it may if fetal respiratory capacity can somehow be enhanced in the future. Whenever it may occur, the attainment of viability may continue to serve as the critical fact, just as it has done since *Roe* was decided; which is to say that no change in *Roe's* factual underpinning has left its central holding obsolete, and none supports an argument for overruling it.

The sum of the precedential inquiry to this point shows *Roe's* underpinnings unweakened in any way affecting its central holding. While it has engendered disapproval, it has not been unworkable. An entire generation has come of age free to assume *Roe's* concept of liberty in defining the capacity of women to act in society, and to make reproductive decisions; no erosion of principle going to liberty or personal autonomy has left *Roe's* central holding a doctrinal remnant; *Roe* portends no developments at odds with other precedent for the analysis of personal liberty; and no changes of fact have rendered viability more or less appropriate as the point at which the balance of interests tips. Within the bounds of normal *stare decisis* analysis, then, and subject to the considerations on which it customarily turns, the stronger argument is for affirming *Roe*'s central holding, with whatever degree of personal reluctance any of us may have, not for overruling it.

In a less significant case, *stare decisis* analysis could, and would, stop at the point we have reached. But the sustained and widespread debate *Roe* has provoked calls for some comparison between that case and others of comparable dimension that have responded to national controversies and taken on the impress of the controversies addressed . . .

Because neither the factual underpinnings of *Roe*'s central holding nor our understanding of it has changed (and because no other indication of weakened precedent has been shown) the Court could not pretend to be reexamining the prior law with any justification beyond a present doctrinal disposition to come out differently from the Court of 1973. To overrule prior law for no other reason than that would run counter to the view repeated in our cases, that a decision to overrule should rest on some special reason over and above the belief that a prior case was wrongly decided . . .

. . . [a] terrible price that would have been paid if the Court had not overruled as it did. In the present case, however, as our analysis to this point makes clear, the terrible price would be paid for overruling. Our analysis would not be complete, however, without explaining why overruling *Roe*'s central holding would not only reach an unjustifiable result under principles of *stare decisis*, but would seriously weaken the Court's capacity to exercise the judicial power and to function as the Supreme Court of a Nation dedicated to the rule of law. To understand why this would be so it is necessary to understand the source of this Court's authority, the conditions necessary for its preservation, and its relationship to the country's understanding of itself as a constitutional Republic.

The root of American governmental power is revealed most clearly in the instance of the power conferred by the Constitution upon the Judiciary of the United States and specifically upon this Court. As Americans of each succeeding generation are rightly told, the Court cannot buy support for its decisions by spending money and, except to a minor degree, it cannot independently coerce obedience to its decrees. The Court's power lies, rather, in its legitimacy, a product of substance and perception that shows itself in the people's acceptance of the Judiciary as fit to determine what the Nation's law means and to declare what it demands.

The underlying substance of this legitimacy is of course the warrant for the Court's decisions in the Constitution and the lesser sources of legal principle on which the Court draws. That substance is expressed in the Court's opinions, and our contemporary understanding is such that a decision without principled justification would be no judicial act at all. But even when justification is furnished by apposite legal principle, something more is required. Because not every conscientious claim of principled justification will be accepted as such, the justification claimed must be beyond dispute. The Court must take care to speak and act in ways that allow people to accept its decisions on the terms the Court claims for them, as grounded truly in principle, not as compromises with social and political pressures having, as such, no bearing on the principled choices that the Court is obliged to make. Thus, the Court's legitimacy depends on making legally principled decisions under circumstances in which their principled character is sufficiently plausible to be accepted by the Nation.

The need for principled action to be perceived as such is implicated to some degree whenever this, or any other appellate court, overrules a prior case. This is not to say, of course, that this Court cannot give a perfectly satisfactory explanation in most cases. People understand that some of the Constitution's language is hard to fathom and that the Court's Justices are sometimes able to perceive significant facts or to understand principles of law that eluded their predecessors and that justify departures from existing decisions. However upsetting it may be to those most directly affected when one judicially derived rule replaces another, the country can accept some correction of error without necessarily questioning the legitimacy of the Court.

In two circumstances, however, the Court would almost certainly fail to receive the benefit of the doubt in overruling prior cases. There is, first, a point beyond which frequent overruling would overtax the country's belief in the Court's good faith. Despite the variety of reasons that may inform and justify a decision to overrule, we cannot forget that such a decision is usually perceived (and perceived correctly) as, at the least, a statement that a prior decision was wrong. There is a limit to the amount of error that can plausibly be imputed to prior courts. If that limit should be exceeded, disturbance of prior rulings would be taken as evidence that justifiable reexamination of principle had given way to drives for particular results in the short term. The legitimacy of the Court would fade with the frequency of its vacillation.

That first circumstance can be described as hypothetical; the second is to the point here and now. Where, in the performance of its judicial duties, the Court decides a case in such a way as to resolve the sort of intensely divisive controversy reflected in *Roe* and those rare, comparable cases, its decision has a dimension that the resolution of the normal case does not carry. It is the dimension present whenever the Court's interpretation of the Constitution calls the contending sides of a national controversy to end their national division by accepting a common mandate rooted in the Constitution.

The Court is not asked to do this very often, having thus addressed the Nation only twice in our lifetime, in the decisions of *Brown* and *Roe*. But when the Court does act in this way, its decision requires an equally rare precedential force to counter the inevitable efforts to overturn it and to thwart its implementation. Some of those efforts may be mere unprincipled emotional reactions; others may proceed from principles worthy of profound respect. But whatever the premises of opposition may be, only the most convincing justification under accepted standards of precedent could suffice to demonstrate that a later decision overruling the first was anything but a surrender to political pressure, and an unjustified repudiation of the principle on which the Court staked its authority in the first instance. So to overrule under fire in the absence of the most compelling reason to reexamine a watershed decision would subvert the Court's legitimacy beyond any serious question . . .

The country's loss of confidence in the judiciary would be underscored by an equally certain and equally reasonable condemnation for another failing in overruling unnecessarily and under pressure. Some cost will be paid by anyone who approves or implements a constitutional decision where it is unpopular, or who refuses to work to undermine the decision or to force its reversal. The price may be criticism or ostracism, or it may be violence. An extra price will be paid by those who themselves disapprove of the decision's results when viewed outside of constitutional terms, but who nevertheless struggle to accept it, because they respect the rule of law. To all those who will be so tested by following, the Court implicitly undertakes to remain steadfast, lest in the end a price be paid for nothing. The promise of constancy, once given, binds its maker for as long as the power to stand by the decision survives and the understanding of the issue has not changed so fundamentally as to render the commitment obsolete. From the obligation of this promise this Court cannot and should not assume any exemption when duty requires it to decide a case in conformance with the

Constitution. A willing breach of it would be nothing less than a breach of faith, and no Court that broke its faith with the people could sensibly expect credit for principle in the decision by which it did that.

It is true that diminished legitimacy may be restored, but only slowly. Unlike the political branches, a Court thus weakened could not seek to regain its position with a new mandate from the voters, and even if the Court could somehow go to the polls, the loss of its principled character could not be retrieved by the casting of so many votes. Like the character of an individual, the legitimacy of the Court must be earned over time. So, indeed, must be the character of a Nation of people who aspire to live according to the rule of law. Their belief in themselves as such a people is not readily separable from their understanding of the Court invested with the authority to decide their constitutional cases and speak before all others for their constitutional ideals. If the Court's legitimacy should be undermined, then, so would the country be in its very ability to see itself through its constitutional ideals. The Court's concern with legitimacy is not for the sake of the Court but for the sake of the Nation to which it is responsible.

The Court's duty in the present case is clear. In 1973, it confronted the already divisive issue of governmental power to limit personal choice to undergo abortion, for which it provided a new resolution based on the due process guaranteed by the Fourteenth Amendment. Whether or not a new social consensus is developing on that issue, its divisiveness is no less today than in 1973, and pressure to overrule the decision, like pressure to retain it, has grown only more intense. A decision to overrule *Roe's* essential holding under the existing circumstances would address error, if error there was, at the cost of both profound and unnecessary damage to the Court's legitimacy, and to the Nation's commitment to the rule of law. It is therefore imperative to adhere to the essence of *Roe's* original decision, and we do so today.

From what we have said so far it follows that it is a constitutional liberty of the woman to have some freedom to terminate her pregnancy. We conclude that the basic decision in *Roe* was based on a constitutional analysis which we cannot now repudiate. The woman's liberty is not so unlimited, however, that from the outset the State cannot show its concern for the life of the unborn, and at a later point in fetal development the State's interest in life has sufficient force so that the right of the woman to terminate the pregnancy can be restricted.

That brings us, of course, to the point where much criticism has been directed at *Roe*, a criticism that always inheres when the Court draws a specific rule from what in the Constitution is but a general standard. We conclude, however, that the urgent claims of the woman to retain the ultimate control over her destiny and her body, claims implicit in the meaning of liberty, require us to perform that function. Liberty must not be extinguished for want of a line that is clear. And it falls to us to give some real substance to the woman's liberty to determine whether to carry her pregnancy to full term.

We conclude the line should be drawn at viability, so that before that time the woman has a right to choose to terminate her pregnancy. We adhere to this principle for two reasons. First, as we have said, is the doctrine of *stare decisis*. Any judicial act of line drawing may seem somewhat arbitrary, but *Roe* was a reasoned statement, elaborated with great care. We have twice reaffirmed it in the face of great opposition. See *Thornburgh v. American College of Obstetricians & Gynecologists*, 476 U.S., at 759; *Akron I*, 462 U.S., at 419–420. Although we must overrule those parts of *Thornburgh* and *Akron I* which, in our view, are inconsistent with *Roe's* statement that the State has a legitimate interest in promoting the life or potential life of the unborn, see *infra*, at ___, the central premise of those cases represents an unbroken commitment by this Court to the essential holding of *Roe*. It is that premise which we re-affirm today.

The second reason is that the concept of viability, as we noted in *Roe*, is the time at which there is a realistic possibility of maintaining and nourishing a life outside the womb, so that the independent existence of the second life can in reason and all fairness be the object of state protection that now overrides the rights of the woman. See *Roe v. Wade*, 410 U.S., at 163. Consistent with other constitutional norms, legislatures may draw lines which appear arbitrary without the necessity of offering a justification. But courts may not. We must justify the lines we draw. And there is no line other than viability which is more workable. To be sure, as we have said, there may be some medical developments that affect the precise point of viability, see *supra,* at ___, but this is an imprecision within tolerable limits given that the medical community and all those who must apply its discoveries will continue to explore the matter. The viability line also has, as a practical matter, an element of fairness. In some broad sense it might be said that a woman who fails to act before viability has consented to the State's intervention on behalf of the developing child.

The woman's right to terminate her pregnancy before viability is the most central principle of *Roe v. Wade*. It is a rule of law and a component of liberty we cannot renounce.

On the other side of the equation is the interest of the State in the protection of potential life. The *Roe* Court recognized the State's "important and legitimate interest in protecting the potentiality of human life." *Roe, supra,* at 162. The weight to be given this state interest, not the strength of the woman's interest, was the difficult question faced in *Roe*. We do not need to say whether each of us, had we been Members of the Court when the valuation of the State interest came before it as an original matter, would have concluded, as the *Roe* Court did, that its weight is insufficient to justify a ban on abortions prior to viability even when it is subject to certain exceptions. The matter is not before us in the first instance, and coming as it does after nearly 20 years of litigation in *Roe*'s wake we are satisfied that the immediate question is not the soundness of *Roe*'s resolution of the issue, but the precedential force that must be accorded to its holding. And we have concluded that the essential holding of *Roe* should be reaffirmed.

Yet it must be remembered that *Roe v. Wade* speaks with clarity in establishing not only the woman's liberty but also the State's "important and legitimate interest in potential life." *Roe, supra,* at 163. That portion of the decision in *Roe* has been given too little acknowledge-ment and implementation by the Court in its subsequent cases. Those cases decided that any regulation touching upon the abortion decision must survive strict scrutiny, to be sustained only if drawn in narrow terms to further a compelling state interest. See, *e.g., Akron I, supra,* at 427. Not all of the cases decided under that formulation can be reconciled with the hold-ing in *Roe* itself that the State has legitimate interests in the health of the woman and in protecting the potential life within her. In resolving this tension, we choose to rely upon *Roe*, as against the later cases.

Roe established a trimester framework to govern abortion regulations. Under this elabo-rate but rigid construct, almost no regulation at all is permitted during the first trimester of pregnancy; regulations designed to protect the woman's health, but not to further the State's interest in potential life, are permitted during the second trimester; and during the third tri-mester, when the fetus is viable, prohibitions are permitted provided the life or health of the mother is not at stake. . . Most of our cases since *Roe* have involved the application of rules derived from the trimester framework . . .

The trimester framework no doubt was erected to ensure that the woman's right to choose not become so subordinate to the State's interest in promoting fetal life that her choice exists in theory but not in fact. We do not agree, however, that the trimester approach is necessary to accomplish this objective. A framework of this rigidity was unnecessary and in its later interpretation sometimes contradicted the State's permissible exercise of its powers.

Though the woman has a right to choose to terminate or continue her pregnancy before viability, it does not at all follow that the State is prohibited from taking steps to ensure that this choice is thoughtful and informed. Even in the earliest stages of pregnancy, the State may enact rules and regulations designed to encourage her to know that there are philosophic and social arguments of great weight that can be brought to bear in favor of continuing the pregnancy to full term and that there are procedures and institutions to allow adoption of unwanted children as well as a certain degree of state assistance if the mother chooses to raise the child herself. "'[T]he Constitution does not forbid a State or city, pursuant to democratic processes, from expressing a preference for normal childbirth.'" *Webster v. Reproductive Health Services*, 492 U.S., at 511 (opinion of the Court) (quoting *Poelker v. Doe*, 432 U.S. 519, 521 (1977)). It follows that States are free to enact laws to provide a reasonable framework for a woman to make a decision that has such profound and lasting meaning. This, too, we find consistent with *Roe*'s central premises, and indeed the inevitable consequence of our holding that the State has an interest in protecting the life of the unborn.

We reject the trimester framework, which we do not consider to be part of the essential holding of *Roe*. See *Webster v. Reproductive Health Services*, *supra*, at 518 (opinion of Rehnquist, C. J.); *id.*, at 529 (O'Connor, J., concurring in part and concurring in judgment) (describing the trimester framework as "problematic"). Measures aimed at ensuring that a woman's choice contemplates the consequences for the fetus do not necessarily interfere with the right recognized in *Roe*, although those measures have been found to be inconsistent with the rigid trimester framework announced in that case. A logical reading of the central holding in *Roe* itself, and a necessary reconciliation of the liberty of the woman and the interest of the State in promoting prenatal life, require, in our view, that we abandon the trimester framework as a rigid prohibition on all previability regulation aimed at the protection of fetal life. The trimester framework suffers from these basic flaws: in its formulation it misconceives the nature of the pregnant woman's interest; and in practice it undervalues the State's interest in potential life, as recognized in *Roe*. As our jurisprudence relating to all liberties save perhaps abortion has recognized, not every law which makes a right more difficult to exercise is, *ipso facto*, an infringement of that right. An example clarifies the point. We have held that not every ballot access limitation amounts to an infringement of the right to vote. Rather, the States are granted substantial flexibility in establishing the framework within which voters choose the candidates for whom they wish to vote . . .

The abortion right is similar. Numerous forms of state regulation might have the incidental effect of increasing the cost or decreasing the availability of medical care, whether for abortion or any other medical procedure. The fact that a law which serves a valid purpose, one not designed to strike at the right itself, has the incidental effect of making it more difficult or more expensive to procure an abortion cannot be enough to invalidate it. Only where state regulation imposes an undue burden on a woman's ability to make this decision does the power of the State reach into the heart of the liberty protected by the Due Process Clause . . .

These considerations of the nature of the abortion right illustrate that it is an overstatement to describe it as a right to decide whether to have an abortion "without interference from the State," *Planned Parenthood of Central Mo. v. Danforth,* 428 U.S. 52, 61 (1976). All abortion regulations interfere to some degree with a woman's ability to decide whether to terminate her pregnancy. It is, as a consequence, not surprising that despite the protestations contained in the original *Roe* opinion to the effect that the Court was not recognizing an absolute right, 410 U.S., at 154–155, the Court's experience applying the trimester framework has led to the striking down of some abortion regulations which in no real sense deprived women of the ultimate decision. Those decisions went too far because the right recognized by *Roe* is a right "to be free from unwarranted governmental intrusion into matters so fundamentally affecting a person as the decision whether to bear or beget a child." *Eisenstadt v. Baird,* 405 U.S., at 453. Not all governmental intrusion is of necessity unwarranted; and that brings us to the other basic flaw in the trimester framework: even in *Roe's* terms, in practice it undervalues the State's interest in the potential life within the woman.

Roe v. Wade was express in its recognition of the State's "important and legitimate interest[s] in preserving and protecting the health of the pregnant woman [and] in protecting the potentiality of human life." 410 U.S., at 162. The trimester framework, however, does not fulfill *Roe's* own promise that the State has an interest in protecting fetal life or potential life. *Roe* began the contradiction by using the trimester framework to forbid any regulation of abortion designed to advance that interest before viability. *Id.,* at 163. Before viability, *Roe* and subsequent cases treat all governmental attempts to influence a woman's decision on behalf of the potential life within her as unwarranted. This treatment is, in our judgment, incompatible with the recognition that there is a substantial state interest in potential life throughout pregnancy . . .

The very notion that the State has a substantial interest in potential life leads to the conclusion that not all regulations must be deemed unwarranted. Not all burdens on the right to decide whether to terminate a pregnancy will be undue. In our view, the undue burden standard is the appropriate means of reconciling the State's interest with the woman's constitutionally protected liberty.

The concept of an undue burden has been utilized by the Court as well as individual members of the Court, including two of us, in ways that could be considered inconsistent . . . Because we set forth a standard of general application to which we intend to adhere, it is important to clarify what is meant by an undue burden.

A finding of an undue burden is a shorthand for the conclusion that a state regulation has the purpose or effect of placing a substantial obstacle in the path of a woman seeking an abortion of a nonviable fetus. A statute with this purpose is invalid because the means chosen by the State to further the interest in potential life must be calculated to inform the woman's free choice, not hinder it. And a statute which, while furthering the interest in potential life or some other valid state interest, has the effect of placing a substantial obstacle in the path of a woman's choice cannot be considered a permissible means of serving its legitimate ends. To the extent that the opinions of the Court or of individual Justices use the undue burden standard in a manner that is inconsistent with this analysis, we set out what in our view should be the controlling standard . . . Understood another way, we answer the question, left open in previous opinions discussing the undue burden formulation, whether a law designed to further the State's interest in fetal life which imposes an undue burden on the woman's decision before fetal viability could be constitutional. . . . The answer is no.

Some guiding principles should emerge. What is at stake is the woman's right to make the ultimate decision, not a right to be insulated from all others in doing so. Regulations which do no more than create a structural mechanism by which the State, or the parent or guardian of a minor, may express profound respect for the life of the unborn are permitted, if they are not a substantial obstacle to the woman's exercise of the right to choose. See *infra*, at ___ ___ (addressing Pennsylvania's parental consent requirement). Unless it has that effect on her right of choice, a state measure designed to persuade her to choose childbirth over abortion will be upheld if reasonably related to that goal. Regulations designed to foster the health of a woman seeking an abortion are valid if they do not constitute an undue burden . . .

That is to be expected in the application of any legal standard which must accommodate life's complexity. We do not expect it to be otherwise with respect to the undue burden standard. We give this summary:

(a) To protect the central right recognized by Roe *v.* Wade while at the same time accommodating the State's profound interest in potential life, we will employ the undue burden analysis as explained in this opinion. An undue burden exists, and therefore a provision of law is invalid, if its purpose or effect is to place a substantial obstacle in the path of a woman seeking an abortion before the fetus attains viability.

(b) We reject the rigid trimester framework of *Roe v. Wade*. To promote the State's profound interest in potential life, throughout pregnancy the State may take measures to ensure that the woman's choice is informed, and measures designed to advance this interest will not be invalidated as long as their purpose is to persuade the woman to choose childbirth over abortion. These measures must not be an undue burden on the right.

(c) As with any medical procedure, the State may enact regulations to further the health or safety of a woman seeking an abortion. Unnecessary health regulations that have the purpose or effect of presenting a substantial obstacle to a woman seeking an abortion impose an undue burden on the right.

(d) Our adoption of the undue burden analysis does not disturb the central holding of *Roe v. Wade,* and we reaffirm that holding. Regardless of whether exceptions are made for particular circumstances, a State may not prohibit any woman from making the ultimate decision to terminate her pregnancy before viability.

(e) We also reaffirm *Roe*'s holding that "subsequent to viability, the State in promoting its interest in the potentiality of human life may, if it chooses, regulate, and even proscribe, abortion except where it is necessary, in appropriate medical judgment, for the preservation of the life or health of the mother." *Roe v. Wade,* 410 U.S., at 164–165.

These principles control our assessment of the Pennsylvania statute, and we now turn to the issue of the validity of its challenged provisions.

The Court of Appeals applied what it believed to be the undue burden standard and upheld each of the provisions except for the husband notification requirement. We agree generally with this conclusion, but refine the undue burden analysis in accordance with the principles articulated above. We now consider the separate statutory sections at issue.

Because it is central to the operation of various other requirements, we begin with the statute's definition of medical emergency. Under the statute, a medical emergency is "[t]hat condition which, on the basis of the physician's good faith clinical judgment, so complicates the medical condition of a pregnant woman as to necessitate the immediate abortion of her pregnancy to avert her death or for which a delay will create serious risk of substantial and irreversible impairment of a major bodily function." 18 Pa. Cons. Stat. (1990). § 3203.

Petitioners argue that the definition is too narrow, contending that it forecloses the possibility of an immediate abortion despite some significant health risks. If the contention were correct, we would be required to invalidate the restrictive operation of the provision, for the essential holding of *Roe* forbids a State from interfering with a woman's choice to undergo an abortion procedure if continuing her pregnancy would constitute a threat to her health. 410 U.S., at 164. See also *Harris v. McRae*, 448 U.S., at 316.

The District Court found that there were three serious conditions which would not be covered by the statute: preeclampsia, inevitable abortion, and premature ruptured membrane. 744 F. Supp., at 1378. Yet, as the Court of Appeals observed, 947 F. 2d, at 700–701, it is undisputed that under some circumstances each of these conditions could lead to an illness with substantial and irreversible consequences. While the definition could be interpreted in an unconstitutional manner, the Court of Appeals construed the phrase "serious risk" to include those circumstances. *Id.*, at 701. It stated: "we read the medical emergency exception as intended by the Pennsylvania legislature to assure that compliance with its abortion regulations would not in any way pose a significant threat to the life or health of a woman." *Ibid.* As we said in *Brockett v. Spokane Arcades, Inc.*, 472 U.S. 491, 499–500 (1985): "Normally, . . . we defer to the construction of a state statute given it by the lower federal courts." Indeed, we have said that we will defer to lower court interpretations of state law unless they amount to "plain" error. *Palmer v. Hoffman*, 318 U.S. 109, 118 (1943). This "'reflect[s] our belief that district courts and courts of appeals are better schooled in and more able to interpret the laws of their respective States.'" *Frisby v. Schultz*, 487 U.S. 474, 482 (1988) (citation omitted). We adhere to that course today, and conclude that, as construed by the Court of Appeals, the medical emergency definition imposes no undue burden on a woman's abortion right.

We next consider the informed consent requirement. 18 Pa. Cons. Stat. Ann. § 3205. Except in a medical emergency, the statute requires that at least 24 hours before performing an abortion a physician inform the woman of the nature of the procedure, the health risks of the abortion and of childbirth, and the "probable gestational age of the unborn child." The physician or a qualified nonphysician must inform the woman of the availability of printed materials published by the State describing the fetus and providing information about medical assistance for childbirth, information about child support from the father, and a list of agencies which provide adoption and other services as alternatives to abortion. An abortion may not be performed unless the woman certifies in writing that she has been informed of the availability of these printed materials and has been provided them if she chooses to view them.

Our prior decisions establish that as with any medical procedure, the State may require a woman to give her written informed consent to an abortion. See *Planned Parenthood of Central Mo. v. Danforth*, 428 U.S., at 67. In this respect, the statute is unexceptional. Petitioners challenge the statute's definition of informed consent because it includes the provision of specific information by the doctor and the mandatory 24-hour waiting period. The conclusions reached by a majority of the Justices in the separate opinions filed today and the undue burden standard adopted in this opinion require us to overrule in part some of the Court's past decisions, decisions driven by the trimester framework's prohibition of all previability regulations designed to further the State's interest in fetal life.

In *Akron I*, 462 U.S. 416 (1983), we invalidated an ordinance which required that a woman seeking an abortion be provided by her physician with specific information "designed to influence the woman's informed choice between abortion or childbirth." *Id.*, at 444. As we later described the *Akron I* holding in *Thornburgh v. American College of Obstetricians and Gynecologists*, 476 U.S., at 762, there were two purported flaws in the Akron ordinance: the information was designed to dissuade the woman from having an abortion and the ordinance imposed "a rigid requirement that a specific body of information be given in all cases, irrespective of the particular needs of the patient. . . ." *Ibid.*

To the extent *Akron I* and *Thornburgh* find a constitutional violation when the government requires, as it does here, the giving of truthful, nonmisleading information about the nature of the procedure, the attendant health risks and those of childbirth, and the "probable gestational age" of the fetus, those cases go too far, are inconsistent with *Roe's* acknowledgment of an important interest in potential life, and are overruled. This is clear even on the very terms of *Akron I* and *Thornburgh*. Those decisions, along with *Danforth*, recognize a substantial government interest justifying a requirement that a woman be apprised of the health risks of abortion and childbirth. *E.g., Danforth, supra,* at 66–67. It cannot be questioned that psychological well being is a facet of health. Nor can it be doubted that most women considering an abortion would deem the impact on the fetus relevant, if not dispositive, to the decision. In attempting to ensure that a woman apprehend the full consequences of her decision, the State furthers the legitimate purpose of reducing the risk that a woman may elect an abortion, only to discover later, with devastating psychological consequences, that her decision was not fully informed. If the information the State requires to be made available to the woman is truthful and not misleading, the requirement may be permissible.

We also see no reason why the State may not require doctors to inform a woman seeking an abortion of the availability of materials relating to the consequences to the fetus, even when those consequences have no direct relation to her health. An example illustrates the point. We would think it constitutional for the State to require that in order for there to be informed consent to a kidney transplant operation the recipient must be supplied with information about risks to the donor as well as risks to himself or herself. A requirement that the physician make available information similar to that mandated by the statute here was described in *Thornburgh* as "an outright attempt to wedge the Commonwealth's message discouraging abortion into the privacy of the informed consent dialogue between the woman and her physician." 476 U.S., at 762. We conclude, however, that informed choice need not be defined in such narrow terms that all considerations of the effect on the fetus are made irrelevant. As we have made clear, we depart from the holdings of *Akron I* and *Thornburgh* to the extent that we permit a State to further its legitimate goal of protecting the life of the unborn by enacting legislation aimed at ensuring a decision that is mature and informed, even when in so doing the State expresses a preference for childbirth over abortion. In short, requiring that the woman be informed of the availability of information relating to fetal development and the assistance available should she decide to carry the pregnancy to full term is a reasonable measure to insure an informed choice, one which might cause the woman to choose childbirth over abortion. This requirement cannot be considered a substantial obstacle to obtaining an abortion, and, it follows, there is no undue burden.

Our prior cases also suggest that the "straitjacket," *Thornburgh, supra,* at 762 (quoting *Danforth, supra,* at 67, n. 8), of particular information which must be given in each case interferes with a constitutional right of privacy between a pregnant woman and her physician. As a preliminary matter, it is worth noting that the statute now before us does not require a physician to comply with the informed consent provisions "if he or she can demonstrate by a preponderance of the evidence, that he or she reasonably believed that furnishing the information would have resulted in a severely adverse effect on the physical or mental health of the patient." 18 Pa. Cons. Stat. § 3205 (1990). In this respect, the statute does not prevent the physician from exercising his or her medical judgment.

Whatever constitutional status the doctor patient relation may have as a general matter, in the present context it is derivative of the woman's position. The doctor patient relation does not underlie or override the two more general rights under which the abortion right is justified: the right to make family decisions and the right to physical autonomy. On its own, the doctor patient relation here is entitled to the same solicitude it receives in other contexts. Thus, a requirement that a doctor give a woman certain information as part of obtaining her consent to an abortion is, for constitutional purposes, no different from a requirement that a doctor give certain specific information about any medical procedure.

All that is left of petitioners' argument is an asserted First Amendment right of a physician not to provide information about the risks of abortion, and childbirth, in a manner mandated by the State. To be sure, the physician's First Amendment rights not to speak are implicated, see *Wooley v. Maynard*, 430 U.S. 705 (1977), but only as part of the practice of medicine, subject to reasonable licensing and regulation by the State. Cf. *Whalen v. Roe*, 429 U.S. 589, 603 (1977). We see no constitutional infirmity in the requirement that the physician provide the information mandated by the State here.

The Pennsylvania statute also requires us to reconsider the holding in *Akron I* that the State may not require that a physician, as opposed to a qualified assistant, provide information relevant to a woman's informed consent. 462 U.S., at 448. Since there is no evidence on this record that requiring a doctor to give the information as provided by the statute would amount in practical terms to a substantial obstacle to a woman seeking an abortion, we conclude that it is not an undue burden. Our cases reflect the fact that the Constitution gives the States broad latitude to decide that particular functions may be performed only by licensed professionals, even if an objective assessment might suggest that those same tasks could be performed by others. . . . Thus, we uphold the provision as a reasonable means to insure that the woman's consent is informed.

Our analysis of Pennsylvania's 24-hour waiting period between the provision of the information deemed necessary to informed consent and the performance of an abortion under the undue burden standard requires us to reconsider the premise behind the decision in *Akron I* invalidating a parallel requirement. In *Akron I* we said: "Nor are we convinced that the State's legitimate concern that the woman's decision be informed is reasonably served by requiring a 24-hour delay as a matter of course." 462 U.S., at 450. We consider that conclusion to be wrong. The idea that important decisions will be more informed and deliberate if they follow some period of reflection does not strike us as unreasonable, particularly where the statute directs that important information become part of the background of the decision. The statute, as construed by the Court of Appeals, permits avoidance of the waiting period in the event of a medical emergency and the record evidence shows that in the vast majority of cases, a 24-hour delay does not create any appreciable health risk. In theory, at least, the waiting period is a reasonable measure to implement the State's interest in protecting the life of the unborn, a measure that does not amount to an undue burden.

Whether the mandatory 24-hour waiting period is nonetheless invalid because in practice it is a substantial obstacle to a woman's choice to terminate her pregnancy is a closer question. The findings of fact by the District Court indicate that because of the distances many women must travel to reach an abortion provider, the practical effect will often be a delay of much more than a day because the waiting period requires that a woman seeking an abortion make at least two visits to the doctor. The District Court also found that in many instances this will increase the exposure of women seeking abortions to "the harassment and hostility of anti abortion protestors demonstrating outside a clinic." 744 F. Supp., at 1351. As a result, the District Court found that for those women who have the fewest financial resources, those who must travel long distances, and those who have difficulty explaining their whereabouts to husbands, employers, or others, the 24-hour waiting period will be "particularly burdensome." *Id.*, at 1352.

These findings are troubling in some respects, but they do not demonstrate that the waiting period constitutes an undue burden. We do not doubt that, as the District Court held, the waiting period has the effect of "increasing the cost and risk of delay of abortions," *id.*, at 1378, but the District Court did not conclude that the increased costs and potential delays amount to substantial obstacles. Rather, applying the trimester framework's strict prohibition of all regulation designed to promote the State's interest in potential life before viability, see *id.*, at 1374, the District Court concluded that the waiting period does not further the state "interest in maternal health" and "infringes the physician's discretion to exercise sound medical judgment." *Id.*, at 1378. Yet, as we have stated, under the undue burden standard a State is permitted to enact persuasive measures which favor childbirth over abortion, even if those measures do not further a health interest. And while the waiting period does limit a physician's discretion, that is not, standing alone, a reason to invalidate it. In light of the construction given the statute's definition of medical emergency by the Court of Appeals, and the District Court's findings, we cannot say that the waiting period imposes a real health risk.

We also disagree with the District Court's conclusion that the "particularly burdensome" effects of the waiting period on some women require its invalidation. A particular burden is not of necessity a substantial obstacle. Whether a burden falls on a particular group is a distinct inquiry from whether it is a substantial obstacle even as to the women in that group. And the District Court did not conclude that the waiting period is such an obstacle even for the women who are most burdened by it. Hence, on the record before us, and in the context of this facial challenge, we are not convinced that the 24-hour waiting period constitutes an undue burden.

We are left with the argument that the various aspects of the informed consent requirement are unconstitutional because they place barriers in the way of abortion on demand. Even the broadest reading of *Roe*, however, has not suggested that there is a constitutional right to abortion on demand. See, *e.g.*, *Doe v. Bolton*, 410 U.S., at 189. Rather, the right protected by *Roe* is a right to decide to terminate a pregnancy free of undue interference by the State. Because the informed consent requirement facilitates the wise exercise of that right it cannot be classified as an interference with the right *Roe* protects. The informed consent requirement is not an undue burden on that right.

Section 3209 of Pennsylvania's abortion law provides, except in cases of medical emergency, that no physician shall perform an abortion on a married woman without receiving a signed statement from the woman that she has notified her spouse that she is about to undergo an abortion. The woman has the option of providing an alternative signed statement certifying that her husband is not the man who impregnated her; that her husband could not be located; that the pregnancy is the result of spousal sexual assault which she has reported; or that the woman believes that notifying her husband will cause him or someone else to inflict bodily injury upon her. A physician who performs an abortion on a married woman without receiving the appropriate signed statement will have his or her license revoked, and is liable to the husband for damages . . .

. . . The American Medical Association (AMA) has published a summary of the recent research in this field, which indicates that in an average 12-month period in this country, approximately two million women are the victims of severe assaults by their male partners. In a 1985 survey, women reported that nearly one of every eight husbands had assaulted their wives during the past year. The AMA views these figures as "marked underestimates," because the nature of these incidents discourages women from reporting them, and because surveys typically exclude the very poor, those who do not speak English well, and women who are homeless or in institutions or hospitals when the survey is conducted. According to the AMA, "[r]esearchers on family violence agree that the true incidence of partner violence is probably *double* the above estimates; or four million severely assaulted women per year. Studies suggest that from one fifth to one third of all women will be physically assaulted by a partner or ex partner during their lifetime." AMA Council on Scientific Affairs, Violence Against Women 7 (1991) (emphasis in original). Thus on an average day in the United States, nearly 11,000 women are severely assaulted by their male partners. Many of these incidents involve sexual assault. *Id.*, at 3–4; Shields &Hanneke, Battered Wives' Reactions to Marital Rape, in The Dark Side of Families: Current Family Violence Research 131, 144 (D. Finkelhor, R. Gelles, G. Hataling, & M. Straus eds. 1983). In families where wife beating takes place, moreover, child abuse is often present as well. Violence Against Women, *supra*, at 12 . . .

The limited research that has been conducted with respect to notifying one's husband about an abortion, although involving samples too small to be representative, also supports the District Court's findings of fact. The vast majority of women notify their male partners of their decision to obtain an abortion. In many cases in which married women do not notify their husbands, the pregnancy is the result of an extramarital affair. Where the husband is the father, the primary reason women do not notify their husbands is that the husband and wife are experiencing marital difficulties, often accompanied by incidents of violence. Ryan & Plutzer, When Married Women Have Abortions: Spousal Notification and Marital Interaction, 51 J. Marriage & the Family 41, 44 (1989).

This information and the District Court's findings reinforce what common sense would suggest. In well functioning marriages, spouses discuss important intimate decisions such as whether to bear a child. But there are millions of women in this country who are the victims of regular physical and psychological abuse at the hands of their husbands. Should these women become pregnant, they may have very good reasons for not wishing to inform their husbands of their decision to obtain an abortion. Many may have justifiable fears of physical abuse, but may be no less fearful of the consequences of reporting prior abuse to the Commonwealth of Pennsylvania. Many may have a reasonable fear that notifying their husbands will provoke further instances of child abuse; these women are not exempt from § 3209's notification requirement. Many may fear devastating forms of psychological abuse from their husbands, including verbal harassment, threats of future violence, the destruction of possessions, physical confinement to the home, the withdrawal of financial support, or the disclosure of the abortion to family and friends. These methods of psychological abuse may act as even more of a deterrent to notification than the possibility of physical violence, but women who are the victims of the abuse are not exempt from § 3209's notification requirement. And many women who are pregnant as a result of sexual assaults by their husbands will be unable to avail themselves of the exception for spousal sexual assault, § 3209(b)(3), because the exception requires that the woman have notified law enforcement authorities within 90 days of the assault, and her husband will be notified of her report once an investigation begins. § 3128(c). If anything in this field is certain, it is that victims of spousal sexual assault are extremely reluctant to report the abuse to the government; hence, a great many spousal rape victims will not be exempt from the notification requirement imposed by § 3209.

The spousal notification requirement is thus likely to prevent a significant number of women from obtaining an abortion. It does not merely make abortions a little more difficult or expensive to obtain; for many women, it will impose a substantial obstacle. We must not blind ourselves to the fact that the significant number of women who fear for their safety and the safety of their children are likely to be deterred from procuring an abortion as surely as if the Commonwealth had outlawed abortion in all cases.

Respondents attempt to avoid the conclusion that § 3209 is invalid by pointing out that it imposes almost no burden at all for the vast majority of women seeking abortions. They begin by noting that only about 20 percent of the women who obtain abortions are married. They then note that of these women about 95 percent notify their husbands of their own volition. Thus, respondents argue, the effects of § 3209 are felt by only one percent of the women who obtain abortions. Respondents argue that since some of these women will be able to notify their husbands without adverse consequences or will qualify for one of the exceptions, the statute affects fewer than one percent of women seeking abortions. For this reason, it is asserted, the statute cannot be invalid on its face. See Brief for Respondents 83–86. We disagree with respondents' basic method of analysis.

The analysis does not end with the one percent of women upon whom the statute operates; it begins there. Legislation is measured for consistency with the Constitution by its impact on those whose conduct it affects. For example, we would not say that a law which requires a newspaper to print a candidate's reply to an unfavorable editorial is valid on its face because most newspapers would adopt the policy even absent the law. . . . The proper focus of constitutional inquiry is the group for whom the law is a restriction, not the group for whom the law is irrelevant.

Respondents' argument itself gives implicit recognition to this principle, at one of its critical points. Respondents speak of the one percent of women seeking abortions who are married and would choose not to notify their husbands of their plans. By selecting as the controlling class women who wish to obtain abortions, rather than all women or all pregnant women, respondents in effect concede that § 3209 must be judged by reference to those for whom it is an actual rather than irrelevant restriction. Of course, as we have said, § 3209's real target is narrower even than the class of women seeking abortions identified by the State: it is married women seeking abortions who do not wish to notify their husbands of their intentions and who do not qualify for one of the statutory exceptions to the notice requirement. The unfortunate yet persisting conditions we document above will mean that in a large fraction of the cases in which § 3209 is relevant, it will operate as a substantial obstacle to a woman's choice to undergo an abortion. It is an undue burden, and therefore invalid.

This conclusion is in no way inconsistent with our decisions upholding parental notification or consent requirements. . . . Those enactments, and our judgment that they are constitutional, are based on the quite reasonable assumption that minors will benefit from consultation with their parents and that children will often not realize that their parents have their best interests at heart. We cannot adopt a parallel assumption about adult women.

We recognize that a husband has a "deep and proper concern and interest . . . in his wife's pregnancy and in the growth and development of the fetus she is carrying." *Danforth, supra,* at 69. With regard to the children he has fathered and raised, the Court has recognized his "cognizable and substantial" interest in their custody. . . . If this case concerned a State's ability to require the mother to notify the father before taking some action with respect to a living child raised by both, therefore, it would be reasonable to conclude as a general matter that the father's interest in the welfare of the child and the mother's interest are equal.

Before birth, however, the issue takes on a very different cast. It is an inescapable biological fact that state regulation with respect to the child a woman is carrying will have a far greater impact on the mother's liberty than on the father's. The effect of state regulation on a woman's protected liberty is doubly deserving of scrutiny in such a case, as the State has touched not only upon the private sphere of the family but upon the very bodily integrity of the pregnant woman. Cf. *Cruzan v. Director, Missouri Dept. of Health*, 497 U.S., at 281. The Court has held that "when the wife and the husband disagree on this decision, the view of only one of the two marriage partners can prevail. Inasmuch as it is the woman who physically bears the child and who is the more directly and immediately affected by the pregnancy, as between the two, the balance weighs in her favor." *Danforth, supra*, at 71. This conclusion rests upon the basic nature of marriage and the nature of our Constitution: "[T]he marital couple is not an independent entity with a mind and heart of its own, but an association of two individuals each with a separate intellectual and emotional makeup. If the right of privacy means anything, it is the right of the *individual*, married or single, to be free from unwarranted governmental intrusion into matters so fundamentally affecting a person as the decision whether to bear or beget a child." *Eisenstadt v. Baird*, 405 U.S., at 453 (emphasis in original). The Constitution protects individuals, men and women alike, from unjustified state interference, even when that interference is enacted into law for the benefit of their spouses.

There was a time, not so long ago, when a different understanding of the family and of the Constitution prevailed. In *Bradwell v. Illinois*, 16 Wall. 130 (1873), three Members of this Court reaffirmed the common law principle that "a woman had no legal existence separate from her husband, who was regarded as her head and representative in the social state; and, notwithstanding some recent modifications of this civil status, many of the special rules of law flowing from and dependent upon this cardinal principle still exist in full force in most States." *Id.*, at 141 (Bradley J., joined by Swayne and Field, JJ., concurring in judgment). Only one generation has passed since this Court observed that "woman is still regarded as the center of home and family life," with attendant "special responsibilities" that precluded full and independent legal status under the Constitution. *Hoyt v. Florida*, 368 U.S. 57, 62 (1961). These views, of course, are no longer consistent with our understanding of the family, the individual, or the Constitution.

In keeping with our rejection of the common law understanding of a woman's role within the family, the Court held in *Danforth* that the Constitution does not permit a State to require a married woman to obtain her husband's consent before undergoing an abortion. 428 U.S., at 69. The principles that guided the Court in *Danforth* should be our guides today. For the great many women who are victims of abuse inflicted by their husbands, or whose children are the victims of such abuse, a spousal notice requirement enables the husband to wield an effective veto over his wife's decision. Whether the prospect of notification itself deters such women from seeking abortions, or whether the husband, through physical force or psychological pressure or economic coercion, prevents his wife from obtaining an abortion until it is too late, the notice requirement will often be tantamount to the veto found unconstitutional in *Danforth*. The women most affected by this law—those who most reasonably fear the consequences of notifying their husbands that they are pregnant—are in the gravest danger.

The husband's interest in the life of the child his wife is carrying does not permit the State to empower him with this troubling degree of authority over his wife. The contrary view leads to consequences reminiscent of the common law. A husband has no enforceable right to require a wife to advise him before she exercises her personal choices. If a husband's interest in the potential life of the child outweighs a wife's liberty, the State could require a married woman to notify her husband before she uses a postfertilization contraceptive. Perhaps next in line would be a statute requiring pregnant married women to notify their husbands before engaging in conduct causing risks to the fetus. After all, if the husband's interest in the fetus' safety is a sufficient predicate for state regulation, the State could reasonably conclude that pregnant wives should notify their husbands before drinking alcohol or smoking. Perhaps married women should notify their husbands before using contraceptives or before undergoing any type of surgery that may have complications affecting the husband's interest in his wife's reproductive organs. And if a husband's interest justifies notice in any of these cases, one might reasonably argue that it justifies exactly what the *Danforth* Court held it did not justify—a requirement of the husband's consent as well. A State may not give to a man the kind of dominion over his wife that parents exercise over their children.

Section 3209 embodies a view of marriage consonant with the common law status of married women but repugnant to our present understanding of marriage and of the nature of the rights secured by the Constitution. Women do not lose their constitutionally protected liberty when they marry. The Constitution protects all individuals, male or female, married or unmarried, from the abuse of governmental power, even where that power is employed for the supposed benefit of a member of the individual's family. These considerations confirm our conclusion that § 3209 is invalid.

We next consider the parental consent provision. Except in a medical emergency, an unemancipated young woman under 18 may not obtain an abortion unless she and one of her parents (or guardian) provides informed consent as defined above. If neither a parent nor a guardian provides consent, a court may authorize the performance of an abortion upon a determination that the young woman is mature and capable of giving informed consent and has in fact given her informed consent, or that an abortion would be in her best interests.

We have been over most of this ground before. Our cases establish, and we reaffirm today, that a State may require a minor seeking an abortion to obtain the consent of a parent or guardian, provided that there is an adequate judicial bypass procedure. . . . Under these precedents, in our view, the one parent consent requirement and judicial bypass procedure are constitutional.

The only argument made by petitioners respecting this provision and to which our prior decisions do not speak is the contention that the parental consent requirement is invalid because it requires informed parental consent. For the most part, petitioners' argument is a reprise of their argument with respect to the informed consent requirement in general, and we reject it for the reasons given above. Indeed, some of the provisions regarding informed consent have particular force with respect to minors: the waiting period, for example, may provide the parent or parents of a pregnant young woman the opportunity to consult with her in private, and to discuss the consequences of her decision in the context of the values and moral or religious principles of their family.

Under the recordkeeping and reporting requirements of the statute, every facility which performs abortions is required to file a report stating its name and address as well as the name and address of any related entity, such as a controlling or subsidiary organization. In the case of state funded institutions, the information becomes public.

For each abortion performed, a report must be filed identifying: the physician (and the second physician where required); the facility; the referring physician or agency; the woman's age; the number of prior pregnancies and prior abortions she has had; gestational age; the type of abortion procedure; the date of the abortion; whether there were any pre-existing medical conditions which would complicate pregnancy; medical complications with the abortion; where applicable, the basis for the determination that the abortion was medically necessary; the weight of the aborted fetus; and whether the woman was married, and if so, whether notice was provided or the basis for the failure to give notice. Every abortion facility must also file quarterly reports showing the number of abortions performed broken down by trimester. See 18 Pa. Cons. Stat. §§ 3207, 3214 (1990). In all events, the identity of each woman who has had an abortion remains confidential.

In *Danforth*, 428 U.S., at 80, we held that recordkeeping and reporting provisions "that are reasonably directed to the preservation of maternal health and that properly respect a patient's confidentiality and privacy are permissible." We think that under this standard, all the provisions at issue here except that relating to spousal notice are constitutional. Although they do not relate to the State's interest in informing the woman's choice, they do relate to health. The collection of information with respect to actual patients is a vital element of medical research, and so it cannot be said that the requirements serve no purpose other than to make abortions more difficult. Nor do we find that the requirements impose a substantial obstacle to a woman's choice. At most they might increase the cost of some abortions by a slight amount. While at some point increased cost could become a substantial obstacle, there is no such showing on the record before us.

Subsection (12) of the reporting provision requires the reporting of, among other things, a married woman's "reason for failure to provide notice" to her husband. § 3214(a)(12). This provision in effect requires women, as a condition of obtaining an abortion, to provide the Commonwealth with the precise information we have already recognized that many women have pressing reasons not to reveal. Like the spousal notice requirement itself, this provision places an undue burden on a woman's choice, and must be invalidated for that reason.

Our Constitution is a covenant running from the first generation of Americans to us and then to future generations. It is a coherent succession. Each generation must learn anew that the Constitution's written terms embody ideas and aspirations that must survive more ages than one. We accept our responsibility not to retreat from interpreting the full meaning of the covenant in light of all of our precedents. We invoke it once again to define the freedom guaranteed by the Constitution's own promise, the promise of liberty.

The judgment in No. 91–902 is affirmed. The judgment in No. 91–744 is affirmed in part and reversed in part, and the case is remanded for proceedings consistent with this opinion, including consideration of the question of severability.

It is so ordered.

SOURCE: *Planned Parenthood of Southeastern Pennsylvania v. Casey* 505 U.S. 833. (1992) (footnotes omitted).

DOCUMENT ANALYSIS

The *Casey* ruling upheld *Roe v. Wade* while simultaneously allowing for greater state restriction of abortion access. For although a bare majority of justices agreed with the central holding in *Roe*, the Court also accepted unprecedented restrictions on abortion access. In *Casey*, the justices upheld three state abortion regulations: informed consent followed by a 24-hour waiting period, a parental consent requirement, and a reporting requirement. Disagreeing with Judge Alito, who was in the minority on the lower court, the decision also struck down Pennsylvania's requirement that a married woman notify her husband prior to ending a pregnancy. But in some ways, the impact of *Casey* is less about the specific state restrictions it upheld, and more about the new standard it created for the adjudication of future restrictions.

The Court in *Casey* instituted its undue burden standard—a far lower hurdle for states to clear in restricting abortion than the fundamental right standard adopted in 1973. Justice O'Connor, in particular, had been developing the undue burden standard since her confirmation to the Court; through dissenting opinions in 1983 and 1986, O'Connor articulated earlier iterations of the standard. In *Casey*, that standard became the guiding principle for states, and the courts that would adjudicate their statutes.

The undue burden standard lowers the threshold over which states must pass in restricting abortion in at least two ways. First, while the old standard presumed that restrictions were unconstitutional when limiting a woman's pre-viability abortion options, the undue burden standard assumes a state interest in fetal life from conception. And although the *Casey* Court retained the traditional perspective that a state's interest would grow with the fetus, this was the first time a majority of the Court asserted a state's right extended to the earliest phases of pregnancy, allowing for a fuller range of restrictions, including but not limited to those

IN HISTORY

A CHANGING COURT

*Supreme Court: 1973 (**Roe**)*

Chief Justice Warren E. Burger

Harry Blackmun
William J. Brennan
William O. Douglas
Thurgood Marshall
Lewis Franklin Powell, Jr.
William Rehnquist (dissent)
Potter Stewart
Byron White (dissent)

*Supreme Court: 1992 (**Casey**)*

Chief Justice William Rehnquist

Anthony Kennedy
Antonin Scalia
Byron White
Clarence Thomas
David Souter
Harry Blackmun
John Paul Stevens
Sandra Day O'Connor

The only justices from *Roe v. Wade* remaining on the Court when the *Casey* decision was issued were William Rehnquist and Byron White, both of whom dissented in *Roe*. All seven justices in the majority had been replaced by 1992.

upheld in the Pennsylvania case. The Court specifically took aim at *Roe*'s trimester system, arguing that it was rigid and unworkable precisely because it did not acknowledge the state's interest in early fetal life.

Second, one of the foundations of the undue burden standard is the perspective that states may articulate their preference for birth over abortion through the adoption of abortion guidelines. In previous rulings, the Court was careful to argue that while states may have positions on abortion, those positions could not be used to manipulate a woman's decision about her pregnancy. Here, the Court argues that so long as those positions do not preclude the option of abortion (and are thus not "undue"), the states may, in fact, use state policy to persuade women to keep their pregnancies.

The policy implications of this shift are unfolding still. Increasingly, as chapter 7 reveals, states are using materials about fetal development, and technology that demonstrates that development, to inform women of their fetus' condition. Under the undue burden standard, these requirements are likely constitutional: for while they appear to some aimed at influencing a woman's abortion decision, and sometimes impose an additional financial burden on the woman, they do not by themselves preclude abortion as an option.

It is noteworthy that Justice Blackmun, the architect of the trimester system and the author of the majority opinion in *Roe*, offered a dissenting view not included here. Along with the separate opinion of Justice Stevens (also not included here), Justice Blackmun argued that the new standard crafted by O'Connor would not fully protect women's freedom. Defending the central concepts of *Roe* against the majority of the Court, Blackmun had traded positions with now-Chief Justice Rehnquist, who was a dissenter in the 1973 landmark.

Finally, four justices declared their willingness to overturn *Roe v. Wade* in the *Casey* decision. Justices White, Scalia, and Thomas, along with Chief Justice Rehnquist, would have overturned the earlier landmark had they a fifth vote. The decision therefore points to the vulnerability of *Roe v. Wade*, and at the same time seems successful in limiting *Roe*'s influence through a strategy of chipping away at that ruling's central concepts.

Document: Freedom of Access to Clinic Entrances Act.
Date: Signed into law, May 26, 1994.
Where: Washington, D.C.
Significance: Congress responded to an increasing number of clinic blockades and clinic-related acts of violence by making it a federal crime to prevent entrance to a women's health facility. Although violence at clinics continues, the number of clinic blockades has declined precipitously since President Clinton signed this bill into law.

TITLE 18 PART 1 CHAPTER 13 248
248 Freedom of Access to Clinic Entrances
(a) Prohibited Activities.—Whoever—
   (1) by force or threat of force or by physical obstruction, intentionally injures, intimidates or interferes with or attempts to injure, intimidate or interfere with any person because that person is or has been, or in order to intimidate such person or any other person or any class of persons from, obtaining or providing reproductive health services;
   (2) by force or threat of force or by physical obstruction, intentionally injures, intimidates or interferes with or attempts to injure, intimidate or interfere with any person law-

Police officer at the Boston women's clinic where four employees were shot in 1994. Getty Images.

fully exercising or seeking to exercise the First Amendment right of religious freedom at a place of religious worship; or

(3) intentionally damages or destroys the property of a facility, or attempts to do so, because such facility provides reproductive health services, or intentionally damages or destroys the property of a place of religious worship, shall be subject to the penalties provided in subsection (b) and the civil remedies provided in subsection (c), except that a parent or legal guardian of a minor shall not be subject to any penalties or civil remedies under this section for such activities insofar as they are directed exclusively at that minor.

(b) Penalties.—Whoever violates this section shall—

(1) in the case of a first offense, be fined in accordance with this title, or imprisoned not more than one year, or both; and

(2) in the case of a second or subsequent offense after a prior conviction under this section, be fined in accordance with this title, or imprisoned not more than 3 years, or both; except that for an offense involving exclusively a nonviolent physical obstruction, the fine shall be not more than $10,000 and the length of imprisonment shall be not more than six months, or both, for the first offense; and the fine shall, notwithstanding section 3571, be not more than $25,000 and the length of imprisonment shall be not more than 18 months, or both, for a subsequent offense; and except that if bodily injury results, the length of imprisonment shall be not more than 10 years, and if death results, it shall be for any term of years or for life.

(c) Civil Remedies.—

(1) Right of action.—

(A) In general.—Any person aggrieved by reason of the conduct prohibited by subsection (a) may commence a civil action for the relief set forth in subparagraph (B), except that such an action may be brought under subsection (a)(1) only by a person involved in providing or seeking to provide, or obtaining or seeking to obtain, services in a facility that provides reproductive health services, and such an action may be brought under subsection (a)(2) only by a person lawfully exercising or seeking to exercise the First Amendment right of religious freedom at a place of religious worship or by the entity that owns or operates such place of religious worship.

(B) Relief.—In any action under subparagraph (A), the court may award appropriate relief, including temporary, preliminary or permanent injunctive relief and compensatory and punitive damages, as well as the costs of suit and reasonable fees for attorneys and expert witnesses. With respect to compensatory damages, the plaintiff may elect, at any time prior to the rendering of final judgment, to recover, in lieu of actual damages, an award of statutory damages in the amount of $5,000 per violation.

(2) Action by attorney general of the United States.—

    (A) In general.—If the Attorney General of the United States has reasonable cause to believe that any person or group of persons is being, has been, or may be injured by conduct constituting a violation of this section, the Attorney General may commence a civil action in any appropriate United States District Court.

    (B) Relief.—In any action under subparagraph (A), the court may award appropriate relief, including temporary, preliminary or permanent injunctive relief, and compensatory damages to persons aggrieved as described in paragraph (1)(B). The court, to vindicate the public interest, may also assess a civil penalty against each respondent—

        (i) in an amount not exceeding $10,000 for a nonviolent physical obstruction and $15,000 for other first violations; and

        (ii) in an amount not exceeding $15,000 for a nonviolent physical obstruction and $25,000 for any other subsequent violation.

(3) Actions by state attorneys general.—

    (A) In general.—If the Attorney General of a State has reasonable cause to believe that any person or group of persons is being, has been, or may be injured by conduct constituting a violation of this section, such Attorney General may commence a civil action in the name of such State, as parens patriae on behalf of natural persons residing in such State, in any appropriate United States District Court.

    (B) Relief.—In any action under subparagraph (A), the court may award appropriate relief, including temporary, preliminary or permanent injunctive relief, compensatory damages, and civil penalties as described in paragraph (2)(B).

(d) Rules of Construction.—Nothing in this section shall be construed—

    (1) to prohibit any expressive conduct (including peaceful picketing or other peaceful demonstration) protected from legal prohibition by the First Amendment to the Constitution;

    (2) to create new remedies for interference with activities protected by the free speech or free exercise clauses of the First Amendment to the Constitution, occurring outside a facility, regardless of the point of view expressed, or to limit any existing legal remedies for such interference;

    (3) to provide exclusive criminal penalties or civil remedies with respect to the conduct prohibited by this section, or to preempt State or local laws that may provide such penalties or remedies; or

    (4) to interfere with the enforcement of State or local laws regulating the performance of abortions or other reproductive health services.

(e) Definitions.—As used in this section:

    (1) Facility.—The term "facility" includes a hospital, clinic, physician's office, or other facility that provides reproductive health services, and includes the building or structure in which the facility is located.

    (2) Interfere with.—The term "interfere with" means to restrict a person's freedom of movement.

(3) Intimidate.—The term "intimidate" means to place a person in reasonable apprehension of bodily harm to him- or herself or to another.

(4) Physical obstruction.—The term "physical obstruction" means rendering impassable ingress to or egress from a facility that provides reproductive health services or to or from a place of religious worship, or rendering passage to or from such a facility or place of religious worship unreasonably difficult or hazardous.

(5) Reproductive health services.—The term "reproductive health services" means reproductive health services provided in a hospital, clinic, physician's office, or other facility, and includes medical, surgical, counseling or referral services relating to the human reproductive system, including services relating to pregnancy or the termination of a pregnancy.

(6) State.—The term "State" includes a State of the United States, the District of Columbia, and any commonwealth, territory, or possession of the United States.

SOURCE: Freedom of Access to Clinic Entrances Act, PL 103–259 (1994).

DOCUMENT ANALYSIS

The Freedom of Access to Clinic Entrances (FACE) Act made it a federal crime to commit acts of violence at reproductive health clinics; the legislation had an immediate impact on clinic protests. Official statistics about clinic violence reported since 1994 show decreasing blockades in the aftermath of the legislation's passage.

The legislative history of FACE reveals new and interesting abortion party dynamics. By 1994, the party divide in Congress on abortion had grown clear, with most abortion-related bills creating obvious light between the parties' position. This bill, however, did not dramatize the differences between the parties and pointed to areas of common ground. Because the legislation was framed as a law and order bill (and not directly about abortion), many conservatives from both political parties voted for the legislation. And while 68 percent of House Republicans voted against the legislation, that unity paled in comparison to the Partial Birth Abortion Ban of 2003, which captured the support of 94 percent of Republicans. For their part, 79 percent of Democrats voted in favor of FACE, allowing the bill to pass with a

IN HISTORY

ABORTION CLINIC VIOLENCE

Although most abortion protest is peaceful dissent, violence has been present in the antiabortion movement since 1976, when the first clinic arson was reported. In 1978 there was a series of arson attacks on abortion clinics, and by the early 1990s violence in the antiabortion movement was becoming more common. Dr. David Gunn became the first abortion provider murdered when Michael Griffin shot him in 1993. Since then, six additional clinic workers and providers have been murdered.

Violence in the movement also includes extreme attempts to intimidate clinic workers and patients through blockades, butyric acid attacks, stalking, and most recently, anthrax threats.

There have been no clinic worker murders in the United States since 1998, and clinic blockades have become almost non-existent since President Clinton signed the Freedom of Access to Clinic Entrances bill in 1994. Still, other forms of clinic harassment have continued unabated.

considerable majority in a Democratic-controlled Congress. President Clinton signed the bill into law and it took effect in May, 1994.

Document: Naomi Wolf, "Our Bodies, Our Souls."
Date: October 16, 1995.
Where: The New Republic.
Significance: Feminist scholar Naomi Wolf caused a great uproar in feminist circles with her article. The piece offers some critical insights into women's experiences with abortion, stirring up questions of strategy for the prochoice movement.

I had an abortion when I was a single mother and my daughter was 2 years old. I would do it again. But you know how in the Greek myths when you kill a relative you are pursued by furies? For months, it was as if baby furies were pursuing me. These are not the words of a benighted, superstition-ridden teenager lost in America's cultural backwaters. They are the words of a Cornell-educated, urban-dwelling, Democratic-voting 40-year-old cardiologist—I'll call her Clare. Clare is exactly the kind of person for whom being pro-choice is an unshakeable conviction. If there were a core constituent of the movement to secure abortion rights, Clare would be it. And yet: her words are exactly the words to which the pro-choice movement is not listening. At its best, feminism defends its moral high ground by being simply faithful to the truth: to women's real-life experiences. But, to its own ethical and political detriment, the pro-choice movement has relinquished the moral frame around the issue of abortion. It has ceded the language of right and wrong to abortion foes. The movement's abandonment of what Americans have always, and rightly, demanded of their movements—an ethical core—and its reliance instead on a political rhetoric in which the fetus means nothing are proving fatal. The effects of this abandonment can be measured in two ways. First of all, such a position causes us to lose political ground. By refusing to look at abortion within a moral framework, we lose the millions of Americans who want to support abortion as a legal right but still need to condemn it as a moral iniquity. Their ethical allegiances are then addressed by the pro-life movement, which is willing to speak about good and evil. But we are also in danger of losing something more important than votes; we stand in jeopardy of losing what can only be called our souls. Clinging to a rhetoric about abortion in which there is no life and no death, we entangle our beliefs in a series of self-delusions, fibs and evasions. And we risk becoming precisely what our critics charge us with being: callous, selfish and casually destructive men and women who share a cheapened view of human life. In the following pages, I will argue for a radical shift in the pro-choice movement's rhetoric and consciousness about abortion: I will maintain that we need to contextualize the fight to defend abortion rights within a moral framework that admits that the death of a fetus is a real death; that there are degrees of culpability, judgment and responsibility involved in the decision to abort a pregnancy; that the best understanding of feminism involves holding women as well as men to the responsibilities that are inseparable from their rights; and that we need to be strong enough to acknowledge that this country's high rate of abortion—which ends more than a quarter of all pregnancies—can only be rightly understood as what Dr. Henry Foster was brave enough to call it: "a failure." Any doubt that our current pro-choice rhetoric leads to disaster should be dispelled by the famous recent defection of the woman who had been Jane Roe. What happened to Norma McCorvey? To judge by her characterization in the elite media and by some prominent pro-choice feminists, nothing very important. Her change of heart about abortion was relentlessly "explained away" as having everything to do with the girlish motivations of insecurity, fickleness and the need for attention, and little to do with any actual moral agency. This dismissive (and, not incidentally, sexist and classist) interpretation was so highly colored by subjective impressions offered up by the very institutions that define objectivity that it bore all the hallmarks of an exculpatory cultural myth: poor Norma—she just needed stroking. She was never very stable, the old dear—first she was a chess-piece for the pro-choice movement ("just some anonymous person who suddenly emerges," in the words of one NOW member) and then a codependent of the Bible-thumpers. Low self-esteem, a history of substance abuse, ignorance—these and other personal weaknesses explained her turnaround. To me, the first commandment of real feminism is: when in doubt, listen to women. What if we were to truly, respectfully listen to this woman who began her political life as, in her words, just "some little old Texas girl who got in trouble"? We would have to hear this: perhaps Norma McCorvey actually had a revelation that she could no longer live as the symbol of a belief system she increasingly repudiated. Norma McCorvey should be seen as an object lesson for the pro-choice movement—a call to us to search our souls and take another, humbler look at how we go about what we are doing. For McCorvey is in fact an American Everywoman: she is the lost middle of the abortion debate, the woman whose allegiance we forfeit by our refusal to use a darker and sterner and more honest moral rhetoric. McCorvey is more astute than her critics; she seems to understand better than the pro-choice activists she worked with just what the woman-in-the-middle believes: "I believe in the woman's right to choose. I'm like a lot of people. I'm in the mushy middle," she said. McCorvey still supports abortion rights through the first trimester—but is horrified by the brutality of abortion as it manifests more obviously further into a pregnancy. She does not respect the black-and-white ideology on either side and insists on referring instead, as I understand her explanation, to her conscience. What McCorvey and other Americans want and deserve is an abortion-rights movement willing publicly to mourn the evil—necessary evil though it may be—that is abortion. We must have a movement that acts with moral accountability and without euphemism. With the pro-choice rhetoric we use now, we incur three destructive consequences—two ethical, one strategic: hardness of heart, lying and political failure. Because of the implications of a Constitution that defines rights according to the legal idea of "a person," the abortion debate has tended to focus on the question of "personhood" of the fetus. Many pro-choice advocates developed a language to assert that the fetus isn't a person, and this, over the years, has developed into a lexicon of dehumanization. Laura Kaplan's The Story of Jane, an important forthcoming account of a pre-Roe underground abortion service, inadvertently sheds light on the origins of some of this rhetoric: service staffers referred to the fetus—well into the fourth month—as "material" (as in "the amount of material that had to be removed . . ."). The activists felt exhilaration at learning to perform abortions themselves instead of relying on male doctors: "When a staffer removed the speculum and said, There, all done,' the room exploded in excitement." In an era when women were dying of illegal abortions, this was the understandable exhilaration of an underground resistance movement. Unfortunately, though, this cool and congratulatory rhetoric lingers into a very different present. In one woman's account of her chemical abortion, in the January/February 1994 issue of Mother Jones, for example, the doctor says, "By Sunday you won't see on the monitor what we call the heartbeat" (my italics). The author of the article, D. Redman, explains that one of the drugs the doctor administered would "end the growth of the fetal tissue." And we all remember Dr. Joycelyn Elders's remark, hailed by some as refreshingly frank and pro-woman, but which I found remarkably brutal: that "We really need to get over this love affair with the fetus. . . ." How did we arrive at this point? In the early 1970s, Second Wave feminism adopted this rhetoric in response to the reigning ideology in which motherhood was invoked as an excuse to deny women legal and social equality. In a climate in which women risked being defined as mere vessels while their fetuses were given "personhood" at their expense, it made sense that women's advocates would fight back by depersonalizing the fetus.

The feminist complaint about the pro-life movement's dehumanization of the pregnant woman in relation to the humanized fetus is familiar and often quite valid: pro-choice commentators note that the pro-life film The Silent Scream portrayed the woman as "a vessel"; Ellen Frankfort's Vaginal Politics, the influential feminist text, complained that the fetus is treated like an astronaut in a spaceship. But, say what you will, pregnancy confounds Western philosophy's idea of the autonomous self: the pregnant woman is in fact both a person in her body and a vessel. Rather than seeing both beings as alive and interdependent—seeing life within life—and acknowledging that sometimes, nonetheless, the woman must choose her life over the fetus's, Second Wave feminists reacted to the dehumanization of women by dehumanizing the creatures within them. In the death-struggle to wrest what Simone de Beauvoir called transcendence out of biological immanence, some feminists developed a rhetoric that defined the unwanted fetus as at best valueless; at worst an adversary, a "mass of dependent protoplasm."

Yet that has left us with a bitter legacy. For when we defend abortion rights by emptying the act of moral gravity we find ourselves cultivating a hardness of heart.

Having become pregnant through her partner's and her own failure to use a condom, Redman remarks that her friend Judith, who has been trying to find a child to adopt, begs her to carry the pregnancy to term. Judith offers Redman almost every condition a birthmother could want: "'Let me have the baby,'" she quotes her friend pleading. "'You could visit her anytime, and if you ever wanted her back, I promise I would let her go.'" Redman does not mention considering this possibility. Thinking, rather, about the difficulty of keeping the child—"My time consumed by the tedious, daily activities that I've always done my best to avoid. Three meals a day. Unwashed laundry. . . ."—she schedules her chemical abortion.

The procedure is experimental, and the author feels "almost heroic," thinking of how she is blazing a trail for other women. After the abortion process is underway, the story reaches its perverse epiphany: Redman is on a Women's Day march when the blood from the abortion first appears. She exults at this: "'Our bodies, our lives, our right to decide.' . . . My life feels luxuriant with possibility. For one precious moment, I believe that we have the power to dismantle this system. I finish the march, borne along by the women. . . ." As for the pleading Judith, with everything she was ready to offer a child, and the phantom baby? They are both off-stage, silent in this chilling drama of "feminist" triumphalism.

And why should we expect otherwise? In this essay, the fetus (as the author writes, "the now-inert material from my womb") is little more than a form of speech: a vehicle to assert the author's identity and autonomy.

The pro-life warning about the potential of widespread abortion to degrade reverence for life does have a nugget of truth: a free-market rhetoric about abortion can, indeed, contribute to the eerie situation we are now facing, wherein the culture seems increasingly to see babies not as creatures to whom parents devote their lives but as accoutrements to enhance parental quality of life. Day by day, babies seem to have less value in themselves, in a matrix of the sacred, than they do as products with a value dictated by a market economy.

Stories surface regularly about "worthless" babies left naked on gratings or casually dropped out of windows, while "valuable," genetically correct babies are created at vast expense and with intricate medical assistance for infertile couples. If we fail to treat abortion with grief and reverence, we risk forgetting that, when it comes to the children we choose to bear, we are here to serve them—whomever they are; they are not here to serve us.

Too often our rhetoric leads us to tell untruths. What Norma McCorvey wants, it seems, is for abortion-rights advocates to face, really face, what we are doing: "Have you ever seen a second-trimester abortion?" she asks. "It's a baby. It's got a face and a body, and they put him in a freezer and a little container."

Well, so it does; and so they do.

The pro-choice movement often treats with contempt the pro-lifers' practice of holding up to our faces their disturbing graphics. We revile their placards showing an enlarged scene of the aftermath of a D & C abortion; we are disgusted by their lapel pins with the little feet, crafted in gold, of a 10-week-old fetus; we mock the sensationalism of The Silent Scream. We look with pity and horror at someone who would brandish a fetus in formaldehyde—and we are quick to say that they are lying: "Those are stillbirths, anyway," we tell ourselves.

To many pro-choice advocates, the imagery is revolting propaganda. There is a sense among us, let us be frank, that the gruesomeness of the imagery belongs to the pro-lifers; that it emerges from the dark, frightening minds of fanatics; that it represents the violence of imaginations that would, given half a chance, turn our world into a scary, repressive place. "People like us" see such material as the pornography of the pro-life movement.

But feminism at its best is based on what is simply true. While pro-lifers have not been beyond dishonesty, distortion and the doctoring of images (preferring, for example, to highlight the results of very late, very rare abortions), many of those photographs are in fact photographs of actual D & Cs; those footprints are in fact the footprints of a 10-week-old fetus; the pro-life slogan, "Abortion stops a beating heart," is incontrovertibly true. While images of violent fetal death work magnificently for pro-lifers as political polemic, the pictures are not polemical in themselves: they are biological facts. We know this. Since abortion became legal nearly a quarter-century ago, the fields of embryology and perinatology have been revolutionized —but the pro-choice view of the contested fetus has remained static. This has led to a bizarre bifurcation in the way we who are pro-choice tend to think about wanted as opposed to unwanted fetuses; the unwanted ones are still seen in schematic black-and-white drawings while the wanted ones have metamorphosed into vivid and moving color. Even while Elders spoke of our need to "get over" our love affair with the unwelcome fetus, an entire growth industry—Mozart for your belly; framed sonogram photos; home fetal-heartbeat stethoscopes—is devoted to sparking fetal love affairs in other circumstances, and aimed especially at the hearts of over-scheduled yuppies. If we avidly cultivate love for the ones we bring to term, and "get over" our love for the ones we don't, do we not risk developing a hydroponic view of babies—and turn them into a product we can cull for our convenience?

Any happy couple with a wanted pregnancy and a copy of What to Expect When You're Expecting can see the cute, detailed drawings of the fetus whom the book's owner presumably is not going to abort, and can read the excited descriptions of what that fetus can do and feel, month by month. Anyone who has had a sonogram during pregnancy knows perfectly well that the 4-month-old fetus responds to outside stimulus—"Let's get him to look this way," the technician will say, poking gently at the belly of a delighted mother-to-be. The Well Baby Book, the kind of whole-grain, holistic guide to pregnancy and childbirth that would find its audience among the very demographic that is most solidly pro-choice reminds us that: "Increasing knowledge is increasing the awe and respect we have for the unborn baby and is causing us to regard the unborn baby as a real person long before birth. . . . "

So, what will it be: Wanted fetuses are charming, complex, REM-dreaming little beings whose profile on the sonogram looks just like Daddy, but unwanted ones are mere "uterine material"? How can we charge that it is vile and repulsive for pro-lifers to brandish vile and repulsive images if the images are real? To insist that the truth is in poor taste is the very height of hypocrisy. Besides, if these images are often the facts of the matter, and if we then claim that it is offensive for pro-choice women to be confronted by them, then we are making the judgment that women are too inherently weak to face a truth about which they have to make a grave decision. This view of women is unworthy of feminism. Free women must be strong women, too; and strong women, presumably, do not seek to cloak their most important decisions in euphemism.

Other lies are not lies to others, but to ourselves. An abortion-clinic doctor, Elizabeth Karlin, who wrote a recent "Hers" column in The New York Times, declared that "There is only one reason I've ever heard for having an abortion: the desire to be a good mother."

While that may well be true for many poor and working-class women—and indeed research shows that poor women are three times more likely to have abortions than are better-off women—the elite, who are the most vociferous in their morally unambiguous pro-choice language, should know perfectly well how untrue that statement often is in their own lives. All abortions occupy a spectrum, from full lack of alternatives to full moral accountability. Karlin and many other pro-choice activists try to situate all women equally at the extreme endpoint of that spectrum, and it just isn't so. Many women, including middle-class women, do have abortions because, as one such woman put it, "They have a notion of what a good mother is and don't feel they can be that kind of mother at this phase of their lives." In many cases, that is still a morally defensible place on the spectrum; but it is not the place of absolute absolution that Dr. Karlin claims it to be. It is, rather, a place of moral struggle, of self-interest mixed with selflessness, of wished-for good intermingled with necessary evil.

Other abortions occupy places on the spectrum that are far more culpable. Of the abortions I know of, these were some of the reasons: to find out if the woman could get pregnant; to force a boy or man to take a relationship more seriously; and, again and again, to enact a rite of passage for affluent teenage girls. In my high school, the abortion drama was used to test a boyfriend's character. Seeing if he would accompany the girl to the operation or, better yet, come up with the money for the abortion could almost have been the 1970s Bay Area equivalent of the '50s fraternity pin.

The affluent teenage couples who conceive because they can and then erase the consequences—and the affluent men and women who choose abortion because they were careless or in a hurry or didn't like the feel of latex—are not the moral equivalent of the impoverished mother who responsibly, even selflessly, acknowledges she already has too many mouths to feed. Feminist rights include feminist responsibilities; the right to obtain an abortion brings with it the responsibility to contracept. Fifty-seven percent of unintended pregnancies come about because the parents used no contraception at all. Those millions certainly include women and men too poor to buy contraception, girls and boys too young and ill-informed to know where to get it, and countless instances of marital rape, coerced sex, incest and couplings in which the man refused to let the woman use protection.

But they also include millions of college students, professional men and women, and middle- and upper-middle-class people (11 percent of abortions are obtained by people in households with incomes of higher than $50,000)—who have no excuse whatsoever for their carelessness. "There is only one reason I've ever heard for having an abortion: the desire to be a good mother"—this is a falsehood that condescends to women struggling to be true agents of their own souls, even as it dishonors through hypocrisy the terminations that are the writer's subject.

Not to judge other men and women without judging myself, I know this assertion to be false from my own experience. Once, I made the choice to take a morning-after pill. The heavily pregnant doctor looked at me, as she dispensed it, as if I were the scum of the earth.

If what was going on in my mind had been mostly about the well-being of the possible baby, that pill would never have been swallowed. For that potential baby, brought to term, would have had two sets of loving middle-income grandparents, an adult mother with an education and even, as I discovered later, the beginning of diaper money for its first two years of life (the graduate fellowship I was on forbade marriage but, frozen in time before women were its beneficiaries, said nothing about unwed motherhood). Because of the baby's skin color, even if I chose not to rear the child, a roster of eager adoptive parents awaited him or her. If I had been thinking only or even primarily about the baby's life, I would have had to decide to bring the pregnancy, had there been one, to term.

No: there were two columns in my mind—"Me" and "Baby"—and the first won out. And what was in it looked something like this: unwelcome intensity in the relationship with the father; desire to continue to "develop as a person" before "real" parenthood; wish to encounter my eventual life partner without the off-putting encumbrance of a child; resistance to curtailing the nature of the time remaining to me in Europe. Essentially, this column came down to: I am not done being responsive only to myself yet.

At even the possibility that the cosmos was calling my name, I cowered and stepped aside. I was not so unlike those young louts who father children and run from the specter of responsibility. Except that my refusal to be involved with this potential creature was as definitive as a refusal can be.

Stepping aside in this way is analogous to draft evasion; there are good and altruistic reasons to evade the draft, and then there are self-preserving reasons. In that moment, feminism came to one of its logical if less-than- inspiring moments of fruition: I chose to sidestep biology; I acted—and was free to act—as if I were in control of my destiny, the way men more often than women have let themselves act. I chose myself on my own terms over a possible someone else, for self-absorbed reasons. But "to be a better mother?" "Dulce et decorum est . . ."? Nonsense.

Now, freedom means that women must be free to choose self or to choose selfishly. Certainly for a woman with fewer economic and social choices than I had—for instance, a woman struggling to finish her higher education, without which she would have little hope of a life worthy of her talents—there can indeed be an obligation to choose self. And the defense of some level of abortion rights as fundamental to women's integrity and equality has been made fully by others, including, quite effectively, Ruth Bader Ginsburg. There is no easy way to deny the powerful argument that a woman's equality in society must give her some irreducible rights unique to her biology, including the right to take the life within her life.

But we don't have to lie to ourselves about what we are doing at such a moment. Let us at least look with clarity at what that means and not whitewash self-interest with the language of self-sacrifice. The landscape of many such decisions looks more like Marin County than Verdun. Let us certainly not be fools enough to present such spiritually limited moments to the world with a flourish of pride, pretending that we are somehow pioneers and heroines and even martyrs to have snatched the self, with its aims and pleasures, from the pressure of biology.

That decision was not my finest moment. The least I can do, in honor of the being that might have been, is simply to know that.

Using amoral rhetoric, we weaken ourselves politically because we lose the center. To draw an inexact parallel, many people support the choice to limit the medical prolongation of life. But, if a movement arose that spoke of our "getting over our love affair" with the terminally ill, those same people would recoil into a vociferous interventionist position as a way to assert their moral values. We would be impoverished by a rhetoric about the end of life that speaks of the ill and the dying as if they were meaningless and of doing away with them as if it were a bracing demonstration of our personal independence.

Similarly, many people support necessary acts of warfare (Catholics for a Free Choice makes the analogy between abortion rights and such warfare). There are legal mechanisms that allow us to bring into the world the evil of war. But imagine how quickly public opinion would turn against a president who waged war while asserting that our sons and daughters were nothing but cannon fodder. Grief and respect are the proper tones for all discussions about choosing to endanger or destroy a manifestation of life.

War is legal; it is sometimes even necessary. Letting the dying die in peace is often legal and sometimes even necessary. Abortion should be legal; it is sometimes even necessary. Sometimes the mother must be able to decide that the fetus, in its full humanity, must die. But it is never right or necessary to minimize the value of the lives involved or the sacrifice incurred in letting them go. Only if we uphold abortion rights within a matrix of individual conscience, atonement and responsibility can we both correct the logical and ethical absurdity in our position—and consolidate the support of the center.

Many others, of course, have wrestled with this issue: Camille Paglia, who has criticized the "convoluted casuistry" of some pro-choice language; Roger Rosenblatt, who has urged us to permit but discourage abortion; Laurence Tribe, who has noted that we place the fetus in shadow in order to advance the pro-choice argument. But we have yet to make room for this conversation at the table of mainstream feminism.

And we can't wait much longer. Historical changes—from the imminent availability of cheap chemical abortifacients to the ascendancy of the religious right to Norma McCorvey's defection—make the need for a new abortion-rights language all the more pressing.

In a time of retrenchment, how can I be so sure that a more honest and moral rhetoric about abortion will consolidate rather than scuttle abortion rights? Look at what Americans themselves say. When a recent Newsweek poll asked about support for abortion using the rare phrasing, "It's a matter between a woman, her doctor, her family, her conscience and her God," a remarkable 72 percent of the respondents called that formulation "about right." This represents a gain of thirty points over the abortion-rights support registered in the latest Gallup poll, which asked about abortion without using the words "God" or "conscience." When participants in the Gallup poll were asked if they supported abortion "under any circumstances" only 32 percent agreed; only 9 percent more supported it under "most" circumstances. Clearly, abortion rights are safest when we are willing to submit them to a morality beyond just our bodies and our selves.

But how, one might ask, can I square a recognition of the humanity of the fetus, and the moral gravity of destroying it, with a pro-choice position? The answer can only be found in the context of a paradigm abandoned by the left and misused by the right: the paradigm of sin and redemption.

It was when I was four months pregnant, sick as a dog, and in the middle of an argument, that I realized I could no longer tolerate the fetus-is-nothing paradigm of the pro-choice movement. I was being interrogated by a conservative, and the subject of abortion rights came up. "You're four months pregnant," he said. "Are you going to tell me that's not a baby you're carrying?"

The accepted pro-choice response at such a moment in the conversation is to evade: to move as swiftly as possible to a discussion of "privacy" and "difficult personal decisions" and "choice." Had I not been so nauseated and so cranky and so weighed down with the physical gravity of what was going on inside me, I might not have told what is the truth for me. "Of course it's a baby," I snapped. And went rashly on: "And if I found myself in circumstances in which I had to make the terrible decision to end this life, then that would be between myself and God."

Startlingly to me, two things happened: the conservative was quiet; I had said something that actually made sense to him. And I felt the great relief that is the grace of long-delayed honesty.

Now, the G-word is certainly a problematic element to introduce into the debate. And yet "God" or "soul"—or, if you are secular and prefer it, "conscience"—is precisely what is missing from pro-choice discourse. There is a crucial difference between "myself and my God" or "my conscience"—terms that imply moral accountability—and "myself and my doctor," the phrasing that Justice Harry Blackmun's wording in Roe ("inherently, and primarily, a medical decision") has tended to promote in the pro-choice movement. And that's not even to mention "between myself and myself" (Elders: "It's not anybody's business if I went for an abortion"), which implies just the relativistic relationship to abortion that our critics accuse us of sustaining.

The language we use to make our case limits the way we let ourselves think about abortion. As a result of the precedents in Roe (including *Griswold v. Connecticut* and *Eisenstadt v. Baird*), which based a woman's right to an abortion on the Ninth and Fourteenth Amendments' implied right to personal privacy, other unhelpful terms are also current in our discourse. Pro-choice advocates tend to cast an abortion as "an intensely personal decision." To which we can say, No: one's choice of carpeting is an intensely personal decision. One's struggles with a life-and-death issue must be understood as a matter of personal conscience. There is a world of difference between the two, and it's the difference a moral frame makes.

Stephen L. Carter has pointed out that spiritual discussion has been robbed of a place in American public life. As a consequence we tend—often disastrously—to use legislation to work out right and wrong. That puts many in the position of having to advocate against abortion rights in order to proclaim their conviction that our high rate of avoidable abortion (one of the highest in developed countries, five times that of the Netherlands, for example) is a social evil; and, conversely, many must pretend that abortion is not a transgression of any kind if we wish to champion abortion rights. We have no ground on which to say that abortion is a necessary evil that should be faced and opposed in the realm of conscience and action and even soul; yet remain legal.

But American society is struggling to find its way forward to a discourse of right and wrong that binds together a common ethic for the secular and the religious. When we do that, we create a moral discourse that can exist in its own right independent of legislation, and we can find ground to stand upon.

Norma McCorvey explained what happened to her in terms of good and evil: she woke in the middle of the night and felt a presence pushing violently down on her. "I denounce you, Satan," she announced. This way of talking about evil is one of the chief class divisions in America: working-class people talk about Satan, and those whom Paul Fussell calls "the X group"—those who run the country—talk instead about neurotic guilt. While the elite scoff at research that shows that most Americans maintain a belief in the embodiment of evil—"the devil"—they miss something profound about the human need to make moral order out of chaos. After all, the only real difference between the experience described by Clare, the Cornell-educated pro-choicer, and McCorvey, the uneducated ex-alcoholic, is a classical allusion.

There is a hunger for a moral framework that we pro-choicers must reckon with. In the Karlin "Hers" column, the author announced proudly that pregnant women are asked by the counselor in the office, "So, how long have you been pro-choice?" Dr. Karlin writes that "Laughter and the answer, About ten minutes,' is the healthiest response. I still don't believe in abortion,' some women say, unaware that refusal to take responsibility for the decision means that I won't do the procedure.'"

How is this "feminist" ideological coercion any different from the worst of pro-life shaming and coercion? The women who come to a clinic that is truly feminist—that respects women—are entitled not only to their abortions but also to their sense of sin.

To use the term "sin" in this context does not necessarily mean, as Dr. Karlin believes, that a woman thinks she must go to hell because she is having an abortion. It may mean that she thinks she must face the realization that she has fallen short of who she should be; and that she needs to ask forgiveness for that, and atone for it. As I understand such a woman's response, she is trying to take responsibility for the decision.

We on the left tend to twitch with discomfort at that word "sin." Too often we have become religiously illiterate, and so we deeply misunderstand the word. But in all of the great religious traditions, our recognition of sin, and then our atonement for it, brings on God's compassion and our redemption. In many faiths, justice is linked, as it is in medieval Judaism and in Buddhism, to compassion. From Yom Kippur and the Ash Wednesday-to-Easter cycle to the Hindu idea of karma, the individual's confrontation with her or his own culpability is the first step toward ways to create and receive more light.

How could one live with a conscious view that abortion is an evil and still be pro-choice? Through acts of redemption, or what the Jewish mystical tradition calls tikkun; or "mending." Laurence Tribe, in Abortion: The Clash of Absolutes, notes that "Memorial services for the souls of aborted fetuses are fairly common in contemporary Japan," where abortions are both legal and readily available. Shinto doctrine holds that women should make offerings to the fetus to help it rest in peace; Buddhists once erected statues of the spirit guardian of children to honor aborted fetuses (called "water children" or "unseeing children"). If one believes that abortion is killing and yet is still pro-choice, one could try to use contraception for every single sex act; if one had to undergo an abortion, one could then work to provide contraception, or jobs, or other choices to young girls; one could give money to programs that provide prenatal care to poor women; if one is a mother or father, one can remember the aborted child every time one is tempted to be less than loving—and give renewed love to the living child. And so on: tikkun.

But when you insist, as the "Hers" column writer did, on stripping people of their sense of sin, they react with a wholesale backing-away into a rigid morality that reimposes order: hence, the ascendancy of the religious right.

Just look at the ill-fated nomination of Dr. Henry Foster for Surgeon General. The Republicans said "abortion," and the discussion was over. The Democrats, had they worked out a moral framework for progressivism, could have responded: "Yes: our abortion rate is a terrible social evil. Here is a man who can help put a moral framework around the chaos of a million and a half abortions a year. He can bring that rate of evil down. And whichever senator among you has ever prevented an unplanned pregnancy—and Dr. Foster has—let him ask the first question."

Who gets blamed for our abortion rate? The ancient Hebrews had a ritual of sending a "scapegoat" into the desert with the community's sins projected upon it. Abortion doctors are our contemporary scapegoats. The pro-lifers obviously scapegoat them in one way: if pro-lifers did to women what they do to abortion doctors—harassed and targeted them in their homes and workplaces—public opinion would rapidly turn against them; for the movement would soon find itself harassing the teachers and waitresses, housewives and younger sisters of their own communities. The pro-life movement would have to address the often all-too-pressing good reasons that lead good people to abort. That would be intolerable, a tactical defeat for the pro-life movement, and as sure to lose it "the mushy middle" as the pro-choice movement's tendency toward rhetorical coldness loses it the same constituency.

But pro-choicers, too, scapegoat the doctors and clinic workers. By resisting a moral framework in which to view abortion we who are pro-abortion- rights leave the doctors in the front lines, with blood on their hands: the blood of the repeat abortions—at least 43 percent of the total; the suburban summer country-club rite-of-passage abortions; the "I don't know what came over me, it was such good Chardonnay" abortions; as well as the blood of the desperate and the unpreventable and accidental and the medically necessary and the violently conceived abortions. This is blood that the doctors and clinic workers often see clearly, and that they heroically rinse and cause to flow and rinse again. And they take all our sins, the pro-choice as well as the pro-life among us, upon themselves.

And we who are pro-choice compound their isolation by declaring that that blood is not there.

As the world changes and women, however incrementally, become more free and more powerful, the language in which we phrase the goals of feminism must change as well. As a result of the bad old days before the Second Wave of feminism, we tend to understand abortion as a desperately needed exit from near-total male control of our reproductive lives. This scenario posits an unambiguous chain of power and powerlessness in which men control women and women, in order to survive, must have unquestioned control over fetuses. It is this worldview, all too real in its initial conceptualization, that has led to the dread among many pro-choice women of departing from a model of woman-equals-human-life, fetus-equals-not-much.

This model of reality may have been necessary in an unrelenting patriarchy. But today, in what should be, as women continue to consolidate political power, a patriarchy crumbling in spite of itself, it can become obsolete.

Now: try to imagine real gender equality. Actually, try to imagine an America that is female-dominated, since a true working democracy in this country would reflect our 54–46 voting advantage.

Now imagine such a democracy, in which women would be valued so very highly, as a world that is accepting and responsible about human sexuality; in which there is no coerced sex without serious jail time; in which there are affordable, safe contraceptives available for the taking in every public health building; in which there is economic parity for women—and basic economic subsistence for every baby born; and in which every young American woman knows about and understands her natural desire as a treasure to cherish, and responsibly, when the time is right, on her own terms, to share.

In such a world, in which the idea of gender as a barrier has become a dusty artifact, we would probably use a very different language about what would be—then—the rare and doubtless traumatic event of abortion. That language would probably call upon respect and responsibility, grief and mourning. In that world we might well describe the unborn and the never-to-be-born with the honest words of life.

And in that world, passionate feminists might well hold candlelight vigils at abortion clinics, standing shoulder to shoulder with the doctors who work there, commemorating and saying goodbye to the dead.

SOURCE: Naomi Wolf, "Our Bodies, Our Souls." *The New Republic*, October 16, 1995, 26–35.

DOCUMENT ANALYSIS

Naomi Wolf's words sent a chill through the prochoice community. Written in 1995, when conservative Republicans in Congress were pursuing antiabortion legislation even with a sitting, prochoice Democratic president in the White House, women in the prochoice community were beginning to take stock of the movement's framework for analysis.

Wolf's piece challenges the prochoice organizations and followers to consider the humanity of the fetus. In part because *Roe v. Wade* had refused to acknowledge the fetus as person, subsequent prochoice arguments have rested on a scientific and often legalistic rationale. As a consequence, antiabortion forces have become increasingly successful in describing the prochoice community as detached and insensitive to the complexities of abortion. Wolf argues that by acknowledging these complexities, the prochoice organizations would be more appealing to the vast majority of Americans who are conflicted about abortion. Moreover, she argues that the prochoice community would do well to acknowledge that even some abortion patients find their decision morally challenging.

Wolf's position would gain a greater footing some years later, when, in the aftermath of the 2004 election, several prominent Democrats, including both Senator Hillary Rodham Clinton and Democratic National Committee Chairman Howard Dean, began softening their abortion rhetoric, making space for a wider range of views.

Document: President Clinton's veto statement of H.R. 1833, the Partial Birth Abortion Ban.
Date: April 10, 1996.
Where: The White House, Office of the Press Secretary.
Significance: President Clinton's veto prevented the Partial Birth Abortion Ban from becoming law, if only temporarily. But it provoked a maelstrom of criticism from antiabortion organizations, intensifying the American abortion debate.

The White House
Office of the Press Secretary
For Immediate Release April 10, 1996
To The House of Representatives:

I am returning herewith without my approval H.R. 1833, which would prohibit doctors from performing a certain kind of abortion. I do so because the bill does not allow women to protect themselves from serious threats to their health. By refusing to permit women, in reliance on their doctors' best medical judgment, to use this procedure when their lives are threatened or when their health is put in serious jeopardy, the Congress has fashioned a bill that is consistent neither with the Constitution nor with sound public policy.

I have always believed that the decision to have an abortion generally should be between a woman, her doctor, her conscience, and her God. I support the decision in *Roe v. Wade* protecting a woman's right to choose, and I believe that the abortions protected by that decision should be safe and rare. Consistent with that decision, I have long opposed late-term abortions except where necessary to protect the life or health of the mother. In fact, as Governor of Arkansas, I signed into law a bill that barred third trimester abortions, with an appropriate exception for life or health.

The procedure described in H.R. 1833 has troubled me deeply, as it has many people. I cannot support use of that procedure on an elective basis, where the abortion is being performed for non-health related reasons and there are equally safe medical procedures available.

There are, however, rare and tragic situations that can occur in a woman's pregnancy in which, in a doctor's medical judgment, the use of this procedure may be necessary to save a woman's life or to protect her against serious injury to her health. In these situations, in which a woman and her family must make an awful choice, the Constitution requires, as it should, that the ability to choose this procedure be protected.

In the past several months, I have heard from women who desperately wanted to have their babies, who were devastated to learn that their babies had fatal conditions and would not live, who wanted anything other than an abortion, but who were advised by their doctors that this procedure was their best chance to avert the risk of death or grave harm which, in some cases, would have included an inability to ever bear children again. For these women, this was not about choice—not about deciding against having a child. These babies were certain to perish before, during or shortly after birth, and the only question was how much grave damage was going to be done to the woman.

I cannot sign H.R. 1833, as passed, because it fails to protect women in such dire circumstances—because by treating doctors who perform the procedure in these tragic cases as criminals, the bill poses a danger of serious harm to women. This bill, in curtailing the ability of women and their doctors to choose the procedure for sound medical reasons, violates the constitutional command that any law regulating abortion protect both the life and the health of the woman. The bill's overbroad criminal prohibition risks that women will suffer serious injury.

That is why I implored Congress to add an exemption for the small number of compelling cases where selection of the procedure, in the medical judgment of the attending physician, was necessary to preserve the life of the woman or avert serious adverse consequences to her health. The life exception in the current bill only covers cases where the doctor believes that the woman will die. It fails to cover cases where, absent the procedure, serious physical harm, often including losing the ability to have more children, is very likely to occur. I told Congress that I would sign H.R. 1833 if it were amended to add an exception for serious health consequences. A bill amended in this way would strike a proper balance, remedying the constitutional and human defect of H.R. 1833. If such a bill were presented to me, I would sign it now.

I understand the desire to eliminate the use of a procedure that appears inhumane. But to eliminate it without taking into consideration the rare and tragic circumstances in which its use may be necessary would be even more inhumane.

The Congress chose not to adopt the sensible and constitutionally appropriate proposal I made, instead leaving women unprotected against serious health risks. As a result of this Congressional indifference to women's health, I cannot, in good conscience and consistent with my responsibility to uphold the law, sign this legislation.

SOURCE: William J. Clinton, the White House, http://clinton6.nara.gov/1996/ot/1996-04-10-statement-on-partial-birth-abortion-veto.html.

DOCUMENT ANALYSIS

When President Clinton vetoed H.R. 1833 in 1996, he surrounded himself with women who, for a variety of "rare and tragic" circumstances, had had the procedure described in the bill. The President chose to underscore repeatedly the rarity of the procedure, a claim that was later challenged, and the official who had provided the president with the data for his argument admitted to falsifying those numbers. The House of Representatives voted to override Clinton's veto but the Senate failed to muster the two-thirds vote necessary to do so.

Clinton's veto message hung on the premise that the procedure was uncommon. He also admitted his discomfort with late-term abortions and explained that his concern for women's health, underscored by *Roe v. Wade* as well as subsequent Supreme Court rulings, was the principle behind his veto decision.

The Partial Birth Abortion Ban returned to Congress the following year. Again, the legislation was passed by both chambers of Congress, and landed on the President's desk. This time, amidst much greater public scrutiny and majority support for the bill in the public, President Clinton vetoed the legislation alone, in the middle of the night.

The legislation would be taken up again after the presidential election of 2000, and was ultimately signed into law by President George W. Bush on November 5, 2003.

Further Reading

Baehr, Ninia. *Abortion without Apology: A Radical History for the 1990s.* Boston: South End Press, 1990.

Condit, Celeste Michelle. *Decoding Abortion Rhetoric: Communicating Social Change.* Urbana: University of Illinois Press, 1990.

Cook, Elizabeth Adell, Ted G. Jelen, and Clyde Wilcox. *Between Two Absolutes: Public Opinion and the Politics of Abortion.* Boulder, Colo.: Westview Press, 1992.

Maguire, Daniel C. *Sacred Choices: The Right to Contraception and Abortion in Ten World Religions.* Minneapolis: Augsburg Fortress, 2001.

McDonagh, Eileen L. *Breaking the Abortion Deadlock: From Choice to Consent.* New York: Oxford University Press, 1996.

7

THE BATTLE CONTINUES INTO THE TWENTY-FIRST CENTURY

The turn of the twenty-first century brought no closure to the abortion debate in America. Instead, the new century ushered in fresh dimensions and a return of old nuances to this age-old policy battle. For the foreseeable future, abortion will continue to be a matter of national interest, with little resolution coming from either the states or from Congress. Rather, the Supreme Court continues to be the final arbiter of abortion policy.

With the addition of Justice Samuel A. Alito and Chief Justice John G. Roberts to the Supreme Court in 2006, fresh attention was drawn to the Court's continued role in abortion policy. Preceding their addition to the Court, the highest court issued a major 2000 decision striking a Nebraska ban on "partial birth" abortion, a procedure used in late-term and high-risk pregnancies, because it did not include an exception to the ban for a woman's health (*Stenberg v. Carhart*). That 5–4 decision did not settle the question of procedural bans, however. Just as the Court struck the Nebraska statute, Congress was creating a federal version of the ban. Once again, the federal version did not create an exception for a woman's health. Still, it was upheld 5–4 by the new Supreme Court in 2007, charting a new course for abortion jurisprudence.

Antiabortion forces benefited from the presidency of George W. Bush. Perhaps more than any other president, he shared the goals of the antiabortion movement; his actions would benefit the movement's aims while extending abortion opposition to new issues. Abortion would remain a national issue in the 2008 election, assured by both the Roberts court's actions and the great divide between the party platforms.

Document: President George W. Bush's Stem Cell Address.
Date: August 9, 2001.
Where: The Bush Ranch—Crawford, Texas.
Significance: This is the first and most complete presidential statement on stem cell research, which is often connected to abortion politics.

Good evening. I appreciate you giving me a few minutes of your time tonight so I can discuss with you a complex and difficult issue, an issue that is one of the most profound of our time.

The issue of research involving stem cells derived from human embryos is increasingly the subject of a national debate and dinner table discussions. The issue is confronted every day in laboratories as scientists ponder the ethical ramifications of their work. It is agonized over by parents and many couples as they try to have children, or to save children already born.

The issue is debated within the church, with people of different faiths, even many of the same faith coming to different conclusions. Many people are finding that the more they know about stem cell research, the less certain they are about the right ethical and moral conclusions.

My administration must decide whether to allow federal funds, your tax dollars, to be used for scientific research on stem cells derived from human embryos. A large number of these embryos already exist. They are the product of a process called in vitro fertilization, which helps so many couples conceive children. When doctors match sperm and egg to create life outside the womb, they usually produce more embryos than are planted in the mother. Once a couple successfully has children, or if they are unsuccessful, the additional embryos remain frozen in laboratories.

Some will not survive during long storage; others are destroyed. A number have been donated to science and used to create privately funded stem cell lines. And a few have been implanted in an adoptive mother and born, and are today healthy children.

Based on preliminary work that has been privately funded, scientists believe further research using stem cells offers great promise that could help improve the lives of those who suffer from many terrible diseases—from juvenile diabetes to Alzheimer's, from Parkinson's to spinal cord injuries. And while scientists admit they are not yet certain, they believe stem cells derived from embryos have unique potential.

You should also know that stem cells can be derived from sources other than embryos— from adult cells, from umbilical cords that are discarded after babies are born, from human placenta. And many scientists feel research on these type of stem cells is also promising. Many patients suffering from a range of diseases are already being helped with treatments developed from adult stem cells.

However, most scientists, at least today, believe that research on embryonic stem cells offer the most promise because these cells have the potential to develop in all of the tissues in the body.

Scientists further believe that rapid progress in this research will come only with federal funds. Federal dollars help attract the best and brightest scientists. They ensure new discoveries are widely shared at the largest number of research facilities and that the research is directed toward the greatest public good.

The United States has a long and proud record of leading the world toward advances in science and medicine that improve human life. And the United States has a long and proud record of upholding the highest standards of ethics as we expand the limits of science and knowledge. Research on embryonic stem cells raises profound ethical questions, because extracting the stem cell destroys the embryo, and thus destroys its potential for life. Like a snowflake, each of these embryos is unique, with the unique genetic potential of an individual human being.

As I thought through this issue, I kept returning to two fundamental questions: First, are these frozen embryos human life, and therefore, something precious to be protected? And second, if they're going to be destroyed anyway, shouldn't they be used for a greater good, for research that has the potential to save and improve other lives?

I've asked those questions and others of scientists, scholars, bioethicists, religious leaders, doctors, researchers, members of Congress, my Cabinet, and my friends. I have read heartfelt letters from many Americans. I have given this issue a great deal of thought, prayer and considerable reflection. And I have found widespread disagreement.

On the first issue, are these embryos human life—well, one researcher told me he believes this five-day-old cluster of cells is not an embryo, not yet an individual, but a pre-embryo. He argued that it has the potential for life, but it is not a life because it cannot develop on its own.

An ethicist dismissed that as a callous attempt at rationalization. Make no mistake, he told me, that cluster of cells is the same way you and I, and all the rest of us, started our lives. One goes with a heavy heart if we use these, he said, because we are dealing with the seeds of the next generation.

And to the other crucial question, if these are going to be destroyed anyway, why not use them for good purpose—I also found different answers. Many argue these embryos are byproducts of a process that helps create life, and we should allow couples to donate them to science so they can be used for good purpose instead of wasting their potential. Others will argue there's no such thing as excess life, and the fact that a living being is going to die does not justify experimenting on it or exploiting it as a natural resource.

At its core, this issue forces us to confront fundamental questions about the beginnings of life and the ends of science. It lies at a difficult moral intersection, juxtaposing the need to protect life in all its phases with the prospect of saving and improving life in all its stages.

As the discoveries of modern science create tremendous hope, they also lay vast ethical mine fields. As the genius of science extends the horizons of what we can do, we increasingly confront complex questions about what we should do. We have arrived at that brave new world that seemed so distant in 1932, when Aldous Huxley wrote about human beings created in test tubes in what he called a "hatchery."

In recent weeks, we learned that scientists have created human embryos in test tubes solely to experiment on them. This is deeply troubling, and a warning sign that should prompt all of us to think through these issues very carefully.

Embryonic stem cell research is at the leading edge of a series of moral hazards. The initial stem cell researcher was at first reluctant to begin his research, fearing it might be used for human cloning. Scientists have already cloned a sheep. Researchers are telling us the next step could be to clone human beings to create individual designer stem cells, essentially to grow another you, to be available in case you need another heart or lung or liver.

I strongly oppose human cloning, as do most Americans. We recoil at the idea of growing human beings for spare body parts, or creating life for our convenience. And while we must devote enormous energy to conquering disease, it is equally important that we pay attention to the moral concerns raised by the new frontier of human embryo stem cell research. Even the most noble ends do not justify any means.

My position on these issues is shaped by deeply held beliefs. I'm a strong supporter of science and technology, and believe they have the potential for incredible good—to improve lives, to save life, to conquer disease. Research offers hope that millions of our loved ones may be cured of a disease and rid of their suffering. I have friends whose children suffer from juvenile diabetes. Nancy Reagan has written me about President Reagan's struggle with Alzheimer's. My own family has confronted the tragedy of childhood leukemia. And, like all Americans, I have great hope for cures.

I also believe human life is a sacred gift from our Creator. I worry about a culture that devalues life, and believe as your President I have an important obligation to foster and encourage respect for life in America and throughout the world. And while we're all hopeful about the potential of this research, no one can be certain that the science will live up to the hope it has generated.

Eight years ago, scientists believed fetal tissue research offered great hope for cures and treatments—yet, the progress to date has not lived up to its initial expectations. Embryonic stem cell research offers both great promise and great peril. So I have decided we must proceed with great care.

As a result of private research, more than 60 genetically diverse stem cell lines already exist. They were created from embryos that have already been destroyed, and they have the ability to regenerate themselves indefinitely, creating ongoing opportunities for research. I have concluded that we should allow federal funds to be used for research on these existing stem cell lines, where the life and death decision has already been made.

Leading scientists tell me research on these 60 lines has great promise that could lead to breakthrough therapies and cures. This allows us to explore the promise and potential of stem cell research without crossing a fundamental moral line, by providing taxpayer funding that would sanction or encourage further destruction of human embryos that have at least the potential for life.

I also believe that great scientific progress can be made through aggressive federal funding of research on umbilical cord placenta, adult and animal stem cells which do not involve the same moral dilemma. This year, your government will spend $250 million on this important research.

I will also name a President's council to monitor stem cell research, to recommend appropriate guidelines and regulations, and to consider all of the medical and ethical ramifications of biomedical innovation. This council will consist of leading scientists, doctors, ethicists, lawyers, theologians and others, and will be chaired by Dr. Leon Kass, a leading biomedical ethicist from the University of Chicago.

This council will keep us apprised of new developments and give our nation a forum to continue to discuss and evaluate these important issues. As we go forward, I hope we will always be guided by both intellect and heart, by both our capabilities and our conscience.

I have made this decision with great care, and I pray it is the right one.

Thank you for listening. Good night, and God bless America.

SOURCE: Office of the Press Secretary, The White House, http://www.whitehouse.gov/news/releases/2001/08/20010809-2.html.

DOCUMENT ANALYSIS

Stem cell policy is admittedly beyond the scope of this text, but it is addressed routinely in the context of abortion. President Bush made clear his opposition to stem cell research in 2001, despite deep public disagreement with his viewpoint, even within his own political party. Stem cell research may be one area of the "human question" that does not divide the parties tidily into Democrat and Republican, but rather, seems to inspire disagreement within the two major parties.

Many Americans mistakenly connect stem cell research with abortion, perhaps fearing that stem cell lines come, or will come in the future, from aborted fetuses, which feeds the fear of so-called abortion mills. In fact, embryonic stem cell research is the result of unwanted embryos created through the invitro fertilization process, as the President's message above indicates. The piece is significant to abortion politics precisely because it indicates how the lines between abortion and other life issues are often blurred.

Document: Presidential statement restoring the Mexico City Policy.
Date: January 22, 2001.
Where: Office of the Press Secretary, The White House.
Significance: This statement indicates the return of an antiabortion administration.

For Immediate Release
Office of the Press Secretary
January 22, 2001
Memorandum
January 22, 2001
MEMORANDUM FOR THE ADMINISTRATOR OF THE UNITED STATES AGENCY FOR INTERNATIONAL DEVELOPMENT

SUBJECT: Restoration of the Mexico City Policy

The Mexico City Policy announced by President Reagan in 1984 required nongovernmental organizations to agree as a condition of their receipt of Federal funds that such organizations would neither perform nor actively promote abortion as a method of family planning in other nations. This policy was in effect until it was rescinded on January 22, 1993.

It is my conviction that taxpayer funds should not be used to pay for abortions or advocate or actively promote abortion, either here or abroad. It is therefore my belief that the Mexico City Policy should be restored. Accordingly, I hereby rescind the "Memorandum for the Acting Administrator of the Agency for International Development, Subject: AID Family Planning Grants/Mexico City Policy," dated January 22, 1993, and I direct the Administrator of the United States Agency for International Development to reinstate in full all of the requirements of the Mexico City Policy in effect on January 19, 1993.

GEORGE W. BUSH

SOURCE: http://www.whitehouse.gov/news/releases/20010123–5.html.

DOCUMENT ANALYSIS

This executive statement is both a marker of presidential authority in abortion policy and an indicator of how that policy can swing from one administration to another. Eight years prior, President Clinton had wielded a similar pen, with a stroke reversing the antiabortion administrative rules of the Reagan and Bush years, including the so-called Mexico City Policy. So in 2001, upon taking office, President George W. Bush exercised a similar authority in reinstating the Mexico City Policy of President Reagan and his father's administrations.

This statement also suggests the reach of American abortion policy: it extends beyond our own borders. Through the Mexico City Policy, any foreign agency that performs abortions may not receive U.S. government dollars, even when those dollars are targeted for nonabortion services. Critics argue that the policy hampers the efforts of family planning organizations in poor nations. Supporters contend that nongovernmental agencies abroad would use

American dollars to support abortion services if they could, and that such a ban provides a necessary protection of American values.

Document: Excerpt from Jimmy Carter's chapter, "Would Jesus Approve Abortions and the Death Penalty?"
Date: 2005.
Where: Our Endangered Values
Significance: The first American president to deal fully with the political and legal aftermath of *Roe v. Wade* explains his views some 30 years later.

Of all the sharply debated moral and political issues in America, abortion is the most divisive. Emotions run deep on both sides of the question, and they permeate both our nation's domestic and foreign policy. At the same time, there is a general consensus within our Christian churches that a developing fetus is a human life and should be protected.

It is practically impossible to meld the two most extreme views on abortion, with one side claiming that this is strictly a decision to be made by a woman about her own body with little or no regard for the fetus, and the other maintaining that a human being exists at the instant of conception and that murder results from any interruption of the embryo's development —or even the female ovum's fertilization by ejaculated sperm. There will never be any reconciliation between these true believers.

I am convinced that every abortion is an unplanned tragedy, brought about by a combination of human errors, and this has been one of the most difficult moral and political issues I have had to face. As president, I accepted my obligation to enforce the *Roe v. Wade* Supreme Court ruling, and at the same time attempted in every way possible to minimize the number of abortions—through legal restrictions, prevention of unwanted pregnancies, the encouragement of expectant women to give birth, and the promotion of foster parenthood.

I was bombarded with questions about abortion from the news media throughout my political campaigns and my presidency. One of my best-remembered and most often quoted remarks came at a presidential press conference in July 1977, when I defended my lack of support for federal funds to be used for abortions among poor mothers, even though wealthier women could afford to have their pregnancies terminated. Without any careful forethought, I responded to a question on this issue by saying, "Life is often unfair."

I could see then, and now, a clear opportunity to make substantial reductions in the need or desire for abortions while protecting the basic rights of a pregnant woman as prescribed by the Supreme Court. I advocated the evolution of more attractive adoption procedures, hoping to encourage the birth of a baby who might be unwanted or unplanned, and at the same time meet the desire of would-be parents to obtain a child. My administration also gave top priority to health care for new mothers and their babies.

In summary, I tried to do everything possible to prevent unwanted pregnancies and to encourage prospective mothers to deliver their babies. Without any apologies, I addressed the issue with the somewhat simple approach that "every baby conceived should be a wanted child." Frank and effective sex education is critical for teenagers, with a primary emphasis on abstinence but also information about safe and proven birth control methods.

SOURCE: Jimmy Carter, *Our Endangered Values: America's Moral Crisis* (New York: Simon and Schuster, 2005), 71–73. Reprinted with the permission of Simon & Schuster Adult Publishing Group. Copyright © 2005 by Jimmy Carter.

DOCUMENT ANALYSIS

Jimmy Carter was elected president as Congress was debating the Hyde Amendment. During his first year in office, the federal ban on abortion funding took effect, virtually ending all federal subsidies of abortion. As a self-identified evangelical Christian, President Carter was clear that he personally opposed the practice of abortion, but also felt compelled by the duty of his office to uphold the law of *Roe v. Wade*.

This selection from Carter's book is interesting in the context of the contemporary party alignments around abortion. While the official position of the Democratic Party has been to protect a woman's right to choose, particular Democratic officials, like Carter, maintain their personal opposition to abortion. In this selection, Carter's distance from his party's official abortion position is apparent, although so too is his commitment to prevention of unwanted pregnancy and implementation of sex education. In the contemporary party divide over abortion, Carter's voice is a unique blend of prevention pragmatism and principled opposition to abortion.

The excerpt is also striking in its candor. Few active political figures can afford to be so transparent about their conflicted views on this subject; fewer still would admit a mistake in an abortion-related comment. The fact that President Carter's statement is striking both in its complexity and lucidity reveals how entrenched the current debate has become.

IN HISTORY

SOUTH DAKOTA BAN AND ITS AFTERMATH

Governor Mike Rounds (R) of South Dakota signed the nation's strictest abortion law in 2006. Designed to challenge *Roe v. Wade,* the provision would have made it a felony to provide an abortion in all cases except to save the life of the woman. But opponents of the law placed a referendum on the November 2006 ballot, and voters rejected the abortion ban 55–45 percent.

One voice was of particular interest in the outcry over the ban. Oglala Sioux Chief Cecilia Fire Thunder offered to place a women's health clinic on her Pine Ridge Reservation; as a sovereign nation the Oglala Sioux could establish such a clinic, which the chief would have named Sacred Choices, had the law taken effect.

Chief Fire Thunder was impeached by her tribe for her actions. A former nurse and the first female chief of the South Dakota Oglala Sioux, Fire Thunder's actions offended many antiabortion Sioux, whose memory of forced sterilization of native women leaves them suspicious of abortion rights.

Document: State of Arkansas ultrasound equipment law.
Date: 2003.
Where: Little Rock, Arkansas.
Significance: This law made Arkansas the ninth in the nation to require physicians to purchase ultrasound equipment and provide women undergoing abortion the option to view their fetus prior to the procedure.

20–16–602. Right to view ultrasound image prior to abortion.

a) All physicians who use ultrasound equipment in the performance of an abortion shall inform the woman that she has the right to view the ultrasound image of her unborn child before an abortion is performed.

A prochoice protestor at the University of Texas holds up a symbol of the prochoice movement. Getty Images.

b) (1) The physician shall certify in writing that the woman was offered an opportunity to view the ultrasound image and shall obtain the woman's acceptance or rejection to view the image in writing.

(2) If the woman accepts the offer and requests to view the ultrasound image, she shall be allowed to view it.

c) The physician's certification together with the woman's signed acceptance or rejection shall be placed in the woman's medical file in the physician's office and kept for three (3) years.

d) Any physician who fails to inform the woman that she has the right to view the ultrasound image of her unborn child before an abortion is performed or fails to allow her to view the ultrasound image upon her request may be subject to disciplinary action by the Arkansas State Medical Board.

History. Acts 2003, No.1189, §§ 1, 2.

SOURCE: http://www.armedialboard.org/support/forms/MPA.pdf.

DOCUMENT ANALYSIS

Arkansas' ultrasound legislation portends a new trend in contemporary abortion politics. Much of the antiabortion activities during previous decades included outright abortion bans and overt restrictions on access; moreover, earlier efforts to curb abortion access generally did not try to engage the pregnant woman in persuasive tactics. With the new wave of ultrasound requirements, the antiabortion movement signals two important trends that will continue to be evident for the foreseeable future.

The first of those trends is an effort to use technology to persuade women to carry their fetuses to term. Activists who support such legislation often argue that by viewing the fetus, a woman is less likely to abort. Thus, the antiabortion movement is focusing on technology and advancing information about fetal life to enlist the help of pregnant women themselves in the antiabortion movement.

Secondly, this emphasis on the pregnant woman generally is packaged in empowering language, signaling the use of prochoice tactics to antiabortion ends. In previous decades, women who sought abortion were often characterized as selfish or immoral. Today, the ultrasound legislation generally uses the language of empowerment to describe the legislation in positive terms. Texas' law, for instance, is the "Woman's Right to Know" statute. The language of rights and women's control over their own bodies is historically the province of the abortion rights community. Efforts to mobilize abortion restrictions through female-centered language signals a new era of antiabortion activism and illustrates the tendency of the antiabortion movement to use to their own ends ways of understanding abortion typically used by abortion rights groups.

IN HISTORY

DATA ON ULTRASOUND EQUIPMENT LAWS

By June 2007, the following nine states had laws requiring abortion providers to purchase ultrasound equipment and give their abortion patients the option of viewing their fetus. Many more states are considering similar legislation, signaling a major nationwide trend in the twenty-first century.

Alabama
Arkansas
Idaho
Indiana
Michigan
Mississippi
Oklahoma
Utah
Wisconsin

Document: Excerpt from *Gonzales v. Carhart,* footnotes omitted.
Date: April 18, 2007.
Where: U.S. Supreme Court.
Significance: This landmark case is the first in which the Supreme Court abandoned its 30-year commitment to putting the consideration of women's health before the state's interest in emerging fetal life.

Justice Kennedy, writing for the majority:

The Act's purposes are set forth in recitals preceding its operative provisions. A description of the prohibited abortion procedure demonstrates the rationale for the congressional enactment. The Act proscribes a method of abortion in which a fetus is killed just inches before completion of the birth process. Congress stated as follows: "Implicitly approving such a brutal and inhumane procedure by choosing not to prohibit it will further coarsen society to the humanity of not only newborns, but all vulnerable and innocent human life, making it increasingly difficult to protect such life." Congressional Findings (14)(N), in notes following 18 U.S.C. §1531 (2000 ed., Supp. IV), p. 769. The Act expresses respect for the dignity of human life.

Congress was concerned, furthermore, with the effects on the medical community and on its reputation caused by the practice of partial-birth abortion. The findings in the Act explain:

President George W. Bush, surrounded by Republican congressmen, as he signs the Partial Birth Abortion Ban of 2003. Getty Images.

"Partial-birth abortion. . . confuses the medical, legal, and ethical duties of physicians to preserve and promote life, as the physician acts directly against the physical life of a child, whom he or she had just delivered, all but the head, out of the womb, in order to end that life." Congressional Findings (14)(J), ibid.

There can be no doubt the government "has an interest in protecting the integrity and ethics of the medical profession." *Washington v. Glucksberg*, 521 U.S. 702, 731 (1997); see also *Barsky v. Board of Regents of Univ. of N. Y.*, 347 U.S. 442, 451 (1954) (indicating the State has "legitimate concern for maintaining high standards of professional conduct" in the practice of medicine). Under our precedents it is clear the State has a significant role to play in regulating the medical profession.

Casey reaffirmed these governmental objectives. The government may use its voice and its regulatory authority to show its profound respect for the life within the woman. A central premise of the opinion was that the Court's precedents after *Roe* had "undervalue[d] the State's interest in potential life." 505 U.S., at 873 (plurality opinion); see also *id.*, at 871. The plurality opinion indicated "[t]he fact that a law which serves a valid purpose, one not designed to strike at the right itself, has the incidental effect of making it more difficult or more expensive to procure an abortion cannot be enough to invalidate it." *Id.*, at 874. This was not an idle assertion. The three premises of *Casey* must coexist. See *id.*, at 846 (opinion of the Court). The third premise, that the State, from the inception of the pregnancy, maintains its own regulatory interest in protecting the life of the fetus that may become a child, cannot be set at naught by interpreting *Casey*'s requirement of a health exception so it becomes tantamount to allowing a doctor to choose the abortion method he or she might prefer. Where it has a rational basis to act, and it does not impose an undue burden, the State may use its regulatory power to bar certain procedures and substitute others, all in furtherance of its legitimate interests in regulating the medical profession in order to promote respect for life, including life of the unborn.

The Act's ban on abortions that involve partial delivery of a living fetus furthers the Government's objectives. No one would dispute that, for many, D&E is a procedure itself laden with the power to devalue human life. Congress could nonetheless conclude that the type of abortion proscribed by the Act requires specific regulation because it implicates additional ethical and moral concerns that justify a special prohibition. Congress determined that the abortion methods it proscribed had a "disturbing similarity to the killing of a newborn infant," Congressional Findings (14)(L), in notes following 18 U. S. C. §1531 (2000 ed., Supp.

IV), p. 769, and thus it was concerned with "draw[ing] a bright line that clearly distinguishes abortion and infanticide." Congressional Findings (14)(G), *ibid*. The Court has in the past confirmed the validity of drawing boundaries to prevent certain practices that extinguish life and are close to actions that are condemned. *Glucksberg* found reasonable the State's "fear that permitting assisted suicide will start it down the path to voluntary and perhaps even involuntary euthanasia." 521 U.S., at 732–735, and n. 23.

Respect for human life finds an ultimate expression in the bond of love the mother has for her child. The Act recognizes this reality as well. Whether to have an abortion requires a difficult and painful moral decision. *Casey, supra*, at 852–853 (opinion of the Court). While we find no reliable data to measure the phenomenon, it seems unexceptionable to conclude some women come to regret their choice to abort the infant life they once created and sustained. See Brief for Sandra Cano et al. as *Amici Curiae* in No. 05–380, pp. 22–24. Severe depression and loss of esteem can follow. See ibid.

In a decision so fraught with emotional consequence some doctors may prefer not to disclose precise details of the means that will be used, confining themselves to the required statement of risks the procedure entails. From one standpoint this ought not to be surprising. Any number of patients facing imminent surgical procedures would prefer not to hear all details, lest the usual anxiety preceding invasive medical procedures become the more intense. This is likely the case with the abortion procedures here in issue. See, e.g., *Nat. Abortion Federation*, 330 F. Supp. 2d, at 466, n. 22 ("Most of [the plaintiffs'] experts acknowledged that they do not describe to their patients what [the D&E and intact D&E] procedures entail in clear and precise terms"); see also *id.*, at 479.

It is, however, precisely this lack of information concerning the way in which the fetus will be killed that is of legitimate concern to the State. *Casey, supra*, at 873 (plurality opinion) ("States are free to enact laws to provide a reasonable framework for a woman to make a decision that has such profound and lasting meaning"). The State has an interest in ensuring so grave a choice is well informed. It is self-evident that a mother who comes to regret her choice to abort must struggle with grief more anguished and sorrow more profound when she learns, only after the event, what she once did not know: that she allowed a doctor to pierce the skull and vacuum the fast-developing brain of her unborn child, a child assuming the human form.

It is a reasonable inference that a necessary effect of the regulation and the knowledge it conveys will be to encourage some women to carry the infant to full term, thus reducing the absolute number of late-term abortions. The medical profession, furthermore, may find different and less shocking methods to abort the fetus in the second trimester, thereby accommodating legislative demand. The State's interest in respect for life is advanced by the dialogue that better informs the political and legal systems, the medical profession, expectant mothers, and society as a whole of the consequences that follow from a decision to elect a late-term abortion.

JUSTICE GINSBURG, with whom JUSTICE STEVENS, JUSTICE SOUTER, and JUSTICE BREYER join, dissenting.

In *Planned Parenthood of Southeastern Pa. v. Casey*, 505 U.S. 833, 844 (1992), the Court declared that "[l]iberty finds no refuge in a jurisprudence of doubt." There was, the Court said, an "imperative" need to dispel doubt as to "the meaning and reach" of the Court's 7-to-2 judgment, rendered nearly two decades earlier in *Roe v. Wade*, 410 U.S. 113 (1973). 505 U.S., at 845. Responsive to that need, the Court endeavored to provide secure guidance to "[s]tate and federal courts as well as legislatures throughout the Union," by defining "the rights of the woman and the legitimate authority of the State respecting the termination of pregnancies by abortion procedures." *Ibid.*

Taking care to speak plainly, the *Casey* Court restated and reaffirmed *Roe*'s essential holding. 505 U.S., at 845–846. First, the Court addressed the type of abortion regulation permissible prior to fetal viability. It recognized "the right of the woman to choose to have an abortion before viability and to obtain it without undue interference from the State." *Id.*, at 846. Second, the Court acknowledged "the State's power to restrict abortions *after fetal viability*, if the law contains exceptions for pregnancies which endanger the woman's life *or health*." *Ibid.* (emphasis added). Third, the Court confirmed that "the State has legitimate interests from the outset of the pregnancy in protecting *the health of the woman* and the life of the fetus that may become a child." *Ibid.* (emphasis added).

In reaffirming *Roe*, the *Casey* Court described the centrality of "the decision whether to bear . . . a child," *Eisenstadt v. Baird*, 405 U.S. 438, 453 (1972), to a woman's "dignity and autonomy," her "personhood" and "destiny," her "conception of . . . her place in society." 505 U.S., at 851–852. Of signal importance here, the *Casey* Court stated with unmistakable clarity that state regulation of access to abortion procedures, even after viability, must protect "the health of the woman." *Id.*, at 846.

Seven years ago, in *Stenberg v. Carhart*, 530 U.S. 914 (2000), the Court invalidated a Nebraska statute criminalizing the performance of a medical procedure that, in the political arena, has been dubbed "partial-birth abortion." With fidelity to the *Roe-Casey* line of precedent, the Court held the Nebraska statute unconstitutional in part because it lacked the requisite protection for the preservation of a woman's health. *Stenberg*, 530 U.S., at 930; cf. *Ayotte v. Planned Parenthood of Northern New Eng.*, 546 U.S. 320, 327 (2006).

Today's decision is alarming. It refuses to take *Casey* and *Stenberg* seriously. It tolerates, indeed applauds, federal intervention to ban nationwide a procedure found necessary and proper in certain cases by the American College of Obstetricians and Gynecologists (ACOG). It blurs the line, firmly drawn in *Casey*, between previability and postviability abortions. And, for the first time since *Roe*, the Court blesses a prohibition with no exception safeguarding a woman's health.

I dissent from the Court's disposition. Retreating from prior rulings that abortion restrictions cannot be imposed absent an exception safeguarding a woman's health, the Court upholds an Act that surely would not survive under the close scrutiny that previously attended state-decreed limitations on a woman's reproductive choices.

I

A

As *Casey* comprehended, at stake in cases challenging abortion restrictions is a woman's "control over her [own] destiny." 505 U.S., at 869 (plurality opinion). See also *id.*, at 852 (majority opinion). "There was a time, not so long ago," when women were "regarded as the center of home and family life, with attendant special responsibilities that precluded full and independent legal status under the Constitution." *Id.*, at 896–897 (quoting *Hoyt v. Florida*, 368 U.S. 57, 62 (1961)). Those views, this Court made clear in *Casey*, "are no longer consistent with our understanding of the family, the individual, or the Constitution." 505 U.S., at 897. Women, it is now acknowledged, have the talent, capacity, and right "to participate equally in the economic and social life of the Nation." *Id.*, at 856. Their ability to realize their full potential, the Court recognized, is intimately connected to "their ability to control their reproductive lives." *Ibid.* Thus, legal challenges to undue restrictions on abortion procedures do not seek to vindicate some generalized notion of privacy; rather, they center on a woman's autonomy to determine her life's course, and thus to enjoy equal citizenship stature. See, *e.g.*, Siegel, Reasoning from the Body: A Historical Perspective on Abortion Regulation and Questions of Equal Protection, 44 Stan. L. Rev. 261 (1992); Law, Rethinking Sex and the Constitution,132 U. Pa. L. Rev. 955, 1002–1028 (1984).

In keeping with this comprehension of the right to reproductive choice, the Court has consistently required that laws regulating abortion, at any stage of pregnancy and in all cases, safeguard a woman's health. See, *e.g.*, Ayotte, 546 U.S., at 327–328 ("[O]ur precedents hold . . . that a State may not restrict access to abortions that are necessary, in appropriate medical judgment, for preservation of the life or health of the [woman]." (quoting *Casey*, 505 U.S., at 879 (plurality opinion))); *Stenberg*, 530 U.S., at 930 ("Since the law requires a health exception in order to validate even a postviability abortion regulation, it at a minimum requires the same in respect to previability regulation."). See also *Thornburgh v. American College of Obstetricians and Gynecologists*, 476 U.S. 747, 768–769 (1986) (invalidating a *post*-viability abortion regulation for "fail[ure] to require that [a pregnant woman's] health be the physician's paramount consideration").

We have thus ruled that a State must avoid subjecting women to health risks not only where the pregnancy itself creates danger, but also where state regulation forces women to resort to less safe methods of abortion. See *Planned Parenthood of Central Mo. v. Danforth*, 428 U.S. 52, 79 (1976) (holding unconstitutional a ban on a method of abortion that "force[d] a woman . . . to terminate her pregnancy by methods more dangerous to her health"). See also *Stenberg*, 530 U.S., at 931 ("[Our cases] make clear that a risk to . . . women's health is the same whether it happens to arise from regulating a particular method of abortion, or from barring abortion entirely."). Indeed, we have applied the rule that abortion regulation must safeguard a woman's health to the particular procedure at issue here—intact dilation and evacuation (D&E).

In *Stenberg*, we expressly held that a statute banning intact D&E was unconstitutional in part because it lacked a health exception. 530 U.S., at 930, 937. We noted that there existed a "division of medical opinion" about the relative safety of intact D&E, *id.*, at 937, but we made clear that as long as "substantial medical authority supports the proposition that banning a particular abortion procedure could endanger women's health," a health exception is required, *id.*, at 938. We explained:

"The word 'necessary' in *Casey*'s phrase 'necessary, in appropriate medical judgment, for the preservation of the life or health of the [pregnant woman],' cannot refer to an absolute necessity or to absolute proof. Medical treatments and procedures are often considered appropriate (or inappropriate) in light of estimated comparative health risks (and health benefits) in particular cases. Neither can that phrase require unanimity of medical opinion. Doctors often differ in their estimation of comparative health risks and appropriate treatment. And *Casey*'s words 'appropriate medical judgment' must embody the judicial need to tolerate responsible differences of medical opinion. . . ." *Id.*, at 937 (citation omitted).

Thus, we reasoned, division in medical opinion "at most means uncertainty, a factor that signals the presence of risk, not its absence." *Ibid.* "[A] statute that altogether forbids [intact D&E]. . . . consequently must contain a health exception." *Id.*, at 938. See also *id.*, at 948 (O'Connor, J., concurring) ("Th[e] lack of a health exception necessarily renders the statute unconstitutional.").

B

In 2003, a few years after our ruling in *Stenberg,* Congress passed the Partial-Birth Abortion Ban Act—without an exception for women's health. See 18 U.S. C. §1531(a) (2000 ed., Supp. IV). The congressional findings on which the Partial-Birth Abortion Ban Act rests do not withstand inspection, as the lower courts have determined and this Court is obliged to concede. *Ante,* at 35–36. See *National Abortion Federation v. Ashcroft,* 330 F. Supp. 2d 436, 482 (SDNY 2004) ("Congress did not . . . carefully consider the evidence before arriving at its findings."), aff'd *sub nom. National Abortion Federation v. Gonzales,* 437 F. 3d 278 (CA2 2006). See also *Planned Parenthood Federation of Am. v. Ashcroft,* 320 F. Supp. 2d 957, 1019 (ND Cal. 2004) ("[N]one of the six physicians who testified before Congress had ever performed an intact D&E. Several did not provide abortion services at all; and one was not even an obgyn. . . . [T]he oral testimony before Congress was not only unbalanced, but intentionally polemic."), aff'd, 435 F. 3d 1163 (CA9 2006); *Carhart v. Ashcroft,* 331 F. Supp. 2d 805, 1011 (Neb. 2004) ("Congress arbitrarily relied upon the opinions of doctors who claimed to have no (or very little) recent and relevant experience with surgical abortions, and disregarded the views of doctors who had significant and relevant experience with those procedures."), aff'd,413 F. 3d 791 (CA8 2005).

Many of the Act's recitations are incorrect. See *ante,* at 35–36. For example, Congress determined that no medical schools provide instruction on intact D&E. §2(14)(B), 117 Stat. 1204, notes following 18 U.S. C. §1531 (2000 ed., Supp. IV), p. 769, ¶(14)(B) (Congressional Findings). But in fact, numerous leading medical schools teach the procedure. See *Planned Parenthood,* 320 F. Supp. 2d, at 1029; *National Abortion Federation,* 330 F. Supp. 2d, at 479. See also Brief for ACOG as *Amicus Curiae* 18 ("Among the schools that now teach the intact variant are Columbia, Cornell, Yale, New York University, Northwestern, University of Pittsburgh, University of Pennsylvania, University of Rochester, and University of Chicago.").

More important, Congress claimed there was a medical consensus that the banned procedure is never necessary. Congressional Findings (1), in notes following 18 U.S. C. §1531 (2000 ed., Supp. IV), p. 767. But the evidence "very clearly demonstrate[d] the opposite." *Planned Parenthood,* 320 F. Supp. 2d, at 1025. See also *Carhart,* 331 F. Supp. 2d, at 1008–1009 ("[T]here was no evident consensus in the record that Congress compiled. There was, however, a substantial body of medical opinion presented to Congress in opposition. If anything . . . the congressional record establishes that there was a 'consensus' in favor of the banned procedure."); *National Abortion Federation,*330 F. Supp. 2d, at 488 ("The congressional record itself undermines [Congress'] finding" that there is a medical consensus that intact D&E "is never medically necessary and should be prohibited." (internal quotation marks omitted)).

Similarly, Congress found that "[t]here is no credible medical evidence that partial-birth abortions are safe or are safer than other abortion procedures." Congressional Findings (14)(B), in notes following 18 U.S. C. §1531 (2000 ed., Supp. IV), p. 769. But the congressional record includes letters from numerous individual physicians stating that pregnant women's health would be jeopardized under the Act, as well as statements from nine professional associations, including ACOG, the American Public Health Association, and the California Medical Association, attesting that intact D&E carries meaningful safety advantages over other methods. See *National Abortion Federation,* 330 F. Supp. 2d, at 490. See also *Planned Parenthood,* 320 F. Supp. 2d, at 1021 ("Congress in its findings . . . chose to disregard the statements by ACOG and other medical organizations."). No comparable medical groups supported the ban. In fact, "all of the government's own witnesses disagreed with many of the specific congressional findings." *Id.*, at 1024.

C

In contrast to Congress, the District Courts made findings after full trials at which all parties had the opportunity to present their best evidence. The courts had the benefit of "much more extensive medical and scientific evidence . . . concerning the safety and necessity of intact D&Es." *Planned Parenthood*, 320 F. Supp. 2d, at 1014; cf. *National Abortion Federation*, 330 F. Supp. 2d, at 482 (District Court "heard more evidence during its trial than Congress heard over the span of eight years.").

During the District Court trials, "numerous" "extraordinarily accomplished" and "very experienced" medical experts explained that, in certain circumstances and for certain women, intact D&E is safer than alternative procedures and necessary to protect women's health. *Carhart*, 331 F. Supp. 2d, at 1024–1027; see *Planned Parenthood*, 320 F. Supp. 2d, at 1001 ("[A]ll of the doctors who actually perform intact D&Es concluded that in their opinion and clinical judgment, intact D&Es remain the safest option for certain individual women under certain individual health circumstances, and are significantly safer for these women than other abortion techniques, and are thus medically necessary."); cf. *ante*, at 31 ("Respondents presented evidence that intact D&E may be the safest method of abortion, for reasons similar to those adduced in *Stenberg*.").

According to the expert testimony plaintiffs introduced, the safety advantages of intact D&E are marked for women with certain medical conditions, for example, uterine scarring, bleeding disorders, heart disease, or compromised immune systems. See *Carhart*, 331 F. Supp. 2d, at 924–929, 1026–1027; *National Abortion Federation*, 330 F. Supp. 2d, at 472–473; *Planned Parenthood*, 320 F. Supp. 2d, at 992–994, 1001. Further, plaintiffs' experts testified that intact D&E is significantly safer for women with certain pregnancy-related conditions, such as placenta previa and accreta, and for women carrying fetuses with certain abnormalities, such as severe hydrocephalus. See *Carhart*, 331 F. Supp. 2d, at 924, 1026–1027; *National Abortion Federation*, 330 F. Supp. 2d, at 473–474; *Planned Parenthood*, 320 F. Supp. 2d, at 992–994, 1001. See also *Stenberg*, 530 U.S., at 929; Brief for ACOG as *Amicus Curiae* 2, 13–16.

Intact D&E, plaintiffs' experts explained, provides safety benefits over D&E by dismemberment for several reasons: *First*, intact D&E minimizes the number of times a physician must insert instruments through the cervix and into the uterus, and thereby reduces the risk of trauma to, and perforation of, the cervix and uterus—the most serious complication associated with nonintact D&E. See *Carhart*, 331 F. Supp. 2d, at 923–928, 1025; *National Abortion Federation*, 330 F. Supp. 2d, at 471; *Planned Parenthood*, 320 F. Supp. 2d, at 982, 1001. *Second*, removing the fetus intact, instead of dismembering it *in utero*, decreases the likelihood that fetal tissue will be retained in the uterus, a condition that can cause infection, hemorrhage, and infertility. See *Carhart*, 331 F. Supp. 2d, at 923–928, 1025–1026; *National Abortion Federation*, 330 F. Supp. 2d, at 472; *Planned Parenthood*, 320 F. Supp. 2d, at 1001. *Third*, intact D&E diminishes the chances of exposing the patient's tissues to sharp bony fragments sometimes resulting from dismemberment of the fetus. See *Carhart*, 331 F. Supp. 2d, at 923–928, 1026; *National Abortion Federation*, 330 F. Supp. 2d, at 471; *Planned Parenthood*, 320 F. Supp. 2d, at 1001. *Fourth*, intact D&E takes less operating time than D&E by dismemberment, and thus may reduce bleeding, the risk of infection, and complications relating to anesthesia. See *Carhart*, 331 F. Supp. 2d, at 923–928, 1026; *National Abortion Federation*, 330 F. Supp. 2d, at

472; *Planned Parenthood*, 320 F. Supp. 2d, at 1001. See also *Stenberg*, 530 U.S., at 928–929, 932; Brief for ACOG as *Amicus Curiae* 2, 11–13.

Based on thoroughgoing review of the trial evidence and the congressional record, each of the District Courts to consider the issue rejected Congress' findings as unreasonable and not supported by the evidence. See *Carhart*, 331 F. Supp. 2d, at 1008–1027; *National Abortion Federation*, 330 F. Supp. 2d, at 482, 488–491; *Planned Parenthood*, 320 F. Supp. 2d, at 1032. The trial courts concluded, in contrast to Congress' findings, that "significant medical authority supports the proposition that in some circumstances, [intact D&E] is the safest procedure." *Id.*, at 1033 (quoting *Stenberg*, 530 U.S., at 932);accord *Carhart*, 331 F. Supp. 2d, at 1008–1009, 1017–1018; *National Abortion Federation*, 330 F. Supp. 2d, at 480–482; cf. *Stenberg*, 530 U.S., at 932 ("[T]he record shows that significant medical authority supports the proposition that in some circumstances, [intact D&E] would be the safest procedure.").

The District Courts' findings merit this Court's respect. See, *e.g.*, Fed. Rule Civ. Proc. 52(a); *Salve Regina College v. Russell*, 499 U.S. 225, 233 (1991). Today's opinion supplies no reason to reject those findings. Nevertheless, despite the District Courts' appraisal of the weight of the evidence, and in undisguised conflict with *Stenberg*, the Court asserts that the Partial-Birth Abortion Ban Act can survive "when . . . medical uncertainty persists." *Ante*, at 33. This assertion is bewildering. Not only does it defy the Court's longstanding precedent affirming the necessity of a health exception, with no carve-out for circumstances of medical uncertainty, see *supra*, at 4–5; it gives short shrift to the records before us, carefully canvassed by the District Courts. Those records indicate that "the majority of highly-qualified experts on the subject believe intact D&E to be the safest, most appropriate procedure under certain circumstances." *Planned Parenthood*, 320 F. Supp. 2d, at 1034. See *supra*, at 9–10.

The Court acknowledges some of this evidence, *ante*, at 31, but insists that, because some witnesses disagreed with the ACOG and other experts' assessment of risk, the Act can stand. *Ante*, at 32–33, 37. In this insistence, the Court brushes under the rug the District Courts' well-supported findings that the physicians who testified that intact D&E is never necessary to preserve the health of a woman had slim authority for their opinions. They had no training for, or personal experience with, the intact D&E procedure, and many performed abortions only on rare occasions. See *Planned Parenthood*, 320 F. Supp. 2d, at 980; *Carhart*, 331 F. Supp. 2d, at 1025; cf. *National Abortion Federation*, 330 F. Supp. 2d, at 462–464. Even indulging the assumption that the Government witnesses were equally qualified to evaluate the relative risks of abortion procedures, their testimony could not erase the "significant medical authority support[ing] the proposition that in some circumstances, [intact D&E] would be the safest procedure." *Stenberg*, 530 U.S., at 932.

II

A

The Court offers flimsy and transparent justifications for upholding a nationwide ban on intact D&E *sans* any exception to safeguard a women's health. Today's ruling, the Court declares, advances "a premise central to [*Casey's*] conclusion"—*i.e.*, the Government's "legitimate and substantial interest in preserving and promoting fetal life." *Ante*, at 14. See also *ante*, at 15 ("[W]e must determine whether the Act furthers the legitimate interest of the Government in protecting the life of the fetus that may become a child."). But the Act scarcely furthers that interest: The law saves not a single fetus from destruction, for it targets only a *method* of performing abortion. See *Stenberg,* 530 U.S., at 930. And surely the statute was not designed to protect the lives or health of pregnant women. *Id.,* at 951 (GINSBURG, J., concurring); cf. *Casey,* 505 U.S., at 846 (recognizing along with the State's legitimate interest in the life of the fetus, its "legitimate interes[t] . . . in protecting the *health of the woman*" (emphasis added)). In short, the Court upholds a law that, while doing nothing to "preserv[e] . . . fetal life," *ante,* at 14, bars a woman from choosing intact D&E although her doctor "reasonably believes [that procedure] will best protect [her]." *Stenberg,* 530 U.S., at 946 (STEVENS, J., concurring).

As another reason for upholding the ban, the Court emphasizes that the Act does not proscribe the nonintact D&E procedure. See *ante,* at 34. But why not, one might ask. Nonintact D&E could equally be characterized as "brutal," *ante,* at 26, involving as it does "tear[ing] [a fetus] apart" and "ripp[ing] off" its limbs, *ante,* at 4, 6. "[T]he notion that either of these two equally gruesome procedures . . . is more akin to infanticide than the other, or that the State furthers any legitimate interest by banning one but not the other, is simply irrational." *Stenberg,* 530 U.S., at 946–947 (STEVENS, J., concurring).

Delivery of an intact, albeit nonviable, fetus warrants special condemnation, the Court maintains, because a fetus that is not dismembered resembles an infant. *Ante,* at 28. But so, too, does a fetus delivered intact after it is terminated by injection a day or two before the surgical evacuation, *ante,* at 5, 34–35, or a fetus delivered through medical induction or cesarean, *ante,* at 9. Yet, the availability of those procedures—along with D&E by dismemberment —the Court says, saves the ban on intact D&E from a declaration of unconstitutionality. *Ante,* at 34–35. Never mind that the procedures deemed acceptable might put a woman's health at greater risk. See *supra,* at 13, and n. 6; cf. *ante,* at 5, 31–32.

Ultimately, the Court admits that "moral concerns" are at work, concerns that could yield prohibitions on any abortion. See *ante,* at 28 ("Congress could . . . conclude that the type of abortion proscribed by the Act requires specific regulation because it implicates additional ethical and moral concerns that justify a special prohibition."). Notably, the concerns expressed are untethered to any ground genuinely serving the Government's interest in preserving life. By allowing such concerns to carry the day and case, overriding fundamental rights, the Court dishonors our precedent. See, *e.g., Casey,* 505 U.S., at 850 ("Some of us as individuals find abortion offensive to our most basic principles of morality, but that cannot control our decision. Our obligation is to define the liberty of all, not to mandate our own moral code."); *Lawrence v. Texas,* 539 U.S. 558, 571 (2003) (Though "[f]or many persons [objections to homosexual conduct] are not trivial concerns but profound and deep convictions accepted as ethical and moral principles," the power of the State may not be used "to enforce these views on the whole society through operation of the criminal law." (citing *Casey,* 505 U.S., at 850)).

Revealing in this regard, the Court invokes an antiabortion shibboleth for which it concededly has no reliable evidence: Women who have abortions come to regret their choices, and consequently suffer from "[s]evere depression and loss of esteem." *Ante,* at 29. Because of women's fragile emotional state and because of the "bond of love the mother has for her child," the Court worries, doctors may withhold information about the nature of the intact D&E procedure. *Ante,* at 28–29. The solution the Court approves, then, is *not* to require doctors to inform women, accurately and adequately, of the different procedures and their attendant risks. Cf. *Casey,* 505 U.S., at 873 (plurality opinion) ("States are free to enact laws to provide a reasonable framework for a woman to make a decision that has such profound and lasting meaning."). Instead, the Court deprives women of the right to make an autonomous choice, even at the expense of their safety.

This way of thinking reflects ancient notions about women's place in the family and under the Constitution—ideas that have long since been discredited. Compare, *e.g.*, *Muller v. Oregon*, 208 U.S. 412, 422–423 (1908) ("protective" legislation imposing hours-of-work limitations on women only held permissible in view of women's "physical structure and a proper discharge of her maternal funct[ion]"); *Bradwell v. State*, 16 Wall. 130, 141 (1873) (Bradley, J., concurring) ("Man is, or should be, woman's protector and defender. The natural and proper timidity and delicacy which belongs to the female sex evidently unfits it for many of the occupations of civil life. . . . The paramount destiny and mission of woman are to fulfil[l] the noble and benign offices of wife and mother."), with *United States v. Virginia*, 518 U.S. 515 , n. 12 (1996) (State may not rely on "overbroad generalizations" about the "talents, capacities, or preferences" of women; "[s]uch judgments have . . . impeded . . . women's progress toward full citizenship stature throughout our Nation's history"); *Califano v. Goldfarb*, 430 U.S. 199, 207 (1977) (gender-based Social Security classification rejected because it rested on "archaic and overbroad generalizations" "such as assumptions as to [women's] dependency" (internal quotation marks omitted)).

Though today's majority may regard women's feelings on the matter as "self-evident," *ante*, at 29, this Court has repeatedly confirmed that "[t]he destiny of the woman must be shaped . . . on her own conception of her spiritual imperatives and her place in society." *Casey*, 505 U.S., at 852. See also *id.*, at 877 (plurality opinion) ("[M]eans chosen by the State to further the interest in potential life must be calculated to inform the woman's free choice, not hinder it."); *supra*, at 3–4.

B

In cases on a "woman's liberty to determine whether to [continue] her pregnancy," this Court has identified viability as a critical consideration. See *Casey*, 505 U.S., at 869–870 (plurality opinion). "[T]here is no line [more workable] than viability," the Court explained in *Casey*, for viability is "the time at which there is a realistic possibility of maintaining and nourishing a life outside the womb, so that the independent existence of the second life can in reason and all fairness be the object of state protection that now overrides the rights of the woman. . . . In some broad sense it might be said that a woman who fails to act before viability has consented to the State's intervention on behalf of the developing child." *Id.*, at 870.

Today, the Court blurs that line, maintaining that "[t]he Act [legitimately] appl[ies] both previability and postviability because . . . a fetus is a living organism while within the womb, whether or not it is viable outside the womb." *Ante*, at 17. Instead of drawing the line at viability, the Court refers to Congress' purpose to differentiate "abortion and infanticide" based not on whether a fetus can survive outside the womb, but on where a fetus is anatomically located when a particular medical procedure is performed. See *ante*, at 28 (quoting Congressional Findings (14)(G), in notes following 18 U.S. C. §1531 (2000 ed., Supp. IV), p. 769).

One wonders how long a line that saves no fetus from destruction will hold in face of the Court's "moral concerns." See *supra*, at 15; cf. *ante*, at 16 (noting that "[i]n this litigation" the Attorney General "does not dispute that the Act would impose an undue burden if it covered standard D&E"). The Court's hostility to the right *Roe* and *Casey* secured is not concealed. Throughout, the opinion refers to obstetrician-gynecologists and surgeons who perform abortions not by the titles of their medical specialties, but by the pejorative label "abortion doctor." *Ante*, at 14, 24, 25, 31, 33. A fetus is described as an "unborn child," and as a "baby," *ante*, at 3, 8; second-trimester, previability abortions are referred to as "late-term," *ante*, at 26; and the reasoned medical judgments of highly trained doctors are dismissed as "preferences" motivated by "mere convenience," *ante*, at 3, 37. Instead of the heightened scrutiny we have previously applied, the Court determines that a "rational" ground is enough to uphold the Act, *ante*, at 28, 37. And, most troubling, *Casey*'s principles, confirming the continuing vitality of "the essential holding of *Roe*," are merely "assume[d]" for the moment, *ante*, at 15, 31, rather than "retained" or "reaffirmed," *Casey*, 505 U.S., at 846.

III

A

The Court further confuses our jurisprudence when it declares that "facial attacks" are not permissible in "these circumstances," *i.e.*, where medical uncertainty exists. *Ante*, at 37; see *ibid*. ("In an as-applied challenge the nature of the medical risk can be better quantified and balanced than in a facial attack."). This holding is perplexing given that, in materially identical circumstances we held that a statute lacking a health exception was unconstitutional on its face. *Stenberg*, 530 U.S., at 930; see *id.*, at 937 (in facial challenge, law held unconstitutional because "significant body of medical opinion believes [the] procedure may bring with it greater safety for *some patients*" (emphasis added)). See also *Sabri v. United States*, 541 U.S. 600, 609–610 (2004) (identifying abortion as one setting in which we have recognized the validity of facial challenges); Fallon, Making Sense of Overbreadth, 100 Yale L. J. 853, 859, n. 29 (1991) ("[V]irtually all of the abortion cases reaching the Supreme Court since *Roe v. Wade*, 410 U.S. 113 (1973), have involved facial attacks on state statutes, and the Court, whether accepting or rejecting the challenges on the merits, has typically accepted this framing of the question presented."). Accord Fallon, As-Applied and Facial Challenges and Third-Party Standing, 113 Harv. L. Rev. 1321, 1356 (2000);Dorf, Facial Challenges to State and Federal Statutes, 46 Stan. L. Rev. 235, 271–276 (1994).

Without attempting to distinguish *Stenberg* and earlier decisions, the majority asserts that the Act survives review because respondents have not shown that the ban on intact D&E would be unconstitutional "in a large fraction of relevant cases." *Ante*, at 38 (citing *Casey*, 505 U.S., at 895). But *Casey* makes clear that, in determining whether any restriction poses an undue burden on a "large fraction" of women, the relevant class is *not* "all women," nor "all pregnant women," nor even all women "seeking abortions." 505 U.S., at 895. Rather, a provision restricting access to abortion, "must be judged by reference to those [women] for whom it is an actual rather than an irrelevant restriction," *ibid*. Thus the absence of a health exception burdens *all* women for whom it is relevant—women who, in the judgment of their doctors, require an intact D&E because other procedures would place their health at risk. Cf. *Stenberg*, 530 U.S., at 934 (accepting the "relative rarity" of medically indicated intact D&Es as true but not "highly relevant"—for "the health exception question is whether protecting women's health requires an exception for those infrequent occasions"); *Ayotte*, 546 U.S., at 328 (facial challenge entertained where "[i]n some very small percentage of cases . . . women . . . need immediate abortions to avert serious, and often irreversible damage to their health"). It makes no sense to conclude that this facial challenge fails because respondents have not shown that a health exception is necessary for a large fraction of second-trimester abortions, including those for which a health exception is unnecessary: The very purpose of a health *exception* is to protect women in *exceptional* cases.

B

If there is anything at all redemptive to be said of today's opinion, it is that the Court is not willing to foreclose entirely a constitutional challenge to the Act. "The Act is open," the Court states, "to a proper as-applied challenge in a discrete case." *Ante*, at 38; see *ante*, at 37 ("The Government has acknowledged that preenforcement, as-applied challenges to the Act can be maintained."). But the Court offers no clue on what a "proper" lawsuit might look like. See *ante*, at 37–38. Nor does the Court explain why the injunctions ordered by the District Courts should not remain in place, trimmed only to exclude instances in which another procedure would safeguard a woman's health at least equally well. Surely the Court cannot mean that no suit may be brought until a woman's health is immediately jeopardized by the ban on intact D&E. A woman "suffer[ing] from medical complications," *ante*, at 38, needs access to the medical procedure at once and cannot wait for the judicial process to unfold. See *Ayotte*, 546 U.S., at 328.

The Court appears, then, to contemplate another lawsuit by the initiators of the instant actions. In such a second round, the Court suggests, the challengers could succeed upon demonstrating that "in discrete and well-defined instances a particular condition has or is likely to occur in which the procedure prohibited by the Act must be used." *Ante*, at 37. One may anticipate that such a preenforcement challenge will be mounted swiftly, to ward off serious, sometimes irremediable harm, to women whose health would be endangered by the intact D&E prohibition.

The Court envisions that in an as-applied challenge, "the nature of the medical risk can be better quantified and balanced." *Ibid.* But it should not escape notice that the record already includes hundreds and hundreds of pages of testimony identifying "discrete and well-defined instances" in which recourse to an intact D&E would better protect the health of women with particular conditions. See *supra*, at 10–11. Record evidence also documents that medical exigencies, unpredictable in advance, may indicate to a well-trained doctor that intact D&E is the safest procedure. See *ibid.* In light of this evidence, our unanimous decision just one year ago in *Ayotte* counsels against reversal. See 546 U.S., at 331 (remanding for reconsideration of the remedy for the absence of a health exception, suggesting that an injunction prohibiting unconstitutional applications might suffice).

The Court's allowance only of an "as-applied challenge in a discrete case," *ante*, at 38—jeopardizes women's health and places doctors in an untenable position. Even if courts were able to carve-out exceptions through piecemeal litigation for "discrete and well-defined instances," *ante*, at 37, women whose circumstances have not been anticipated by prior litigation could well be left unprotected. In treating those women, physicians would risk criminal prosecution, conviction, and imprisonment if they exercise their best judgment as to the safest medical procedure for their patients. The Court is thus gravely mistaken to conclude that narrow as-applied challenges are "the proper manner to protect the health of the woman." Cf. *ibid.*

IV

As the Court wrote in *Casey*, "overruling *Roe*'s central holding would not only reach an unjustifiable result under principles of *stare decisis*, but would seriously weaken the Court's capacity to exercise the judicial power and to function as the Supreme Court of a Nation dedicated to the rule of law." 505 U.S., at 865. "[T]he very concept of the rule of law underlying our own Constitution requires such continuity over time that a respect for precedent is, by definition, indispensable." *Id.*, at 854. See also *id.*, at 867 ("[T]o overrule under fire in the absence of the most compelling reason to reexamine a watershed decision would subvert the Court's legitimacy beyond any serious question.").

Though today's opinion does not go so far as to discard *Roe* or *Casey*, the Court, differently composed than it was when we last considered a restrictive abortion regulation, is hardly faithful to our earlier invocations of "the rule of law" and the "principles of *stare decisis*." Congress imposed a ban despite our clear prior holdings that the State cannot proscribe an abortion procedure when its use is necessary to protect a woman's health. See *supra*, at 7, n. 4. Although Congress' findings could not withstand the crucible of trial, the Court defers to the legislative override of our Constitution-based rulings. See *supra*, at 7–9. A decision so at odds with our jurisprudence should not have staying power.

In sum, the notion that the Partial-Birth Abortion Ban Act furthers any legitimate governmental interest is, quite simply, irrational. The Court's defense of the statute provides no saving explanation. In candor, the Act, and the Court's defense of it, cannot be understood as anything other than an effort to chip away at a right declared again and again by this Court—and with increasing comprehension of its centrality to women's lives. See *supra*, at 3, n. 2; *supra*, at 7, n. 4. When "a statute burdens constitutional rights and all that can be said on its behalf is that it is the vehicle that legislators have chosen for expressing their hostility to those rights, the burden is undue." *Stenberg*, 530 U.S., at 952 (GINSBURG, J., concurring) (quoting *Hope Clinic* v. *Ryan*, 195 F. 3d 857, 881 (CA7 1999) (Posner, C. J., dissenting)).

For the reasons stated, I dissent from the Court's disposition and would affirm the judgments before us for review.

SOURCE: *Gonzales v. Carhart.* 550 U.S. 1 (2007) (footnotes omitted).

DOCUMENT ANALYSIS

The Court's majority opinion in this case is offered not by Chief Justice Roberts, who would customarily render the opinion, but by his new colleague Justice Alito. The opinion is reminiscent of Alito's 1991 dissenting opinion in *Casey*, when it was before him as a lower court judge. In this case, as in the earlier opinion, Justice Alito hangs his opinion on a twofold logic: first, that the undue burden standard created by his predecessor Justice O'Connor would permit the acceptance of the federal abortion ban, and that evidence of harm to women's health of such a ban is scant.

Alito maintains that O'Connor's undue burden standard satisfactorily justifies upholding the federal ban on a single abortion procedure. His read of O'Connor's definition allows government, including the federal government, to prefer birth over abortion and to use its considerable authority to persuade women seeking abortion of that viewpoint. Moreover, argues Alito, the scientific data gathered by three lower courts is insufficient to prove that the banned procedure is superior in protecting women's health than its still-legal alternative. Alito relies on controversial scientific evidence presented at congressional hearings to argue that banning the procedure without a health exception is constitutional.

The importance of the Court's ruling to uphold the federal procedure ban has been lost on many abortion-weary observers. While most Americans agree with Congress' ban, and most analysts argue that the ban will likely not alter the number of abortions provided in this country, the Court's decision is remarkable for at least two reasons.

First, this is the first time in abortion jurisprudence that does not require the abortion restriction to contain an exception to protect women's health. As such, court observers can reasonably expect that future legislatures will attempt similar restrictions, as the court has stepped away from nearly four decades of commitment to women's health as the central concept of abortion policy.

Secondly, the ruling is notable for one particular passage. In arguing that "it seems unexceptionable to conclude some women come to regret their choice to abort the infant life they once created and sustained. . . . Severe depression and loss of esteem can follow." Without scientific evidence, Justice Alito has affirmed a new perspective in antiabortion rhetoric from the bench: that abortion is bad for *women*, not just fetuses. More than any other passage in the decision, this one has been called out by prochoice forces as the most disappointing.

That perspective is articulated by Justice Ginsburg. In her dissent, the only woman on the Supreme Court argues both that the majority has misunderstood the undue burden test created by her former colleague Sandra Day O'Connor, and that the majority has taken a major step in displacing its commitment to women's health.

IN HISTORY

NEW HAMPSHIRE REPEALS PARENTAL NOTIFICATION LAW

In June 2007, New Hampshire became the first state in the nation to repeal its parental involvement law. Passed in 2003, New Hampshire's 48-hour parental notification law was among the strictest of its kind because, like the federal Partial Birth Abortion Ban, it contained no exception for the teen's health. A federal court had rejected the law, arguing that without the health exception the law is unconstitutional. In 2006, the Supreme Court unanimously sent the case back to lower court to determine whether the exception could be added. In the meantime, a prochoice Democratic majority took control of the state legislature as a consequence of the 2006 election. Rather than add a health exception, the new majority repealed the law entirely.

Document: Remarks by Senator Hillary Rodham Clinton to Family Planning Advocates of New York State.

Date: January 24, 2005.

Where: Empire State Plaza Convention Center, Albany, New York.

Significance: Senator Clinton's remarks shifted prochoice rhetoric by acknowledging the complexities of abortion, and set the tone for the 2008 presidential election.

Thank you all very much for having me. I am so pleased to be here two days after the 32nd anniversary of *Roe v. Wade*, a landmark decision that struck a blow for freedom and equality for women. Today Roe is in more jeopardy than ever, and I look forward to working with all of you as we fight to defend it in the coming years. I'm also pleased to be talking to people who are on the front lines of increasing women's access to quality health care and reducing unwanted pregnancy—an issue we should be able to find common ground on with people on the other side of this debate.

We should all be able to agree that we want every child born in this country and around the world to be wanted, cherished, and loved. The best way to get there is do more to educate the public about reproductive health, about how to prevent unsafe and unwanted pregnancies.

My own views of family planning and reproductive rights are heavily influenced by my travels as First Lady. I saw firsthand the costs to women when the government controls their reproductive health decisions.

In pre-democratic Romania, they had a leader named Ceausescu, a Soviet style Communist dictator, who decided it was the duty of every Romanian woman to bear five children so they

Abortion protestors, with a contemporary antiabortion slogan. Getty Images.

could build the Romanian State. So they eliminated birth control, they eliminated sex education, and they outlawed abortions.

Once a month, Romanian women were rounded up at their workplaces. They were taken to a government-controlled health clinic, told to disrobe while they were standing in line. They were then examined by a government doctor with a government secret police officer watching. And if they were pregnant, they were closely monitored to make sure you didn't do anything to that pregnancy.

If a woman failed to conceive, her family was fined a celibacy tax of up to 10 percent of their monthly salary. The terrible result was that many children who were born were immediately abandoned, and left to be raised in government-run orphanages.

Now go to the other side of the world and the opposite side of this debate. In China, local government officials used to monitor women's menstrual cycles and their use of contraceptives because they had the opposite view—no more than one child. If you wanted to have a child in China, you needed to get permission or face punishment. After you had your one allotted child, in some parts of China, you could be sterilized against your will or forced to have an abortion.

So whether it was Romania saying you had to have children for the good of the state, or China saying you can only have one child for the good of the state, the government was dictating the most private and important decisions we make as families and as women. Now with all of this talk about freedom as the defining goal of America, let's not forget the importance of the freedom of women to make the choices that are consistent with their faith and their sense of responsibility to their family and themselves.

I heard President Bush talking about freedom and yet his Administration has acted to deny freedom to women around the world through a global gag policy, which has left many without access to basic reproductive health services.

This decision, which is one of the most fundamental, difficult and soul searching decisions a woman and a family can make, is also one in which the government should have no role. I believe we can all recognize that abortion in many ways represents a sad, even tragic choice to many, many women. Often, it's a failure of our system of education, health care, and preventive services. It's often a result of family dynamics. This decision is a profound and complicated one; a difficult one, often the most difficult that a woman will ever make. The fact is that the best way to reduce the number of abortions is to reduce the number of unwanted pregnancies in the first place.

As many of you know, I have worked on these issues throughout my career and I continue to work on them in the Senate. One of the most important initiatives I worked on as First Lady and am proud to continue to champion in the Senate is the prevention of teen pregnancy. I worked alongside my husband who launched the National Campaign to Prevent Teen Pregnancy in the mid-1990s. This organization, which has proven to be a tremendous success, was really was born out of my husband's 1995 State of the Union address, which declared teenage pregnancy to be one of the most critical problems facing our country. We set a national goal of reducing unwanted pregnancies by one-third over the decade. We knew, though, that this goal could not be reached with a government-only effort. That's why we invited private sector sponsors to join the board and use their organizations to send a powerful message to teens to be responsible about their futures.

Now back when the National Campaign was getting off the ground, I actually came to New York City and gave a speech before high-profile members of the media—essentially challenging the media to embrace this issue and use its power to send strong, clear messages to teenagers to be responsible. Back then I used the phrase "teenage celibacy" over and over. Of course, no one talks about "teenage celibacy" anymore, but the message remains relevant and necessary today. I think it's a synonym for abstinence.

The good news is that the National Campaign, which has nourished many new and fruitful partnerships like those with Time Warner and with the faith community, has helped achieve the goal that my husband set in his State of the Union in 1995. Between 1991 and 2003, the teen birth rate fell 32.5 percent to a record low. The National Campaign has also conducted and disseminated some critical research on the important role that parents can play in encouraging their children to abstain from sexual activity.

So I'm very proud of the work of the National Campaign. We'll be celebrating its 10th anniversary this year and I will continue working with them to keep the number of unwanted pregnancies among our teenagers falling until we get to zero. But we have a long road ahead.

Today, even with the recent decline, 34% of teenage girls become pregnant at least once before their 20th birthday, and the U.S. has the highest teen pregnancy rate of any industrialized country. Children born to teen moms begin life with the odds against them. They are more likely to be of low-birth weight, 50 percent more likely to repeat a grade, and significantly more likely to be victims of abuse and neglect. And girls who give birth as teenagers face a long, uphill battle to economic self-sufficiency and pride. Clearly we do have our work cut out for us.

Research shows that the primary reason that teenage girls abstain is because of their religious and moral values. We should embrace this—and support programs that reinforce the idea that abstinence at a young age is not just the smart thing to do, it is the right thing to do. But we should also recognize what works and what doesn't work, and to be fair, the jury is still out on the effectiveness of abstinence-only programs. I don't think this debate should be about ideology, it should be about facts and evidence—we have to deal with the choices young people make not just the choice we wish they would make. We should use all the resources at our disposal to ensure that teens are getting the information they need to make the right decision.

We should also do more to educate and involve parents about the critical role they can play in encouraging their children to abstain from sexual activity. Teenagers who have strong emotional attachments to their parents are much less likely to become sexually active at an early age.

But we have to do more than just send the right messages and values to our children. Preventing unwanted pregnancy demands that we do better as adults to create the structure in which children live and the services they need to make the right decisions.

A big part of that means increasing access to family planning services. I have long been a strong supporter of Title X, the only federal program devoted solely to making comprehensive family planning services available to anyone interested in seeking them. Each year, approximately 4.5 million people receive health-care services at Title X-funded clinics. Nearly two-thirds of Title X clients come from households with incomes below the poverty level. And just to remind you, the poverty level is currently set for a family of three at $15,620. So where do these two-thirds of Title X clients go to receive the services they need? Unfortunately, despite the Clinton Administration working to obtain a 58% increase during the 1990s, the Bush Administration proposed level funding for Title X at $265 million for the 2003 and 2004 budgets, and Congress appropriated only $275 million in 2003. So even as our population has grown and the need has increased, the funding has remained stagnant. In fact, if Title X funding had increased at the rate of inflation from its FY 1980 funding level of $162 million, it would be at approximately $590 million now, but because its been held flat and we don't even know yet what the next budget holds for Title X funding. Title X cannot keep pace with basic services, let alone meet the growing cost of diagnostic tests and new forms of contraception.

It's also important that private insurance companies do their part to help reduce unwanted pregnancies. That is why I am a proud co-sponsor of the Equity in Prescription Insurance and Contraceptive Coverage—the so-called EPICC. The legislation would require private health plans to cover FDA-approved prescription contraceptives and related medical services to the same extent that they cover prescription drugs and other outpatient medical services. This bill simply seeks to establish parity for prescription contraception. Thanks to so many of the people in this room and the advocates, the EPICC law is now in effect in New York State having been passed and signed in 2002. It's a real role model for the nation. And it's about equal rights and simple justice. After all, if insurance companies can cover Viagra, they can certainly cover prescription contraceptives.

Contraception is basic health care for women, and the burden for its expense cannot fall fully on all women, many who after all live below that poverty rate, and in many instances above it, but not by very much and have a hard time affording such prescriptions. Just think, an average woman who wants two children will spend five years pregnant or trying to get pregnant, and roughly 30 years trying to prevent pregnancy. As I said earlier, and you know so well, the U.S. has one of the highest rates of unintended pregnancy in the industrialized world. Each year, nearly half of the six million pregnancies in this country are unintended, and more than half of all unintended pregnancies end in abortion.

The use of contraception is a big factor in determining whether or not women become pregnant. In fact, this is a statistic that I had not known before we started doing the research that I wanted to include in this speech, 7% of American women who do not use contraception account for 53% of all unintended pregnancies. So by preventing unintended pregnancy, contraception reduces the need for abortion. Improving insurance coverage of contraception will make contraception more affordable and reduce this rate of abortion. And expanding coverage and resources for Title X will do the same.

Another form of family planning that should be widely available to women is "Plan B," Emergency Contraception. I agree with the scientists on the Food and Drug Administration's Advisory Panel who voted overwhelmingly that Plan B is safe and effective for over the counter use. And I worked to launch a GAO investigation into the process of denying Barr Laboratories' application because I believe the decision was influenced more by ideology than evidence.

I am hopeful that the FDA will come to its senses and announce a new policy making Plan B available. Information about Plan B should be available over the counter, which is exactly what the FDA's Advisory Committee recommended. It should also be made available —automatically—to women who are victims of sexual assault and rape. I have to confess that I never cease to be surprised but last week, I joined with 21 of my colleagues in sending a letter to the Director of the Office on Violence Against Women—that's the name of the office at the Department of Justice—urging the Director to revise the newly-released first-ever national protocol for sexual assault treatment to include the routine offering of emergency contraception. Right now, this 130-page, otherwise comprehensive document fails to include any mention of emergency contraception, a basic tool that could help rape victims prevent the trauma of unintended pregnancies, avoid abortions, and safeguard their reproductive and mental health. Every expert agrees that the sooner Plan B is administered, the more effective it is. Once a woman becomes pregnant, emergency contraception obviously will have no effect.

Yet nowhere does the DOJ Protocol mention emergency contraception or recommend that it be offered to sexual assault victims. According to the Alan Guttmacher Institute, there are 15,000 abortions a year from rape. How is it possible that women who have been so victimized by violence can be victimized again by ideology? And how can we expect to reduce the number of unwanted pregnancies if we lose this most obvious opportunity to help women who may have had an unwanted pregnancy physically forced upon them?

I hope that whatever one believes or whatever side of the aisle one is, in either the NY State Legislature or the Congress, or anywhere in our country, we all at least agree that the Department of Justice must immediately revise its protocol to include strong recommendations about emergency contraception.

And the final building block of our effort to increase women's health includes ensuring that once women become pregnant, they have access to high-quality pre-natal care so that they can bring healthy children into the world.

One bill that provides a comprehensive approach to the problem of unintended pregnancies encapsulates many of these efforts. It's called "The Putting Prevention First Act." It provides a roadmap to the destination of fewer unwanted pregnancies—to the day when abortion is truly safe, legal, and rare. The Putting Prevention First Act, which I was proud to co-sponsor in the last Congress, increases funding for Title X; expands Medicaid family-planning services to provide access for more low-income women; ensures that health plans that cover prescription drugs also cover prescription contraceptives; funds emergency contraception public-education campaigns for doctors, nurses and women; ensures that hospital emergency rooms offer emergency contraception to victims of sexual assault; and establishes the nation's first-ever federal sex-education program.

A very similar version of the Putting Prevention First Act is being introduced today, one of the first bills introduced by Minority Leader Harry Reid, to lay out the Democratic plan for women's reproductive healthcare. I am proud to be a co-sponsor of this bill and I will work very hard to see that it is enacted. Because I know we can make progress on these issues; the work of the Clinton Administration and so many others saw the rate of abortion consistently fall in the 1990's. The abortion rate fell by one-fourth between 1990 and 1995, the steepest decline since Roe was decided in 1973. The rate fell another 11 percent between 1994 and 2000, from about 24 to 21 abortions for every 1,000 women of childbearing age.

But unfortunately, in the last few years, while we are engaged in an ideological debate instead of one that uses facts and evidence and commonsense, the rate of abortion is on the rise in some states. In the three years since President Bush took office, 8 states saw an increase in abortion rates (14.6% average increase), and four saw a decrease (4.3% average), so we have a lot of work still ahead of us.

I think it's important that family planning advocates reach out to those who may not agree with us on everything to try to find common ground in those areas where, hopefully, emergency contraception, more funding for prenatal care and others can be a point of common ground.

As an advocate for children and families throughout my life, as a lawyer who occasionally represented victims of sexual assault and rape, as a mother, as a wife, as a woman, I know the difference that good information, good education, and good health care can make in empowering women and girls to make good decisions for themselves.

So in addition to the work that lies ahead of us here at home I would just put in a word for the work that we should be doing around the world. It has been tragic to see so much of the good work that provided family planning assistance and resources to physicians and nurses to deliver to women in places where there was no family planning, where in fact abortion was the only means of contraception. But during the 90's we reached out to women and girls in other parts of the world. When my husband rescinded the global gag rule we began to work on behalf of women's health, though the infant mortality and maternal mortality rate is way too high in so many parts of the world. When I was in Afghanistan last year, I met with a group of women and their number one plea was what can the United States Government do to help save the lives of Afghan women who have one of the highest rates of maternal mortality in the world? Is there some way that more education could be brought in so that women could possibly have more control over their own lives? In places I've traveled I've cut the ribbons on clinics—that were partially funded by money from our government and money from private givers in our country—that for the first time would provide the full range of health services to women and girls. Because of the reinstatement of the global gag rule under President Bush that work has stopped. Those resources have dried up. The lives of so many women and girls have been put at risk. We can do better not only here at home but around the world.

Yes we do have deeply held differences of opinion about the issue of abortion. I for one respect those who believe with all their hearts and conscience that there are no circumstances under which any abortion should ever be available. But that does not represent even the majority opinion within the anti-abortion community. There are exceptions for rape and for incest, for the life of the mother. Those in the pro-choice community who have fought so hard for so many years, not only to protect *Roe v. Wade* and the law of the land, but to provide the resources that would effectuate that constitutional right, believe just as strongly the point of view based on experience and conscience that they have come to. The problem I always have is what is the proper role of government in making this decision? That is why I started with two stories about Romania and China. When I spoke to the conference on women in Beijing in 1995—ten years ago this year—I spoke out against any government interfering with the reproductive rights and decisions of women and families.

So we have a lot of experience from around the world that is a cautionary tale about what happens when a government substitutes its opinion for an individual's. There is no reason why government cannot do more to educate and inform and provide assistance so that the choice guaranteed under our constitution either does not ever have to be exercised or only in very rare circumstances. But we cannot expect to have the kind of positive results that all of us are hoping for to reduce the number of unwanted pregnancies and abortions if our government refuses to assist girls and women with their health care needs, a comprehensive education and accurate information.

So my hope now, today, is that whatever our disagreements with those in this debate, that we join together to take real action to improve the quality of health care for women and families, to reduce the number of abortions and to build a healthier, brighter more hopeful future for women and girls in our country and around the world.

Thank you very much.

SOURCE: Remarks by Senator Hillary Rodham Clinton to the New York State Family Planning Providers, January 24, 2005, available at: http://clinton.senate.gov/~clinton/speeches/2005125A05.html.

DOCUMENT ANALYSIS

Senator Clinton's remarks at a gathering commemorating the anniversary of *Roe v. Wade* sent shockwaves through the political world with one sentence: "we can all recognize that abortion in many ways represents a sad, even tragic choice to many, many women." With this statement, Senator Clinton acknowledged the complexity of abortion, which for some abortion rights advocates conceded a point to prolife forces that would create a strategic hurdle for the movement.

While most of the speech is traditionally prochoice and celebratory in tone, with this one sentence the senator touched a nerve within the prochoice organizations, much as Naomi Wolf had a decade prior. Still, with her emphasis on pregnancy prevention, the senator positioned herself as a moderate on abortion and in doing so, challenged the popular perception that Democratic candidates are *proabortion* rather than prochoice. This positioning both makes Clinton a viable candidate in the presidential election as a moderate on social policy, and widens Democratic rhetoric on abortion policy, possibly influencing the tenor of the election itself.

Further Reading

Ehrlich, J. Shoshanna. *Who Decides? The Abortion Rights of Teens*. Westport, Conn.: Praeger, 2006.

McFarlane, Deborah R., and Kenneth J. Meier. *The Politics of Fertility Control: Family Planning and Abortion Policies in the American States*. New York: Chatham House Publishers, 2001.

Roth, Rachel. *Making Women Pay: The Hidden Costs of Fetal Rights*. Ithaca, N.Y.: Cornell University Press, 2000.

Saletan, William. *Bearing Right: How Conservatives Won the Abortion War*. Berkeley: University of California Press, 2004.

Schroedel, Jean Reith. *Is the Fetus a Person? A Comparison of Policies across the Fifty States*. Ithaca, N.Y.: Cornell University Press, 2000.

CONCLUSION

In 1800, there was not a single abortion statute in America. By 1900, there were dozens of state abortion restrictions and a single federal proscription against sending obscene materials through the U.S. postal service—which had implications both for abortion advertisements as well as birth control devices. By 2000, the Supreme Court was considering a state ban on abortion against the backdrop of a midcentury liberalization of abortion policy. In 2006, South Dakota became the first state in the nation to ban abortion in a half-century.

When seen from aloft, these transformations in American public policy speak to the intensity of debate surrounding the issue. This text has used primary sources in the arenas of law, religion, science, and politics to reveal the tensions existing both historically and presently in American abortion policy. For many, the text is a useful touchstone for a meaningful document here and there; for others, it gives the broad sweep of abortion policy and practice over a 200-year span of time and from dozens of points of view.

America, it seems, finds itself at a crossroads once again in abortion policy. In 1973, seven justices out of nine voted to extend national abortion rights to America's women. This shift reflected the product of a long-standing social movement and the culmination of medical and legal trends. In 2007, five justices upheld a federal abortion procedure ban that did not contain an exception to protect women's health: a requirement under the 1973 decision. How far the nation had traveled between 1973 and 2007 is reflected in the documents here, and while the full explanation of how the nation could return to restrictive abortion policy is well beyond the scope of this work, most of the explanation lies within the arguments laid out in these primary source documents.

The next stage in American abortion politics will contain similar sources: legal, religious, scientific, and poetic, and the debate will encompass an equally varied array of voices. Whether dissonant or melodious depends on the audience, but each of the voices in this chorus reveals tensions within the American political landscape that must be addressed through policy.

What appears certain is that the 2008 election will address the abortion issue. Abortion has had an increasingly prominent role in national elections since *Roe v. Wade* nationalized the issue in 1973. While federal candidates prior to that year preferred to side-step the issue when possible, in the post-*Roe* world, abortion divides the two major political parties as interest groups put pressure on candidates to commit to policy outcomes. As long as Congress votes on abortion-related bills dozens of times per year, and as long as presidents have the opportunity to nominate justices to the Supreme Court, American voters will want to know where the candidates stand on the issue.

Still, although the voices may be new, the themes will remain largely the same as in past generations. Women's control over their bodies, acknowledgement of the fetus, the role of states and federal government, and the appropriate roles for medicine and politicians remain the constant wedges in the abortion controversy over the span of American history. And if America has a chance of resolving this dilemma for the greater good, it must address the only truth about abortion politics discovered by all parties: that the incidence of abortion practice remains unrelated to the policies of the day. Far from affecting the demand for abortion, abortion policy changes does little but change where women have abortions. Perhaps the twenty-first century will discover the illusive solution to one of America's most vexing policy dilemmas.

BIBLIOGRAPHY

Print Sources

Atwood, Margaret. *The Handmaid's Tale*. New York: Fawcett Crest, 1986.

Bachiochi, Erika, ed. *The Cost of "Choice": Women Evaluate the Impact of Abortion*. San Francisco: Encounter Books, 2004.

Baehr, Ninia. *Abortion without Apology: A Radical History for the 1990s*. Boston: South End Press, 1990.

Balkin, Jack M., ed. *What* Roe v. Wade *Should Have Said: The Nation's Top Legal Experts Rewrite America's Most Controversial Decision*. New York: New York University Press, 2005.

Barnett, Ruth, as told to Doug Baker. *The Weep on My Doorstep*. Beaverton, Ore.: Halo Publishers, 1969.

Condit, Celeste Michelle. *Decoding Abortion Rhetoric: Communicating Social Change*. Urbana: University of Illinois Press, 1990.

Cook, Elizabeth Adell, Ted G. Jelen, and Clyde Wilcox. *Between Two Absolutes: Public Opinion and the Politics of Abortion*. Boulder, Colo.: Westview Press, 1992.

Craig, Barbara Hinkson, and David M. O'Brien. *Abortion and American Politics*. Chatham, N.J.: Chatham House Publishers, Inc., 1993.

Critchlow, Donald T. *Intended Consequences: Birth Control, Abortion, and the Federal Government in Modern America*. Oxford, England: Oxford University Press, 1999.

Critchlow, Donald T., ed. *The Politics of Abortion and Birth Control in Historical Perspective*. University Park: The Pennsylvania State University Press, 1996.

Doan, Alesha E. *Opposition & Intimidation: The Abortion Wars and Strategies of Political Harassment*. Ann Arbor: University of Michigan Press, 2007.

Ehrlich, J. Shoshanna. *Who Decides? The Abortion Rights of Teens*. Westport, Conn.: Praeger, 2006.

Faux, Marian. Roe v. Wade: *The Untold Story of the Landmark Supreme Court Decision That Made Abortion Legal*. New York: Macmillan Publishing Company, 1988.

Feldt, Gloria. *The War on Choice: The Right-Wing Attack on Women's Rights and How to Fight Back*. New York: Bantam Books, 2004.

Garrow, David J. *Liberty and Sexuality: The Right to Privacy and the Making of* Roe v. Wade. New York: Macmillan Publishing Company, 1994.

Glendon, Mary Ann. *Abortion and Divorce in Western Law: American Failures, European Challenges*. Cambridge, Mass.: Harvard University Press, 1987.

Gordon, Linda. *Woman's Body, Woman's Right*. New York: Penguin Books, 1974.

Gorney, Cynthia. *Articles of Faith: A Frontline History of the Abortion Wars*. New York: Simon and Schuster, 1998.

Hull, N.E.H., and Peter Charles Hoffer. Roe v. Wade: *The Abortion Rights Controversy in American History*. Lawrence: University Press of Kansas, 2001.

Hull, N.E.H., Williamjames Hoffer, and Peter Charles Hoffer, eds. *The Abortion Rights Controversy in America: A Legal Reader*. Chapel Hill: The University of North Carolina Press, 2004.

Irving, John. *The Cider House Rules*. New York: William Morrow and Company, Inc., 1985.

Joffee, Carole. *Doctors of Conscience: The Struggle to Provide Abortion before and after* Roe v. Wade. Boston: Beacon Press, 1995.

Kaplan, Laura. *The Story of Jane: The Legendary Underground Feminist Abortion Service*. Chicago: University of Chicago Press, 1995.

Lader, Lawrence. *RU 486: The Pill That Could End the Abortion Wars and Why American Women Don't Have It*. Reading, Mass.: Addison-Wesley Publishing Company, Inc., 1991.

Maguire, Daniel C. *Sacred Choices: The Right to Contraception and Abortion in Ten World Religions*. Minneapolis: Augsburg Fortress, 2001.

McCorvey, Norma, with Andy Meisler. *I am Roe: My Life*, Roe v. Wade, *and Freedom of Choice*. New York: HarperCollins Publishers, 1994.

McDonagh, Eileen L. *Breaking the Abortion Deadlock: From Choice to Consent*. New York: Oxford University Press, 1996.

McFarlane, Deborah R., and Kenneth J. Meier. *The Politics of Fertility Control: Family Planning and Abortion Policies in the American States*. New York: Chatham House Publishers, 2001.

McKeegan, Michele. *Abortion Politics: Mutiny in the Ranks of the Right*. New York: The Free Press, 1992.

Mohr, James C. *Abortion in America: The Origins and Evolution of National Policy*. Oxford, England: Oxford University Press, 1978.

O'Connor, Karen. *No Neutral Ground? Abortion Politics in an Age of Absolutes*. Boulder, Colo.: Westview Press, 1996.

Page, Cristina. *How the Pro-Choice Movement Saved America: Freedom, Politics, and the War on Sex*. New York: BasicBooks, 2006.

Petchesky, Rosalind. *Abortion and Woman's Choice: The State, Sexuality, and Reproductive Freedom*, 2nd ed. Boston: Northeastern University Press, 1990.

Reagan, Leslie J. *When Abortion Was a Crime: Women, Medicine, and Law in the United States, 1867–1973*. Berkeley: University of California Press, 1997.

Reiterman, C. *Abortion and the Unwanted Child: The California Committee on Therapeutic Abortion*. New York: Springer Publishing Inc., 1971.

Risen, James, and Judy L. Thomas. *Wrath of Angels: The American Abortion War*. New York: Basic Books, 1998.

Rose, Melody. *Safe, Legal, and Unavailable?* Washington, D.C.: Congressional Quarterly Press, 2007.

Roth, Rachel. *Making Women Pay: The Hidden Costs of Fetal Rights*. Ithaca, N.Y.: Cornell University Press, 2000.

Rowland, Debran, esq. *The Boundaries of Her Body: A History of Women's Rights in AMERICA*. Naperville, Ill.: Sphinx Publishing, 2004.

Saletan, William. *Bearing Right: How Conservatives Won the Abortion War*. Berkeley: University of California Press, 2004.

Sanger, Alexander. *Beyond Choice: Reproductive Freedom in the 21st Century*. New York: PublicAffairs Books, 2004.

Schroedel, Jean Reith. *Is the Fetus a Person? A Comparison of Policies across the Fifty States*. Ithaca, N.Y.: Cornell University Press, 2000.

Solinger, Rickie. *The Abortionist: A Woman Against the Law*. Berkeley: University of California Press, 1996.

Solinger, Rickie. *Beggars and Choosers: How the Politics of Choice Shapes Adoption, Abortion, and Welfare in the United States*. New York: Hill and Wang, 2001.

Solinger, Rickie. *Pregnancy and Power: A Short History of Reproductive Politics in America*. New York: New York University Press, 2005.

Solinger, Rickie. *Wake Up Little Susie: Single Pregnancy and Race Before* Roe v. Wade. New York: Routledge, 1992.

Terry, Randall A. *Operation Rescue*. Springdale, Penn.: Whitaker House, 1988.

Tribe, Laurence H. *Abortion: The Clash of Absolutes*. New York: W.W. Norton and Company, 1990.

Tushnet, Mark. *Constitutional Issues: Abortion*. New York: Facts on Files, Inc., 1996.

Weddington, Sarah. *A Question of Choice*. New York: Putnam's, 1992.

Web sites

Alan Guttmacher Institute: www.agi-usa.org/

American College of Obstetricians and Gynecologists: www.acog.org

American Life League: www.all.org/

American Medical Association: www.ama-assn.org

Americans United for Life: www.aul.org

Catholics for Free Choice: www.catholicsforchoice.org/

Center for Reproductive Rights: http://www.reproductiverights.org

Choice USA: http://www.choiceusa.org

Christian Coalition of America: http://www.cc.org/

Concerned Women for America: www.cwfa.org

Democrats for Life of America: www.democratsforlife.org

Eagle Forum: www.eagleforum.org/

Elliot Institute: www.afterabortion.com

Family Research Council: www.frc.org/

Feminists for Life: www.feministsforlife.org/

Feminist Majority Foundation: www.feminist.org

Focus on the Family: http://www.family.org/

Life Dynamics: www.ldi.org

Life Issues Institute, Inc.: www.lifeissues.org

NARAL Pro-Choice America: www.naral.org/

National Abortion Federation: www.prochoice.org/

National Black Women's Health Project: http://www.blackwomenshealth.org

National Coalition of Abortion Providers: www.ncap.com

National Network of Abortion Funds: http://www.nnaf.org/

National Organization for Women: www.now.org/

National Right to Life Committee: http://www.nrlc.org/

Operation Rescue/Operation Save America: www.operationsaveamerica.org

Planned Parenthood Federation of America: www.plannedparenthood.org/

Religious Coalition for Reproductive Choice: www.rcrc.org/

Republicans for Choice: http://www.republicansforchoice.com/

Roe No More: http://www.crossingover.bravehost.com

The Silent Scream: www.silentscream.org

Sister Song: http://www.sistersong.net

Traditional Values Coalition: www.traditionalvalues.org/

United States Catholic Conference: www.usccb.org/

Writings of Paul Hill: www.armyofgod.com

INDEX

Index

About the Author

MELODY ROSE is chair of political science at the Hatfield School of Government at Portland State University. She holds degrees from U.C. Santa Cruz (B.A. with honors and Phi Beta Kappa, 1988) and Cornell University (Masters in Public Affairs, 1991; M.A. in Government, 1995; Ph.D. in Government, 1997). She is the author of a number of articles and books on social and election policy, most recently including *Safe, Legal, and Unavailable?* (2007, CQ Press), a book evaluating American abortion policy. Dr. Rose is also Founder and Director of NEW Leadership Oregon, which offers political and leadership training programs to college women in Oregon. This program is dedicated to inspiring and educating the next generation of women leaders in our nation.